AGONISTICS
Arenas of Creative Contest

I0884789

SUNY Series, The Margins of Literature
Mihai I. Spariosu, Editor

AGONISTICS

Arenas of Creative Contest

Edited by

Janet Lungstrum and Elizabeth Sauer

STATE UNIVERSITY OF NEW YORK PRESS

Cover art: Hanna Höch, "Starke Männer," © 1997, reprinted with permission of the Artists Rights Society (ARS), New York/VG Bild-Kunst, Bonn.

Published by
State University of New York Press

© 1997 State University of New York

All rights reserved

Printed in the United States of America

No part of this book may be used or reproduced
in any manner whatsoever without written permission.
No part of this book may be stored in a retrieval system or
transmitted in any form or by any means including electronic,
electrostatic, magnetic tape, mechanical, photocopying,
recording, or otherwise without the prior permission in
writing of the publisher.

For information, address the State University of New York Press,
State University Plaza, Albany, NY 12246

Marketing by Fran Keneston • Production by Bernadine Dawes

Library of Congress Cataloging-in-Publication Data

Agonistics : arenas of creative contest / edited by Janet Lungstrum & Elizabeth Sauer.
p. cm. — (SUNY series, the margins of literature)
Includes bibliographical references and index.
ISBN 0-7914-3411-7 (hc : alk. paper). — ISBN 0-7914-3412-5 (pbk. : alk. paper)
1. Struggle. 2. Contests. 3. Competition. 4. Philosophy.
5. Aesthetics. I. Lungstrum, Janet, 1963– . II. Sauer, Elizabeth, 1964– . III. Series.
BD437.A36 1997
190—dc21 97-1951
CIP

1 2 3 4 5 6 7 8 9 10

For

Walter H. Sokel

and

Balachandra Rajan

in continuing gratitude and friendship

Table of Contents

Creative Agonistics: An Introduction

Janet Lungstrum and Elizabeth Sauer

Every talent must unfurl itself struggling . . .
—Nietzsche, "Homer's Contest"

I

"I am afraid that we do not understand these things in a sufficiently 'Greek' way," complains Nietzsche in his essay "Homer's Contest" (1872). By this, Nietzsche means modernity's problem with thinking agonistically.[1] Specifically, he refers to the late nineteenth century's unhealthy, "softish" attitude toward competitiveness, contest, strife, creativity, and conflict:[2] in short, toward all phenomena inspired by the Greek *agōn*.[3] In his essay, Nietzsche is voicing not only an idealization of the ancient Greeks for their total incorporation of the agon into daily life, philosophy, art, sport, and war; he is also and more importantly projecting his own vision of an age to come in which the agon would recur. The age he is speaking of and to is postmodernity; Nietzsche is the agonal prophet of the postmodern world.

Not everyone shares Nietzsche's vision for postmodernity as a new agonal age. For Jean Baudrillard, the agon in Nietzsche's predicted neo-Greek format would appear to be dead or stillborn. This is how we should absorb Baudrillard's recent account, in *The Transparency of Evil* (1990),[4] of current Western culture's decidedly non-creative fall from agonistic grace. In this post-orgiastic, deflated era after the loss of faith in modernity (something he sees as occurring in 1968, but which could conceivably be understood as happening much earlier), there is in the Baudrillardian vision of things no more birthing of ideas, no more new invention, no more struggle in the active sense. Where Nietzsche had once called for the "re-evaluation of values" in modernity, Baudrillard is now saying this has since happened and that we now exist uniquely in a rather repetitive postmodern aftermath or in a no-man's-land following such agonistic, creative re-evaluation. It is of course possible to take issue with Baudrillard's nihilistically inclined "black-hole" analysis of postmodernity,[5] where only the bleak prospect of hyperreal competition or performance exists. For Baudrillard, "total confusion" has overtaken real, engaged difference and agonal critique (8); technology has brought us to a stage where we can know only an agon of inauthenticity.

However, not all scenes of contemporary postmodern struggle and creativity are virtual or fractal in the technologically simulated sense that Baudrillard depends upon. At the same time, it is equally possible to disagree with Nietzsche's warlike call for a renewed postmodern agon out of the conceptual dullness of modernity. While most people would not dispute that these are indeed agonistic times, there seems to be a guilt-ridden, taboo-like hesitancy to name the human need to play and fight (and to play-fight) for what it is. Part of our post-Nietzschean conceptual paralysis before this characteristic has to do with the *Materialschlacht* of World War I and the Holocaust and Hiroshima of World War II, all of which demonstrated only too well that the agon in its original sense of combative honor has long been overtaken and dishonored by technologized procedures of impersonal, instantaneous mass extermination. In a parallel sense, the institutional work ethic has so overwhelmed our (late-) capitalistic society that the agonal play drive and the festivities it used to inspire are demoted, almost wholly commercialized, and openly acknowledged only when channelled into pre-accepted ritual functions that remain subservient to the routinization of postindustrial society.[6]

At the end of the millennium, it is more difficult than ever to answer the question about what is worth struggling for and against. The issue is broader than even Nietzsche and Baudrillard have configured it. To use Fredric Jameson's phrase, the pedagogical endeavor of "cognitive mapping"[7] that this volume sets itself is to chart postmodernity and its relation to modernity in terms of the agonal problematic. If anything, people today are increasingly beset by a self-perpetuating, contradictory set of notions about agonal meanings and possibilities pertaining to postmodernized lives. The processes and arenas of the agon—here termed "agonistics"—are opened up in this volume of essays as a partial answer to such questions as: which aspects of existence are contestatory, and which (if any) are not? Are all forms of the agon integral to the play drive, as Johan Huizinga claims in his cultural-anthropological study *Homo Ludens* (1944),[8] or can some (non-)agonal environments be traced that are differential in character? If the agon is a biologically determined trait that humans have always shared with predatory-yet-playful animals, can (or should) it ever be totally transcended? What forms of sublimation does it take? How do we re-chart the agonal drive to suit the transformed playing field of human existence amidst high-tech productivity and bureaucracy, and to suit ourselves? Can any pragmatic truth be drawn from agonistic behavior's evolutionary gift of adaptability[9] and hence survival? How can boundaries be established and rules be set to avoid harm being done? To what degree is it ever preferable to allow open creative contest, and in which situations are restrictions necessary? What are the spatiotemporal configurations of the agon in modern and postmodern society? Where is the agon actively engaged in, and where is it passively enjoyed as entertainment or spectator sport? How does agonistics function in human discourse and artistic creativity? These are the kinds of speculative issues addressed by the contributors to this volume as well as by the major theorists of the agon that we refer to in this introduction, such as Jean-François Lyotard, Jacob Burckhardt, Michel Foucault, Sigmund Freud, Harold Bloom, and Mikhail Bakhtin.

We turn initially to Lyotard, who, in *The Postmodern Condition* (1979), explicitly defines postmodernity in terms of agonistics. Lyotard declares that the postmodern age is undeniably agonistic in the sense of a new liberation born of the loss of former stable monoliths in narrative, meaning, and the social bond, but for him this "delegitimation of knowledge" does not lead to "barbarity";[10] on the contrary, he charts the social, creative, and educational advantages inherent in throwing out Socratic-Hegelian dialectics. This can be seen as a heraldic statement of the contemporary age: where once metanarrative and binary opposition ruled, we now have an " 'atomization' of the social into flexible networks of language games" (17), and these performance-based language games follow the Nietzscho-Wittgensteinian rule that "to speak is to fight, in the sense of playing, and speech acts fall into the domain of a general agonistics" (10). Lyotard's emphasis is on the introduction of the new, of the inventive, via such agonistic language "moves" (16)—"[I]nvention is always born of dissension" (xxv)—an epistemological version of Derridean playful *différance.* In a scarcely veiled attack on Jürgen Habermas's consensus-theory, Lyotard declares that the aim of collective dialogue is not consensus but "paralogy" operating within both the "heterogeneity of the rules and the search for dissent" (66).

For Lyotard's neo-Marxist and feminist readers, the most obvious limit of *The Postmodern Condition* is that its indubitably positive agon verges on stasis in societal terms, that it is not sufficiently politically conscious, and does not enable marginalized groups to develop their own voices or to effect collective change. In response to Lyotard's pro-dissent attack on Habermas, Terry Eagleton, for example, critiques Lyotard for a lack of prescription and communality.[11] The feminist arguments of Seyla Benhabib, Nancy Fraser, and Linda J. Nicholson[12] take Habermas's side against Lyotard, decrying the latter's dependency on rhetorical performativity; his anti-social lack of participatory care; his silence on race, gender, and class; and the inability of his agonistic language games to differentiate between manipulative and non-manipulative uses of speech (e.g., in the abortion debate).

The Lyotardian postmodern agon is therefore perceived to be empty and meaningless unless it is also serving a justifiable, communal goal, particularly as part of emancipatory, multicultural aesthetics and politics. That is to say, advocates of cultural studies are wholly supportive of the collapse of metanarrative and the construction in its place of a non-hegemonic framework. Cultural critics clearly perceive the vitality and inherent health of agonistic desires within and between social groups. Edward Said, for example, explains in *Culture and Imperialism* (1993) how there was always an intensely agonal relation between colonizer and colonized, and how this relation was by no means one-sided.[13] Moreover, our present-day condition is an agonistic blend of this cross-cultural hybridity: "Partly because of empire, all cultures are involved in one another; none is single and pure, all are hybrid, heterogeneous, extraordinarily differentiated, and unmonolithic" (xxv). Said is at pains to demonstrate that "culture" and "power" are at no time free of each other (57)—for culture *is* agonistic. Hybridity is the latest transformational term applied to the human agonal condition, one that no longer "isolate[s] cultural and aesthetic realms from the worldly domain" (58). In the same vein, as Louis A. Montrose states, literature and the enterprise of literary criticism become significant for New Historicists and cultural critics primarily as "unstable and agonistic field[s] of verbal and social practices."[14] Indeed, Chris Jencks has defined the practice of cultural studies as "predicated upon conflict rather than order. It investigates and anticipates conflict both at the level of face-to-face interaction but also, and more significantly, at the level of meaning. Culture cannot be viewed as a unifying principle, a source of shared understanding of a mechanism for legitimating the social bond."[15] Contemporary analysts of culture as well as minority activists operate, then, within agonistic spheres that freely defy the former unity of Enlightenment principles which so conveniently propped up the hegemonic majority.

It is to this beneficial, essentially *creative* side of social and written agonistics under the sign of postmodernity that the attention of the present volume is turned. Aggressively agonistic behavior cannot be continually or effectively eradicated, avoided, or sublimated without strict censure; at best, under postmodern scrutiny, it can be utilized, transformed, or made self-aware. The regeneration of the postmodern agon, as displayed in the essays of this volume, is intended as a guide for the current post-Wall paradigm shift of postmodernism's journey from the intertext to the extra-textual cultural and historical world. Rather than fading, postmodernism is changing its linguistic focus and becoming more cognizant of social structures. The mode of the agon that we trace in this volume effectively provides a bridge from deconstructionist philosophies of language to studies of culture and history. Agonistics serves as a transition between paradigms in literary theory because it is inclusive and equally and interconnectedly operational both in language and in society. An explicit analysis of agonal activities in our own academic arenas will prove to be a major step toward improving our self-awareness as critics of any transferences between personal and written histories, between the age we live and the books we write.

These considerations inform *Agonistics: Arenas of Creative Contest* in its examination of agonal poetics and politics. The contributors to this essay collection focus on agonistics both as social struggle and as creative gesture, and demonstrate just how provocative the cathectic spectrum of agonistics can be. While the concept of the agon has been invoked by literary theorists and continental philosophers alike, and is firmly entrenched within classical studies, it has until recently remained relatively neglected—with the welcome exceptions of the work on the history of the play-concept in Western thought by Mihai Spariosu or the "méthodagonie" [*sic*] of Jean-Luc Boilleau—as the *explicit* subject of a broadly focused study of (post)modern intellectual thought.[16]

II

The ancient Greeks experienced first-hand the agonal arenas in art and life, and it is this world that provides an optimal parallel context for the present volume's more recent emphasis.[17] The first scholar to analyze Greek culture in terms of the agon was Nietzsche's mentor and teacher Jacob Burckhardt, in his posthumous *Griechische Kulturgeschichte* (1902).[18] Burckhardt saw Greek culture evolving in cycles that produced various types: "heroic" man, "colonial" man, and "agonal" man, then fifth-century man, fourth-century man, and finally, Hellenistic man, respectively. The agonal era, for Burckhardt, was the sixth century B.C. (namely at the height of the Panhellenic games at Olympia, held under a sacred truce of all warfare).[19] But Burckhardt's theory that the agon pertained only to this specific time in Greek history is something that Huizinga wishes to demote. Huizinga details how the "spirit of the contest dominated Hellenic culture both before . . . [the sixth century] and after" (73). Moreover, Huizinga states that Burckhardt may have coined the term "the agonal" but was not, as a cultural historian of the German nineteenth century, "equipped to perceive the widespread sociological background of the phenomenon" (71). Certainly, the archaic era of the agon refers by no means *only* to the ancient Greeks, as Huizinga amply demonstrates by giving countless worldwide examples—such as the rivalry and boastful generosity found in the gift-giving custom of the potlatch (59)—and by indicating how humans share agonistic behavioral traits with the entire animal kingdom. Nevertheless, Huizinga is overly harsh on Burckhardt, since the latter did in fact dare to suggest that the agon defined the entirely of Greek culture and was not just confined to its most obvious arenas, namely sports (especially wrestling and the race-events of the Olympic games),[20] rhapsodic singing contests, or dramatic contests held in honor of Dionysus. Moreover, Burckhardt's theory of the agon displays an awareness of its presence throughout the entirety of Greek culture, even as it peaked during the archaic (what Nietzsche would call Dionysian) period. Huizinga perhaps overreaches in his extension of the agon to all cultures in almost equal dosage: clearly, not all cultures are as agonal as others, and no other culture in the history of the West has so intertextually defined itself as agonal as did that of the ancient Greeks.

The multiple expressions of the agon in Greek society assert the term's significance as an enforcer of social, philosophy, and physical discipline that was applied to the benefit of all citizens. The agon is indeed visible in such varied Greek arenas as the Sophists' competitions of public rhetoric (*agōnes logōn*), male beauty contests, drinking contests, Spartan youth initiation ceremonies, accounts of heroism in the Homeric epic, the agon of the Greek lawsuit, the Heraclitean view of the agonistically wrestling and eternally self-becoming nature of the universe, the poetic contest between Hesiod and Homer, and the Sphinx's riddle-contest with Oedipus. As Foucault demonstrates, even the code of Hellenic male sexuality was determined by an "agonistic relationship with oneself"—indeed the agonal arena of the Greeks was in its entirety a uniquely male phenomenon.[21] In *Twilight of the Idols* (1888), Nietzsche's Burckhardtian praise knows no bounds as he maintains that the agon represents the "*supreme cultural* event of history": for the agon formulated the development of healthy cultures as sites of positive, creative strife and anti-tyrannical, plural contention.[22] Benjamin C. Sax affirms that the agon "represents the central value system of the Greeks: for from it arises the quest for *aretē* [virtue/excellence]"; and what is amazing about the Greeks' agonistic understanding is that through it they created a society that was "at once nature and culture" (i.e., which knew nothing of the latter-day guilt of combining the one with the other).[23]

This indivisibility and non-contradictoriness of nature and culture in Greek society is demonstrated by Carrie L. Asman, who explains how one actual source of the agon, at least as far as tragic drama is concerned, may be traced back to the court trial of antiquity. Citing Florens Christian Rang's 1922 journal entry, "Agon und Theater" (penned by his disciple Walter Benjamin),[24] Asman explains how potential victims of human sacrifice could escape their fate if they successfully outran their pursuers in a diagonal race across the amphitheater to reach the altar. Rang perceives in this earlier practice the origin of the transformation from *Wettlaufen* to the verbalized altercation (*Wettreden*) of two protagonists on the stage, each aided and abetted by the alienation-effect of the chorus.[25] The Hellenic agonal act of human sacrifice (deed/body) was thus transformed into the contest of drama (word/representation).

III

What, then, happened to Western civilization's agonistics after its Greek prerational apex? Nietzsche blames Socrates for having introduced "a new kind of *agon*" with his synthesis-oriented dialectics and philosophy of virtue (*Twilight of the Idols* 42). As Spariosu indicates in *God of Many Names*, Socrates favored "median [classical] over archaic agon" (174), using the techniques of the latter to introduce the scientific-philosophical ethos of the former, by adopting the Sophists' agonal art of verbal gymnastics in his dialogic arguments against poetry as a ludic-cum-mimetic form (168–69). Through Plato's rational form of play, the prerational agon was internalized and weakened from its former state of exteriorized social value.[26] As Nietzsche mythically stages it in *The Birth of Tragedy* (1872), the agonal congeniality of the Dionysian and Apollonian art drives was subsumed by the Socratic. In Hellenistic Greek thought, mankind was increasingly separated from its instincts, which came to be depicted as "evil" in relation to the Christian "good": in short, a process began that made the agon into something wholly negative (literally: antagonistic) rather than something life-affirming through the organic cycle of creation and destruction. Expressions of power began to get a bad name, so to speak. Michel Foucault tells a parallel tale regarding the discourses of power. In "The Discourse on Language," Foucault explains the linguistic fall from agonal, Hesiodic grace to Platonic logocentrism: with the onset of Plato, "true discourse was no longer considered precious and desirable, since it had ceased to be discourse linked to the exercise of power. And so the Sophists were routed."[27] For Foucault, there remains, however, an indivisible link between discourse and the agon (his terms here are "desire and power" [219]) that the Platonic belief-system has since done its best to disguise: "[S]peech is no mere verbalization of conflicts and systems of domination, but . . . the very object of man's conflicts" (216).

Foucault's thought on the history of power in fact tells us a lot about the post-Platonic agon. Foucault dedicated himself to undoing public preconceptions of power as something inevitably destructive, emanating uniquely from the "system of Law-and-Sovereign," as he states in his *Introduction* to *The History of Sexuality*. He shows that power, defined essentially as the "multiplicity of force relations immanent in the sphere in which they operate and which constitute their own organization; as the process which, through ceaseless struggles and confrontations, transforms, strengthens, or reverses them," is not a superstructural phenomenon but a producer of effects "from below" that are "local and unstable."[28] In this wholly agonistic, Heraclitean-Nietzschean field of force relations, power can give rise to a "plurality of resistances" (96) in the same way Said claims for minority cultures. As Gilles Deleuze emphasizes, Foucauldian power is "not essentially repressive . . . ; it passes through the hands of the mastered no less than through the hands of the masters."[29]

On the other hand, most readers of Foucault take away with them strong impressions of the decidedly *non*-agonistic apparatus of the modern State in its various institutionalized configurations. In his depictions of the panoptic architectures of social control in the penal system, schools, hospitals, etc., Foucault has charted a trajectory of modern discipline that advocates solely the "power of normalization."[30] But precisely within these arenas of repression, he detects that from the eighteenth century onward there exists a "synaptic regime of power, a regime of its exercise *within* the social body, rather than *from above* it."[31] The question here is whether the agonistic force relations he sees simultaneously operating within repressive systems do in fact serve as sites of effective resistance (as generators of "power-knowledge" for all), so much as they end up merely legitimating institutional control.[32] Foucault's agonal understanding of power from the onset of the modern age onward is too neutral for its own good. The critique of Foucault offered by Richard Rorty, for example, is based on Rorty's need for philosophy to provide "social hope" and Foucault's refusal to do the same.[33]

IV

Perhaps the primary descendant of the Socratic agon, and the theorist closest to most people's clearly *negative* associations with the agonistic principle—as an exploitative will to power, or as psychic pain (the later sense of the term *agōnia*)—is in fact Freud. In a metapsychological text written in the wake of World War I and during the rise of Nazism and rabid antisemitism in Germany and Austria, namely *Civilization and its Discontents* (1930), Freud turns Nietzsche's positive reevaluation of creative agonistics on its head and prefers instead to interpret the modern psyche as locked in an eternal agon between the life instinct, *Eros* (libido, or sexuality), and the death drive, *Thanatos*. In this dualistic-agonistic interplay of the two forces,[34] the death instinct is witnessed in all destructive, aggressive acts and desires, and indeed comes eventually for Freud to dominate the entire process of modern existence.[35] Spariosu has noted in *Dionysus Reborn* how Freud's theory initially requires the "primacy of Eros," but "later on it requires the primacy of Thanatos" (182). While Freud believes that the benefits of Eros-serving modern civilization far outweigh the disadvantages, he nonetheless charts how civilization imposes inevitable restrictions on the individual's sexual desires, resulting in a sociopathic impairment or neurotic inversion of the latter if these are not successfully sublimated: "In consequence of this primary mutual hostility of human beings, civilized society is perpetually threatened with disintegration" (69). The concept of *homo ludens* has been dominated by Freud's deeply pessimistic vision of *homo homini lupus*,[36] and the consequences of Social Darwinism are not far behind.

A literary version of the Freudian spin on agonistic theory is found in the work of Harold Bloom. Bloom has basically suggested a *Leviathan*-esque literary history of inspirational wrestling between "strong poets" and an Oedipal agony or "anxiety of influence" that goads the former into creating and the weak poets into giving up. Implicitly inserting himself, in *Agon: Towards a Theory of Revisionism* (1982), into the agonistic order of those who have theorized or prophesized the agon (Burckhardt, Nietzsche, Freud, Huizinga,[37] and now Bloom), he displays strong traces of Freud's notion of sublimation as he analogizes artistic creativity to a neurosis with one's precursors. As he states in *The Anxiety of Influence* (1973), "Influence is *Influenza*—an astral disease. . . . Health is stasis."[38] Bloom's is indeed a theory for an Oedipally guilt-ridden, post-Homeric age: he presents us in *Agon* with a structure of creative agonistics that is—in its debt to Freud and its indirect debt to the priest-mentality of Nietzsche's *Genealogy of Morals* (1887)—wholly a decadent, even "contaminated" one: "[O]ur instinctual life is agonistic and ultimately self-destructive and . . . our most authentic moments tend to be those of negation, contraction and repression. Is it so unlikely that our creative drives are deeply contaminated by our instinctual origins?" (99). It is possible to trace a chronological self-postmodernizing shift in Bloom's texts away from his original notion of author-to-author influence and the "desperate insistence upon priority" after the post-Miltonic modern fall (AI, 13), and toward "relationships between texts" in which the writer's intertextual "misreading" in the creative moment resembles the act of criticism.[39]

But Bloom remains resilient to change in one significant area: his faith in the literary canon as an infallible product of the agonal scene of literary production and reception has remained intact, despite its current state of siege in the age of multiculturalism.[40] This view follows from his insistence on divorcing literary identity from extra-literary influences that shape humanity. In *The Western Canon* (1994), Bloom politicizes for bestseller consumption the literary agon as an integral conservative support of the canon of "aesthetic value" against what he perceives as the "School of Resentment"[41]—whose cultural studies members are, he claims, out to destroy the agonistic nature of literature when they revise the canon to include e.g., more African-American or women's texts.[42] He continues to believe ardently in the system of literary production that "cripples weaker talents but stimulates canonical genius" (10), and dismisses these alternative texts as weak. He wants to remain in a purified aesthetic realm, and will not entertain the notion that the reason a work of minority literature did not enter the canon at the time of its origin might have had something to do with its ideological suppression by a canon-forming hegemony. Bloom is hence missing the irony of the current situation: as past and present minority literature is entering the canon and changing the entire canonization process, it is demonstrating that the agonistic forces of literary production and reception are indeed alive and well and are fully engaged in the simultaneous field of social resistance.

Bakhtinian narrative theory, always a highly agonistic scene, offers a useful indirect response to the Bloomian *Angst*-ridden model. Bakhtin analyzes how words, discourses, and voices become de-privileged in their association with competing definitions and authorial and narrative voices.[43] All writers must contend with the agonistics of language, that is, with the dialogic nature of the single word and the tongues that recite it. Here we may refer again to Lyotard in *The Postmodern Condition* on the "agonistics of [creative] language" that breaks through the Jaussian horizon of expectations: "Great joy is had in the endless invention of turns of phrase, of words and meanings, the process behind the evolution of language on the level of *parole*. But undoubtedly even this pleasure depends on a feeling of success won at the expense of an adversary—at least one adversary, and a formidable one: the accepted language, or connotation" (10). An awareness of the ways in which the agon operates in literary texts leads as well to an examination of the cultural and historical conditions that informed their creation. Literature not only dramatizes exchanges between voices in the text but also dialogizes with other voices of the culture through intertextual references and also by establishing for the participants in this dialogue "positions of compliance or resistance with respect to those other 'voices.' "[44] Indeed, Huizinga reminds us that *poiesis* has always been an agonistic "play-function" oriented in the social function (119)—comedy and tragedy were born of ancient Dionysian festivities; Greek dramas were judged competitively for the feast of Dionsysus; and in German, drama is literally a *Spiel* (144–45). This is matched by Bakhtin's emphasis in *Problems of Dostoevsky's Poetics* on carnivalization, a process of free play where "opposites come together, look at one another, are reflected in one another, know and understand one another"; the carnival as agonistic scene "strives to encompass and unite within itself both poles of becoming or both members of an antithesis" (176).

Bakhtin postulates a plural, dialogic self that complements his view of texts as carnivalesque polyphony. The text is produced through dialogue, involving for Bakhtin not only the exchange of viewpoints but also matters of cultural politics. The critic, in turn, defines dialogism, double-voicedness, in terms of a collision of contexts in a single utterance—textual contexts as well as immediate material (socio-historical) conditions. As a site for the dialogic interaction of a multiplicity of verbal / social voices, the text thus bears the marks of social groups, classes, and diverse discursive communities. Agonal dialogism, then, identifies the complex interrelationship of languages "when they face one another with appropriate force, and the struggle implicit in heteroglossia and stratification becomes visible."[45] The act of reading establishes a dialogic tension between reader and text, text and context. In analyzing this activity, Bakhtin emphasizes the interpretative community and the concrete social and historical milieu in which the reader/critic is situated. Bakhtin's concept of the interpretative community is radically different from that of Stanley Fish, whose model of the operations of inter-communal persuasion precludes agonal conflict and change and is regraded from the outset as essentially authoritative.[46]

V

Evidently, the agon is far from being the very opposite of community and culture, as Bloom would prefer it to be. Indeed, the goal of *Agonistics: Arenas of Creative Contest* is precisely to show the agon as a practice of life and culture, not of the work of art in any rarified sphere. The essays of this volume may best be understood as agonistic contexts, arenas or applications that interrogate various aspects of the theory and history of the agon in familiar and new settings. They are arranged according to four interrelated groupings, "Contests in Cultural Philosophy," "Psychoanalytic and Racial Conflicts," "Agonal Aesthetics and Narrative Theory," and "Agons of Gender and the Body"; each grouping thereby re-orientates, in an expanding concentric manner, the introductory comments of this chapter on the evolutionary history and theory of agonistics into larger areas of interest. These four comprehensive sections also reflect the diverse fields our contributors occupy: literary criticism and theory in various national literatures, intellectual history, gender studies, Jewish studies, continental philosophy, psychology, and sports studies. Their topics are even more far-reaching, ranging from criminology to chaos theory, film studies to mythicism, ancient Greece to science fiction, and Surrealism to social theory. Indeed, the wider spectrum of disciplines in which the agon is an active concept is a net extending yet further to include political science, zoology, art history, neurochemistry, materials science, and law. Each of our contributors provides rich comparative-intertextual readings of the agonistics of language and culture as creative contest. Each sets her- or himself the task of coming to terms with the acute problematic of the agonal drive, by suggesting a new ethos that best deals with the respective contextual situations of conflict under analysis. Even as the contributors to this volume are joined by their communal agonal outreach, they inevitably also disagree both within and between their respective groupings over a definitive mode of analyzing and resolving representations of conflict. For the essays of this collection are struggling with the very notion of struggle.

Our volume opens with Nietzsche's posthumously published essay "Homer's Contest" (chapter 1), translated here especially for this volume. Nietzsche's essay, a vital *mise-en-scène* of the agon, effectively anchors the volume since it serves as a significant point of entry into investigations of agonistics in both its ancient and (post)modern contexts. Precisely because Nietzsche's essay is as symptomatic as it is paradigmatic, we have included it in the first part of this essay collection, entitled "Contests in Cultural Philosophy." This first cluster of essays posits the agon as a social and post-metaphysical agency in modern Western thought. Nietzsche's is not so much a backward-looking essay on ancient Greece as it is a wake-up call for modernity and beyond via a historicist idealization of the Greeks.[47] The iconoclastic function of Nietzschean agonistics serves to break up worn-out patterns of language, thought, and behavior and to invigorate genealogically those cultural and artistic practices deemed worthy of new life. Contestatory creativity in Nietzsche embraces at once literary moments of the struggle of intertextual and interpersonal influences, the educational formation of competing individuals, historical and cultural constructions, the push toward warlike transformatory stances, and the fate for the writer or performer of becoming imprisoned in language or in the historical continuum.

We leave it to Benjamin C. Sax's essay, "Cultural Agonistics: Nietzsche, the Greeks, Eternal Recurrence" (chapter 2), to provide—via the lens of Burckhardt—an in-depth interpretation of Nietzsche's seminal text on the agon as well as its companion-piece, "Philosophy in the Tragic Age of the Greeks." Sax argues that the significance that Nietzsche attributes to struggle and even violence is neither merely a playful inversion of modern values nor a vague and groundless call for an aggressive form of creativity. Rather, Nietzsche employs such terms as "creativity," "ascending values," and even "culture" in terms of his understanding of the position of the agon in the formation of archaic Greece. Mediated through the philosophy of Heraclitus, this positive notion—one that transformed natural aggression into the culturally creative form of the agon—also gave rise to a non-Eliatic and non-Platonic understanding of the relation between thought and world. For Sax, this notion of the agon, once translated into a modern context, forms the basis of Nietzsche's notion of the relation between the will to power and the thought of eternal recurrence. Sax concludes that in its historical, philosophical, and poetic form, Nietzsche's agon provides one of the strongest arguments—even when unacknowledged or unappreciated—for an agonistic understanding of intellectual and artistic creativity.

Arkady Plotnitsky's essay, "Closing the Eye: Hegel, Derrida, and the Closure of Metaphysics" (chapter 3), is a deconstructionist study of how philosophy and the act of philosophizing become the topic of agonistic interplay and transference by means of two interrelated cultural economies involved in the creative agon between Hegel and Derrida. The first is the economy of the closure or enclosure (*clôture*) of philosophy—in contrast to its end. The second economy is that of an infinitesimal proximity to and a radical distance from (specifically Hegel's) philosophy. For Plotnitsky, the creative agon for postmodern philosophy remains a struggle under the Medusan eye of Hegel: the closure of metaphysics can re-open at any time. While Plotnitsky engages both economies in terms of Bloom's theory of creative agonistics as the "anxiety of influence," he also reconfigures Bloom within the matrix defined by these two economies and their interrelationships. The scene of agonal influence is here wholly transformed from the traces of the Bloomian Oedipal scene into a Derridean, intertextual agonistics that best characterizes philosophy's ongoing relationship to the (Hegelian) precursor-texts as simultaneously divergent and convergent.

Chapter 4, the concluding essay in the "Contests in Cultural Philosophy" section, is Marcus Paul Bullock's "Walter Benjamin: The Prophet's War against Prophecy." Bullock suggests through his reading of Benjamin's letters to Gershom Scholem and the "Theses on the Philosophy of History" that the site of the agon can be located, in the case of Benjamin, as an intense, inner, indeed tragic experience for the cultural philosopher. Benjamin's curiosity drives him to discover how the world looks when tested for its worthiness for destruction. But the grand enterprise of laying bare the forces at work in cultural modernity always draws

Benjamin back to the intricacies of his own entanglement in the processes of that inheritance. The decision to take up a Marxist position only intensified these conflicts in a more overt form. Bullock goes on to explain how the Marxist demand led Benjamin to turn against his own situation as a bourgeois scholar and against his own contemplative subjectivity. In this way, Benjamin projects an idealized "destructive character" whose Apollonian serenity and youthful ability to act appears in stark contrast to his own disabling, suicidal melancholy. Bullock's reading of Benjamin demonstrates how the letter's self-imposed, agonal contest with the world of myth-bound modernity necessarily returned him to that troubled condition. As Bullock concludes, all such agonistic struggle involves that reflective confrontation with itself.

VI

The essays of Part II of *Agonistics: Arenas of Creative Contest*, a section entitled "Psychoanalytic and Racial Conflicts," resituate the agon in the individually experiential fields of identity-formation in both psychoanalysis and racism. In psychoanalysis, agonistics may occur in the internal struggles of the patient as well as in the external conflicts between therapist and patient; in racism, it occurs in the stereotyping of the outsider who is culturally or racially different. As Bakhtin states, the "content of the individual psyche is just as social as is ideology," and "ideological phenomena are just as individual . . . as are psychological phenomena."[48] Evidently, the making of the Other occurs both within the psyche and without, and the process of agonal demonization is most often associated with transferentially inspired fantasies of aggression associated with sex and race. The essays of this section all contextualize this problematic in new ways.

In the first essay of this part, "Interpretation Interminable: Agonistics in Psychoanalysis" (chapter 5), Volney P. Gay reexamines Freud's devotion to an agonistic theory of mind as anticipated by Nietzsche, with whom he shared a common idealization of the Greek models. Freud named his most famous clinical concept, the Oedipus Complex, after the greatest hero of

Greek agonistic drama. The role of the Greeks as partial validation of psychoanalysis itself also emerges when Freud cites Empedocles' doctrine of eternal strife and melds it to his own metapsychology. Gay examines Freud's famous essay "Analysis Terminable and Interminable" for its agonistic view of the human mind and of the inherent, endless struggle between patient and analyst. Gay charts how the concept of agonistic struggle helps us delineate two traditions of response to inner struggle and turmoil, especially to new discoveries about human nature. One tradition Freud identifies when he traces his thought back to Empedocles and the doctrine of eternal struggle between love and strife. The other opposing tradition is that of religious and mythical solutions to agonal struggles, wherein Gay examines the mysticism proposed by Pythagoras (or his disciples) and the metaphysics of Aristotle and Paul.

The unconscious versus the preconscious, the pleasure principle versus the reality principle, Eros versus the death instinct, civilization versus aggression—through Freud's work runs a concatenation of dualities. This is Freud's version of the agon: the notion of a clash between two antithetical entities, and the insight that this clash is a powerful explanatory key. Lorna Martens's essay, "The Institutionalization of Conflict as an Interpretative Strategy in Freud's *The Interpretation of Dreams*" (chapter 6), examines the birth of Freudian agonistic dualism in its earliest form, namely conflict psychology, in the 1890s. The idea that the normal, healthy psyche is in conflict with itself emerges initially and tentatively in *Studies on Hysteria* (1895), where Freud introduces the concept of repression, and definitively in *The Interpretation of Dreams* (1900), where Freud "discovers" the unconscious. Martens shows how Freud initially conceived of trauma almost in racial terms as an entry from the outside. As Martens suggests, Freud then redefined his trauma theory into the more successfully agonistic battle between unconscious and conscious wills. The dream is the product of the conflict between two psychic systems that Freud adopts as a new and versatile hermeneutic tool. Martens argues that conflict psychology is the product of a convergence between Freud's hermeneutic and metapsychological projects. She demonstrates that long before Freud would anchor the notion of a conflicted psyche in the empirical antagonisms of the family romance in *The Ego and the Id* (1923), the agonistic idea of the dual psyche at this early stage served at once as a hermeneutic strategy that helped Freud interpret hysterical symptoms and then dreams, and as a model of the mind that accounted for its dynamic functioning.

The last two essays of this section provide two new arenas for revealing the surreptitious influence of racial stereotyping on both psychoanalytical and criminological methods of investigation. Specifically chapter 7, "The Jewish Genius: Freud and the Jewishness of the Creative" by Sander L. Gilman, examines contending cultural and racial discourses about creativity by analyzing Freud's assessment of the same as an arena of irrationality and psychological abnormality. Gilman charts how Freud, particularly in response to Otto Weininger and Cesare Lombroso, challenges *fin-de-siècle* agonal representations of the essentially non-original, deviant, mad, and hypersexed Jew. Freud's own brand of resistance takes the form of universalizing—but not normalizing—the entire question of the creative by locating such energies within the sexual drives and psychic phenomena of *all* humans, not just of the agonal Jewish Other. In this way, Freud reappropriates the potential of creativity for himself and for his theories of psychoanalysis. For Gilman, race and sexuality become blurred in Freud's thesis, however, insofar as both the Jew and the artist undergo maskings of assimilation and sublimation.

The projection of racial and social anxieties onto an outsider or stranger is also the subject of Nancy A. Harrowitz's contribution in chapter 8, the last essay of the section "Psychoanalytic and Racial Conflicts." In "Criminality and Poe's Orangutan: The Question of Race in Detection," Harrowitz demonstrates how Edgar Allan Poe's 1841 detective story, "The Murders in the Rue Morgue," reveals racial anxieties through the author's curious choice of an orangutan as the perpetrator. Poe displaces the figure of the threatening outsider, a figure hinted at by a discussion of Asians and Africans in the story, onto this exotic ape. Through an analysis of the agonistics of race and the cracks in the detective Dupin's epistemological method, Harrowitz leads us to Poe's state of equivocation on the subject of race, criminal classification, and the semiotic detection of the criminal through the use of the orangutan. Her analysis is further contextualized through an examination of the relation between the developing discipline of criminology (specifically, the establishment of genetic controls by the developer of eugenics, Francis Galton) and the detective genre. She also turns to Nietzsche's opposition of civilization and savagery found in his definition of agon, in order to highlight its dissociation from the oppressively xenophobic culture of criminology emerging in nineteenth-century Europe.

VII

Part III of this essay collection, "Agonal Aesthetics and Narrative Theory," addresses the discursive-dialogic agon both in the interminable acts of creative writing and reading as well as in the literary or philosophical text itself. John A. McCarthy's essay, " 'A Chain of Utmost Potency': On the Agon and the Creative Impulse" (chapter 9), is a study of philosophical, scientific, and literary creativity as it is depicted in *Faust*, Goethe's other writings, and in Nietzsche from an unusual viewpoint—that of chaos and complexity theory in the natural sciences. By means of this unconventional rapprochement of creators from different fields and eras, McCarthy interprets the term "agonistic" as designating a particular intellectual attitude that is not strictly and merely oppositional in the sense of "antagonistic." It is seen rather as a mirroring and convergence of an overall economy of existence without reducing each movement to a purely mechanical or linear relationship. Dynamically interactive and autopoietic systems thus stand at the forefront of McCarthy's investigation. His cross-disciplinary study of chaos theory in the text and in nature exposes the agonal tension that underlies creative performance both in the artistic and scientific worlds.

Elizabeth Sauer in chapter 10, "The Partial Song of Satanic Anti-Creation: Milton's Discourses of the Divided Self," examines the epic of the poet whom Bloom identified as the precursor and source of anxiety for all future poets. By reassessing John Milton's *Paradise Lost* in the light of the agonistic processes of reading and writing, Sauer discusses the complex attempts at self-representation in the poem's soliloquies that challenge the hegemony of cultural and literary expression established in the epic.

Milton's soliloquies destroy, in favor of a dialogic relationship, what Bakhtin calls in *Problems of Dostoevsky's Poetics* the "naive wholeness of one's notions about the self" that lies at the heart of the classical epic, lyric, and tragedy (120). *Paradise Lost*, a multi-genre poem, registers its anxiety about the authority of monological voice in the contest between the demonic epic poet and the inspired poet-narrator. The characterization in the poem of Satan as an actor (an *agonistes*) and, simultaneously, as a defeated champion (which invokes another definition of *agonistes*) testifies to the conflict between the carnivalesque and the tragic in the poem, and, in turn, anticipates Samson's *agonistes* in Milton's Greek tragedy of the same name.

The multivocal and metafictional discourses of James Joyce are the subject of Andrew Schmitz's essay of chapter 11, "The Penman and the Postal-Carrier: Preordained Rivalry in Joyce's *Finnegans Wake*." With reference to Lyotard and Nietzsche, Schmitz discusses the representation of the game-playing artist in the novel in terms of the agonistic relationship between Shaun and his twin warring brother, Shem, the writer and forger on whose body the text and the narrative of its composition are inscribed. Schmitz finds that *Finnegans Wake* is preordained to do agonistic battle with the very formulations and codes it is producing. That is, as soon as the *Wake* becomes "properly" literature, it disappears as the radical modernist experiment it claimed to be. By means of the private language ("idiolect" or "idioglossary") associated with the brothers, especially Shem, as well as the work's continuous reference to forgery and counterfeit, Schmitz detects that the *Wake* constructs a language so private it can only parodically quote itself—an act of writing as self-subversion, a mastering gesture that transcends its own mastery.

The agonization over artistic performance is also the subject of the last essay of Part III, but in a way that focuses more on the writer's own self-reflexivity as literary producer. In chapter 12, "The Gender of Fiction: Henry James's 'Backward Glance' at the Agon of Composition," Cecile Mazzucco-Than examines James's agonistic attempts at self-expression and authorship as they are worked out in a series of retrospective Prefaces to his collected works. In these Prefaces James plays out the creative contest at the center of the composition for each work.

Mazzucco-Than finds that the Prefaces suggest a series of opposing forces that vie for mastery; while their struggle remains unresolved, they are vital for James's creativity. At the root of the conflict is the gender of James's agon of composition, i.e., the gendered metaphors that James uses to describe his art. James's programmatic stance toward usurping the feminine elements of his work in order to gain high-art, patriarchal status for the genre of the novel is revealed by Mazzucco-Than to be continually precluded by a pre-Oedipal identification with the maternal on the part of the author, as well as by what may be termed a type of *écriture féminine* where the writing process is an end in itself.

VIII

The essays of Part IV, "Agons of Gender and the Body," raise a few of the unavoidable spectres of agonistics that touch upon the very physicality and cathexis of the agon. These questions include: is the agon not the (exclusive) property of a males-only club? Does feminism signify an end to agonistics, or can there be such a thing as a feminist agon? How does postmodernism affect the interplay of agonistic forces in gender relations? Does the (post)modern sportive agon impose a healthy neo-Greek discipline upon the human body, or its very opposite? In a society of the future, should the agon be disposed of or re-worked? This section of *Agonistics: Arenas of Creative Contest* addresses these questions as it retraces a history of agonistics inscribed in human social and gender roles, sexuality, and physical performance.

As Sandra M. Gilbert and Susan Gubar state in *No Man's Land*, the agonal "plot of sexual battle is of course as old as literature itself."[49] Feminists like Gilbert and Gubar have not failed to notice the eagerness with which our aesthetic and philosophical tradition makes femininity a fetishized surrogate for agonal alterity, ultimately for death—a tension that was exacerbated by the mid-nineteenth-century onset of feminist rebellion and women's changed social roles in the twentieth century's two World Wars. The scene of agonistic creativity, in turn, is frequently feminized, with the concept of the Muse-like feminine offering (male) authors and critics a useful means for defining possibilities and forms of linguistic play. In a reading of André Breton's romance, *Nadja*, Lisabeth During narrates the account of the feminine birth of the Surrealist artist in terms of a murder masquerading as love. During's "The Muse Abused" (chapter 13) reads *Nadja* as a case study of the modernist engagement with death and the unconscious, one that bears the name of Orpheus. Here a mediating woman—muse, angel, beloved sacrifice—intervenes to protect the artist from disintegration and the loss of inspiration. If the woman he lets go can negotiate the underworld for him, the Orphic artist escapes. Bloom's males-only Oedipal agon between the strong father-poet and the ambitious epigone intends to take seriously the real risks of challenging the father, of refusing repression. The Surrealist impersonator of Orpheus, while non-Oedipal, eludes the ban of repression and keeps death and madness at a safe distance only by underwriting the sacrifice of the female body in the act of male authorship.

The next essay in the section "Agons of Gender and the Body" addresses a different form of sacrifice, one that is shared these days by both genders in varying ways, namely the extreme effects of high-performance sport. John Hoberman in "The Sportive Agon in Ancient and Modern Times" (chapter 14) discusses the body as a prime site of agonal self-definition and cultural struggle, and, moreover, returns us to a Nietzscho-Greek definition of the agon by means of a comparison of such ideals with recent theories of sport. While, for example, Huizinga complains (already half a century ago) of the loss of spontaneity and amateurism in modern professionalized, over-disciplined sport—for him, the agonistically "pure play-quality" has been lost, and sport now occupies a zone unrelated to the "structure of society" (197, 198)—others, such as sports sociologists John W. Loy and Graham L. Hesketh, insist that despite the fact that contemporary sport bears certain signs of post-feudal society's "pseudo-agon," this need not necessarily be seen as a loss of the agon entirely. Loy and Hesketh point to the survival of certain key agonal characteristics in sport today, such as action, peer review, prestige processes, and a gift mode of exchange.[50] Hoberman's contribution responds to this dichotomous portrayal of modern sport's effect on the body. He neither sets up the ancient Greeks as an ideal (acknowledging, for example, that practices of brutality were integral to Greek sport), nor does he avoid the unfortunate extremes visible in the pharmacological trend of latter-day physiological performance and its general effects on body image. Hoberman thus charts how the meaning of the agon, defined as the fusing of physical and mental exertion in pursuit of an athletic goal, has evolved since the time of the ancient Greek Olympic games. Over the past century since the Olympics' reinstatement in 1896, increasing levels of stress have made high-performance sport a physiological, disciplinary agon waged panoptically against human limits as well as a contest with one's human competitors. The ultimate physical agon at the end of the twentieth century is thus directed against oneself in the form of self-surveillance rather than neo-Nietzschean "self-overcoming."

Cynthia Willett in "Baudrillard, *After Hours*, and the Postmodern Suppression of Socio-Sexual Conflict" (chapter 15) also offers a critique of the agon as it operates in contemporary society. Willett finds that the postmodern condition offers a dead-end for agonistic social change, particularly for gender relations. She investigates how encounters between male and female values and sexualities have shifted from their previous modern setting, as depicted in Hollywood screwball comedies, to a new postmodern context of the hyperreal. Drawing on the theory of Baudrillard, Willett offers a critical reading of Martin Scorsese's acclaimed film *After Hours* (1985) by suggesting how high-tech postmodernism's loss of metanarrative has in fact contributed to a dehumanizing loss of plot and character development found in comic dialectic, i.e., to a representational loss of the instigators necessary for genuine socio-sexual agons. In the Manhattan environment of the white-collar, male yuppie (the protagonist of Scorsese's film), inescapable postmodern matrices of power displace modern narrative and historical dialectic; these power matrices are depicted in terms of castrating women and are, thereby, represented as emasculating and socially static. Willett provides us with a richly ironic filmic scenario of the dangers of precluding social change and genuine male-female agonistic interaction—in short, an encapsulation of the Baudrillardian endgame of late capitalism.

The visionary possibilities for a new agonistics in the arena of postmodern democracy form the focus of George A. Trey's study,

"Agonal Politics in Space and Time: Arendt and Le Guin on World Creation" (chapter 16), which concludes this section and the volume as a whole. Trey achieves this utopian vision of the agon by focusing on gender and social participation in the context of political debate. Concentrating on dispossession and discursive politics in the science fiction novels *The Dispossessed* and *The Eye of the Heron*, Trey argues that Ursula Le Guin's feminist model ultimately resists the aristocratic exclusivity inherent in Hannah Arendt's views of the public sphere in ancient Greece and in the latter's patriarchally elitist forms of world creation. For Trey, Le Guin thus depicts a new configuration: a Habermassian, egalitarian form of agonistics. Trey is, however, alert to the fact that there can be no *final* resolution of social conflict—no overriding, absolute consensus, only temporary contracts. A pluralist society must, in the words of Chantal Mouffe, necessarily project a "self-refuting ideal";[51] for democracy would in fact come to an end if all its ideals were met. As Mouffe states: "In the realm of politics, [this requires that] the 'other' is not seen as an enemy to be destroyed, but as an 'adversary' with whose ideas we are going to struggle, but whose right to defend those ideas will not be put into question. We could say that the aim of democratic politics is to transform an antagonism into an 'agonism' " (120). In the agonistic pluralism conceived of by Le Guin in Trey's analysis, emancipatory action is depicted as a successful, feminine (but not females-only) metaphor.

IX

In this way—both through this Introduction's explicit revalorization of the creative-regenerative aspect of contestatory struggle, as well as through the individual analyses that follow, each exploring the agon's philosophical, psychological, literary, or political applications—we hope to indicate to our readership the acute relevance of agonistics for the postmodern *Zeitgeist*. It is in the nature of the agon neither to render its participants mute nor to attain the conquering finality of *telos*. The agonistic paradigm allows texts, authors, historical events, and cultural voices to engage in a creative and regenerative contest. This is by no means an easy hermeneutic journey—there exists an undeniably very fine line between the positive benefits wrought by active resistances of gender battles, racial antagonisms, or class struggle on the one hand, and the (self-)destructive and decadent transmutations of the agon in ideological polarization, the cult of warfare, and surveillance-mechanisms of power on the other. As a basic mode of action, the agon represents the conflicted and conflicting nature of human self-expression, and precisely because of the urgency and vitalism involved in these clashes, it always speaks for creativity and extends to all aspects of life.

Moreover, agonistics is an ongoing phenomenon of which this volume is also a part: for each writer and each era reinvents the creative in an act of agonal self-definition and sociohistorical intervention. The agon is not only an object of research across the (inter)disciplinary board; on a more self-reflexive level, it is simultaneously the contestatory mode of university research itself.[52] Agonistics is most certainly present in the (unfortunately too often *ressentiment*-laden)[53] arena of academic discourse—such as in the award-system of tenure and peer review, in the obsession with (inter)national research status in one's field, in conference performances, or in the politicized feuds of different methodologies and schools of thought. "All knowledge," states Huizinga, "is polemical by nature, and polemics cannot be divorced from agonistics" (156). Said reminds us, however, of the need for intellectuals to "speak . . . truth to power"[54]—as academic agonists we should base what we do in ethical authenticity, social relevance, and accountability.[55] Hence we remain resistant to Fish's recent call for agonistically inclined literary scholars of culture in the late 1990s (on both the left and the right) to leave the academy if they want the public to hear them.[56]

Our arenas of creative contest include, then, not only the text, body, and psyche of the author, but also *wirkliche Histoire*, the outsider or the marginalized, and cultures as they are constructed and linguistically reconstructed. The radically multifaceted nature of creative agonistics requires that any discussion of the same be equally multivocal and cross-disciplinary. The collection of essays that follows responds to that demand.

X

We would like to thank Carola Sautter and her assistants at the State University of New York Press for their constant helpfulness and efficiency. Our essay collection has benefitted greatly from the penetrating and insightful comments of the two anonymous SUNY readers. Special thanks go to Henry Sussman for his longstanding support for the original concept behind this essay collection. We thank all our contributors for their input in this Introduction, and especially for their patience and flexibility with their editors' myriad requests. Benjamin C. Sax provided valuable advice on this Introduction in its penultimate version. Janet Lungstrum's husband Richard knows precisely just how ineffable is the debt owed him for all he has done to help us in assembling the multiple voices of this volume. Finally, as two editors who are in several ways mirror-images of each other (one a scholar of German literature born and raised in Britain of English parents, the other a scholar of English literature born and raised in Canada of German parents), we can testify that our personal experience in editing this volume has been an agonistic enterprise in truly the best spirit of the word.

Notes

1. For a study of Nietzschean agonistics in German modernity, cf. Janet Lungstrum, *In Agon with Nietzsche: Studies in Modernist Creativity*, Ph.D. diss. (Charlottesville: Univ. of Virginia, 1993).

2. Friedrich Nietzsche, "Homer's Contest," this volume, 35.

3. Various Greek meanings of the noun 'αγω´ν are: assembly, in the sense of meeting at the games; place of assembly or contest (including the arena or stadium at the Olympic games); action at a law trial (*agonistes* refers to an advocate); battle; and, most generally, struggle or contest in the verbal or physical sense. Cited from Henry George Liddell and Robert Scott, *Greek-English Lexicon: Abridged Edition* (New York: Oxford Univ. Press, 1984). As Thomas F. Scanlon notes in his etymological study of the term, agon is formed from the Indo-European root *ag-* (to drive, to set in motion, to lead); "The Vocabulary of Competition: *Agon* and *Aethlos*, Greek Terms for Contest," *Arete: The Journal of Sport Literature* 1.1 (1983): 148. Scanlon states that the earliest meaning of the agon may be translated as " 'the place where men compete like leaders' "

(154). For another etymology of the word, see James Dennis Ellsworth, *Agon: Studies in the Use of a Word*, Ph.D. diss. (Berkeley: Univ. of California, 1971).

4. Jean Baudrillard, "After the Orgy," *The Transparency of Evil. Essays on Extreme Phenomena*, trans. James Benedict (New York: Verso, 1993), 3–13.

5. For a critique of Baudrillard's "catastrophic theology," see Andreas Huyssen, "In the Shadow of McLuhan: Baudrillard's Theory of Simulation," *Twilight Memories: Marking Time in a Culture of Amnesia* (New York: Routledge, 1995), 190.

6. Cf. Johan Huizinga: "During the growth of a civilization the agonistic function attains its most beautiful form, as well as its most conspicuous, in the archaic phase. As a civilization becomes more complex, more variegated and more overladen, and as the technique of production and social life itself becomes more finely organized, the old cultural soil is gradually smothered under a rank layer of ideas, systems of thought and knowledge, doctrines, rules and regulations, moralities and conventions which have all lost touch with play. Civilization, we then say, has grown more serious; it assigns only a secondary place to playing." *Homo Ludens: A Study of the Play-Element in Culture* (New York: Roy Publishers, 1950), 75.

7. Fredric Jameson, *Postmodernism, or, The Culture Logic of Late Capitalism* (Durham: Duke Univ. Press, 1991), 54.

8. Cf. also Roger Caillois, *Man, Play, and Games*, trans. Meyer Barash (New York: Free Press of Glencoe, 1961).

9. Agonistic behavior in animals and humans alike is not the same as aggression *per se* but is an *adaptive* trait, a "system of behaviour patterns having the common function of adaptation to situations involving physical conflict." J. P. Scott and E. Fredericson, *Physiological Zoology* 24 (1951); quoted by Felicity A. Huntingford and Angela K. Turner in *Animal Conflict* (New York: Chapman & Hall, 1987), 9.

10. Jean-François Lyotard, *The Postmodern Condition: A Report on Knowledge,* trans. Geoff Bennington and Brian Massumi (Minneapolis: Univ. of Minnesota Press, 1984), 41.

11. Terry Eagleton, *The Ideology of the Aesthetic* (Cambridge: Basil Blackwell, 1990), 396–400.

12. Seyla Benhabib, "Epistemologies of Postmodernism: A Rejoinder to Jean-François Lyotard"; Nancy Fraser and Linda J. Nicholson, "Social Criticism without Philosophy: An Encounter between Feminism and Postmodernism"; both in *Feminism/Postmodernism*, ed. Linda J. Nicholson (New York: Routledge, 1990): 107–30, 21–26.

13. "[T]here was *always* some form of active resistance, and in the overwhelming majority of cases, the resistance finally won out." Edward Said, *Culture and Imperialism* (New York: Vintage, 1993), xii.

14. Louis A. Montrose, "The Poetics and Politics of Culture," *The New Historicism*, ed. H. Aram Veeser (New York: Routledge, 1989), 30.

15. Chris Jencks, *Culture* (New York: Routledge, 1993), 157–58.

16. See Mihai I. Spariosu, *Dionysus Reborn: Play and the Aesthetic Dimension in Modern Philosophical and Scientific Discourse* (Ithaca: Cornell Univ.

Press, 1989); Spariosu, *God of Many Names: Play, Poetry, and Power in Hellenic Thought from Homer to Aristotle* (Durham: Duke Univ. Press, 1991); and Jean-Luc Boilleau, *Conflict et lien social: La rivalité contre la domination* (Paris: Editions La Découverte, 1995). Cf. also two volumes on literary and philosophical representations of strife: *Violence and Mediation in Contemporary Culture*, ed. Ronald Bogue and Marcel Cornis-Pope (Albany: State Univ. of New York Press, 1996); and *Intimate Conflict: Contradiction in Literary and Philosophical Discourse*, ed. Brian G. Caraher (Albany: State Univ. of New York Press, 1992).

17. Cf. Spariosu's *God of Many Names* for a study of the agon in Greek life and poetics, especially 4–27, 57–75, 87–98, 142–63, and 168–93. Cf. also Alvin Ward Gouldner, *Enter Plato: Classical Greece and the Origins of Social Theory* (London: Routledge and Kegan Paul, 1967); Ingomar Weiler, *Der Agon im Mythos. Zur Einstellung der Griechen zum Wettkampf* (Darmstadt: Wissenschaftliche Buchgesellschaft, 1974); and Karl Meuli, *Der griechische Agon: Kampf und Kampfspiel im Totenbrauch. Totentanz, Totenklage und Totenlob* (Cologne: Historisches Seminar der Deutschen Sporthochschule Köln, 1968).

18. Jacob Burckhardt, "Der koloniale und agonale Mensch," *Griechische Kulturgeschichte*, vol. 3, ed. Rudolf Marx (Stuttgart: A. Kroner, 1941). Burckhardt's influence on Nietzsche at Basel was significant; but Nietzsche wrote an early agonal essay, "The Contest of Homer and Hesiod," before his move to Basel.

19. For a history of the Olympic games in both Greek and modern society, see Richard D. Mandell, *The First Olympic Games* (Berkeley: Univ. of California Press, 1976).

20. As Spariosu states in *God of Many Names*, from the very onset the Hellenic games were a mixed bag of athletic competitions alongside the verbal contests of the Sophists, dramatic poets, and singers of tales (97). Likewise, Mandell points to a conflation of sportive and musical agon in that several Olympic events (like the weapons race and the pancration [fighting]) were done to musical accompaniment and hence were spectacles or performances in the same sense as a dance (10).

21. Michel Foucault, *The History of Sexuality, Volume II: The Use of Pleasure*, trans. Robert Hurley (New York: Vintage, 1990), 67. States Foucault: "In the ethics of the *aphrodisia*, the inevitability and difficulty of the combat derived . . . from the facts that it unfolded as a solo contest," i.e., without the need for a Christian Other to be invoked as sexual sin or the Devil (68). He defines the Greek *aphrodisia* as "pleasurable [sexual] acts situated in an agonistic field of forces difficult to control" (67). See also Sax's chapter on the Foucauldian agon in "The Fruit of the Garden," forthcoming in *The Radical Return: Postmodernity/Nietzsche/Modernity*, ch. 7.

22. Nietzsche, *Twilight of the Idols*, trans. R. J. Hollingdale (Harmondsworth, UK: Penguin, 1971), 111.

23. Sax, "Zeus' Dice Throw," forthcoming in *The Radical Return: Postmodernity/Nietzsche/Modernity*, ch. 5.

24. Carrie L. Asman, "Theater and *Agon/Agon* and Theater: Walter Benjamin and Florens Christian Rang," *MLN* 107 (1992): 612–13.

25. Cf. Mikhail Bakhtin, who affirms the agonistic origin of tragedy in *Problems of Dostoevsky's Poetics*, ed. and trans. Caryl Emerson (Minneapolis: Univ. of Minnesota Press, 1984), 125 g.

26. Cf. Walter J. Ong's account of the inward turn from Hellenic agonistic orality to modern literacy on the "narrative and the scholarly-scientific fronts." *Fighting for Life: Contest, Sexuality, and Consciousness* (Ithaca: Cornell Univ. Press, 1981), 186.

27. Foucault, "The Discourse on Language," *The Archaelogy of Knowledge*, trans. A. M. Sheridan Smith (New York: Pantheon, 1972), 218.

28. Foucault, *The History of Sexuality, Volume 1: An Introduction*, trans. Robert Hurley (New York: Random House, 1978), 97, 92, 94, 93.

29. Gilles Deleuze, *Foucault*, trans. Seán Hand (Minneapolis: Univ. of Minnesota Press, 1988), 71.

30. Foucault, *Discipline and Punish. The Birth of the Prison*, trans. Alan Sheridan (New York: Vintage, 1979), 308.

31. Foucault, *Power/Knowledge. Selected Interviews and Other Writings 1972–1977*, ed. Colin Giordon, trans. Colin Giordon, Leo Marshall, John Mepham, and Kate Soper (New York: Pantheon, 1980), 39.

32. For a balanced assessment of Foucault, see Joan W. Scott's comments in "Deconstructing equality-versus-difference: Or, the uses of poststructuralist theory for feminism," *The Postmodern Condition: New Perspectives on Social Theory*, ed. Steven Seidman (New York: Cambridge Univ. Press, 1994), 284–85.

33. Richard Rorty, "Method, social science, and social hope," in Seidman, 57–64.

34. Volney P. Gay sees this recognition of Freud's as occurring in his last post-1918 period in which Freud "explained conflict behaviors as products of the interaction between contrary structures, the ego-superego versus the id." *Freud on Sublimation: Reconsiderations* (Albany: State Univ. of New York Press, 1992), 61.

35. Freud's former disciple, Alfred Alder, developed an agonistic theory of the psyche that can be based not on the death instinct but on social interest (*Gemeinschaftsgefühl*). See Randolph Severson's Adlerian critique of Freud's "talking cure" for its negation of the dialogic agon, in "Alder, Agon, and Aggression," *Individual Psychology* 46.3 (1990): 333.

36. Sigmund Freud, *Civilization and Its Discontents*, trans. & ed. James Strachey (New York: W. W. Norton, 1961), 69.

37. Harold Bloom, *Agon: Towards a Theory of Revisionism* (New York: Oxford Univ. Press, 1982), vii.

38. Bloom, *The Anxiety of Influence: A Theory of Poetry* (New York: Oxford Univ. Press, 1973), 95. Abbreviated in the main text as AI.

39. Bloom, *A Map of Misreading* (New York: Oxford Univ. Press, 1975), 3.

40. Of this infallibility, Bloom insists, for example, that "[i]t remains not arbitrary nor even accidental to say that everyone who now reads and writes

in the West, of whatever racial background, sex or ideological camp, is still a son or daughter of Homer" (*A Map of Misreading* 33).

41. Bloom, *The Western Canon: The Books and School of the Ages* (New York: Riverhead Books, 1994), 1, 7.

42. Cf. Paul Gray, "Hurrah for Dead White Males!" *Time* 144.15 (October 10, 1994): 52–53.

43. Bakhtin, *The Dialogic Imagination*, ed. Michael Holquist, trans. Caryl Emerson and Michael Holquist (Austin: Univ. of Texas Press, 1981), 427.

44. Gunther Kress and Terry Threadgold, "Towards a Social Theory of Genre," *Southern Review* 21 (1988): 234.

45. Patricia Yaeger, "Afterword," *Feminism, Bakhtin and the Dialogic*, ed. Dale M. Bauer and Susan J. McKinstry (Albany: State Univ. of New York Press, 1991), 241.

46. David Shepherd, "Bakhtin and the Reader," *Bakhtin and Cultural Theory*, ed. Ken Hirschkop and David Shepherd (New York: Manchester Univ. Press, 1989), 96–97. See Stanley Fish, *Is There a Text in This Class? The Authority of Interpretive Communities* (Cambridge: Harvard Univ. Press, 1980).

47. Cf. Peter Levine's critique of Nietzsche's *Weltanschauung*-historicist method of reading Greek culture, in *Nietzsche and the Modern Crisis of the Humanities* (Albany: State Univ. of New York Press, 1995), 49–57.

48. V. N. Volosinov, *Marxism and the Philosophy of Language*, trans. Ladislav Matejka and I. R. Titunik (Cambridge: Harvard Univ. Press, 1986), 34. Bakhtin is at least a coauthor of this text.

49. Sandra M. Gilbert and Susan Gubar, *No Man's Land: The Place of the Woman Writer in the Twentieth Century, Volume 1: The War of the Words* (New Haven: Yale Univ. Press, 1988), 5.

50. John W. Loy and Graham L. Hesketh, "The Agon Motif: A Prologemon for the Study of Agonetic Behavior," *Contribution of Sociology to the Study of Sport,* ed. Kalevi Olin (Juväskylä, Finland: Univ. of Juväskylä, 1984), 44–45.

51. Chantal Mouffe, "For a Politics of Agonistic Pluralism," *Identity, Authority and Democracy*, ed. James Donald and Stephanie Donald, Culcom Research Papers in Media & Cultural Studies (Brighton: Univ. of Sussex, 1995), 119.

52. It is also true, however, that precisely this agonistic tradition of research in American academe, particularly in the humanities and social sciences, is becoming increasingly endangered in the late 1990s by economic downsizing, the predicted demise of tenure in favor of a contract-based system, and a heightened control (by university administrations, state legislatures, and public opinion) over the standards of performance for faculty, particularly in setting the percentile "agon" between teaching and research responsibilities.

53. On the agonistic tradition in academia, see "Academic and Intellectual Arenas," chapter 4 of Walter J. Ong's *Fighting for Life,* 119–48. Cf. also Cynthia Haynes-Burton's critique of a(nta)gonistic academic discourse in "The Ethico-Political Agon of *Other* Criticisms: Toward a Nietzschean Counter-Ethic," *Pre/Text* 11:3–4 (1990). Haynes-Burton proposes an alternative, neo-Nietzschean

agonistics that goes beyond reactionary herd behavior in the academy, and suggests that we "bear . . . witness to agonistic, combative discourse operating within academic discussions and name it for what it is: anethical and overly political" (304).

54. Said, *Representations of the Intellectual* (New York: Vintage, 1994), 85–102.

55. "The mode of being of the new intellectual can no longer consist in eloquence, which is an exterior and momentary mover of feelings and passions, but in active participation in practical life, as constructor, organizer, 'permanent persuader,' and not just simple orator." Antonio Gramsci, *Selections from the Prison Notebooks*, ed. & trans. Quintin Hoare and Geoffrey Nowell-Smith (London: Lawrence & Wishart, 1973), 161.

56. Fish, *Professional Correctness: Literary Studies and Political Change* (New York: Oxford Univ. Press, 1996).

I Contests in Cultural Philosophy

"Only contest made me a poet, a sophist, an orator!"
Nietzsche (Plato), "Homer's Contest"

Homer's Contest

Friedrich Nietzsche

Translated by Jordan Dieterich and Janet Lungstrum

Preface

When one speaks of *humanity,* the basic concept implied is that this is meant to be what *differentiates* and distinguishes mankind from nature. But such a distinction does not exist in reality: "natural" attributes and those that are called truly "human" have grown inseparably into one another. Man, in the highest and noblest of his strengths, is wholly Nature, and carries her uncanny dual character within him. His terrible capacities that are deemed inhuman may even be that fertile ground out of which alone all of humanity can grow forth in emotions, deeds, and accomplishments.

Thus do the Greeks, the most humane people of antiquity, have a tendency within themselves toward cruelty, toward a tiger-like pleasure in destruction: a tendency that is also clearly visible in that grotesquely enlarged reflection of the Hellenes, Alexander the Great; and that, however, in their entire history, as well as in their mythology, must terrify all of us who encounter them with our softish notion of modern humanity. When Alexander has the feet of Batis,[1] that heroic defender of Gaza, pierced, and his body bound alive to his chariot in order to drag him around amidst the jeering of his soldiers, this is thus a sickening caricature of Achilles, who mishandles the cadaver of Hector at night by similarly dragging it around; yet even this tendency offends and fills us with horror. Here we peer into the abyss of hatred. We also experience this same sensation when we look upon, say, the bloody and insatiable self-slaughter of two Greek parties, for example in the Corcyrean revolution.[2] When the victor in a battle between cities, adhering to the *rights* of war, executes the entire male population and sells all of the women and children into slavery, we can see in the very sanctioning of such rights that the Greek viewed a full discharge of his hatred as a vital necessity; in such moments was the cramped and swollen sensation released: the tiger sprang forth, a lustful ferocity gleaming from his terrifying eyes. Why did the Greek sculptor need again and again to carve out scenes of war and battles in endless repetitions, with outstretched human corpses whose tendons had been torn in hatred or in the wanton frenzy of triumph, with the writhing wounded and the dying in their death-cries? Why did the entire Greek world rejoice over the battle scenes of the *Iliad*? I am afraid that we do not understand these things in a sufficiently "Greek" way; indeed, that we would shudder were we ever to understand them from a Greek perspective.

What, however, lies as the wellspring of everything Hellenic, *behind* the Homeric world? In the *latter,* the unique artistic certainty, peace, and purity of the lines lift us beyond that which is purely material; their colors appearing, through an artistic illusion, to be lighter, milder, warmer; their people, in this colorful warm illumination, to be better and friendlier—but what do we gaze upon when we stride backward into the pre-Homeric world, no longer guided and protected by the hand of Homer? Nothing other than night and dread, the products of an imagination fully accustomed to the hideous. What kind of worldly existence is reflected in these repulsively horrid theogonic legends? A life that is swayed only by the *children of the night:* strife, lust, deceit, old age, and death. Let us imagine the stifling air of the Hesiodic poetry in its compressed and darkened state, and without all of the modifications and purifications that flowed throughout Hellas from Delphi and from countless abodes of the gods; let us mix this thickened Boeotian air with the dark voluptuousness of the Etruscans; then such a reality would *extort* from us a world of myth in which Uranus, Cronus, Zeus, and the battles of the Titans must appear as a relief. In this brooding atmosphere, struggle signifies well-being and salvation; the cruelty of victory is the peak of life's glories. And, as the concept of Greek rights evolved in truth from *murder* and from atonement for murder, so does the nobler culture also take its first victory wreath from the altar of atonement for murder. Closely behind that bloody age follows a wake, deeply carved into Hellenic history. The names of Orpheus, Musaeus,[3] and their cults reveal to which consequences the never-ending spectacle of a world of struggle and cruelty can lead—toward a disgust with existence, toward the comprehension of this state of existence as an unatoneable penalty, toward belief in the co-identity of existence and guilt. These particular consequences, however, are not specifically Hellenic; in this, Greece follows along with India and with the Orient in general. The Hellenic genius had yet another answer ready for the question "What is a life of struggle and of victory really for?"—and it gives this answer in the complete breadth of Greek history.

In order to understand them, we must begin with the fact that the Greek genius validated the existence of this once-terrible drive and considered it to be *legitimate:* while in the Orphic period it was thought that a life rooted in such a drive would not be worth living. The struggle and joy of victory were acknowledged: and nothing separates the Greek world so much from our own as the *coloring,* thus derived, of individual ethical concepts, for example those of *Eris* and of *Envy.*

In his wanderings through Greece, as the traveller Pausanias[4] visited Mount Helicon,[5] he was shown an ancient copy of the first didactic poem of the Greeks, the "Works and Days" of Hesiod,[6] inscribed on lead plates and badly spoiled by time and weather. Still he could recognize that, in contrast to the normal copies, at its head was *not* that little hymn to Zeus, rather it began immediately with the declaration: "There are *two* goddesses of Eris[7] on earth." This is one of the most striking Hellenic concepts, and it is worthy of being impressed right away upon the newcomer at the entrance gate of the Hellenic ethic. "The one Eris would a man praise, if he has any sense, likewise the other would he rebuke; for these two goddesses have an entirely distinct character. For the one fosters awful war and strife, the cruel woman! No mortal can stand her; only under the yoke of necessity does one show any respect to the oppressive Eris, according to the counsel of the immortals. This one, as the elder, was brought forth by the black night;[8] the high-throned Zeus, however, placed the other Eris in the roots of the earth and among men, as a much better one. She drives even the inept man to work; and should one man lacking in property look upon another man who is wealthy, he will then rush to sow and to plant in the same fashion and to put his house in order; neighbor competes with neighbor, striving toward affluence. Good is this Eris for men. The potter also resents the potter and the carpenter the carpenter; the beggar envies the beggar and the poet the poet."

The last two verses, which deal with the *odium figulinum,*[9] appear at this point incomprehensible to our scholars. In their judgment, the attributes "resentment" and "envy" are suitable only to the character of the bad Eris. They therefore have no hesitation in designating the verses as either spurious or placed here by accident. In this regard, however, a different ethic from the Hellenic must have inspired them, unobserved: for Aristotle is not repulsed by these verses about the good Eris. And not only Aristotle but the whole of Greek antiquity thinks differently than we do about resentment and envy. Its judgment parallels that of Hesiod, who first designates one Eris as evil, namely the one who leads men to fight hostile wars of extermination against each other; and then again he praises another Eris as good, who as jealousy, resentment, and envy stirs men to action—not, however, to the action of wars of extermination but to the action of *contest.* The Greek is *envious* and perceives this quality not as a flaw but as a consequence of a *beneficent* deity: what a chasm of ethical judgement between us and him! Because he is envious, he also feels the envious eye of a god resting upon him at every abundance of honor, wealth, glory, and success, and he fears this envy. In this case, he reminds the god of the passing of every man's lot and shudders at his own success; sacrificing the best of it, he bows before the divine envy. This conception does not at all alienate his gods from him: on the contrary, their significance is apparent insofar as man may *never* venture the contest with them, while against every other living being his soul burns with jealousy. In the battle of Thamyris[10] with the Muses, in that of Marsyas[11] with Apollo, in the gripping fate of Niobe,[12] appeared the terrible confrontation of the two powers never allowed to fight each other: man and god.

The greater and more magnificent a Greek man is, however, the more brightly does the flame of ambition break forth from him, consuming anyone in his path. Aristotle once made a list of such hostile contests in the grand style: the most striking example therein is that even a dead man can still provoke a living one to all-consuming jealousy. This is how Aristotle designates the relation of Xenophanes of Colophon[13] to Homer. We do not understand the strength of this attack upon the national hero of poetry if we do not recognize, as later also with Plato, that at the root of this attack is a monstrous craving to take up the place of the fallen poet and to inherit his glory. Every great Hellene passes on the torch of the contest; with every great virtue a new greatness is kindled. When the young Themistocles[14] could not sleep from thinking of the laurels of Miltiades,[15] it was not until the long rivalry with Aristides that his drive, so early awakened, was unleashed into that uniquely remarkable, purely instinctive genius of his political action, as described for us by Thucydides.[16] How characteristic a question and answer, when a renowned opponent of Pericles[17] is asked whether he or Pericles is the best wrestler in the city, and he responds: "Even if I knock him down, he will deny that he has fallen, and so reach his objective, persuading those who saw him fall."

If one wants to see that feeling properly unveiled in its naive manifestations—the feeling of the necessity of contest, a precondition for the well-being of the state—then one should think of the original meaning of *ostrakismos:*[18] how, for example, the Ephesians declare at the banishment of Hermodorus:[19] "Among us no one shall be the best; if anyone is, however, then he should be so elsewhere and among others." Why is it, then, that no one should be the best? Because the contest would be exhausted thereby, and the eternal foundation of life for the Hellenic state would be endangered. Later, *ostrakismos* receives a different position regarding contest: it is employed when there is evident danger that one of the great politicians and party leaders battling in contest feels provoked, in the heat of battle, to use harmful and destructive methods and dubious *coups d'ètat.* The original sense of this extraordinary device is, however, not one of an outlet, rather one of a stimulant: one does away with an outstanding individual, so that once again the competing game of strengths may awaken: a concept that is hostile to the "exclusivity" of genius in the modern sense, but presupposes that in the natural order of things there are always *several* geniuses, who mutually incite each other to act, as they also mutually hold themselves within the bounds of moderation. That is the core of the Hellenic concept of contest: it abhors sovereign mastery, and fears its dangers; it desires, as *protection* against the one genius—a second genius.

Every talent must unfurl itself struggling, requires the Hellenic popular pedagogy: while more recent educators are afraid of nothing more than the unleashing of so-called ambition. Today one fears egoism as "evil in itself"—with the exception of the Jesuits, who like the ancients are predisposed to it, and for this reason may well possibly be the most effective educators of our time. They seem to believe that egoism, i.e., individualism, is only the strongest agency, with its character as "good" and "evil" being received essentially from those goals to which it aspires. For the ancients, however, the goal of agonal education was the welfare of the whole or of the civic state. Every Athenian, for example, had to develop himself in contest, so much so as to be of the highest benefit to Athens and to bring it the least harm. It was not an unmeasured and unmeasurable ambition, as modern ambition mostly is: the young man thought of the well-being of his native city whenever he ran or threw or sang in contest. He wanted to increase its glory through his own; to the gods of the city he dedicated the wreaths that the judges placed upon his head in honor. In contests between the cities, every Greek sensed from childhood on the burning desire within himself to be an instrument for the good of his city; in this way was his ambition kindled; in this way was it restricted and restrained. For this reason the individuals of antiquity were freer because their goals were closer and more tangible. In contrast, modern man is traversed everywhere by infinity, like the swift-footed Achilles in the parable of the Eleatic Zeno:[20] infinity impedes him; he does not even overtake the tortoise.

As the young men to be educated were raised in contest with each other, however, so were their educators, in turn, in rivalry amongst themselves. Distrustful and jealous, the great musical masters Pindar and Simonides took their stand next to each other; the sophist, the advanced educator of antiquity, meets the other sophist in rivalry; even the most general type of instruction, that given through drama, was imparted to the people only in the form of a colossal wrestling among the great musical and dramatic artists. How wonderful! "Even the artist resents the artist!" And modern man fears nothing in an artist so much as the indication of a personal struggle, while the Greek knows an artist *only in personal struggle.* Where modern man suspects weakness in a work of art, the Greek seeks the source of his highest strength! With Plato, for example, that which is of particular artistic significance in his dialogues is mostly the result of a rivalry with the art of the orators, sophists, and dramatists of his time, invented with the aim of being able to say in the end: "Behold, that which my great competitors can do, I can do, too; yes, I can do it better than they. No Protagoras[21] has written such beautiful myths as I; no dramatist such an animated and captivating entirety as the *Symposium;* no orator has composed such orations as I set down in the *Gorgias*—and now I discard it all together and condemn all imitative art! Only contest made me a poet, a sophist, an orator!" What a problem unfolds for us here, when we ask about the relation of contest to the conception of a work of art!

If, on the other hand, we take contest away from Greek life, then we peer instantly into that pre-Homeric abyss of a dreadful wildness of hatred and pleasure in destruction. This phenomenon unfortunately often appears when, because of an exceedingly brilliant deed, a great personality was suddenly removed from the contest and made, in his and his fellow-citizens' judgment, *hors de concours.* The effect is almost without exception one of horror; and if one usually concludes from these reactions that the Greek was incapable of enduring glory and success, then one should speak more precisely: that without further contest he was not able to endure the glory, the success at the conclusion of the contest. There is no clearer example than the final fate of Miltiades. Because of his incomparable success at Marathon, when he was placed on a lonely pinnacle and raised far above every fellow-contestant, he feels awaken within him a low, revenge-seeking craving against a Parian citizen, with whom he had had a feud long ago. To satisfy this craving, he misuses reputation, state property, and civic honor, and dishonors himself. With a feeling of failure he stoops to unworthy machinations. He enters into a secret and godless relationship with Timo, a priestess of Demeter, and at night trespasses into the holy temple, which every man was forbidden to enter. After he jumps over the wall and comes ever nearer to the sanctuary of the goddess, suddenly the terrible dread of a panicked fright overcomes him: near collapse and out of his mind, he feels driven back, and jumping back over the wall he falls down, paralyzed and badly injured. The siege has to be lifted, the people's court awaits him, and a shameful death impresses its seal upon a brilliant heroic career, to darken it for all posterity. After the battle at Marathon, the envy of the heavens seizes him. And this godly envy is kindled when it beholds man without any competitor, devoid of opponents upon a lonely height of glory. Only the gods are by him now—and therefore they are against him. These gods, however, mislead him to a deed of hubris, and under its weight he collapses.

Let us observe well that, just as Miltiades is ruined, so too are the noblest Greek states ruined when, through merit and good fortune, they reach the temple of Nike from the race-track. Athens, which had destroyed the independence of its allies and severely punished the rebellions of its subjugated peoples, and Sparta, which after the battle of Aigospotamoi[22] asserted its ascendancy over Hellas in a much more cruel and severe manner, also brought about their ruin through deeds of hubris, following the example of Miltiades. Herein lies proof that without envy, jealousy, and competitive ambition, the Hellenic state degenerates, likewise the Hellenic man. He becomes evil and cruel, he becomes revenge-seeking and godless; in short, he becomes "pre-Homeric"—and then no more than a panicked fright is required in order to make him fall and shatter. Sparta and Athens surrender to Persia, as Themistocles and Alcibiades[23] have done; they betray the Hellenic principle after they have given up the noblest Hellenic fundamental idea—the contest; and then Alexander, the coarsened copy and abbreviation of Greek history, invents the cosmopolitan Hellene and so-called "Hellenism."

Finished on December 29, 1872.

TRANSLATORS' NOTES

We would like to thank John Gibert for his helpful comments on these notes.

"Homers Wettkampf," written as a Preface, is from "Fünf Vorreden zu fünf ungeschriebenen Büchern" (1872), in Friedrich Nietzsche, *Sämtliche Werke. Kritische Studienausgabe,* ed. Giorgio Colli and Mazzino Montinari, 15 vols. (New York and Berlin: de Gruyter, 1967–1977), 1: 783–92. Translated with the permission of the German publisher. The first translation of this essay was by Maximilian A. Mügge in *Early Greek Philosophy and Other Essays,* vol. 2 of *The Complete Works of Friedrich Nietzsche,* ed. Oscar Levy (London: T. N. Foulis, 1911; rpt., New York: Russell & Russell, 1964; rpt., New York: Gordon Press, 1974); there is also a partial translation of this essay by Walter Kaufmann in *The Portable Nietzsche,* ed. Walter Kaufmann (New York: Penguin, 1982). A more recent translation appears under the title "Homer on Competition" in Friedrich Nietzsche, *On the Genealogy of Morality,* ed. Keith Ansell-Pearson, trans. Carol Diethe (New York: Cambridge Univ. Press, 1994). Another translation of this essay will appear in a future volume of *The Complete Works of Friedrich Nietzsche,* ed. Ernst Behler (Stanford: Stanford Univ. Press, forthcoming).

1. Batis: the commander of Gaza, who resisted Alexander's siege for two months in 332 BCE. This and subsequent explanations of Nietzsche's Greek references are drawn from *Der kleine Pauly. Lexikon der Antike,* ed. Konrat Ziegler and Walther Sontheimer, 5 vols. (Munich: Alfred Druckenmüller Verlag, 1975), and *The Oxford Classical Dictionary,* ed. M. Cary, J. D. Dennison et al., 2nd ed. (Oxford: Clarendon, 1970).

2. Nietzsche refers to Thucydides' famous depiction of Corcyrean civil strife. Corcyra (now Corfu), the model for the Phaecia of the *Odyssey,* was in constant warfare with Corinth, especially after 435 BCE, and received protection from Athens.

3. Musaeus: a mythical bard. Aristophanes distinguishes Musaeus from Orpheus by saying that the former taught cures of diseases and oracles, and the latter mysteries and abstinence.

4. Pausanias: a Greek traveller and geographer, who wrote "Description of Greece," which contains the history and topography of cities as well as a depiction of local customs and mythology.

5. Mount Helicon: the largest mountain of Boeotia, with the sancturary of the Muses at its summit. Hesiod's native town was Ascra, located on its slopes.

6. Hesiod was often contrasted with Homer as the other main representative of early epic. The "Works and Days" gives training on how to live a life of honest labor.

7. Eris was the goddess who personified "bad" strife and discord (βαρεῖα) as well as 'good" emulation and healthy competition (ἀγαθή).

8. Richard Lattimore renders correctly: "But the other one was born / the elder daughter of black Night. / The Son of Kronos, who sits on high and /

dwells in the bright air, / set her in the roots of the earth and among men; / she is far kinder." *Hesiod: The Works and Days, Theogony, The Shield of Herakles* (Ann Arbor: Univ. of Michigan Press, 1959), 19–21. Hesiod means us to understand that both good and bad Eris are children of Night; he is only explicit about the good Eris. Nietzsche's version is not a mistake, but the result of unjustified textual intervention to remove the apparent oddity.

9. "Rivalry of potters" (Nietzsche's Latin phrase).

10. Thamyris: a Thracian bard, who boasted that he could beat the Muses in a contest. They promptly blinded him and made him forget his talent.

11. Marsyas: a satyr, whose name derives from the river of the same name (a tributary of the Maeander). Athena discarded the oboe after having invented it, because it distorted her face to play it; Marsyas picked up the instrument and learned to play it so beautifully that he challenged Apollo to a musical contest. The conditions of the contest were that whoever won could do with the loser as he saw fit. The victory was Apollo's, who whipped Marsyas to death. The river sprang forth from his blood or from the tears of his mourners.

12. Niobe's six sons and six daughters were killed by Apollo and Artemis after Niobe had boasted that she was equal to or better than Leto, the mother of Apollo and Artemis. Zeus turned Niobe's children into stone; and Niobe herself, in her bereavement, metamorphosed into a stone (which is still on Mt. Sipylon).

13. Xenophanes: an epic poet and philosopher who engaged in severe criticism of Homer and Hesoid. He affirmed a single God or Consciousness and rejected the Homeric / Hesiodic pantheon of gods who resemble human beings in their behavior and form.

14. Themistocles (528–462 BCE): an Athenian democratic statesman, who rose to supremacy in 487 BCE. He was behind the ostracism of fellow statesman and rival Aristides in 482 BCE. Later, however, the two cooperated to repel Persia's attack on Athens.

15. Miltiades (550–489 BCE): an Athenian nobleman who, after ruling the Thracian Chersonese as absolute monarch, rose to become the most influential politician in Athens. He became famous for his victory over Persia at the battle of Marathon in 490 BCE—the first time that the Athenians had defeated the Persians. As Herodotus records, his political fall came one year later with a failed expedition to capture Paros; soon afterward he died of his wounds. Nietzsche takes over Herodotus' highly embellished version of Miltiades' demise at the end of "Homer's Contest."

16. Thucydides inserted a eulogy of Themistocles in his "History of the War between Athens and Sparta" (431–404 BCE).

17. Pericles (495–429 BCE): An Athenian statesman renowned for his incorruptibility and skills at oratory.

18. *Ostrakismos:* ostracism as a collective Athenian policy was first introduced c. 487 BCE. It was a method of banning an unpopular prominent citizen for a ten-year period, after which he could return with no loss to his property, status, or citizenship. Each year, citizens voted on whether to hold an ostracism, and, if a majority agreed, citizens wanting to vote would write the name of the

citizen they wished to be ostracized on a potsherd *(ostrakon)*. If the total number of potsherds reached six thousand, the citizen named on the greatest number had to leave Athens within ten days. Ostracism was sometimes an effective way of getting rid of political opponents: on occasion, masses of potsherds were marked in advance with a citizen's name and then distributed to voters.

19. Heraclitus, who lived in Ephesus, a coastal city in Asia Minor, writes contemptuously how the philosopher Hermodorus was banished by the Ephesians, precisely for being their most valued citizen.

20. Zeno: a major representative of the Eleatic School of philosophy; Aristotle called him the founder of dialectic, but he is most famous for a series of paradoxes involving continua.

21. Protagoras, born c. 485 BCE, was one of the earliest sophists, intellectuals and educators who came to prominence in the second half of the fifth century BCE, especially in Athens. Protagoras professed to teach "moral and practical wisdom" ('αρετή), and is known for his dictum, "Man is the measure of all things."

22. Aigospotamoi: a place and river on the coast of the Thracian Chersonesus peninsula, known through the decisive defeat of the Athenian fleet there in 405 BCE at the hands of the Peloponnesians.

23. Alcibiades (450–404 BCE): an Athenian general and statesman, and also the pupil and friend of Socrates. After a turbulent career that had seen him waging the Peloponnesian War from both sides, he escaped to Persia (as had Themistocles before him), where he was eventually murdered.

Cultural Agonistics: Nietzsche, the Greeks, Eternal Recurrence

Benjamin C. Sax

The Homeric Culture of the Agon

While acknowledging the significance of the doctrine of eternal recurrence in *Thus Spake Zarathustra* as well as in other works, interpreters of Nietzsche[1] are, however, in disagreement about the text's philosophical status and even its basic meaning. The debates over the interpretation of eternal recurrence have also stirred up as much controversy as any other "theme" in Nietzsche's writings. Is eternal recurrence a cosmological truth (Stambaugh), or a metaphysical truth (Heidegger), or an "anti-Hegelian" doctrine (Deleuze)?[2] Is eternal recurrence a variant of pragmatic truth (Danto), or the demands of an "existential imperative" (Magnus), or a stylized expression of individual truth (Nehamas)?[3] Some have even claimed that there is no truth whatsoever in this doctrine (de Man, Derrida).[4] Allan Megill finds the idea of the eternal recurrence "extravagant and unreasonable." For him, it is totally "incomprehensible."[5]

Nietzsche himself provided several aids to the interpretation of eternal recurrence. He placed special emphasis upon its origins:

> Now I shall relate the history of *Zarathustra*. The fundamental conception of this work, the idea of the eternal recurrence, this highest formula of affirmation that is at all attainable, belongs in August 1881: it was penned on a sheet with the notation underneath, "6000 feet beyond man and time." That day I was walking through the woods along the lake of Silvaplana; at a powerful pyramidal rock not far from Surlei I stopped. It was then that this idea came to me. (EH 295)

The event of August 1881 is well known to readers of *Ecce Homo*. Yet the thought of eternal recurrence is not only revealed to or intuited by Nietzsche: it is also remembered. In an earlier section of *Ecce Homo*, Nietzsche evaluates his own contribution to the history of philosophy: "I have the right to understand myself as the first *tragic philosopher*."[6] Even the Greeks had not construed such a position: "Before me this transposition of the Dionysian into a philosophical pathos did not exist: *tragic wisdom* was lacking; I even looked in vain for signs of it even among the *great* Greeks in philosophy, those of the two centuries *before* Socrates." Nietzsche, however, makes one important exception among the early Greek philosophers. He admits a special relation to one archaic thinker: "I retained some doubt in the case of *Heraclitus*, in whose proximity I feel altogether warmer and better than anywhere else" (EH 273). "The doctrine of the 'eternal recurrence,' that is, of the unconditional and infinitely repeated circular course of all things—this doctrine of Zarathustra *might* in the end have been taught already by Heraclitus" (EH 274).

The word "might" in the above statement invites various readings. In the uncompleted text, "Philosophy in the Tragic Age of the Greeks" (1873), Nietzsche presented an interpretation of Heraclitus' philosophy. At first glance, he seems to set up an opposition between being and becoming. Against Anaximander's concept of being, Nietzsche's Heraclitus declares, "I see nothing other than becoming" (PTA 51). Heraclitus' philosophy of becoming seems to be uncomplicated and rather straightforward, but how far does it go in explicating Zarathustra's doctrine of eternal recurrence? Is eternal recurrence simply an acceptance of becoming over being and an affirmation of what Nietzsche calls "the innocence of becoming"? If this seems to be the case, then why is the doctrine of eternal recurrence so difficult to understand, and why does Nietzsche place so much emphasis upon the personal pain and suffering involved in accepting it?

Nietzsche's "might" opens another possibility, a less direct and less limited line of interpretation. In "Philosophy in the Tragic Age," Nietzsche places Heraclitus within the history of pre-Socratic thinkers from Thales to Anaximander. But he is concerned with the truth of ancient philosophy and the history of this philosophy only to the extent that they speak to another issue and address a larger problem. Whoever wishes to justify philosophy, Nietzsche declares, must show "to what ends a healthy culture uses and has used philosophy" (PTA 27). The archaic Greeks for Nietzsche simply provide us with a model of the relation between philosophy and a healthy culture. On one level, the question of philosophy is a question of timing: "[T]he Greeks knew precisely how to begin at the proper time, and the lesson of how one must start out in philosophy they demonstrate more plainly than any other people." The pre-Socratics philosophized in the "midst of good fortune" (PTA 28). But on a deeper level, this timing is a cultural phenomenon: "Only a culture such as the Greeks possessed can answer our question as to the task of the philosopher" (PTA 33). The highest philosophical thoughts arise when the culture is at its height.

In this essay, Nietzsche poses a general question of philosophy and culture and the relationship between "true" philosophy and "healthy" cultures. This question of cultural health determines the path of philosophy and the content of its truths. The first task of the philosopher, then, is extra-philosophical: he must ascertain whether he exists in a healthy or a sick culture. Not to ask this question has its consequences. Philosophy never, he argues, made a sick society healthy: "[W]here could we find an instance of cultural pathology which philosophy returned to health?" Philosophy was helpful to healthy cultures: "The sick, it made ever sicker" (PTA 27). Nietzsche makes the point clear by contrasting the archaic Greek to the modern European philosopher: "The philosopher's mission when he lives in a genuine culture (which is characterized by unity of style) cannot be properly derived from our circumstances, for we have no genuine culture" (PTA 33).

In other words, an interpretation of Greek philosophy leads to an understanding of Greek culture. But what precisely does Nietzsche mean by "healthy" culture, and why does Greek culture constitute for him "*the* supreme event of culture," the norm of every "healthy culture"?[7] Nietzsche's writings of the early 1870s provide an answer to these questions.[8] Even when interpreters of Nietzsche have acknowledged the impact of Greek culture upon his thinking, they have often failed to comprehend what Nietzsche valued in this culture. In part this lack of understanding arises from a misconception of Nietzsche's view of the Greeks. It is well known that Nietzsche developed his own philosophical position (independent, that is, of Schopenhauer, Wagner, and Hegel) only after writing *The Birth of Tragedy* (1872), his first interpretation of Greek culture. But the sources of the stance that Nietzsche later adopted (as in the new preface to *The Birth of Tragedy* of 1886 or the section on this work in *Ecce Homo* of 1888) can in fact be located much earlier in his work. They originated in a reinterpretation of Greek culture.[9]

Immediately after completing *The Birth of Tragedy*, Nietzsche began work on this new interpretation in a series of essays. In the earliest of these, "Homer's Contest" (1872), Nietzsche turned away from the idea that he could understand Greek culture through an interpretation of Greek tragedy. And, more importantly, he rejected the problematic upon which *The Birth of Tragedy* was based. The metaphysical contrast between the Apollonian and the Dionysian was abandoned not because he found them philologically or historically questionable, but because he no longer accepted the Schopenhauerian notion that art is an escape from the pains of individuation, that "only as an *aesthetic phenomenon* . . . [are] existence and the world . . . eternally justified" (BT 52). He came to see that the struggle of individuation is life itself, and he abandoned the Hegelian dialectical logic that joined the opposing Apollonian and Dionysian principles within a higher reconciling unity.

"Homer's Contest" *(Homers Wettkampf)* is oddly titled. Nietzsche deals neither with the texts of the Homeric epics nor, as one might suppose, with the funeral games with which the *Iliad* concludes (although the movement in this epic from warfare to athletic contests fits well with Nietzsche's argument). Perhaps

Nietzsche still associated Homer's epos with the Apollonian world of light and clarity, as he did in *The Birth of Tragedy*, or perhaps he found in Homer a world too free from the conflict of values and therefore without the need for thought.[10] In any event, in "Homer's Contest" Nietzsche investigates the non-Homeric and pre-Homeric origins of Greek myths. He finds in these archaic myths the unity and greatness of Greek culture. In the world of pre-Homeric myths, there is only "night and dread, the products of an imagination fully accustomed to the hideous" (HC 36). This is the world of the theogenic myths, a world of "strife, lust, deceit, old age, and death," in which "struggle signifies well-being and salvation; the cruelty of victory is the peak of life's glories" (HC 37). In "Homer's Contest," Nietzsche emphasizes that violence is not merely pre-Homeric; it is *hinter*, both prior to and ever-present in the highest achievements of the Greeks. In stressing the constancy of violence, Nietzsche reverses his earlier interpretation in *The Birth of Tragedy*. Violence and cruelty are no longer identified solely with Dionysus, who is understood as a relatively late Asiatic intruder into an essentially Apollonian world. Cruelty is now understood as the source of and constant background to Greek culture.

Hesiod and not Homer dominates this essay. Nietzsche points to the significance of *Works and Days* for the entire development of Greek culture. Hesiod, he claims, did not just transform a perception of cruelty into a mythic image; he also taught the Greeks how to evaluate this cruelty. More than the *Iliad*, *Works and Days* is "the first didactic poem of the Greeks." Nietzsche provides a translation of the opening section of the poem. It begins, he claims, not with the hymn to Zeus as it is usually reconstructed, but with the simple, bold declaration: "'There are *two* goddesses of Eris [discord] on earth'" (HC 37). Nietzsche then provides his own translation:

> [T]he one [Eris] fosters awful war and strife, the cruel woman! No mortal can stand her; only under the yoke of necessity does one show any respect to the oppressive Eris, according to the counsel of the immortals. . . . the high-throned Zeus, however, placed the other Eris in the roots of the earth and among men. . . . She drives even the inept man to work; and should

> one man lacking in property look upon another man who is wealthy, he will then rush to sow and to plant in the same fashion and to put his house in order; neighbor competes with neighbor, striving toward affluence. Good is this Eris for men. The potter also resents the potter and the carpenter the carpenter; the beggar envies the beggar and the poet the poet. (HC 37–38)

The Greeks, then, distinguished between the evil goddess Eris who leads to violence and fights of annihilation and the good goddess Eris who spurs men to activity and work. Beneficial Eris found her most powerful cultural expression in the agonal contest *(Wettkampf)*. The agon arose, Nietzsche acknowledges, in the wrestling match and other athletic contests; but it soon pervaded, he argues, all of Greek life. It animated Greek pedagogy for both students and educators: "[T]he sophist, the advanced educator of antiquity, meets the other sophist in rivalry; even the most general type of instruction, that given through drama, was imparted to the people only in the form of a colossal wrestling *[Ringen]* among the great musical and dramatic artists. How wonderful! 'Even the artist resents the artist!' " (HW 790; HC 41). Philosophers, even the sick Plato, engaged in the agon. What is the "particular artistic significance" of Plato's dialogues but "a rivalry with the art of the orators, sophists, and dramatists of his time, invented with the aim of being able to say in the end: 'Behold, that which my great competitors can do, I can do, too; yes, I can do it better than they. . . . Only contest made me a poet, a sophist, an orator!' " (HC 41).

Nietzsche extends this definition of the agon even further. Contention led to the accumulation of possessions, to the development of agriculture, and to the invention of the mechanical and fine arts. The agon also structured politics. Within aristocratic and democratic *poleis*, it prevented one single individual from dominating all others. The institution of ostracism, Nietzsche advises us, should be seen in this light: "The original sense of this extraordinary device is, however, not one of an outlet, rather one of a stimulant: one does away with an outstanding individual, so that once again the competing game of strengths may awaken" (HC 39–40). "Why is it, then, that no one should be the best?" Nietzsche asks: "Because the contest would be exhausted thereby, and the eternal foundation of life for the Hellenic state would be endangered" (HC 39). Simply stated, the beneficial goddess Eris defined culture in the broadest sense as an arena for contest.

In the 1886 preface to *The Birth of Tragedy*, "Attempt at Self-Criticism," Nietzsche faults himself for having "deified" art. But he also chides himself for failing to understand the relation between culture and ethics (BT 25). Already in "Homer's Contest" he begins to correct this failure. In fact—in a move that anticipates his later thinking—he equates culture with ethics. For the Greeks, the archaic myths opened the world as an ethical world. *Works and Days* is the great ethical work of Greek culture. These myths created Greek ethics, not in the direct form of prescribing rules of conduct, but indirectly through the establishment of the agon. The agon releases the vital energies into an acceptable ethical form: "Every talent must unfurl itself struggling" was the central ethical principle (HC 40). Constant competition pressed the individual to realize himself in all of his activities to the limits of his capabilities: "The greater and more magnificent a Greek man is, however, the more brightly does the flame of ambition break forth from him, consuming anyone in his path" (HC 39). The agon, therefore, created the dominant personality type, which for Nietzsche gave value to the culture as a whole. All of Greek culture provides an answer to the question "'What is a life of struggle and of victory really for?'—and it gives this answer in the complete breadth of Greek history" (HC 37).

The agon also set limits to competition. Remove the agon—even scratch its surface—and the Greek, Nietzsche claims, sank back into the violent world of bad Eris, "into that pre-Homeric abyss of a dreadful wildness of hatred and pleasure in destruction." He fell out of the ethical community and was left directly confronting the gods. Nietzsche offers the example of Miltiades, who after his great victories over the Persians, found himself towering above all others with no one left to compete with and thus felt "awaken within him a low, revenge-seeking craving" (HC 41–42): "After the battle at Marathon, the envy of the heavens seizes him. . . . Only the gods are by him now—and therefore they are against him. These gods, however, mislead him to a deed of hubris, and under its weight he collapses" (HC 42). And elsewhere, with the unbounded energies of Alexander the Great, Nietzsche notes: "Here we peer into the abyss of hatred" (HC 36).

As with individual heroes, so with Greeks: *polis*, hubris, and chaos always lay close beneath the surface. Without the agon, bloody political strife prevailed both within the *polis* and among the *poleis*: "[T]he Greek viewed a full discharge of his hatred as a vital necessity; in such moments was the cramped and swollen sensation released: the tiger sprang forth, a lustful ferocity gleaming from his terrifying eyes" (HC 36). Athens, having destroyed the independence of her allies, and Sparta, after defeating Athens, brought about their own destruction through hubris: "Herein lies proof that without envy, jealousy, and competitive ambition, the Hellenic state degenerates, likewise the Hellenic man. He becomes evil and cruel, he becomes revenge-seeking and godless; in short, he becomes 'pre-Homeric'—and then no more than a panicked fright is required in order to make him fall and shatter" (HC 42).

Powerful as this interpretation of Greek culture is, Nietzsche was not the first to see in the agon the unity of Greek culture as a whole. Nietzsche acknowledges as much in the *Twilight of the Idols*. Significantly, in speaking of the "older Hellenic instinct, an instinct still exuberant and even overflowing," he points to the similar interpretation by (and acknowledges a personal debt to) a friend and colleague: "Whoever has investigated the Greeks, such as that profoundest student of their culture now living, Jacob Burckhardt of Basel, realizes at once the value of this line of approach" (TI 108). Nietzsche specifically identifies Burckhardt's understanding of Greek pessimism and the Greeks' "*excess* of energy." As Nietzsche goes on to claim in this passage, Burckhardt's *History of Greek Culture (Griechische Kulturgeschichte)* goes far beyond the current scholarly interpretations.[11] In this study of the Greeks as a cultural phenomenon, Burckhardt gains a greater understanding of the Greeks than the so-called specialists in the field, the classical philologists who proceed with "scientific" accuracy in their analysis of ancient texts. Like Nietzsche, Burckhardt intends, beyond the many facts and events of Greek history, to understand the meaning of Greek culture. And he finds this meaning by interpreting this culture as a unitary whole.

In the *History of Greek Culture*, Burckhardt finds this unity, not in the products of Greek art or thought and not in the political organization of the polis of the classical period. Like Nietzsche, Burckhardt perceives this unity in the Greek agon. Burckhardt is, in fact, the first scholar to extend the notion of the agon from the limited areas of athletic and musical competition—as it was recognized by others—into the dominant cultural form of Greek life:

> [T]he whole of Greek existence was animated by a spirit we shall learn to know by the term agonistic in the broadest sense. In time a conscious mode of education was based on this concept, and when grammar, gymnastics, and cithara playing dominated the youth of the cities, everyone early understood what this Greek life was all about. (HGC 114)

The agon was most clearly represented in athletic contests, but it also defined competitions among dramatic and non-dramatic artists, less formal contests among sculptors and architects, and philosophical discussions. It also gave definition to the polis. The agon was the product of the aristocratic culture of the *Kalo Kagathia*, but the amazing thing is that agonistic values came to dominate the entire democratic polis.

Like Nietzsche, Burckhardt emphasizes the moral values associated with the agon. The agon was "the wholly individual fusion of a moral, aesthetic, and material dedication to an idea which we can only imitate and not define sharply" (HCG 106). Burckhardt emphasizes that culture in Athens was based upon the free expression of individuals. The ideal of the free individual established the measure for the entire culture. In Athens, "men's supreme ambition was to distinguish themselves there, and the struggle for that goal was terrible."[12] The free individual strove after self-expression, but this striving was always contained by the rules of the agon. The agon touched all aspects of Greek life: "The agonistic mentality, that spirit of competition among equals, which permeated all thought and action of the Hellenes."[13] It distinguishes the Greeks from all other peoples of the world and fifth-century Athens from all other forms of culture.

Although it is somewhat unfair to compare Nietzsche's short essay with Burckhardt's three volume *History of Greek Culture*, still the contrast is illuminating. Whereas Burckhardt is—or at least appears to be—concerned only with a historical reconstruction of Greek culture, Nietzsche uses his interpretation of Greek culture to make direct comments upon modern culture, and employs Greek culture as a measure for the present.[14] In "Homer's Contest," this contrast and this measure are made explicit from the start. They govern the entire essay. To us moderns, the Greeks—the most humane people of antiquity"—must terrify us "in their entire history, as well as in their mythology" (HC 35). And, Nietzsche adds, this is particularly true if we "encounter them with our softish notion of modern humanity" (HC 35). Here Nietzsche reaches the main point of the essay—the contrast between the ancient struggle for humanity in a violent world and our modern, weak concept of so-called humanity. Nietzsche's point is clear: "The struggle and joy of victory were acknowledged: and nothing separates the Greek world so much from our own as the *coloring*, thus derived, of individual ethical concepts, for example those of *Eris* and of *Envy* " (HC 37). "The Greek is *envious* and perceives this quality not as a flaw but as a consequence of a *beneficent* deity: what a chasm of ethical judgment between us and him!" (HC 38).

This contrast results in a misreading of Greek values. Nietzsche singles out our inability to understand the ethical value of the agon. The Greeks found that every talent was only unfolded in the agon, "while more recent educators are afraid of nothing more than the unleashing of so-called ambition" (HC 40). We moderns fear "egoism as 'evil in itself.' " The ancients, however, found in selfishness the source of all action; and character could only be evaluated not in an innate essence but in the ends of actions that were chosen. "For the ancients, however, the goal of agonal education *[der agonalen Erziehung]* was the welfare of the whole or of the civic state" (HW 789; HC 40). Selfishness was not "unmeasured and unmeasurable" as modern selfishness is. It was given restraint and measure by the city and the struggle among the cities. "Every Athenian, for example, had to develop himself in contest, so much so as to be of the highest benefit to Athens and to bring it the least harm. . . . the young man thought of the well-being of his native city whenever he ran or threw or sang in contest. He wanted to increase its glory through his own; to the gods of the city he dedicated the wreaths that the judges placed upon his head in honor" (HC 40). The culture of the agon made selfishness socially beneficial.

The purpose of Nietzsche's essay is to lead us in the modern world, with our high evaluation of Greek culture and its artistic and philosophical monuments, to a reflection upon our own values. Nietzsche is directly concerned with our ethics and with the ways in which these values prevent us from understanding other cultures, even ones we value highly. Our "softish notion of modern humanity" distorts our knowledge of Greek culture and, more significantly, limits our ability to learn anything of ourselves. Inadvertently, we downplay or dismiss those components of Greek culture that do not conform to our notion of humanity. We pick and choose only those aspects of Greek humanity that conform to our own. Nietzsche asks: "Why did the entire Greek world," as opposed to modern interpretations of it, "rejoice over the battle scenes of the *Iliad*?"[15] And Nietzsche answers: "I am afraid that we do not understand these things in a sufficiently 'Greek' way; indeed, that we would shudder were we ever to understand them from a Greek perspective" (HC 36). Nietzsche does not simply mean that we must read them in the original; we must understand them in Greek terms, feel them as the Greeks did.[16]

What lies behind Nietzsche's strategy in "Homer's Contest," which at first appears so simple and direct—to understand the cultural significance of the Greek agon and the contrast between antiquity and modernity—is a vastly different conception of culture. We moderns approach the ancient Greeks either as the origins of our own values, the beginnings of Western civilization or as a model—in its arts, politics, or culture in general—to be imitated in the present. Nietzsche breaks from both these interpretations.[17] The Greeks are neither an early version of us moderns (a form of identity) nor a goal to be striven after (a form of classicism). In "Homer's Contest," Nietzsche places ancient Greece directly in opposition to the modern world. By drawing out the contrasts between the two cultures, he breaks from all attempts at constructing a distorting notion of tradition. But behind the contrast between ancient and modern culture, he wants to establish a new definition of culture as a measure to evaluate both past and present.[18]

The essay opens with a paradox: "Thus do the Greeks, the most humane people of antiquity, have a tendency within themselves toward cruelty, toward a tiger-like pleasure in destruction" (HC 35). The combination of high humanity and animal cruelty is something we in the modern world can barely understand. Nietzsche then proceeds to his central concern: "When one speaks of *humanity*, the basic concept implied is that this is meant to be what *differentiates* and distinguishes mankind from nature" (HC 35). "Homer's Contest" is an essay on the definition of "humanity" and the ways in which culture has been defined in opposition to nature. Nietzsche validates the opposition only to turn it against itself: "But such a distinction does not exist in reality: 'natural' attributes and those that are called truly 'human' have grown inseparably into one another." There is, in fact, no opposition nature/culture; but our continued use of this polarity has distorted our judgments. We continue to evaluate the anti-natural in man and culture as the truly valuable, the truly human.

Nietzsche's next move is significant. He neither simply inverts this judgment, claiming that nature is "higher" than culture, nor collapses the opposition, arguing that culture is nature. Rather, he restructures the very opposition that makes our evaluations of culture possible. Nature and culture are not opposed to each other; they work together. And this interaction provides him with a new framework for conceiving culture and with a new scale for its evaluation. This new framework, in turn, leads to a new conclusion: "Man, in the highest and noblest of his strengths, is wholly Nature, and carries her uncanny dual character within him" (HC 35). The transition to a discussion of the Greek culture is introduced only now: "His terrible capacities that are deemed inhuman may even be that fertile ground out of which alone all of humanity can grow forth in emotions, deeds, and accomplishments" (HC 35). The remainder of "Homer's Contest" follows from this. The Greeks never considered culture as the opposite of nature. The agon—the unity of their entire culture—constantly combined the two. Through the agon they directed violence into positive action, and formed a culture that did not separate nature from culture. In the agon a culture was created that was, in a remarkable combination, at once nature and culture.

The Greeks, then, provided Nietzsche with a model for the redefinition and reevaluation of culture. The Greeks, it could be said, established for him the basic economy of the relation between nature and a healthy culture. The archaic myths originally opened this world. Good Eris contends with bad Eris, but this contention is not a relation of opposites, a dialectical opposition. Bad Eris is cruel, annihilating nature, inimical to man. Good Eris also originates in jealousy, hatred, and envy; but she does not lead to senseless destruction, but rather spurs individuals on to action and creativity through competition. Violence and cruelty could be controlled and made to serve human ends. The specifically "Greek genius," which was to tolerate the impulse for violence and revenge, "considered it to be *legitimate*" (HC 37). Nietzsche is emphatic on this point. Although good Eris offered an alternative to annihilating violence, she did not abolish or suppress cruelty in all its forms. The two goddesses of Eris are, in fact, not two separate deities. They are two faces of the selfsame goddess. In these faces, the Greeks mythically perceived not an opposition of nature and culture but a double face of nature.

In this way, the Greeks offered Nietzsche an example of a specific cultural "economy." The Greeks did not to attempt to negate this "brooding atmosphere" of bad Eris and try to escape through imagining what Nietzsche calls an orphic counter-world or cultivating an oriental-style withdrawal from life; nor did they indulge themselves in a Schopenhauerian-type pessimism. These are all responses of "sick" cultures. Opposed to these Nos to life, the Greeks develop a "healthy" culture by saying Yes to Nature, Yes to Eris. The Greeks accept nature even in its destructiveness and meaninglessness. But healthy Greek culture is not simply nature or the acceptance of nature. Good Eris is also a No to annihilating Eris, but a No of a particular type. The Greek No only functions in relation to the resounding affirmation of bad Eris. Violence and cruelty were constants in Greek culture; but once accepted, they said No to it only to the extent that a human world could be constructed in coordination with it. This No, in fact, intensifies nature; this intensification is, in fact, culture. By channelling, transforming, and humanizing those aspects of Eris that could be formed for human ends, nature is heightened and shaped into far superior forms than were originally given.[19]

Hence, Nietzsche no longer conceives of Greek culture according to *The Birth of Tragedy*'s opposition of two gods and the synthesis of Apollo and Dionysus in a form of art. He now understands Greek culture as this affirmative economy and the agon as the highest expression of this intensified cultural economy.[20] But beyond the description of Greek culture, Nietzsche establishes in "Homer's Contest" a problematic in which he could evaluate cultures. What forces are at work beneath the surface of a culture and open up this world as basically healthy or sick, affirmative or negative? The basic economy of Yes and then No of Greek culture provides Nietzsche with both a paradigm of culture and a measure of cultural health.

Heraclitus and Eternal Recurrence

The problem of cultural health raised in "Homer's Contest" leads to the related essay "Philosophy in the Tragic Age of the Greeks" and the problem of the normative relationship between culture and thought. In this second essay, Nietzsche claims: "Whoever wishes to justify it [philosophy] must show . . . to what ends a healthy culture uses and has used philosophy" (PTA 27). In "Philosophy in the Tragic Age," Nietzsche was no longer concerned, as he was in "Homer's Contest," with the problem of defining Greek culture. In this essay, he asked what it was to think in this culture and what the task of philosophy in this healthy culture was. Because the Greeks exist in a healthy culture, they tell us the proper time and the proper way to raise the question of truth. But what is the proper relationship between thought and culture? And, more significantly, why does Nietzsche pose the question of truth only in relation to the condition of culture?

Although Nietzsche sketches the "progression" of Greek philosophy among the pre-Socratics in this essay, it quickly becomes clear that its centerpiece is the thought of Heraclitus. The contrast with the philosophy of Parmenides goes to the core of

"Philosophy in the Tragic Age." Parmenides equates being with logic: "This is a conclusion which rests on the assumption that we have an organ of knowledge which reaches into the essence of things and is independent of existence" (PTA 82). Parmenides' power of thinking arose from this independence, this distancing from the world. Thought sets itself apart from experience, establishes a set of criteria against which the world is not just perceived but evaluated. The world experienced and known through the senses is a confused and a lesser world. Logic and conceptual thought opens the "true" world and establishes the criteria for all truth. In this simple move, Parmenides separates a known object from a knowing subject, grounds philosophy as the sole source of truth upon this thinking subject, and posits truth as a problem of the mental representations of this subject. At base, Nietzsche claims, this move is moral. The world as experienced is unjust, evil, and needs to be corrected, reformed by thought. For him, the thought of Parmenides not only marks a major dividing point between all those philosophers who came before him and those who came after, but also determines the future course of philosophy (PTA 90). It opens a path to Plato, to a philosophy that sees the world justified only in terms of logic and a world, Nietzsche claims, devalued in the face of being.[21]

For Nietzsche, Heraclitus offers another path of thinking. Like Parmenides, he rejects Anaximander's distinction between a physical world and a metaphysical one, a finite from an infinite realm. Heraclitus did not, in other words, regard the relation between being and becoming in terms of some Kant-like duality. Like Parmenides, Heraclitus viewed the world as a unity; he denied the duality of being and becoming. But unlike Parmenides, Heraclitus did not posit this unity in being. Instead, he was led to a "far bolder negation: he altogether denied being" (PTA 51). Instead, Heraclitus contemplated becoming and only becoming, becoming for its own sake. Nietzsche maintained the significance of this move. Heraclitus claimed that being, the order of the unchanging, is only apparent—the result of confusing the nature of things for the names of things. For Heraclitus, names and not the world are rigid, persistent, enduring. Logic has little contact with the world.

But what does it mean to posit becoming and only becoming? Heraclitus did not comprehend becoming as did Anaxagoras after him, as a Hegelian-type synthesis of all opposites. There was no dialectical movement in becoming, no unity of opposites, no logic of becoming. In fact, Heraclitus denied all forms of logic. Aristotle criticized Heraclitus for not understanding the basic law of contradiction. According to Nietzsche, Heraclitus "seems to feel pleasure whenever he can contradict it with intuitively arrived-at truth"; he proclaims: "'Everything forever has its opposite along with it'" (PTA 52). Denying logic, Heraclitus denied the basic move of separating the mind from the world; thinking was always in the world and part of the world. Heraclitus broke the hold of logic and conceptual thought upon existence, but as an alternative he did not turn to empirical observation. Heraclitus always "spoke deprecatingly of such questing, fact-gathering, 'historical' men" (PTA 67).

In contrast, Heraclitus' notion of becoming came "in a divine stroke of lightning" (PTA 50). To achieve the insight into becoming, Nietzsche has Heraclitus declare: "'I sought and consulted myself'" (PTA 67). The thought of becoming, in other words, arose from within Heraclitus, from pure intuition. For Nietzsche this is a vital point. There is another form of truth at work in intuition, a truth not open to logic and observation. Denying the power of logic, the thought of Heraclitus remained closer to mythical thinking. His starting point was the world of creating and annihilating violence, the amoral world of bad Eris. This world is inimical to man, destructive of his life and actions, a world in which man constantly suffers for sins he never committed. Heraclitus asks: "Is not the entire world process now an act of punishment for hubris? . . . . Is guilt not now transplanted into the very nucleus of materiality and the world of becoming and of individuals thereby unburdened of responsibility, to be sure, but simultaneously sentenced to carry the consequences of evil forever and anew?" (PTA 61). And Nietzsche answers Heraclitus' question with a resounding No. The world appears as unjust, Heraclitus claims, only for the limited human mind; to the divine mind the world process is justice itself.

For Nietzsche, Heraclitus' intuition, while remaining closer than Parmenides to the wisdom of mythic intuition, also breaks from such intuition. Instead of simply positing symbols, he interprets and critically thinks these symbols. Heraclitus' thinking begins with an interpretation of "Hesiod's good *Eris*" (PTA 55). This goddess opens the world not in terms of the struggle of opposites. Instead, Heraclitus thinks the world—in a way that mirrors Nietzsche's working out of the relation between nature and culture in "Homer's Contest"—as the struggle of the goddess with herself. The world might appear as the play of oppositions; but it is the play itself and not the opposites that must be thought through. For Heraclitus the world is conceived "as being the diverging of a force into two qualitatively different opposed activities that seek to reunite. Everlastingly, a given quality contends against itself and separates into opposites; everlastingly these opposites seek to reunite" (PTA 54). The thought of Heraclitus is opposed to that of Anaximander and Anaxagoras and diametrically opposed to that of Parmenides; his thinking did not impose a cognitive pattern onto the world, and it did not mentally project a counter-world from which the world of experience could be evaluated. For to think through the process of becoming is to accept the world of creating and destroying Eris.

Heraclitus perceives, in other words, only agonistic flux, a world of constant creating and destruction, destruction and creation. To others such a world may appear as a world of "guilt, injustice, contradiction and suffering," a world morally illegitimate (PTA 61); but Heraclitus proclaims that this perception is merely a human perspective, the world made visible "only for the limited human mind which sees things apart." In the face of this flux, "all contradictions run into harmony, invisible to the common human eye," for a god and "to one who, like Heraclitus, is related to the contemplative god. Before his fire-gaze not a drop of injustice remains in the world poured all around him" (PTA 62). From the divine standpoint of Heraclitus, "everything that happens, happens in accordance with this strife, and it is just in the strife that eternal justice is revealed" (PTA 55). Heraclitus did not turn way from this world of becoming; instead, he found the law within becoming. Becoming is lawful; becoming is eternal.

Heraclitus perceived becoming as a necessary interplay of good and bad Eris. But he arrived at even a higher intuition. The initial image that came to Heraclitus' mind was that of a wrestling match. The world is a pair of "wrestlers of whom sometimes the one, sometimes the other is on top" (PTA 54). This wrestling match is lawful but, as Nietzsche emphasizes, not refereed by stern judges, for "a still greater intuition overtook . . . [Heraclitus]. He could no longer see the contesting pairs and their referees as separate; the judges themselves seemed to be striving in the contest and the contestants seemed to be judging them." And Heraclitus thought becoming through to its own resolution as divine justice, proclaiming: " 'The struggle of the many is pure justice itself!' " (PTA 57). This greater intuition perceives in the struggle of opposites—that is, in the world—a higher struggle in which the world itself is destroyed and rebuilt. "Heraclitus characterizes, with notable emphasis, [the world] as a desire, a want, or lack," Nietzsche writes, and notes how this lack is overcome: "[T]he full consumption in fire he calls satiety. It remains for us to ask how he interpreted and what he might have called the newly awakening impulse toward cosmic formation, the new outpouring into the forms of plurality."

Nietzsche asks how this higher unity is to be enacted, and he finds an answer in the Greek proverb: "'Satiety gives birth to hubris'." Hubris breaks the natural order, and Heraclitus derives the "return to the many from hubris." The overthrow of good Eris returns the world to bad Eris, the world of annihilation; but from this annihilation a new world arises. Heraclitus believed "in a periodically repeated end of the world, and in an ever renewed rise of another world out of the all-destroying cosmic fire" (PTA 60). This world of struggle is itself a chance formation within the flux of forces; it is destroyed only in order for another world to appear: another chance formation of a necessary order. Heraclitus therefore recognized not just that the world is a world of constant becoming but that this world itself is the necessary chance formation of becoming. The world we know is only the "beautiful innocent game of the aeon," the game becoming plays with time (PTA 63). This is why Nietzsche declares: "The dangerous word hubris is indeed the touchstone for every Heraclitan" (PTA 61). The thought of Heraclitus arises from this double affirmation: the affirmation of becoming and the affirmation of the law of becoming (the becoming of becoming). Heraclitus' "teaching of *law in becoming* and of *play in necessity* . . . must be seen from now on in all eternity. He raised the curtain on this greatest of all dramas," namely the drama of eternal recurrence (PTA 68). Heraclitus transposed the contention of good and bad Eris into the higher thought of eternal recurrence, which constitutes this second level affirmation.

The acceptance of the thought of the eternity of becoming brings Nietzsche to the main problematic of "Philosophy in the Tragic Age." As his future writings also demonstrate, Nietzsche defines thinking not in terms of its method or abstract content but in the ways in which thinking shapes values. His is not just a dispassionate analysis of the cosmologies of pre-Socratic philosophy; nor does he evaluate the truth claims of these cosmologies. Instead, he addresses the ways in which natural philosophy influences, molds, and creates a particular personality type. Truth is not measured by its capacity to represent the conditions of the external world; it does not point outward to some "true" state of affirms. Rather truth reflects back onto the thinker himself; it is a gauge by which an individual life is shaped. The question here is the relation between thought, values, and the life of the individual.

How, then, is this thought related to Greek culture? Why does Nietzsche claim that Heraclitus is able to conceive of eternal recurrence only because he lived in the midst of healthy Greek culture at its height? The answer to these questions lies not just in the fact that Heraclitus did not remove himself from the world to construct a counter-world in logic or that his intuitions revolved in the orbit of mythical thinking. To think the truth of eternal recurrence is to place oneself within the world, the world of becoming and the becoming of becoming, in order to accept and affirm it in "sublimity and the feeling of blessed astonishment" in thought (PTA 54). Nietzsche argues that Heraclitus' thought of eternal recurrence has little to do with an intuition of a natural or cosmic order. Rather, Heraclitus thought the entirety of Greek culture. Both in form and content, he thought the plurality of this world, its becoming and individuation, as a unity. In other words, Heraclitus thought the world of becoming in terms of the unity of the Greek agon. Nietzsche makes this point clear: Heraclitus' cosmic intuition "is the contest-idea of the Greek individual and the Greek state, taken from the gymnasium and the palaestra, from the artist's *agon*, from the contest between political parties and between cities—all transformed into universal application so that now the wheels of the cosmos turn on it"

(PTA 55). Heraclitus accepted Greek life, thought it in its totality, and transformed it into the thought of eternal recurrence.

Heraclitus' concept of the agon is different from the dialectical agon of Socrates. He did not think the agon by transforming it into linguistic games. His notion of beneficial Eris is the goddess of the agon, "transformed into the cosmic principle" (PTA 55). Eternal recurrence is the agon understood in cosmic terms:

> Just as the Greek individual fought as though he alone were right and an infinitely sure measure of judicial opinion were determining the trend of victory at any given moment, so the qualities [of the cosmos] wrestle with one another, in accordance with inviolable laws and standards that are immanent in the struggle. The things in whose definiteness and endurance narrow human minds, like animal minds, believe have no real existence. They are but the flash and spark of drawn swords, the quick radiance of victory in the struggle of the opposites. (PTA 55)

This means that the questions of the specific content, truth status, and mode of Heraclitus' idea can be posed only in relation to the agon. His philosophy is the "welling up from the purest strings of Hellenism, the idea that strife embodies the everlasting sovereignty of strict justice bound to everlasting laws" (PTA 55).

In "Philosophy in the Tragic Age," Nietzsche is not interested in proving the truth of eternal recurrence according to some Parmenidean or Socratic definition of "logical" truth. The truth of eternal recurrence, as we have seen, operates within a different problematic. The Greeks themselves, at least in their healthy period, did not approach the question of truth so crudely as to ask whether it conforms to logic or dialectics. They did not even seek knowledge for its own sake—"an unrestrained thirst for knowledge for its own sake barbarizes men just as much as a hatred of knowledge" (PTA 30–31). They were insatiable for knowledge; but they controlled it "by their ideal need for and consideration of all the values of life" (PTA 31). Thought was not measured in its truth by its correlation to some external condition. Rather, it was measured according to its ability to enhance values and, beyond this, in its capacity to create and enhance a culture. Cultural truths create truth; they do not reflect given states of affairs. According to Nietzsche, the archaic philosophers asked: "'And what is life worth, after all?'" (PTA 33). In answering this question, they asserted that a healthy culture is one with healthy values and healthy instincts. Heraclitus thereby provides Nietzsche with a means of evaluating thought and culture: thought is truth to the degree that it enhances healthy values and creates a culture. Nietzsche's attack against Plato and Platonism in "Philosophy in the Tragic Age" is only understood against this background. Even with its great consequences for the entire tradition of the West, Platonic philosophy is in its origins and lineage an expression of Socratic cultural sickness.

Nietzsche's early studies of the Greeks provide a way into interpreting the major "themes" of his later writings. Hence, his interpretation of Greek culture did not reach its culmination in *The Birth of Tragedy*. In fact, the essays he wrote immediately after completing this work do not so much extend or modify this interpretation as reject its overt "Hegelianism" and "aestheticism." Rethinking Greek culture not as an artistic response to violence but as the direct acceptance of violence and the transformation of this violence into the cultural forms of the agon, Nietzsche defines a paradigm for all "healthy cultures." To think this paradigm and not just live it also redefines the nature of philosophy. Opposed to the rejection of the world of chaos and violence and the creation of a philosophical counter-world, Heraclitus created the doctrine of eternal recurrence as the acceptance of this world. Zarathustra will rethink this doctrine. The truth of eternal recurrence does not rely upon its accommodation to the metaphysical and hence nihilistic criterion of a concept of cyclical time or recurrence of worlds. Rather, Nietzsche will find via Zarathustra the "truth" of the metaphor of eternal recurrence in its affirmation *(Jasagen)* to life. It is measured only to the degree it opens a world, shapes values, molds personalities, and produces a culture. This acceptance itself is "founded" upon the prior acceptance and the further affirmation of culture as a realm of violence, struggle, and contention, even when it does not take the "healthy," life affirming forms of cultural values and institutions as in the Greek agon. Under the condition of the "sick," life-denying world of modernity, for Zarathustra's doctrine of eternal recurrence to be understood and accepted, a critical and destructive strategy is demanded. Genealogy is that method that reveals, beyond the metaphysical search for unity and continuity and all the other nihilistic modes of modern culture, a world of contending forces. To accept the world as dominated by the will to power is the only way to affirm eternal recurrence.

Notes

1. I abbreviate Nietzsche's works as follows: BT = *The Birth of Tragedy*, trans. Walter Kaufmann (New York: Vintage, 1966); EH = *Ecce Homo*, trans. Walter Kaufmann (New York: Vintage, 1968); HC = "Homer's Contest," this volume; HW = "Homer's Wettkampf," *Friedrich Nietzsche: Samtliche Werke, Kritische Studienausgabe in 15 Bänden*, vol. 1, ed. Giorgio Colli and Mazzino Montinari (Berlin: de Gruyter, 1980); PTA = *Philosophy in the Tragic Age of the Greeks*, trans. Marianne Cowan (Chicago: Regnery, 1962); TI = *Twilight of the Idols*, trans. R.J. Hollingdale (Harmondsworth, UK: Penguin, 1971); WKG = *Werke. Kritische Gesamtausgabe*, ed. Giorgio Colli and Mazzino Montinari (Berlin: de Gruyter, 1967). All translations are my own unless otherwise noted.

2. Joan Stambaugh, *Nietzsche's Thought of Eternal Return* (Baltimore: Johns Hopkins Univ. Press, 1972); Martin Heidegger, *Nietzsche*, trans. David Krell, 4 vols. (New York: Harper and Row, 1982); Gilles Deleuze, *Nietzsche and Philosophy*, trans. Hugh Tomlinson (New York: Columbia Univ. Press, 1983).

3. Arthur C. Danto, *Nietzsche as Philosopher* (New York: Columbia Univ. Press, 1965); Bernd Magnus, *Nietzsche's Existential Imperative* (Bloomington: Indiana Univ. Press, 1978); Alexander Nehamas, *Nietzsche: Life as Literature* (Cambridge: Harvard Univ. Press, 1985). See also Ivan Soll, "Reflections on Recurrence: A Re-examination of Nietzsche's Doctrine, *die ewige Wiederkehr des Gleichen*," *Nietzsche: A Collection of Critical Essays*, ed. Robert Solomon (Garden City, N.Y.: Doubleday, 1973), 322–42.

4. Paul de Man, "Rhetoric of Tropes (Nietzsche)" and "Rhetoric of Persuasion (Nietzsche)," *Allegories of Reading* (New Haven: Yale Univ. Press, 1979); Jacques Derrida, *Spurs: Nietzsche's Styles*, trans. Barbara Harlow (Chicago: Univ. of Chicago Press, 1982).

5. Allan Megill, *Prophets of Extremity: Nietzsche, Heidegger, Foucault, Derrida* (Berkeley: Univ. of California Press, 1985), 83.

6. Nietzsche's italics. All italics in Nietzsche's quotations are his own.

7. This is true not only in his early philological and cultural essays but also in his later philosophical writings. Even when not thematized or mentioned only in passing, as in the major writings after *The Birth of Tragedy*, the Greeks serve as a constant background to Nietzsche's thought in general and his

definition of culture in particular. As he remarks in the *Twilight of the Idols* (1888), "the Greeks remain the *supreme cultural event* of history" (TI 101).

8. For a brief overview of Nietzsche's writings on the Greeks, see Alan D. Schrift, *Nietzsche and the Question of Interpretation: Between Hermeneutics and Deconstruction* (New York: Routledge, 1990), 160–64.

9. For a different interpretation of Nietzsche's understanding of the Greeks, especially in relation to tragic drama, see M.S. Silk and J.P. Stern, *Nietzsche on Tragedy* (Cambridge, UK: Cambridge Univ. Press, 1981), 107–31; Tracy B. Strong, "Aesthetic Authority and Tradition: Nietzsche and the Greeks, "*History of European Ideas* 11 (1989): 989–1008.

10. For Nietzsche's double-edged criticism of Homer's impact upon Greek culture, see "Homer und die klassische Philologie" (WKG 2.1: 249–69; cf. also WKG 4.1: 154–55, 157).

11. Jacob Burckhardt, *History of Greek Culture* (hereafter abbreviated as HGC), trans. Palmer Hilty (New York: Ungar, 1963). The *Griechische Kulturgeschichte* (publ. post., 1902) arose from the lectures Burckhardt gave at the University of Basel between 1870–1878; I use the edition edited by Rudolf Marx (Leipzig: Alfred Kroner Verlag, n.d.). It is unfortunate that Burckhardt never completely edited this work for publication, since even in comparison with *The Civilization of the Renaissance in Italy* (1860), it is in many ways his masterpiece. The *History of Greek Culture* is a more ambitious work than *The Culture of the Renaissance*. It not only wants to present an interrelated tableau of this civilization but also to portray it in its transformation. As such, it presents a more comprehensive vision of the entire course of this culture by describing the general transformations that at first brought harmony to Greek life and then those causes that led to its disintegration. See Rarl J. Weintraub, *Visions of Culture* (Chicago: Univ. of Chicago Press, 1966), 146–52.

12. HGC 2: 92; cf. 123, 147–48, 285, 308.

13. Burckhardt, *Gesamtausgabe*, ed. Emil Duerr *et al.*, 14 vols. (Stuttgart: Deutsche Verlags, 1929–34), 7: 96–97.

14. See Nietzsche (WRG 4.1: 107).

15. This is Nietzsche's only reference to Homer in "Homer's Contest."

16. Nietzsche also contrasts modernity with antiquity in his other writings of this period (cf. WRG 2.1: 2449–50).

17. Nietzsche writes: "[I]t is a task: to whom it is impossible to bring back Greece and thus also Christianity and the earlier foundations of our society and our politics" (WRG 4.1: 159).

18. In the essay of the previous year, "The Greek State," the culture of antiquity is hardly mentioned. The ancient city is merely a pretext to investigate the modern ideals of the "dignity of man" and the "dignity of labor" which only lead to the power-state and the modern form of slavery. In this essay, as in "Homer's Contest," antiquity serves only as a foil to the present.

19. Compare Deleuze's interpretation of Nietzsche on this point. Deleuze understands Nietzsche as simply opposing "affirmation," the Yes to all forms of "negation" and the No.

20. The importance of this interpretation of Greek culture for Nietzsche's thought cannot be overestimated. In a note of 1875, he notes: "The lust for revenge, the lust for the cunning for revenge, for envy, for vindictiveness, for obscenity—all this was recognized by the Greeks as manly, and on this they arranged the structure of their society and morals. The wisdom of their institutions lay in the mixture of the boundary between good and evil, black and white. Nature, as it showed itself, was not lied about but ordered, concentrated in specific cults and days. This is the root of all the freedom of antiquity; one sought for the forces of instinct and nature a measured discharge, not annihilation and denial—the entire system of new order is then the state" (WRG 4.1: 154–55).

21. Nietzsche returns to Heraclitus in *Twilight of the Idols*. Here he contrasts the thought of Heraclitus to that of other philosophers. For Heraclitus, it is not the senses that lie but reason. By adding the notions of "unity and duration" onto the evidence of the senses, reason creates the lie called being. And more suggestively, Nietzsche concludes: "Heraclitus will always be right in this, that being is an empty fiction. The 'apparent' world is the only one: the 'real' world has only been *lyingly added* . . . " (TI 36).

Closing the Eye: Hegel, Derrida, and the Closure of Philosophy

Arkady Plotnitsky

As he was contemplating the exhibition he was invited to curate at the Louvre, Jacques Derrida was afflicted with a form of viral paralysis called *a frigore* (disfiguration), which left his face temporarily disfigured and his left eye unable to close. In the essay that he wrote for the catalogue of the exhibition, *Mémoires d'aveugle: L'autoportrait et autres ruines (Memoirs of the Blind: Self-Portrait and Other Ruins),* Derrida, alluding to Bataille's *Story of the Eye,* refers to the episode and the story of the exhibition as a whole as his *"story of the eye."*[1] This chapter is also concerned with the ability or inability to close our eyes—at least our philosophical eyes. The connection of the present analysis to Derrida's illness is, however, more or less fortuitous. To the degree that it can be meaningfully approached, the psychosomatic economy of such an affliction could, of course, be of considerable interest, especially in view of other autobiographical connections explored by Derrida in *Memoirs* and throughout his recent writings. The economy of the (un)blinking eye—and of the blindness and insight of thinking and writing—can be traced to many of Derrida's works, beginning not with *Memoirs* but with the earliest of his texts. It is developed in an important analysis in chapter 5 of *Speech and Phenomena,* entitled "Signs and the Blink of an Eye."[2]

This chapter is concerned with themes and authors that are found throughout Derrida's work, and in particular with certain key figures (both authors and tropes) in *Memoirs*. Moreover, the chapter focuses on the creative agon between Derrida and Hegel and on two interrelated economies involved in it (although it also refers to the scenes of few other creative agons). The first is the economy of the closure or enclosure *(clôture)*, in contrast to the end of philosophy. The second economy is defined by the relation of simultaneous proximity to and distance from philosophy and, specifically, Hegel. One can see both economies and their relationship in terms of Harold Bloom's theory of creative agon as anxiety of influence defined through what he calls revisionary ratios between the figures involved.[3] From the Bloomian perspective, both economies—that of closure and that of proximity-distance—would be introduced by Derrida, at least in part, in order to triumph or to survive in his agon with Hegel, even if unconsciously repeating Hegel's own insights (or blindness) in the process. As I shall suggest here, one can in turn reevaluate Bloom's theory within the matrix of these two economies.

Figures

It is difficult to turn our philosophical eyes away from Hegel or to keep them closed for long once Hegel enters the field of our vision. However, by making ourselves deliberately or unknowingly blind to Hegel or by trying to avoid him, we risk surrendering to his gaze all the more.[4] And yet, even in confronting Hegel by keeping our eyes open or being unable to close them, we cannot avoid a certain blindness either; we cannot avoid reading Hegel. We become stones under its Medusa-like gaze—statues with our eyes forever open and unable to blink—and make Hegel a stone, a statue, under Medusa-like gazes of our monumentalization (historical, philosophical, or other). This must have been true for Hegel himself, who, according to Derrida in *Glas*, must become a Medusa to himself in his attempt simultaneously to pursue and escape from a self-monumentalization.[5] One can also think of Hegel in this pursuit-escape as at once Achilles and the turtle, and of his work as the great manifestation of the famous paradox of Zeno, the student of Parmenides and the inventor of dialectic.[6]

Hegel's proximity demands that we close our eyes from time to time, metaphorically and physically (as we must actually do in reading his, or any, text), but also that we must, at times, confront Hegel without blinking an eye. This proximity is both threatening and unavoidable, and the distance of Hegel may be even more so. According to Derrida, " '*Hegelianism*' " is the "finest scar" of a "battle" against writing, one of the great wars waged by philosophy (and not philosophy alone) and a great subject of Derrida's own project.[7] "What is at stake [and in play] here is enormous" *(L'enjeu est ici énorme),* Derrida says, in defining the difference or again proximity-difference between what he calls *différance* and the *Aufhebung* of Hegel's dialectics.[8] Hegel is not the only name of the problem of writing, but is one of the greatest, along with Plato and Rousseau, both of whom have momentous significance in Derrida, so much so that Derrida calls Hegel "the first thinker of writing" (OG 26). Elsewhere he "name[s] the necessity of a deconstruction" with the "proper name" Hegel, in view of Hegel's "determinant role . . . in the *construction* of the French University and its philosophical institution" *(emphasis added).*[9] It is, then, not surprising that Derrida sees the stakes in his confrontation with Hegel as enormous.

The history of *Geist* and Absolute Knowledge (or later the Idea) is told and, hence, constructed by Hegel through many figures and stories, some deliberately used and some unperceived. I have already suggested several such figures and stories, and I shall comment on the accumulation (or loss) of figures presently.[10] Hegel's is certainly both a story of the eye and a story of the ear—the story of self-gazing and self-listening—and, of course, of self-thinking, the history of reflecting, within the overall process on all such processes themselves. In this sense Hegel's philosophy, the philosophy of absolute reflection, provides the closure of post-Kantian philosophy, extending Fichte's and Schelling's philosophies of reflection and indeed of the history of Western philosophy beginning with (and before) Plato. It does so in part because it introduces history itself—the figure and/of the idea of history—into philosophy, which is Hegel's arguably greatest contribution, as seen by Hegel himself.[11] Hegel's becomes the philosophy and/as history of the all encompassing I, the I or the eye seeing and capable of absorbing all figures.

While the pun on I/eye is very old and has become a commonplace in recent history, in the present context the conjunction of "I" and "eye" may be uniquely fitting: Hegel connects the subjectivity (the self-interiorization) and vision or gaze (the self-vision or self-gaze) of the Hegelian subject, *Geist*—the absolute subject (in either sense). Human philosophical subject and vision are, then, connected by the model developed by Hegel for *Geist* (which is the ideal manifestation or realization of that model). Hegel's text thus reworks the story of the self-solidifying, self-monumentalizing gaze or following Derrida (in *Glas*) and keeping the French word *méduse* in mind, of the self-meduse-fying gaze of *Geist,* of philosophy, and of Hegel. *Geist*'s self-gazing petrifies the whole of history and medusefies itself into a pillar of ice or stone, or—to complement a Greek narrative with a Biblical one—becomes, like Lot's wife, the pillar of salt turning toward the pillar of fire behind it. Or rather this is what may be necessary in order to complete its project, but what never quite takes place. This "almost" realizable possibility both shapes and works against Hegelian reflection, while suggesting only a medusa-like, gel-like "congealment" rather than a full solidification of (absolute) knowledge.[12] This gel-like or medusa-like quality is indicated by Derrida, alongside the figure of Hegel as the eagle, at the opening of *Glas:*

> From the eagle it draws imperial or historic power. Those who still pronounce his name like the French (there are some) are ludicrous only up to a certain point: the restitution (semantically infallible for those who have read him a little—but only a little) of magisterial coldness and imperturbable seriousness, the eagle caught in ice and frost, glass and gel *[gel].*

Let the emblanced *[emblémi]* philosopher be so congealed *[figé].*[13] It becomes quickly apparent that the accumulation of sometimes contradictory figures is unavoidable either in approaching Hegel or in general terms. Derrida's multi-figured description here, the project of *Glas,* and Derrida's overall philosophical argument leading to his concept of writing show that this accumulation is irreducible and irreducibly excessive. While it is not necessarily unstructured at any given point and in practice can never be for theoretical, historical, or political reasons, no structure can fully contain the accumulation of figures.[14]

One can also think of Hegel, at least at the time of his finishing the *Phenomenology,* as trying to run from the gaze and to run after it (and one can again invoke the figure of Zeno's paradox). The book announces both the apocalyptic end or closure and the apocalyptic (new) beginning of philosophy, the (re)birth of philosophy out of the spirit of philosophy. In doing so, it becomes simultaneously both philosophy's self-gazing Medusa, enclosing itself within itself, and its own Tower of Babel, its spirals and labyrinths. It becomes the story of the eye and the story of the ear of philosophy, both suggested by these figures.[15]

These figures, however, suggest much more. Hegel's famous spiral, first invoked at the end of the *Phenomenology,* brings to mind Dante's spirally terraced Mountain of Purgatorio and Peter Breughel's painting of the Tower of Babel, rising in spirals toward heaven. The *Phenomenology* announces the multiplicity of the languages of philosophy and what may be called the structural translation. Pre-logically rather than ontologically, this translation and the plurality of languages resist the notion of a single original text or language. We are certainly far from finished with translating the *Phenomenology* itself, including, and perhaps even particularly, into German. This work of translation was begun by Hegel himself. A certain translation or a certain simultaneous translatability-untranslatability defines all of Hegel's work and, as Derrida suggests, the very enterprise of philosophy. This translation represents another facet of Derrida's economy of "writing"—a Tower-of-Babel economy of concepts and figures, histories and stories, languages and translations, theories and practices, openings and enclosures, blindness and insight, and so forth. It radically refigures the *theos* of Hegelian *Geist* into a *techné* by means of what may be called the theo-technology or techno-theology of *writing.* Or, to return to geologico- or architectonico-architectural figures suggested earlier, it entails a very different relation between Dante's Mountain of Purgatorio and Brueghel's Tower of Babel, and indeed a very different conception of both. This *writing* holds our towers together and, at the same time, enables us to escape becoming dead statues under the unblinking eyes of philosophy for as long as possible.

Suspended between the Medusa's gaze and gazing, like Lot's wife, at the apocalyptic fire of destruction, the history of philosophy is "the story of the eye"—the story of our ability or inability to close one's eyes or to turn them away. It is also the story of the ear, of its hidden labyrinths and architecture. The eye and the ear can also exchange roles and narratives as they interminably pass into each other. To know, see, or hear "too much" can paralyze one's perceptions, let alone one's philosophizing. One might think of, as it were, micro-towers of Babel at each point or of micro-Medusas of perception. This excess of vision can even make one go mad. The economy, or at least the figure, of madness plays an interesting and important role in the present context, as figures continually accumulate to the point of madness. A certain "madness," or the vertigo of oscillations between reason and madness, shapes the economy of philosophy in Hegel, in part via Hölderlin, as Hegel is ascending his spirals or is climbing (or building) his towers of Babel.[16] This madness is also blindness, sometimes resulting from an excess of vision—insight and, as it were, out-sight. Or to be more precise, madness and blindness are interconnected in the conceptual, metaphorical, and narrative (en)closure of our discourse. The figures of Samson (moving from blindness to mad rage) and Oedipus (moving from mad rage to blindness) suggest these interconnections and the economies—the gaze, the sexual, the political, the feminine, and so forth—accompanying them. Both Samson and Oedipus are among the key references in Derrida's *Memoirs.* Both may be seen as manifestations of Hegel's negativity, or a still more radical negativity, which emerges in Hölderlin's work on tragedy, and especially in his analysis of Oedipus, his Anti-Oedipus. This is the negativity that Hegel tries to circumvent (or the power of which he tries to contain, at least in principle), but which he continuously reinscribes in his text, as he climbs or builds simultaneously both the Mountain of Purgatorio and the Tower of Babel, simultaneously turning away and looking into the eye of Medusa or becoming a Medusa (for) himself. From the *Phenomenology* on, one can trace connections between madness and blindness in Hegel's writing. Both *Geist* and human self-consciousness appear to pass through madness and blindness in their journey through "the night of [their] self-consciousness" invoked at the end of the *Phenomenology* (492), as Hegel conjoins philosophy and history, and hence the figures of *Geist* and Oedipus.

In initiating his project with the history of madness, and thus the initiating a paradigmatic model of the contemporary historical project, Michel Foucault discovered the madness of history or the blindness of history and also a certain commonality, rather than only the difference, between history and madness. The history of blindness still remains to be written, although blindness—the blindness of Samson, the blindness of Oedipus, the blindness of Tiresias—has, of course, been written many times in the margins of other histories. Foucault and Hegel are also creative agonists, as are Derrida and Foucault. Derrida's early essay on Foucault and Descartes, "Cogito and the History of Madness" (in *Writing and Difference*), can be read from that perspective and applied to the (inter-)relationships of Foucault, Hegel, and Derrida. The figure of Descartes overshadows all these creative agonistic relationships between and among Derrida, Foucault, Heidegger, Hegel, Descartes, and several other figures, especially Kant and Husserl (the thinkers of consciousness) on the one hand, and Nietzsche, Freud, Bataille, Blanchot, Lacan, and Genet (the thinkers of the unconscious) on the other. "Descartes, ce penseur de l'oeil," the thinker of the eye, Derrida calls him in *Mémoires* (21; M 13), obviously referring to both his specific investigations in optics and his philosophical vision. This description defines the figure of the philosopher and the enterprise of philosophy itself, including Derrida and (Derrida's) deconstruction. As Derrida recalls (slightly misquoting Nietzsche) immediately following his remark on Descartes, Nietzsche speaks of Socrates as possessing "the eye of the Cyclops"—the eye perhaps unable to blink, but finally blinded by the practical, street-smart, thinking of Odysseus (Nietzsche?).[17]

In contrast to philosophers—thinkers of and with the eye—most literary authors invoked in *Memoirs of the Blind*—Homer, Milton, Borges, and Joyce—are blind or partially blind; and these blind and half-blind writers appear to possess the sharpest vision. This vision, however, always needs blindness, the ability to close one's eyes, according to Nietzsche's famous elaboration in *On the Genealogy of Morals* (GM 57–58).[18] Philosophy, seemingly endowed with or claiming for itself the eagle vision, seems unable to close its eyes, thus making itself blind to its own blindness, too reasonable or not mad enough to see its own madness, although Hegel is positioned ambiguously or ambivalently in this respect. To a degree, Derrida's creative agonistics or "Derrida Agonistes" (Milton's *Samson Agonistes* is another key text in the *Memoirs*) is suspended in this space, perhaps specifically between Joyce and Hegel, who are in turn great creative agonists. Among the several junctures of Joyce and Hegel that one encounters throughout Derrida's works, the one in "Ulysses Gramophone" may be the most pertinent here:

> *My Experiences* is both my "phenomenology of mind" in the Hegelian sense of a "science of the experience of consciousness" and the great circular return, the autobiographic-encyclopedic circumnavigation of Ulysses: there has often been talk of the Odyssey of the phenomenology of mind. Here the phenomenology of mind would have to form a diary of the conscious and the unconscious in the chance form of letters, telegrams, newspapers called, for example, *The Telegraph* (long-distance writing), and also of postcards whose only text, sometimes, taken out of a sailor's pocket, exhibits nothing but a phantom address.[19]

Hegel's *Phenomenology* (at some point subtitled "the science of the experience of consciousness") is already, if implicitly, such a project, as are all his major works and in particular the *Encyclopedia* (defined as the encyclopedia of ideas, rather than of facts or contents, and constituting the first and the last project of that type), to which Derrida alludes here. It is obviously many other things as well, but so is in fact Leopold Bloom's *My Experience,* a projected series of newspaper articles. Nothing prevents one from reading each in terms of the other. Sailors, Michel Serres tells us, are the best philosophers, and in particular the best philosophers of temporality since they, unlike more traditional philosophers, know how to navigate in any weather or how to circumnavigate it. Time and weather are the same in French—*temps*—a point of departure (in either sense) for Serres (who was a sailor at one point of his life).[20] Ulysses-Odysseus, the sailor, is of course the one who blinded the Cyclops, another key figure in *Memoirs* (M 88–94), just as the semi-blind Joyce blinds the eyes of Cyclops or philosophy itself. Derrida's *Memoirs* and most his recent (and many earlier) works aim to negotiate these different strategies and territories—times and weathers—to which we must add Oedipus' many journeys.[21]

Levinas, Derrida reminds us, calls Joyce "the most Hegelian of modern novelists." The Hegel-Joyce axis emerges very early in Derrida's writing, for example, in "Violence and Metaphysics: An Essay on the Thought of Emmanuel Levinas" (originally published in 1964). Derrida himself may well be the most Joycean of modern philosophers—a point often suggested in recent literature. The creative agon between Derrida and Hegel can be linked to Derrida's creative agon with Joyce, whose text is the most blinding, the most medusefying text ever. The network of supplementary substitutions or what Derrida in *The Post Card: From Socrates to Freud and Beyond* conceives of as the postal circulations emerging here, is also a network of creative agonistics, from Socrates or Homer (or Hesiod) to Joyce and Derrida and beyond. (Nietzsche himself traces creative agonistics to the contest of Homer and Hesiod.) In "Ulysses Gramophone," *Ulysses* is called "an immense postcard" (AL 260), which clearly refers to Derrida's *The Post Card,* examined elsewhere in the essay. Derrida's "post card" is also to Joyce and it proceeds via the uncircumventable Hegel and a long line of creative agonists, many of whom—Lacan and Freud, Heidegger and Nietzsche, and Socrates/Plato—are discussed by Derrida in *The Post Card.* It is, however, the postal economy of Joyce's writing that is especially significant here. For this type of economy may well be the greatest and the most unfulfilled ambition of philosophy, which places it both in a proximity to and radical difference from literature. At least from Plato and Aristotle, to Kant and Hegel, to Heidegger and Derrida, this is, of course, one of the great agons of western intellectual history, which acquired in turn an immense—interminable and incalculable—"calculus" of proximities, distances, ambivalences, reversals, and so forth. Joyce might have tried to—and, according to Derrida, did—"calculate" these relationships better than philosophy ever could. The first relationship, that between Derrida and Joyce, becomes via *The Post Card* a complex (conscious and unconscious) difference-repetition—a kind of *différance*—of the relationship between Socrates or Socrates/Plato and Homer. In Derrida's texts, literary figures such as Mallarmé, Blanchot, Ponge, Genet, or Joyce become weapons and also shields—like that of Perseus (another important reference in *Memoirs*)—made of the head of the Medusa, that is, of Derrida's creative agon with Hegel, which is invoked in all these readings.

Hegel's textual economy refuses to see its blindness and madness, at least to the degree (some) literary economies do.[22] At best, Hegel can see this without seeing, show it while concealing it, even though Hegel may have believed himself to be going mad as he was trying to close the *Phenomenology*. Only a philosopher, however, can go mad—or blind—never philosophy itself, making it possible to assume the absolute difference between reason and madness or insight and blindness. This possibility—and, finally, this impossibility—defines every philosophical economy from Descartes' (or Socrates') Cogito to Hegel's *Geist* and its self-conscious Cogito, to Husserl's transcendental consciousness and Heideggerian *Dasein,* or the economies of thinking developed in his later works. As Derrida's analysis in "Cogito and the History of Madness" suggests (in part against Foucault), Descartes is by no means unaware of the interrelationship of madness and reason (WD 53–54). Nor was Hegel, who suggests the possibility of fully suspending both blindness and madness only *in principle* and only at the level of *Geist. Geist* never closes its eyes. It has no unconscious. It never sleeps and never forgets. The Medusa, too, never closes her eyes. Even when dead and transformed into Perseus' shield, she still retains the spellbinding, medusefying power of her dead gaze. But is this gaze dead, then?

Derrida's own meditation on the Medusa in *Glas* proceeds via Freud (and possibly Lacan) and is situated between Hegel and Genet—the column of Freud alongside the columns of Hegel and Genet. In the architecture of *Glas,* one would expect the Medusa to appear, at any point, Imaginary or Symbolic or Real, to use Lacan's famous registers. The giants are turned into stone and *erected* as columns, by the Medusa's eyes or by turning back toward the apocalyptic fire of Sodom: "The Medusa provides for no off-scene *(hors-scène)*. She sees, shows only stony columns." Much of the thematics of *Glas* can be reinscribed through a certain Medusan economy, beginning with its opening lines: "What, after all, of the remain(s), for us, here, now, of Hegel?" To begin with, as we have seen, there is "magisterial coldness and imperturbable seriousness, the eagle [Hegel] caught in ice and frost, glass and gel," as Derrida places the petrified eagle or column of Hegel—the column of Hegel's text—next to the column of Genet's text. "Let the emblanched *[emblémi]* philosopher be so congealed" (G 1a), Derrida says here:

> But as a stone, a firestone, a silex, verily an uncuttable *[inentamable]* diamond. Let that fall *[ça tombe]* to dust, but as funerary slab, so natural that it would reconstitute itself, and always harder. He is Medusa *[se méduse]* to himself [he medusefies himself]. (G 202b)

The last passage actually occurs in the Genet, rather than the Hegel, column of the text. By this point, however, and from the outset, one cannot unequivocally differentiate between Hegel and Genet; instead one must recognize a *différance*—an interplay of differences, commonalities, and interactions—between them. The Medusan economy of *Glas* proceeds by way of the question of self-consciousness—whose proper name is finally Hegel, for whom the proper and final name of absolute self-consciousness is Absolute Knowledge *(Sa—savoir absolut):*

> How can one be Medusa to oneself? One has to understand that *he* is not *himself* before being Medusa to himself. He occurs to himself since the Medusa. To be oneself is to-be-Medusa'd, and from then on the Medusa'd-being constitutes itself, that is, defends itself, bands itself erect, and elaborates itself only in being Medusa'd by oneself, in eating-Medusa'ing oneself, in making oneself a bit *[mors]* that gives oneself/itself up as lost *[fait son deuil]*. Dead sure of self. No *logic* is more powerful than this apotropic. No absolutely general economy, no exposition or pure expenditure: a strict-ure more or less strong. His *(Sa)* Medusa('s), always *[Sa méduse toujours]*. (G 202b)

One can imagine the portrait of Hegel or Genet as simultaneously both Perseus and the Medusa (cf. M 73–87). Their texts and our readings both conquer the Medusa as Perseus did and medusefy themselves, converting themselves into stone monuments by their unblinking eyes—the eyes of the Medusa. Unless they build another Tower of Babel, as they climb the Mountain of Purgatorio. The question is, how many such mountains are we climbing and how many such towers are we building at any given point?

Enclosures

The (en)closure *(clôture)* of metaphysics or philosophy in Derrida designates our dependence on the language, concepts, and strategies developed throughout the history of philosophy but operative elsewhere as well. This extension compels him to speak of the closure of philosophy. According to Derrida, this dependence itself is fundamental and irreducible. In many ways, Derrida's deconstruction is defined as an investigation of this closure, which may be an interminable project: "What is held within the demarcated closure may continue indefinitely" (P 13; cf. WD 250). Although the term "closure" would naturally suggest conclusion, end, or termination, the closure of philosophy (as the metaphysics of presence) as understood by Derrida implies simultaneously an enclosure and interminability, suggested by the double meaning of the French *clôture* as well as the English word "closure." The economy of closure, however, is also conceived by Derrida in terms of the model of Freud's interminable analysis, and Derrida distinguishes the end and the closure from the outset of his introduction of the term.

While the question of the closure of metaphysics or philosophy may not be *Hegel*'s question, it is certainly a *Hegelian* question; and it is, in fact, possible to speak of the closure of philosophy as the post-Hegelian closure. It is not that this closure did not exist before Hegel. Just as in confrontation with writing, this closure has no more an absolute beginning than an absolute end.[23] It is post-Hegelian because, even if without realizing it, Hegel, in his attempt to define the conceptual and historical functioning of *philosophy* itself, inscribed the functioning of the *closure* of philosophy, along with the functioning of writing in Derrida's sense. He would be the first thinker of this closure in the same sense as he is the first thinker of writing, even if in part against himself. What is claimed by Hegel for philosophy can in fact be claimed only for a certain closure of philosophy as the metaphysics of presence, which, according to Derrida, may be seen as culminating in Hegel (OG 24). The closure of philosophy replaces Hegel's conception of philosophy as having a primary role in the history of knowledge. Derrida's understanding that this economy is an economy of closure—and that without realizing it, Hegel in fact inscribes this closure—is one of Derrida's most profound insights.

This replacement or displacement from a given field toward the closure of that field is the first revisionary ratio I want to introduce. One could in principle argue, following a type of argument Harold Bloom has often used, that Hegel already inscribes such a closure. Derrida must repress or displace Hegel in order to produce what Bloom would call a strong theory. I do not think that this is quite the case, except in the sense (which is closer to de Man or, again, Derrida himself than to Bloom) indicated above. As I said, Hegel saw this without seeing, revealed it while concealing it. Hegel is blind to this closure as closure, quite possibly because, in his philosophical vigilance, his philosophical eyes remain wide open and unable to blink. By introducing this closure as closure, Derrida introduces a certain *différance* in Hegel's philosophy and thus points to a radical difference from, rather than only a repetition of and proximity to, it. This relation of close proximity and radical difference is the second revisionary ratio that I want to introduce and connect to the first ratio defined above. If Derrida's closure reinstates an instance of Hegelianism, it does so by surrendering too much to the closure of philosophy rather than to philosophy itself, as Hegel does.

What would be the relation of a deconstructive text, such as Derrida's, to the *text* of philosophy and its margins? Would it be a necessary or unique relation? And, then, how would such a relation define a relation, for example, like that of creative antagonism or agon between Derrida and Hegel? While the field of philosophy as the metaphysics of presence is unified to a degree, it may not be seen as fully unified, certainly not as unified as philosophy's own disciplinary self-concept would have it. But it is sufficiently unified to join the historico-theoretical forces of its many contingents. What then would relate and differentiate different "margins" and "exteriors" of philosophy or different engagements with its text, such as Derrida's, against the forces of philosophy? Such differences may engage margins that may not be defined as the margins of philosophy. Perhaps we are no longer quite "caught within the metaphysical closure." Derrida writes:

> I think that *all concepts hitherto proposed in order to think the articulation of a discourse and of an historical totality are caught within the metaphysical closure [clôture] that I question here,* as we do not know of any other concepts and cannot produce any others, and indeed shall not produce any so long as this closure limits our discourse; as the primordial and indispensable phase, in fact and in principle, of the development of this problematic, consists in questioning the internal structure of these [metaphysical] texts as symptoms . . . *themselves* in the totality of their metaphysical appurtenance. (OG 99)

This (interminable) questioning of "the internal structure of these texts as symptoms" is necessary for the production of new concepts that one could in turn question here.[24] The operation of the closure or closures of that type cannot be suspended, and might in fact need a more multiple economy of closure than Derrida suggests here and elsewhere. The concept of the closure of philosophy is, as I said, one of Derrida's most important contributions. One can argue, however, that there can be no untransformed or undifferentiated configuration of closure, such as the closure of metaphysics or philosophy; and, crucial as this qualification may be, it may not be enough to insist, as Derrida does elsewhere, on the heterogeneity of closure itself or the heterogeneity of a given field, such as philosophy.[25] There can be no totality of closure, particularly of a given theoretical closure, such as the closure of metaphysics, just as there can never be an absolute historical totality—*the* historical totality. In this sense, Derrida's usage of the indefinite article "an" in "*an historical totality*" (99), quoted above, is significant. A certain, and here one may say Hegelian, globalization of the closure of metaphysics may, however, be detected here and elsewhere in Derrida: "*ALL concepts hitherto proposed* . . . we do not know of any other concepts and cannot produce any others, and indeed shall not produce any so long as this closure limits our discourse." It appears that more than his own project is at stake here (which would localize this economy). In Derrida, the closure of metaphysics leads in the style of psychoanalysis to an *interminable* "questioning [of] the *internal* structure of these symptoms" in the text of philosophy, at least "as the primordial and indispensable phase, in fact and in principle, of the development of this problematic." Like all neuroses, philosophy itself would remain incurable, even though some of its symptoms might be treated and controlled.

We cannot produce new concepts "as long as this closure limits our discourse," Derrida says. We might however have to supplement this claim by maintaining a plurality and heterogeneity of closures. We might also be able to locate the areas of discourse where the notion cannot apply. Besides, new concepts—or neither terms nor concepts, such as *différance*—are produced in Derrida and elsewhere. The main questions, however, are whether this closure still limits our discourse and whether, crucial and effective as this project has been in Derrida and elsewhere, the project of the *interminable* questioning of the *internal* structure of certain philosophical symptoms is an irreducible project or an irreducible counterpart of any effective theoretical project. And if there is no unstratified or untransformed closure of any kind, philosophical or other, if the economy of closure is irreducibly heterogeneous, what would be required in order to transgress or transform a given closure? The concepts produced within the history of philosophy continue to constrain our discourse, leading Derrida to the idea of the closure of philosophy. Derrida does not speak of the transformation or stratification of closure—or, in his own terms, dissemination of closures. His position on this issue is closer to both Hegel and Heidegger than to Nietzsche.

Derrida's *positions* are always complex and rarely unequivocal. One could argue, however, that his positions are also on the margins of *philosophy,* and thus simultaneously in infinitesimal proximity to and radical difference from philosophy or a given author, such as Hegel. Derrida himself speaks of "a relation of profound affinity" with and of "infinitesimal and radical displacement" of "Hegelian discourse":

> *[D]ifférance* thus written, although maintaining the relations of profound affinity with Hegelian discourse (such as it must be

> read), is also, up to a certain point, unable to break with that discourse (which has no kind of meaning or chance); but it can operate a kind of infinitesimal and radical displacement of it. (MP 14)

It follows that, if one proceeds by reading and following Hegel's text very closely, one can, at a certain point, displace his conceptual chain—ever so slightly, *infinitesimally.* The results, however, are radical to the point, for example, of making "concepts" no longer possible. Instead, one encounters structures such as *différance* which are neither words nor concepts, which at a certain point make concepts, including Hegelian concepts, possible, but in the end also dislocate them. The displacement is so radical that, if *différance* could be defined, it would be defined *at the limit* of Hegel's *Aufhebung* (P 40–41). Once only infinitesimal, however, a displacement is also a proximity. This proximity is defined in part through the economy of the closure of philosophy, whereby a certain Hegelian field reemerges, but one that is different from Hegel's own in being a certain metaphysics of *closure* rather than a form of the metaphysics of *presence* itself. One keeps as it were one's eyes, at least one eye, afraid to blink upon Hegel and philosophy. But this desire also triggers a reverse force that freezes the movement of one's eye and pen—one's writing—medusefied by the gaze of Hegel and philosophy.

I am not arguing here that Derrida makes Hegel or philosophy into his own *Geist.* Neither do I think that Derrida translates Hegel's economy of the relationship between philosophy and *Geist* or later the Idea into the relationship between "Derrida" and "Hegel." Hegel's economy is, however, that of an infinitesimal proximity and a radical difference between (human) philosophy and *Geist,* which returns me to my second revisionary ratio. This ratio may be seen as pre-comprehending Bloom's matrix of the anxiety of influence and the psycho-socio-political relationships between "tradition and the individual talent," whether in literature or philosophy. For all these relationships—and Oedipal politics itself—are defined in terms of infinitesimal proximity and radical difference or distance.[26] The main precursor of Derrida in this respect could be Heidegger, whose meditation remains according to Derrida "uncircumventable" (MP 22). Heidegger speaks of the economy of *Dasein* as at once the closest and the most distant from Being. On the one hand, Derrida exposes this economy as a form of metaphysics of presence, most specifically in "The Ends of Man" (MP 109–136). On the other hand, he translates it into a relation between deconstruction and philosophy, and, particularly, between Hegel and Heidegger. And yet in this respect, too, the ultimate precursor may still be Hegel, who inscribes this economy from the *Phenomenology* on. The ultimate precursor could be Socrates, if not Parmenides; the philosophies of both defined by the same relation or ratio. Or it could be Plato, whose relationship to Socrates is also that of infinitesimal proximity and radical difference.

This relationship may also be seen as recomprehending the relationship between absolute originality and absolute traditionality, which has served to define many a tradition and many individual talents throughout Western history, from the pre-Socratics to the postmodernists. It certainly defines much of deconstruction—its relationship to and difference from Hegel and philosophy. Deconstruction, too, has become a tradition by now, with its many individual talents, perhaps even a Hegelian—or simultaneously Hegelian and anti-Hegelian—tradition, enclosing and enclosed by Hegel and philosophy, as deconstruction and philosophy continue to keep their eyes upon each other.

The question remains whether this closure and this continuous re-enclosure (for example, via the proximity-distance economy just discussed) into philosophy are unavoidable. I would be compelled to answer in the negative and suggest that one needs a more diverse stratification and a more radical economy of transformation of closure than suggested by Derrida. In the wake of, if against, Derrida's analysis, the question of theoretical transformations acquires a new dimension; the most radical transformations can transform not only theories themselves or fields where such theories primarily operate but also the closures of theories or fields. In the course of such a transformation, that is, a point may be reached when one no longer remains within the closure or configuration of closures dominating the field where the transformation has taken place, such as the closure of philosophy. The latter extends far and along a broad and varied front; and it may not be possible as yet to claim that a transformation escaping this closure or altering it radically enough has taken place. One cannot, however, maintain the possibility of a unitary closure at any point. The economy suggested by the preceding analysis allows for relationships between successive, or parallel configurations or closures, but prevents one from containing them within any single closure, even if the latter is transforming and heterogeneous within itself, as appears to be the case in Derrida's economy of closure.

A transformation may, in the end, be so radical that no given form of philosophical discourse and no extension of philosophy or its closure can control the resulting configuration, however crucial both might have been during preceding stages of the process. Naturally, such new configurations may be reabsorbed by or reconnected to philosophy (or any "old" field that may be in such a position) and then transform that old field or restratify it in relation to an "old" configuration. In short, whether they have philosophical genealogies or not, such new configurations may exceed philosophy itself and even its closure at some point, and leave them behind—assuming that one wishes to do so. Moreover, such genealogies, including the genealogy of philosophy itself, can never be purely philosophical. These new configurations result from other developments, exterior to philosophy, understood, let me stress, as a demarcated institutional field and ensemble of texts (and, again, as the metaphysics of presence). In the wake of Derrida's analysis, the "inside" and the "outside" of anything are no longer unequivocally separable (OG 44–65). But they are no longer unconditionally inseparable either. Hence, no absolute (en)closure of anything appears to be possible, however complex the topology or distribution of such an (en)closure might be.

The closure of philosophy is no longer as powerful and pervasive as it has been hitherto. This closure cannot be seen at any moment of history as omnipotent or omnipresent (or present), even in fields such as the social and human sciences or literary criticism and theory, where the influence of philosophy has been felt most, or within philosophy itself, which is always invaded by other forces and closures. These fields are invaded from within and without and taken over by forces and fields that philosophy could not foresee or master. Or rather, such radical transformations emerge from an interplay of networks inside and outside philosophy, as philosophy is invaded by other fields or, conversely, as it invades other fields, particularly through the closure of philosophy.

"There is a duration to the blink, and it closes the eye *[elle ferme l'oeil]*" (SP 65), Derrida says. This duration *(une durée)* may be made to last long enough to open our eyes to a different vision, for example, to still another mountain with terraces, like Dante's Mountain of Purgatorio, or even a mountain range, or another Tower of Babel, or a cityscape, or a landscape that combines both. "I am building a mountain range out of ever more sacred mountains," Nietzsche says of Zarathustra and of himself (GM 304), very likely with both Dante, the poet, and Hegel, the philosopher, in mind, or with a glance back on the mountains and towers that they built—mountains out of mountains, towers out of towers. We must build both, moving at times fast, at times slow; and at certain points we must make difficult decisions, sometimes without blinking an eye.

Notes

1. Jacques Derrida, *Mémoires d'aveugle: L'autoportrait et autres ruines* (Paris: Editions de la Réunion des musées nationaux, 1990), 23; *Memoirs of the Blind: The Self-Portrait and Other Ruins,* trans. Pascale-Anne Brault and Michael Naas (Chicago: Univ. of Chicago Press, 1993), 17; abbreviated as M in the text. Georges Bataille, "Histoire de l'oeil," *Madame Edwarda, Le Mort, Histoire de l'oeil* (Paris: Pauvert, 1967); *Story of the Eye,* trans. Joachim Neugroschel (San Francisco: City Lights Books, 1987). For Derrida's description of his illness, see the French and English versions, 37–38 and 32 respectively. One can argue that much of the discussion of *Memoirs,* including the theme of the ruins, has been influenced by Bataille's "economy of the eye" (M 17 n.10). A number of ideas introduced by Bataille, especially his concept of general economy, are crucial for Derrida, and Derrida's encounter with Hegel proceeds via Bataille (and a creative agon with Bataille).

2. Derrida, *Speech and Phenomena and Other Essays on Husserl's Theory of Science,* trans. David B. Allison. (Evanston: Northwestern Univ. Press, 1973). Abbreviated in the text as SP. These thematics also emerge in *Memoires: For Paul de Man,* trans. Cecile Lindsay, Jonathan Culler, and Eduardo Cadava (New York: Columbia Univ. Press, 1986), whose title shares the word "memoires" with *Mémoires d'aveugle* (although it is translated as "memoirs" in *Memoirs of the Blind*). The latter contains key references to de Man's *Blindness and Insight: Essays in the Rhetoric of Contemporary Criticism,* 2nd ed.

(Minneapolis: Univ. of Minnesota Press, 1983), and many de Manian themes. Derrida's earlier text on Nietzsche is entitled, conversely, *The Ear of the Other: Otobiography, Transference, Translation. Texts and Discussions with Jacques Derrida,* ed. Christie V. McDonald (Lincoln: Univ. of Nebraska Press, 1985). Autobiography is, however, a major theme there as well.

3. This theory has been developed by Bloom in many of his works beginning with *The Anxiety of Influence: A Theory of Influence* (New York: Oxford Univ. Press, 1973).

4. Cf. Bataille's elaborations in *Guilty (Le Coupable),* trans. Bruce Boon (Venice, Calif.: Lapis Press, 1988), and Derrida's "From Restricted to General Economy: Hegelianism without Reserve," *Writing and Difference,* trans. Alan Bass (Chicago: Univ. of Chicago Press, 1978). Abbreviated in the text as WD.

5. To one degree or another this monumentalization may be unavoidable. Cf. Paul de Man's discussion of monumentalization, which has many Hegelian overtones, in "Shelley Disfigured," *The Rhetoric of Romanticism* (New York: Columbia Univ. Press, 1984), 121–23.

6. Hegel's famous Preface to the *Phenomenology* refers to Plato's *Parmenides* as "(surely the greatest artistic achievement of the ancient dialectic)" (*Phenomenology of Spirit,* trans. A. V. Miller [Oxford: Clarendon Press, 1977], 44).

7. Derrida, *De la grammatologie* (Paris: Editions de Minuit, 1967), 148; *Of Grammatology,* trans. Gayatri C. Spivak (Baltimore: Johns Hopkins Univ. Press, 1976), 99. Abbreviated in the text as OG.

8. Derrida, *Positions,* trans. Alan Bass (Chicago: Univ. of Chicago Press, 1981), 41. Abbreviated in the text as P. The economy of the *Aufhebung,* based on the triple meaning of the German word itself—(selective) negation, conservation, and supersession—governs Hegel's dialectic throughout.

9. Derrida, *The Truth in Painting,* trans. Geoffrey Bennington and Ian McLeod (Chicago: Univ. of Chicago Press, 1987), 19.

10. The term general economy can also be used here in Bataille's sense of a theoretical framework. See my *In the Shadow of Hegel: Complementarity, History and the Unconscious* (Gainesville: Univ. Press of Florida, 1993), and *Reconfigurations: Critical Theory and General Economy* (Gainesville: Univ. Press of Florida, 1993).

11. I have considered this issue extensively in *In the Shadow of Hegel.*

12. The apocalypse of letters in Derrida's "Envois" may be similarly allegorized. See *The Post Card: From Socrates to Freud and Beyond,* trans. Alan Bass (Chicago: Univ. of Chicago Press, 1987), 254–56. The economy of "almost" plays a crucial role throughout Derrida's analysis.

13. Derrida, *Glas,* trans. John P. Leavey Jr. and Richard Rand (Lincoln: Univ. of Nebraska Press, 1986), 1. Abbreviated in the text as G.

14. This list admits no termination or taxonomical closure. It thematizes that peculiar space between infinity and finitude, which these structures are in part designed to account for. Cf. Derrida (SP 101–02); Derrida, at one point, speaks of writing as metaphoricity itself (OG 15). See also his "The *Retrait* of Metaphor," *Enclitic* 2 (Fall 1978): 5–33; and especially "White Mythology:

Metaphor in the Text of Philosophy," in *Margins of Philosophy,* trans. Alan Bass (Chicago: Univ. of Chicago Press, 1982); abbreviated in the text as MP. Some of de Man's work is also significant here, especially again "Shelley Disfigured." On translation, see "Des Tours de Babel" in *Difference in Translation,* ed. Joseph F. Graham (Ithaca: Cornell Univ. Press, 1985), 165–207, and "Living on: Border Lines," trans. James Hulbert, *Deconstruction and Criticism,* ed. Harold Bloom *et al.* (New York: Seabury Press, 1979), 75–176.

15. On the economy of the ear in Derrida, usually proceeding via Nietzsche, see *The Ear of the Other* and "Tympan" (in *Margins*). More conventional psychoanalytic implications of these metaphors—the Medusa and the Tower—and the connections between blindness and castration are not to be ignored. Derrida refers to Freud in this context (M 73; G 202).

16. Cf., on the one hand, de Man's analysis in "The Rhetoric of Temporality" (mentioned earlier) and, on the other, Gilles Deleuze and Felix Guattari's economy of schizophrenia, as developed especially in *Anti-Oedipus: Capitalism and Schizophrenia,* trans. Robert Hurley, Mark Seem, and Helen R. Lane (Minneapolis: Univ. of Minnesota Press, 1983).

17. Friedrich Nietzsche, *The Birth of Tragedy,* trans. Walter Kaufmann (New York: Vintage, 1967), 15 n.7, 89.

18. Nietzsche, *On the Genealogy of Morals and Ecce Homo,* trans. Walter Kaufmann (New York: Vintage, 1967), 57–58. Abbreviated in the text as GM.

19. Derrida, *The Acts of Literature,* ed. Derek Attridge (New York: Routledge, 1992), 262. Abbreviated in the text as AL.

20. See Michel Serres, *The Natural Contract,* trans. Elizabeth MacArtur and William Paulson (Ann Arbor: Univ. of Michigan Press), 27–28.

21. Cf. also Derrida's recent *The Other Heading: Reflections of Today's Europe,* trans. Pascale-Anne Brault and Michael B. Naas (Bloomington: Indiana Univ. Press, 1992), where this problematic emerges in the context of the contemporary geopolitical landscape.

22. See Derrida (P 68–71; AL 33–75); and his "The Double Session," *Dissemination,* trans. Barbara Johnson (Chicago: Univ. of Chicago Press, 1981).

23. See, especially, P 13–14. Obviously an inscription of such a closure *as* closure, or of writing as a certain economy of writing (as in Derrida) is crucial. It allows one to see the functioning of the closure as closure throughout the history of philosophy. In this sense Derrida's contribution remains decisive.

24. I have considered the question of closure in Derrida in detail in my *Reconfigurations* (194–214) and *Complementarity: Anti-epistemology After Bohr and Derrida* (Durham: Duke Univ. Press, 1994), 225–69. The problematics of closure was also considered, from a different perspective, mostly via Levinas, by Simon Critchley in *The Ethics of Deconstruction: Derrida and Levinas* (Cambridge: Blackwell, 1992).

25. See, in particular, "The *Rétrait* of Metaphor" (4) and MP (172 n.16). This point is, however, transparent throughout Derrida's work.

26. It also allows one to consider constructive continuities, building upon traditions, rather than only antagonistic or agonistic economies, which can, of course, be constructive as well, just as continuity may be nonconstructive. In general, we need as rich a dynamics of transformations—of proximities and distances, continuities and breaks, and so forth—as possible. I have considered this dynamic in *In the Shadow of Hegel* (84–95).

Walter Benjamin: The Prophet's War against Prophecy

Marcus Paul Bullock

Between the time when Walter Benjamin completed his doctoral studies in 1919 and his first statements in 1924 announcing his turn to Marxist themes, his letters already revealed his interest in formulating a position within the terms of political struggle. A consideration of this early development and the process of transition from what he refers to as the anarchism of those years throws much light on the difficulties we now have in mapping his path from the politics of culture through theological and materialist terrain. The dialectical climate that reigns in the landscape of these explorations introduces such great atmospheric extremes that no perspective can gather all the features of his later work into a single image identifying him with one category of political convictions. We can let Gerschom Scholem speak for the many voices whose desire to draw Benjamin's genius close prompted them to strain against the complexity that always reimposed a last, irreducible distance. In his book *Walter Benjamin: The Story of a Friendship,* Scholem calls this turn toward communism "the beginning of a split" in his friend.[1] And later, when the split did not close again, Scholem wrote to Benjamin in 1931 that "the tension of this ambiguity" would cause him to be "destroyed because . . . the morality of any insights achieved in such an existence must degenerate."[2]

Scholem's letter to Benjamin concludes with what appears to be a psychological explanation of the "self-deception" (C 373, 375, 379) of which he accuses him: "Your desire for community places you at risk," Scholem states (C 379). Yet even if this were the motivation—and one may assume a desire for community animates any existence that does not already enjoy its share in this universal necessity—it does nothing to explain any of the choices, decisions, and intuitions that shape Benjamin's work, for his responsibility as a critic to engage error and combat myth determines every intellectual relationship. For him, no framework of relations can take precedence over this responsibility. That is why during the period when he speaks most explicitly about a decision to join the Communist Party he can also declare communist goals to be "nonsense and nonexistent" (C 301). Benjamin's struggle against a larger rule of nonsense corrupting every domain of experience justified this affiliation, and the pervasive effect of a shattered language within which truth of all kinds was nonexistent outweighed any opportunism at work in the party structure itself.

From September 1924, in his first comments to Scholem expressing a philosophical interest in studying Marxist writing, to the more extensive remarks in May 1926, he makes it clear that he values only the terms of the contest that could be mounted from Communist positions. His continued rejection of any authoritative positive viewpoint restricts the shift toward Marxism explicitly to a development of his earlier positions. In 1924, contemplating a study of Georg Lukács's book *History and Class Consciousness,* he observes: "I would be surprised if the foundations of my nihilism were not to manifest themselves against communism in an antagonistic confrontation with the concepts and assertions of Hegelian dialectics" (C 248). In 1926, he states: "I am not thinking of 'renouncing' the things that I supported; . . . I am not ashamed of my 'early' anarchism" (C 301).

Even if Benjamin had not questioned the rationality of socialist goals or the reality of the history in which they were framed, we would have great difficulty in asserting how the language of political conflict he adopts does truly refer to what we ordinarily call politics, especially what we call materialist politics. The temptation is strong and the tendency widespread to acknowledge but also neglect the evident divergence between what he understands by those terms and how we, in the ordinary exchange on issues of broad historical and social questions, identify what makes our discourse political. Benjamin's rhetoric is heavily colored by its messianic and theological overtones and undertones, and apocalyptic in its vision of historical forces expressed in agencies like "the masses" or the "proletariat" that brook no equivocation in their absolute contest with reigning powers. Thus the language of his dialectical images leaps well beyond any interest that might unite him and his readers in the benefit to be gained by a tangible political decision within some definite political process.

Yet the overwhelming effect of his arguments against the conditions of modernity from which all the afflictions of our experience must stem appeals irresistibly to the desire that it should enlighten what we decide and how we act. We who find ourselves exposed to political forces desire that the authority of his formulations should accrue to our own interests and bring the goal of real benefits within reach. But the rejection of political goals in his remarks to Scholem does not restrict itself to his reticence before the form or the content of a particular set of ideological formulae. His hesitation to join the Communist Party does not spring from some fine philosophical discrimination on his part that might have been satisfied by critique and refinement of the party's expressed position, or even that he might have preferred the party to embrace other goals. Far from it, the senseless and vacuous character of communist goals, he writes, "does not diminish the value of Communist action one iota" (C 301). He gives two reasons for this. First, the opportunity for action takes precedence over the goals because its conflict with reigning conditions achieves a prior degree of reality by virtue of the real process of acting, so that communist action becomes "the corrective for its goals" (C 301). Second, motivations limited to realizing an imaginary state of affairs will always curtail the vitality of action in response to an actual history of experience. As he puts this much later in his "Theses on the Philosophy of History," the "greatest strength" of a revolutionary class will be "nourished by the image of enslaved ancestors rather than that of liberated grandchildren."[3] In the letter, he observes simply that "there are no meaningfully *political* goals" (C 301).

Communist action, therefore, must be grasped entirely beyond the Hegelian element in its dialectics. Two years after Benjamin suggested this expectation in the letter of 1924, he confirms among his "irrefutable insights" the view "that materialist metaphysics or, indeed, even the materialist conception of history is irrelevant" (C 300). Without this irrelevant burden of mythic sequences in historical time, communist action proceeds with a different promise and on a different basis, namely, the conflict defined primarily by "the mechanism through which things (and conditions) and the masses interact" (C 300). The struggle itself constitutes the cognitive process. Knowledge comes about in the conflict, and the agonistic engagement in this interaction opens the way to an unforeseeable dispensation of understanding. For this reason, he calls this form of political action an "observance," thereby relating it to the practice of a religion.

The principle of action that may "proceed ruthlessly and with radical intent" overcomes the false positivism of a secular ideology and allows a complex "identity" between "religious or political observance" (C 300). It achieves this remarkable identity in the release of forces defined by neither theological nor political dogma as enclosed domains of knowledge. The manifestation of energies and interactions that are incompatible with such enclosures as myth also necessarily contests the fixed laws in unjust worldly orders, the rule of arbitrary secular or of theocratic authority. Radical politics are "just" (C 301) in this sense because they unbind the full energy of the mechanism through which things and the masses interact, but this mechanism cannot be reduced to the irrelevant dogmas of party policy. The principle of "observance" preserves the knowledge thus realized from becoming mechanical, which would occur where human interaction with things took the same form as the interaction of things from a perspective purged of human engagement. That is to say, this activity moves far beyond the realm of facts, and preserves itself as the direct encounter among persons where politics "are intended as nothing but politics" (C 301).

Benjamin's point here echoes that which Friedrich Nietzsche made in the essay from his *Untimely Meditations,* "On the Uses and Disadvantages of History for Life." Nietzsche, too, attacks the Hegelian reduction of all events in history entirely to an expression of the law by which history unfolds everything as unified. That singularity in the form of knowledge destroys its capacity to express human freedom. Just as Benjamin found it essential to uphold the observances of politics and religion against a unified theory of metaphysics and history, Nietzsche objects to the way the iron process of history under Hegelian influence establishes itself "in place of the other spiritual powers, art and religion, as the sole sovereign power." And he notes that "History understood in this Hegelian fashion has been mockingly called God's vicissitudes on earth, though the god referred to has been created only by the history."[4] The identification of a transcendent process ("God's vicissitudes") manifest in the realm of facts prevents the development of any procedure that might uncover a truth not yet fixed in that realm by theory. The mechanism of which Benjamin speaks only permits the historian to approach it in the radical experience of that interaction itself. This is why the initial concern that Benjamin voices to explain to Scholem why politics continues to demand a full place in his thinking takes the form of "attempting to leave the purely theoretical sphere" (C 300).

The purity of theory falsely raises itself above politics, which Benjamin regards here as the enactment of a relationship that has yet to find an explicit character. He sees this relationship as "the study and the practice" that one understands "not as mere words, but as a battle" (C 300). The value of communist action, therefore, depends on that stipulation which Benjamin insists on for the only "human" possibility of overcoming the limitations of theory (C 300). Nietzsche's target in his attack on the counter-critical sense of history among his contemporaries differs from that aspect of the communist heritage to which Benjamin objects because a "sole sovereign power" cannot offer the spectacle of battle. This simplifies the question of Nietzsche's proposed corrective, which falls to an agonism of personal resistance to history, not to a complex maneuver among sites of struggle between contesting historical forces. The Hegelian "Idea" to whose priority Nietzsche never accedes, passes through "vicissitudes" but not reversals. There are no opposing sites that might gather up support and eclipse this sovereignty, but only stages of veiling and obscuring through which the Idea penetrates into the consciousness of theory and reveals its constant preponderance of power. Whatever comes about in history does so as the expression of that power moving through the medium of facticity. For the practice of historical interpretation, declares Nietzsche, this "transforms every moment into a naked admiration for success and leads to an idolatry of the factual" (UM 105). In this accommodation to the facts, he sees nothing but the reinstatement of a thinking that is entirely "mythological" because it controls the minds of men and women through their enfeebled spirit of orthodoxy. He mockingly responds to the modernity of his time that looks back on the mythologies and religions of the past as a vanishing form, and admonishes his contemporaries to "behold the religion of the power of history, regard the priests of the mythology of the idea and their battered knees!" Under the weight of such a faith in facts, the individual "nods 'Yes' like a Chinese mechanical doll to every power, whether it be a government or public opinion or a numerical majority, and moves his limbs to the precise rhythm at which any 'power' whatever pulls the strings" (UM 105).

With this image in mind, we must distinguish between Benjamin's decision to take up a Marxist vocabulary as it looks in retrospect from his final positions, and the way it looks against the background of developments prior to 1924. A primary political concern that preceded his first Marxist leanings is brought to light in 1921 with the essay, "Critique of Violence." The principal idea of true political action is derived from Georges Sorel's notion of a general strike undertaken not with the negotiation of any specific demands but only in response to bringing down the structure of state and laws as the situation of labor. The initial moves toward communism display a similar spirit in setting aside its unrealistic claims in favor of its real possession of a negative capability. The capacity to struggle against ruling conditions outweighed all other concerns for Benjamin because he attached an importance to any act of negation that exceeded the value of any imaginable alternative to what the struggle might thereby remove. The anarchistic transformation of the world has no interest in unrolling a future of lesser evils, or, for that matter, in presenting the better of any two possible choices, but rather is only concerned with the absolute end of what is in order to permit an entirely different and unknowable future to unfold.

What happened during the subsequent crises in European history made it even more difficult to consider the open-textured activity of politics without goals: the rise of fascism imposed an entirely different set of tactical constraints. Moreover, the failure of communism to distinguish itself adequately from fascism drove Benjamin's rhetorical struggles back ever deeper into renewed densities of negation, culminating in 1940, after the Hitler-Stalin Pact and the outbreak of World War II, with the astoundingly rich text of the "Theses on the Philosophy of History." The first of the "Theses on the Philosophy of History" notoriously not only invokes theology as a source of authoritative ideas in the philosophical rivalry between historical materialism and bourgeois theories, but explicitly uses the image of an oriental doll (albeit Turkish, not Chinese) manipulated by strings pulled in order to control the movements of its limbs and thereby ensure its success in the contest with its opposition. The complexity of all that this image suggests, together with the further unfolding of the messianic idea in the remaining "Theses," and the full context of Benjamin's efforts to accommodate his thinking to the materialist interpretation of history beyond the limitations of theory can scarcely be reduced to a single formula. Nonetheless, one can contrast his earlier thinking and this position reached at the catastrophic interaction with conditions at the close of his life by pointing out the significance of his having introduced a finality, a goal, beyond politics merely as politics, in describing how the chess-playing automaton that represents historical materialism in the first "Thesis" is to "win all the time" (I 253).

Even though the "Theses" protest explicitly against the notion that the course of progress is a logical necessity in the development of history (I 260), his own position cannot find much space for "action" free of very doubtful political goals. Certainly, the transposition of images from the past to enliven the consciousness of the political present suggests an even more doubtful conception of winning. He focuses attention on Robespierre's justification of terror by citing the historical parallel between the ancient Roman and contemporary French republics. This illustration seems better adapted to show how a regime falls prey to the madness of myth, abandons the values of human life and justice, and thereby ensures that the people will abandon it and cause its downfall and defeat. The messianic disposition of change as a victory for that supposedly just power against an opposed force, which Benjamin explicitly names "the Antichrist" (I 255), has therefore changed profoundly from the kind of political views he appeared still to have had in mind in 1926.

In the conflict between these two forces, a correct alignment depends on the "discipline" he invokes in the tenth "Thesis," a discipline he models in this context on a religious observance whereby the individual decision to be made and remade as ruthlessness and radicalism in 1926 ("not to decide once and for all, but to decide at every moment" [C 300]) appears much modified and chastened—that of medieval friars whose themes of meditation "were designed to turn them away from the world and its affairs" (I 258). These practices resemble the use Benjamin proposes for his own thoughts now, which he has formulated as a means to extract his readers from the entanglements with those self-deceptions to which politicians have fallen prey. The hopes for an active critical engagement with socialism in the interest of justice give way now before the fear of taint and betrayal in any contact, for he accepts "the high price" we will have to pay to avoid "any complicity with the thinking to which these politicians continue to adhere" (I 258).

The shift in his use of the religious idea had already been conditioned by his acceptance years before of the belief that effective political engagement would also have to depend on discipline. His essay on the Surrealists written in 1929 contrasts the anarchic freedom on which their literary movement took its stand with a different "methodical and disciplinary preparation" for "the other revolutionary experience that we have to acknowledge because it has been ours, the constructive, dictatorial side of revolution."[5] Yet he agrees that the method by which surrealism secures its experience of ecstatic freedom does indeed turn away from conformism with the ruling state of affairs in the world, and in this matter, it bears a close relationship to the esoteric asceticism of courtly love in the medieval world. His objection at this time depends on the "undialectical" (R 189) reluctance to subject this intoxicated aestheticism to the critical perspective of materialist politics. His position in the "Theses" does not give the positive discipline of political action the decisive critical role, but reserves this for the negation of political engagement in reinstating an entirely messianic foundation for history. This use of theology serves as an antidote to the mythic consolations of "the politicians' stubborn faith in progress" (I 258).

The misfortune of this reasoning emerges exactly where Walter Benjamin seeks an explicit connection in his text to Nietzsche's critique of history. Moreover, it happens exactly where Benjamin finally abandons the element of agonism, of direct struggle by human agency against the ruling context that constrains and reduces the domain of human experience. For Nietzsche, the diminution of the concept of man in the context of history represented the triumph of the very worst forms of self-abnegation in human understanding. Therefore, from his perspective, the distinction between the messiah as the redeemer of history and the continuing triumph of the antichrist merely put separate faces on their singular opposition as mythology to the human. Faith in history as progress or faith in history as messianic redemption entails abandonment of the human, that ruthless and radical component of freedom by which alone philosophy separates the seductions of mythology from the promise of emancipation. In either case, the priority of an absolute historical power reduces human expression in politics to the workings of a mechanical doll whose powers over human particularity allow it to "win all the time" or to "succeed" in every instance. In Nietzsche's view, the record of such victories over human struggle cannot but present history as "a compendium of factual immorality" (UM 105).

In "Thesis" XII, Benjamin begins with an epigraph from Nietzsche's essay that reads: "*We need history, but not the way a spoiled loafer in the garden of knowledge needs it.*"[6] Yet he immediately turns his point away from Nietzsche's meaning when he opens his own remarks with the statement that "Not man or men but the struggling, oppressed class itself is the depository of historical knowledge" (I 260). By separating the oppressed class from "man or men," not just as a distinct focus of social power but as the source and vessel of knowledge, Benjamin turns historical knowledge into a contradictory term. The knowledge of history that takes the form of conscious action, decision, or even interpretation of actions and decisions in an effort to look forward, depends on intellectual labor. The forms of action that

Benjamin calls historical no longer include those that fulfill the will and understanding of an individual man or woman, or express that aspect in which their situation contains knowledge of a human experience beyond that enclosure. Another form of knowledge animates the oppressed class in its role "as the avenger that completes the task of liberation in the name of generations of the downtrodden" (I 260). Such knowledge can only be gathered in retrospect, after the mechanism of history has unfolded its messianic potential through this means. That is why the historical materialist cannot look forward but only backward.[7]

We need history, Nietzsche explains in the completion of the thought that Benjamin quotes, "for the sake of life and action, not so as to turn comfortably away from life and action" (UM 59). By identifying with the oppressed class, Benjamin does not choose history for the sake of bourgeois passivity and comfort, but he does derive comfort from the understanding that his abandonment of one stream of history, that of bourgeois historicism, and his abandonment of the rationalistic notion of causes in history, connect him with the depository of historical knowledge that will "win all the time." It wins all the time in its philosophical claim to justice by losing all the time to worldly injustice. It is precisely by turning away from complicity with politicians, and thus by refraining from all activity in the name of "man or men," that it gains the upper hand in philosophy when this automaton is guided by the strings of theology, which is to say, knowledge denied to actively thinking man or men. The philosophical disputation adumbrated in the first "Thesis," therefore, no longer takes place within the arena of competing theories. The indefensible theological origin of this critical mechanism exposes the narrow enclosure and inadequate basis of the knowledge opposed to it. It rises above that self-defeating limitation because it stands outside the process whereby theories collude in establishing their common ground in the arena of philosophical dispute. While Nietzsche's Chinese doll nods its head in universal assent, Benjamin's Turkish doll shakes its head in an unyielding radicalism of refusal.

If this is so, then we must reread the rhetorical connection Benjamin makes between the apparent dynamism of "blast[ing] open the continuum of history" and the inaction of "a present . . .

in which time stands still and has come to a stop" (I 262). The text of the "Theses" repeats formulations indicating that the past has to be "seized" ("Thesis" V, VI), that the need "to brush history against the grain" involves "grasping and holding" (VII), and that "a tiger's leap into the past" (XIV) to "blast a specific era" free (XVII) will make "history explode" (XV). These terms establish the rhythm by which Benjamin stirs his reader to recognize the urgency of the "fight for the oppressed past" (XVII). Amid all this welter of phrases invoking the release of decisive political forces, we should not lose sight of the passive role that has finally overcome the historian. He does not wield the explosive power in historical understanding for the same reason that he cannot unfold the depository of true historical knowledge. His part in history limits him to challenging the false language of historicism by resisting the temptations to continue the existence of a historicist consciousness. "Thinking involves not only the flow of thoughts, but their arrest as well," Benjamin states (I 262), though without addressing the question of how the effect on a thinking being of ceasing to think might affect the world. Here, he limits his remarks to the effect on the thoughts only, which he has exposed to a new critical distance by their appearing now cut off from an ongoing experience of subjective life: "Where thinking suddenly stops in a configuration pregnant with tensions, it gives that configuration a shock, by which it crystallizes into a monad" (I 262–63). The separation of the monad now alerts the thinker to the falsity of the time that he had previously packed out with the "mass of data" produced by the "additive" (I 262) process of historicist thought.

This "shock" alerts him to the vacuity of his own time and to his incapacity to experience a fuller time. He knows of a real time when he discovers that it eludes him: "The nourishing fruit of the historically understood contains time as a precious but tasteless seed" (I 263). Armed with this insight, he "establishes a conception of the present" that takes into account what it cannot possess as knowledge (I 263). His concept reflects its position outside the truth because it bears the traces of another dimension—shivered fragments of messianic time—of which he can form a conception negatively, like the seed he cannot taste. That is to say, by disrupting the deluded continuity of a false and empty mythic narrative of causal history encountered in historicism, he develops a sense of the present whose very isolation now resembles its disrupted relationship to a true history. Only the final active break of a revolution can instate messianic time in place of myth and consummate objective relations of history. That transformation depends on the quite separate active power of the revolutionary class.

The power to which "thinking" as its own consummation has access achieves its most decisive moment by not continuing but by refraining from the activity that joins the thinker to the world that is closest to him. The significance of that abstinence emerges primarily by the difference it establishes between him and those who do not turn away from the world and its affairs in this monastic discipline: "The historical materialist leaves it to others to be drained by the whore called 'Once upon a time' in historicism's bordello" (I 262). The conclusion Benjamin draws here can only extend that refusal to the meaning of a decisive act by drawing on the blurred meaning in the word "history." He can indeed point to the dubious nature of all history as knowledge, especially when the narrative work of recreating the past as a story ties up the record of events into the orderly motifs of a causal structure. The desires at work will always transfigure any representation of the past to make it fit the world of the historian and his audience as a precisely modelled frame. Therefore, the historian who chooses not to "historicize" can always defeat the claim by any "philosophy" or world of thought that endeavors to justify itself within the intimacy of such complementary frameworks. But this must represent the extent to which Benjamin modifies his claims when he writes that such a figure "remains in control of his powers, man enough to blast open the continuum of history" (I 262). The extremity of the rhetoric itself contains the reinstatement of history in precisely the same debilitating form. The irresistible presence of desire speaks at this moment, swells the voice, and gives itself over to the mythological domain of messianic dispensations by laying claim to a share in historical powers that decide the future in politics.

Benjamin has reduced himself to the service of this theological vision because he fears that opposition to history on its own terms would not be opposition at all. He chooses to submit his language to the terms of theology because the fear overwhelms him that confidence in the process of deliberate judgment entails the "threat . . . of becoming a tool of the ruling classes" (I 255). But by denying the process of subjective construction in which the striving of "a man or men" rises up against history, he has denied the only course of independent action open to human struggle (I 260). He has denied it, however, only in theory. The rhetoric of struggle, of blasting away at the illusions of conformism, that reverberates through these passages, raises up its architecture of independent intellectual labor far beyond the fantasy of salvation it encloses as the nominal object of its service. What he has surrendered in political judgment, he has recovered against his own declarations in the language enframing his final reckoning with the catastrophe that had swallowed up all parties in the political world.

This corresponds significantly to the warning Scholem gives Benjamin in his letter of May 1931 against "the imagery with which you are cheating yourself out of your calling" (C 379). Scholem concedes, he says, the possibility of writing like Lenin, but admonishes his friend, "I am attacking only the fiction of pretending to do this while doing something totally different" (C 379). This retreat into fiction continued the split that Scholem dates back to Benjamin's first efforts to assimilate Marxism. However, while Scholem was right in observing that it threatened Benjamin's ability to sustain his personal existence where it caused the "morality" of his insights to "degenerate," the achievement of the "Theses" themselves confirms Benjamin's talents insofar as the text gives precise expression to his experience of that split itself. When Benjamin had asked him for a "counterproposal" (C 378), Scholem wrote, "I can only suggest that you acknowledge your genius, which you are currently so hopelessly attempting to deny" (C 379). That self-denial by genius took the form of genius in the "Theses," but Scholem had foreseen correctly: "Self-deception turns all too easily into suicide" (C 379).

In thus ascribing a value to genius as a counterbalance to the threat of self-denial before materialist history, Scholem allies himself with Nietzsche in his defense of that which is most living in human life. His position, like Nietzsche's, asserts that when history rises above other fields of human knowledge and lays claim to its own ultimate objectivity, it subverts the place of creative life in art and religion. By enthroning itself on earth, where the visible creations of art should appear, and by the usurping the role of religion as the repository of all possibilities beyond the visible, it crushes the human experience of time under the weight of myth. Earlier, Scholem had expressed his fear that Benjamin might become a "sacrifice to the confusion of religion and politics" by the false connection established in a doctrine that asserts an objective process in history. This would be a paradox because, he tells Benjamin, this error arose from that very issue of two domains "whose true connection no one could have been expected to work out more clearly than you" (C 376). This idea of a betrayal of one's own genius conveys precisely what Nietzsche had objected to in the false religion of history, the self-deception of this modern mythology that manifests itself in the way "historical man lets himself be emptied"; "by worshipping" the force of history, "one renounces all force of one's own in heaven and upon earth" (UM 105). Nietzsche clearly distinguishes between this force of myth that denies human genius, and the "other spiritual powers, art and religion," which the "sole sovereign power" of the modern mythology has thrust aside (UM 104). While one approach to the past as an accumulation of triumphant facticity empties us and deprives us of our own forces, the past also records what Nietzsche here calls the great moral repudiations of fact, of mere event, in the achievements of art and religion wherever history "also preserves the memory of the great fighters *against history,* that is to say against the blind power of the actual" (UM 106).

As expressions of dynamic human force, these spiritual powers sustain precisely the same elements of radicalism and ruthlessness that identified religious and political observance as the human alternatives to theory for Benjamin in 1926. There can be no doubt that Benjamin always held the distinction between myth and theology to constitute a polar opposition within the realm of knowledge,[8] but to understand what drove him to endanger his own position between these two, we have to look back to his earlier attempts to stake out a political position. The essay "Critique of Violence" demonstrates the difficulty he hoped to overcome by turning to Marxism, because that text failed to enlarge the basis of his argument beyond two founding ideas. He first asserts that the law in its present form establishes its own domain of ends in order to exclude what Benjamin calls "natural ends." In setting up this order, the legal system ensures that individuals may only use legal means to the attainment of those ends. The purpose of law does not lie primarily with those ends, but in "preserving the law itself." Violent activity by individuals threatens the law merely by opening up a domain exterior to that defined by the enclosed system of law: "violence, when not in the hands of the law, threatens it . . . by its mere existence outside the law" (R 281).

The system of laws and the legal forms of violence that uphold it remain entirely self-defining and mythic. Therefore, Benjamin can propose his second principle, namely, that struggle to destroy mythic laws fulfills itself as the expression of divine purpose by ending mythic violence: "Just as in all spheres God opposes myth, mythical violence is confronted by the divine. And the latter constitutes its antithesis in all respects" (R 297). The contradiction in this attempt to envision a divine expression of politics could scarcely be more obvious. There is no human form of action that might serve as that divine expression. Even if one holds true to the idea of ultimate, complete, and universal justice as the only final resting point of a political commitment, and Benjamin certainly repeats his conviction about this often enough throughout his career, there remains the question of mediation or of method. That is indeed the question to which he returns when, while weighing the values of communism, he declared he was neither renouncing his past nor ashamed of his anarchist leanings, but now simply had to "consider anarchist methods to be useless" (C 301).

His argument in formulating an anarchist conception of social relations begins with the function of violent means under "contemporary European conditions . . . as far as the individual as legal subject is concerned" (R 280). But of course Benjamin excludes the activity of the criminal from his concern by parenthetically noting that, although he may arouse "the secret admiration of the public," his ends remain "repellent" (R 281). The criminal's ends actually lead him entirely away from the suspension of law since he benefits by its control over others. On the other hand, this does leave the question of how individual aims or individual actions can ascend to the level he defines as "divine." He writes that "If mythical violence is lawmaking, divine violence is law-destroying; if the former sets boundaries, the latter boundlessly destroys them" (R 297). But what does it mean to destroy laws by violence?

The German word *Gewalt* that Benjamin uses throughout does not specify aggressive acts against property or persons so clearly as does the English translation "violence." The distinction lies in that the German also admits the idea of a seizure of control. One might read this as the forceful displacement of another force. Nietzsche preserves the memory of the struggle against a reigning mythological force by the contrary force whose moral condemnation of an unjust history upholds "that which in the past was able to expand the concept 'man' and make it more beautiful" (UM 68). But this only determines a shift of relations between striving individuals and the reigning order so that the striving itself rises up as an example of human life in the beauty of its fulfillment.

That achievement does not put an end to the mythology, but returns eternally as an inspiration in the intimate antagonism through which human life joins myth and resists myth and makes myth again as the struggle we recognize across the expanses of history. Individual achievements in turn make history significant as an object of contemplation and "do not carry forward any kind of process but live contemporaneously with one another" (UM 111). The struggle that this inspires and fails to resolve takes us back once more to the only "counterproposal" Scholem could find when challenged by Benjamin. The moral substance on which Benjamin's survival depended would "degenerate," Scholem wrote, if he did not acknowledge his own genius. The self-destructive risk was "not that you are fighting, but that you are fighting under a disguise" (C 379). Even though one may agree that this disguise did carry the risk that it could turn "all too easily into suicide," and that his suicide must be counted part of the factual immorality (in Nietzsche's phrase) of all history, the necessity that history imposed on Benjamin in his fight, and the genius that fought on to the last moment of each defeat, must be counted precisely as what still raises his life to contemporaneity with our own.

Notes

1. Gershom Scholem, *Walter Benjamin: The Story of a Friendship,* trans. Harry Zohn (Philadelphia: Jewish Publication Society of America, 1981), 123.

2. Gershom Scholem and Theodor W. Adorno, eds., *The Correspondence of Walter Benjamin, 1910–1940,* trans. Manfred R. Jacobson and Evelyn M. Jacobson (Chicago: Chicago Univ. Press, 1994), 379. Abbreviated in the text as C.

3. Walter Benjamin, "Theses on the Philosophy of History," *Illuminations,* trans. Harry Zohn, ed. Hannah Arendt (New York: Schocken, 1969), 260. Abbreviated in the text as I.

4. Friedrich Nietzsche, *Untimely Meditations,* trans. R. J. Hollingdale (New York: Cambridge Univ. Press, 1983), 104. Abbreviated in the text as UM.

5. Walter Benjamin, "Surrealism," *Reflections: Essays, Aphorisms, Autobiographical Writings,* trans. Edmund Jephcott, ed. Peter Demetz (New York: Schocken, 1986), 189. Abbreviated in the text as R.

6. *Illuminations,* 260. The translation here is slightly different from that given on page 59 of the *Untimely Meditations* edition from which other quotations from Nietzsche have been taken. Notable: the German "Müßiggänger" is translated simply as "idler" rather than "spoiled loafer."

7. In his working notes for the "Theses," Benjamin revives an idea from Friedrich Schlegel that "the historian is a prophet turned backward." Walter Benjamin, *Gesammelte Schriften,* ed. Theodor W. Adorno and Gerschom Scholem (Frankfurt a.M.: Suhrkamp, 1974), 1.3: 1232. My translation.

8. This principle runs deeply through the essay on Goethe's *Wahlverwandtschaften,* but also occurs in simple and unambiguous declarations, for example the remarks on Bachofen and Klages to Scholem (C 288). Scholem mentions this theme as a continuing topic of discussions with Benjamin in *Walter Benjamin: The Story of a Friendship,* 61.

II Psychoanalytic and Racial Conflicts

If on the other hand, we take contest away from Greek life, then we peer instantly into that pre-Homeric abyss of a dreadful wildness of hatred and pleasure in destruction.

Nietzsche, "Homer's Contest"

Interpretation Interminable: Agonistics in Psychoanalysis

Volney P. Gay

For psychoanalysts, the collective intellectual past is primarily founded on the traditions upon which Freud drew and which, in turn, rest upon Europe's idealization of the Greeks. As heirs to Freud, we are also bound, if not indentured, to his heroes, especially the classical Greeks. Like Friedrich Nietzsche, his chief rival as the premier psychologist of the past century, Freud referred incessantly to the Greeks and typically drew upon them for both inspiration and validation.[1] Their inspiration is evident in both the name and the content of Freud's most famous discovery, the "Oedipus complex." Their significance for contemporary psychoanalysts is less obvious. It becomes apparent when Freud cites Empedocles' doctrine of eternal strife and melds it to his metapsychology, his grand theory of the mind.

The concept of agonal contests animated both Nietzsche and Freud when they attempted to portray the deepest part of human nature. Freud's famous essay "Analysis Terminable and Interminable"[2] retains an agonistic view of the human mind and of the inherent, endless struggle between patient and analyst. The concept of agonistic struggle helps us understand two traditions that inform psychoanalysis. Freud outlines one tradition when he traces his thought back to Empedocles and the doctrine of eternal struggle between love and strife. The other, opposing tradition develops out of religious and mythical solutions to agonal struggles. The mysticism proposed by Pythagoras (or his disciples) and the metaphysics of Aristotle and Paul constitute this second tradition.

Zeno, Nietzsche, and Freud

The Greek philosophers who preceded Socrates do not fit into exclusive categories, such as theologian, mathematician, or poet. The following fragment from Empedocles is both philosophical and poetic. His philosophical claim is, roughly, that what Aristotle calls "Being" is composed of four elements (earth, air, fire, water), which are controlled by two principles, love and strife. When mixed in differing combinations, these irreducible elements make up the transient and changing world of appearances:

> With earth do we see earth, with water water, with
> air bright air, with fire consuming fire,
> With Love do we see Love, Strife with dread Strife.[3]

Love, the impulse toward union, rules human life, especially when personified as Aphrodite. As the goddess of love, she is the "cause of all pairing, both in the realm where we are accustomed to distinguish male and female and far beyond this in the whole structure of nature."[4] These verses evoke images of nurturing and the essential unity between all things: for "by earth we perceive earth" means that our commonality permits us to perceive elements that are like us. By implication, everything we perceive must be like us and we like it. This humanizes the cosmos and makes human beings actors in a cosmic drama. Like human beings, the cosmos experiences the ecstasy and despair of self-consciousness.[5]

Out of Aristotelian philosophy, rigorous schools of thought developed, each with specific doctrines and arguments. Among their successes was the discovery of non-rational numbers; among their failures was the inability to account for these kinds of numbers.

The Discovery of Non-Rational Numbers

The Greeks discovered or re-discovered non-rational numbers, that is, numbers that cannot be reduced to a ratio of two whole integers. A non-specialist, I bring together aspects of Greek thought that are often separated: the rise of geometry, Zeno's paradoxes, and the ubiquity of mythic dualism. Many authors, including specialists in the history of Greek science, Greek philosophy, and Greek religion do not make the kind of leaps I am guilty of making in this chapter.[6]

By the fifth century BCE, Greek mathematicians had discovered that the magnitudes of certain line segments, like the edge and diagonal of a square, were not commensurable with one another. How they discovered this is a fascinating story in its own right and, like many issues in the history of Greek thought, a disputed one.[7] Two magnitudes were considered "commensurable" *(symmetra)* with one another if there was a measure that divided each magnitude an exact number of times, designated by an integer *(arithmos)*. If there was no such integer, then the two magnitudes were considered incommensurable *(asymmetra)*. For example, in a square with one unit sides, the diagonal's *length* is the square root of the sum of the two sides, which is the square root of 2. Charles H. Edwards explains:

> Today we simply say that $\sqrt{2}$ is an irrational number. However, for the Greeks, the discovery of incommensurability meant that there existed geometric magnitudes that could not be measured by numbers! For, as we have seen, their conception of numbers as integers alone was *discrete* in character, whereas the phenomenon of incommensurable lengths implied that geometric magnitudes have some sort of inherently (and unavoidable) *continuous* character.[8]

Greek mathematicians solved their dilemma by refusing to term the length of the diagonal a number:

> Whereas such a simple equation as $x^2 = 2$ has no solution in the domain of (Greek, rational) numbers, the equation $x^2 = ab$

> where *a* and *b* are given lengths can be solved geometrically by constructing a square with edge *x* whose area is equal to that of the rectangle with sides *a* and *b*. (Edwards 11)

In other words, while they could not designate an irrational number, Greek mathematicians could designate a quantity, namely an area corresponding to that number.[9]

This geometric solution meant that the Greeks had to retain a conceptual gulf that separated arithmetic from geometry. This gulf was not bridged until the modern period, when philosophers including Leibniz and Newton developed methods and notations that gave rise to the modern calculus (Boyer 26–27). Historians of Greek science and mathematics note that in struggling with incommensurables, Greek geometers proposed diverse solutions. Some were pragmatic, others were conceptual. Pragmatically, some Greek mathematicians refined the Egyptian and Babylonian practices of approximating quantities they could not calculate directly. A common example is "squaring the circle," that is, approximating the area of a circle by imagining an ever larger number of polygons inscribed in it. By using basic geometry to find the area of this set of polygons, we can approximate the area of the circle that they occupy.

Conceptually, Greek thinkers attempted to unite mathematics with geometry through the notion of the "infinitesimal." Democritus suggested the infinitesimal was a monad or "unit of such a nature that an indefinite number of them will be required for the diagonal and for the side of the square" (Boyer 21). The notion of an infinitely small unit saves the concept of ratios for it permits us to say that the ratio of the diagonal to the side of a square (which we now designate as $\sqrt{2}:1$) is a ratio of one set of infinitesimal units to another set of such units.

Zeno, a student of Parmenides, challenged this solution. In *Metaphysica,* Aristotle attributed to Zeno a brilliant polemic against Democritus' concept of the infinitesimal: " . . . that which neither when added makes a thing greater nor when subtracted makes it less" (W 1001b).[10] In addition, Zeno elaborated on his famous paradoxes. As a set, they demonstrate that a class of infinite temporal or spatial units could not possibly exist. For example, in his *Achilles* paradox, Zeno showed that if a tortoise had a head start in a race with a superior runner, like the great athlete Achilles, then Achilles would have to cover that distance before he overtook the tortoise. But if there is an infinite number of actual spatial units between the tortoise and Achilles that must be traversed, then Achilles would require an infinite length of time to catch up. This he could never do. Refinements of this paradox show that the tortoise could never traverse the infinitely divisible space stretching out in front of him. Indeed, if space and time are infinitely divisible, then all motion is impossible. Since this is impossible, Zeno dismisses the concept of infinitesimal units of space and time.

A satisfactory answer to Zeno emerged through the development of the calculus, the "principal quantitative language of Western science" (Edwards v). First, by not accepting the notion of infinitely divisible "real space" and "real time," we reject Democritus' amalgamation of mathematical entities with actual entities. Second, the concept of an infinite set of rational *numbers* lying, for example, between integer 1 and integer 2, readily becomes a mathematical truth. It has no immediate claim upon natural space and time that we arbitrarily measure with fixed units of distance, like the marks on a piece of wood called a ruler. What was difficult for minds as refined as those of Greek geometrists to accept is, then, simple for post-eighteenth-century geometrists who possess concepts not available to their predecessors. For example, one can read Aristotle's struggle with Zeno's paradoxes as the consequence of Aristotle's common sense metaphysics. This rests upon "the cardinal weakness of Greek logic and geometry: a naive realism which regarded thought as a true copy of the external world" (Boyer 45).

"Naive realism" appears eminently plausible, since so much of Euclid's *Elements,* for example, seems not just logically consistent but offers "true" and "accurate" descriptions of the world as we experience it. One can sympathize with Aristotle's wish for a truly unified metaphysics in which all the sciences, including geometry, had a fixed and reasonable place in a hierarchy of thought. That this hierarchy matched perfectly the Greek sense of the world only added luster to its claims. Further, if one could prove the validity of syllogistic reasoning with dialectical thinking, and if one began with true (apparently valid) assumptions about the "real world," then one could establish new truths about the world by reasoning alone.

In contrast to the *wish* for a unified metaphysics, Archimedes, usually regarded as the greatest of all Greek mathematicians, perceived that fundamental gaps in geometry continued to exist. Specifically, in response to central problems, like the "squaring of the circle" (and other problems that we now solve through the use of π and real numbers, like $\sqrt{2}$), Archimedes developed heuristic methods. One method we have seen was that of "exhaustion." Another was the use of *reductio ad absurdum* arguments; by showing, for example, that the sum of approximations could not be more than or less than the figure arrived at, Archimedes supported the validity of the figure itself. Yet these remained *indirect* proofs. To these methods, derived from previous geometrists, Archimedes added his contribution to mechanics, the "law of the lever" (Boyer 49).

By combining pragmatic methods, Archimedes discovered formulae for finding the center of gravity of semicircle parabolas and other geometric figures. Historians of Greek mathematics conclude that even these solutions were inadequate, because they resulted from the ban on discourse about the infinite: "The reasons for this ban are obvious: intuition could at that time afford no clear picture of it, and it had as yet no logical basis" (Boyer 53). Aristotle's solutions to the problems posed by Zeno were for the time satisfactory.[11]

Nietzsche and the Rediscovery of Agon

In *The Birth of Tragedy,* written in 1872 when he was twenty-seven years old, Nietzsche gave himself the heroic task of explaining the rise of Greek tragic theater. Nietzsche felt that this magical period of the flowering of the Western mind could be revived in Richard Wagner's operatic theater. Given the magnitude of Nietzsche's question and the achievements of the Greek tragedians, this attempt to recover the past was a bold undertaking. To do justice to Nietzsche's method, his "grandiose" questions, and his seductive ability to overpower the reader requires a much larger study than this. It is nevertheless important to address Nietzsche's question: what is the nature of Greek genius?

In 1872, Nietzsche also wrote a short essay, "Homer's Context," in which he continued his quest to find the origins of the classical Greek spirit. He located that idealized entity in the combat or "agonistic" events that took place both at battle and at the great games. Indeed he centers *most* of Greek genius, artistic, philosophic, and creative at the juncture of agonistic encounters: "[T]he Greek knows an artist *only in personal struggle.*"[12] In both pieces, Nietzsche identifies agonistics as being central to the preservation of the Greek ideals of contest, struggle, and health. Hence, he says the Greeks dreaded absolute superiority: "Because the contest would be exhausted thereby, and the eternal foundation of life for the Hellenic state would be endangered" (HC 39). By searching for the origins, as Freud so often searched for the single, great origins of the neuroses, Nietzsche presupposed a dramatic, indeed tragic, structure: there once was a golden age, an age of heroic, impassioned, lusty, men and women who lived briefly, struggled, and then died out, giving rise to lesser, debased races. Answering his own question, which was constrained by his demand to find idealizable heroes, Nietzsche was forced to conceive of an equally radical *antithesis.* He did so by evoking, in *The Birth of Tragedy,* two gods—Dionysus and Apollo—whom he opposed to one another and who represented, therefore, a fundamental antithesis within the human being itself, one that was also reflected in the poetic structure of the tragedy:

> Accordingly we recognize in tragedy a complete stylistic opposition: the language, color, flexibility and movement of the dialogue fall apart into two entirely separate realms of expression, into the Dionysian lyrics of the chorus on the one hand, and the Apollonian dream-world of the scene on the other.[13]

Having established that these antithetical gods exemplify our antithetical nature, Nietzsche pours out a stream of metaphors that contrast the clarity of Apollonian discourse with the mythic darkness upon which the plays were built:

> [L]et us enter into the myth which is projected in these bright mirrorings. We shall suddenly experience a phenomenon which

> has an inverse relation to one familiar in optics. When, after trying hard to look straight at the sun, we turn away blinded, we have dark-colored spots before our eyes as restoratives, so to speak; while, reversing the colors, those light-picture phenomena of the Sophoclean hero,—in short, the Apollonian of the mask,—are the inevitable consequences of a glance into the secret and terrible things of nature. (BT 993)

This paean to the archaic Greek turns on the metaphor of sight: just as our eyes, by nature, adjust themselves to too much "vision," so too our psyches demand compensatory structure, the extra clarity and calmness of Apollo. Greek "cheerfulness," Nietzsche deduces, is not the result of comfort and pleasure but the product of having seen into these depths, into these permanent features of the human mind.

Immediately following these comments about the Greeks' fascination with the agon, Nietzsche offers his interpretation of Oedipus, whom he identifies with a superlative, "the most sorrowful figure of the Greek stage" (BT 993). To achieve its cathartic effect, tragic theater presents a character who plumbed the depths of human nature and nature itself. Oedipus' agon involved him in a struggle with nature. By committing incest and patricide, he tried to force her "to surrender her secrets" (BT 995).

Freud Agonistes

In the early 1920s, Freud observed that some well-analyzed patients reverted, in later life, to neurotic symptoms of which they had supposedly been cured. (Anti-Freudians and non-Freudians might claim simply that psychoanalysis is a faulty technique based upon faulty theories. Patients return to therapy because therapy failed to cure them in the first place.) Freud would not have accepted this rejection of his science. He hearkened back to an "agonistic" theory of mind, one remarkably similar to that invoked in Nietzsche's text. True to his metapsychology or theory of mind, Freud explained his patients' relapses in terms of the resurgence of instinctual energies and their imposition upon the ego of new struggles against two opposing sets of instincts, sexuality and aggression. These he named Eros and Destructiveness, just as Sophocles gave to the human characteristic strength the name "Bia" in *Prometheus Bound.* Human nature, according to Freud, is inherently agonistic. The task of psychoanalysis is to bring together opposing sides whose struggles are eternal. Treatment is thus inherently "unnatural," in the same way that Nietzsche says that it was "unnatural" for Oedipus to plumb the questions to which the answer was "human being." In *Beyond the Pleasure Principle,* Freud *reverts* to the thought and language of Empedocles:

> Our speculations have suggested that Eros operates from the beginning of life and appears as a "life instinct" in opposition to the "death instinct" which was brought into being by the coming to life of inorganic substance. These speculations seek to solve the riddle of life by supposing that these two instincts were struggling with each other from the very first.[14]

Seventeen years later, Freud cites Empedocles directly in "Analysis Terminable and Interminable." He notes how similar his notions of two types of instincts, the love instincts and aggressive instincts, are to Empedocles' concepts of the powers of love *(philia)* and strife *(nexos).* They are, Freud says:

> [B]oth in name and function, the same as our two primal instincts, *Eros* and *destructiveness,*[15] the first of which endeavors to combine what exists into ever greater unities, while the second endeavours to dissolve those combinations and to destroy the structures to which they have given rise. (SE 23: 246)

Concerned with the originality of his thought, Freud adds that he did not know of Empedocles when he composed *Beyond the Pleasure Principle* in 1919. Or, if he had known, he had forgotten. In either case, "I am ready to give up the prestige of originality for the sake of such a confirmation" (SE 23: 245). It is striking and puzzling that Freud would consider a poem by an ancient Greek writer a "confirmation" of a twentieth-century scientific proposition. There are many ancient Greek poems by many ancient Greek philosophers whose opinions are often at odds with one another. They cannot all be true. To cite one among these many poetic verses as a "confirmation" of his grand theory of the duality of human nature is to misuse the concept of confirmation.

Freud wished to ground his discoveries upon the partial insights of the past and its idealized thinkers, as he had done in his earliest writings on the "Oedipus complex." Yet he also wished to be original; he would blaze new trails, not merely revise past thinkers, no matter how illustrious. Freud often resolved this narcissistic tension typical of a person of genius by connecting his insights with the theories of others, especially his collaborators, like Wilhelm Fliess, Joseph Breuer, Carl Jung, and others. However, these composite formations failed him, and a "falling out" took place between Freud and his former devoted companions.

Freud's penchant for dualistic thinking, which one might term "splitting" in another context, does not immediately indicate a peculiar psychopathology. Rather, his reversion to Empedocles defines the nature of the task he had assigned himself in both *Beyond the Pleasure Principle* and in "Analysis Terminable and Interminable." In both he attempted to "go beyond" the evidence afforded him by psychoanalytic experience to offer a view of "life itself" or, as he put it, the riddle of life that centers upon the fact that from death comes life and from living things comes death.

Evidence for the existence of these two classes of instincts derives from psychoanalytic reflection upon the ubiquity and depth of internal conflict even in those who seem most civilized. Freud tells us these instincts drive the "unconscious" psyche which, in turn, controls conscious experience. We must suspect manifest discourse about a patient's self. This does not mean that the analyst is hostile and belittling. Central to Freud's theory is the claim that the ego perceives discord within itself as well. An empathic and accurate analyst confirms a patient's correct self-understanding by recognizing that there are parts of the patient's self that the patient wishes to disown. To deny that a patient has intrapsychic conflicts is to fragment the patient's sense of self. To join the patient in this moment of denial damages the patient's ego. For example, when a patient feels murderous rage toward the analyst it is harmful to deny this rage, for that strengthens the patient's fear that such feelings cannot be handled by speech alone. By denying that speech is adequate to such feelings, the analyst who avoids naming this wish to murder drives the patient to either actions (such as increased threats to the analyst) or attacks on the patient's self (such as ending treatment prematurely or even suicide attempts). To speak directly about the patient's rage is to contain it and to reinforce the patient's self-understanding that these impulses will diminish as they are understood and thus detoxified.

Religious and Mystical Solutions

By the Hellenistic period, Greek and Jewish authors expanded the notion of "agon" to mean struggles between parts of the self, struggles that may continue in the afterlife, and struggles between the forces of good and the forces of evil. Ethelbert Stauffer presents a lucid and condensed discussion of "agon" in Paul, who uses the term frequently to refer to a large range of conflicts, from the struggles each Christian must undertake to avoid indolence, to the denial of self-centered wishes, to the contemplation of obstacles and forces that oppose one's mission, and to the battles of martyrdom. Finally, "The supreme goal for which [Christians] fight and work and suffer is not our own salvation alone: it is the salvation of many."[16]

Arlene Croce says that Igor Stravinsky named his last ballet *Agon* (1957) and retained the Greek spelling of the title *agon* because it contained "alpha" and "omega," the first and last letters of the Greek alphabet thus encompassing the beginning and end of time.[17] The "beginning and end" are not per se agonistic: they become so only in the context of the battles at Armageddon and other similar titanic clashes. We recall the famous passage in Revelation 1:8 when, speaking of the totality of Christ's meaning, John calls Jesus the alpha and the omega of all human history. The end of history is the end of the "agon," when Christ shall finally have triumphed over his enemies.

In contrast to the distress that Zeno, Nietzsche, and Freud induced in their public, any metaphysical solutions to this notion are typically grand and "synthetic." For example, there is a certain majesty in Aristotle's attempt to unify all the Greek sciences within an *intelligible* framework. Here "intelligible" refers both to the evidence of ordinary human senses and to the Greek "horror of the infinite." Classical and later medieval theology and philosophy looked enthusiastically to Aristotle's synthesis as a summing up of the "knowable." Aristotle's concept of god, as the unmoved mover, was, it is true, highly abstract and remote, especially when compared to the full-blooded passion of the Jewish Christian deities. Yet by locating god within an intelligible and knowable framework, Aristotle reinforced the hope that nothing was, finally, irrational about the world of human beings. While Aristotle's theory of nature, his physics, could not address concepts of dynamics and change, it proved immensely supportive of a theocentric world view: god ruled nature and human lives. Persons who were modest, moderate in their passions, and committed to reason and inquiry could learn to recognize this marvelous pattern.

The history of the discovery of the "irrational" numbers is marked much more by conflict. According to Greek legends, when the Pythagoreans discovered the horrible truth of the incommensurable, they decided "in their bewilderment . . . to treat the information as a top secret, to be revealed only to trusted members of the school who had taken the vow of silence."[18] Breaking the "taboo," Zeno (and Nietzsche and Freud) revealed our obsession with imposing a sense of order on the world, no matter the consequences. To gaze directly at the libidinal and aggressive parts of the self, our agonistic core, frightens us because we imagine our divided self emerging and threatening the fragile alliance with which we preserve our psyches. Metaphysicians defend themselves against this profound anxiety by naming these agonistic sides and then creating a "higher" synthesis out of them.

This notion of a "higher" synthesis was central for Pythagoreans and Aristotle who claimed that the natural harmonies of music, which are pleasing and soothing to human beings, are themselves expressions of an underlying order in nature designated by simple ratios. Francis M. Cornford effectively describes this philosophical view: "The infinite variety of quality in sound is reduced to order by the exact and simple law of ratio in quantity . . . the unlimited is no longer an orderless continuum; it is confined within an order, a *cosmos*, by the imposition of Limit or Measure."[19] Nietzsche and Freud, like their hero Sophocles, challenged this position because it preserved peace at the expense of direct contact with the most vital, immediate realities.[20]

To resolve the abovementioned anxiety, some thinkers turn to paradox as a device for understanding and even enabling personal and emotional transformation. By *affirming* paradoxes, we can "transcend" them. This leads us to a new state of mind and a new "higher" consciousness. Jung makes essentially this point in his studies of European and Chinese alchemists who, he claims, were not proto-scientists but proto-psychologists. Their quest was not really to turn lead into gold, for example, but to find eternal life via the philosopher's stone.[21] Not accidentally, this response evolves into forms of worship, secrecy, and esoteric teachings. A paradigmatic instance of this transformation is the development of Pythagorean mysticism.

Mysticism and Transformation in Pythagoras

The theories of Pythagoras, approximately 570 BCE to 495 BCE, illustrate well the processes by which logical or "ego based" failures yield to mythic dualisms. Pythagoras was both a first-rate mathematician and the founder of a school that developed into a cult and a religion. The means by which this event took place was the celebration of paradox and the elaboration of mythic dualisms. In *Metaphysica* (W 986a22ff), Aristotle describes Pythagorean principles:[22] "Others of this same school say that there are ten principles, which they arrange in twin columns, namely":

limited	unlimited
odd	even
one	plurality
right	left
male	female
at rest	moving
straight	crooked
light	darkness
good	bad
square	oblong

These lists represent the most reductive forms of reasoning. They resolve "agonistic" tensions between observed differences, like the "one" and the "many," by reclassifying the two opposing principles as two constituents of nature. Concepts generated out of mythological and binary reasoning become, in this way, "principles" that admit of no further reduction. All sense of conflict is resolved and the quest is ended. Guthrie remarks that this list represents a "religious belief in the essential unity of nature" since the "one" and "limit" appear with "good" (1: 246).

It appears that Aristotle used this list in his essay on biology, *De Partibus Animalium,* when he noted:

> [T]he left side of the body is more watery and colder than the right. For each of two contraries has been so placed as to go together with that which is akin to it in another pair of contraries. Thus right and left, hot and cold, are pairs of contraries; and right is conjoined with hot, after the manner described, and left with cold. (W 5: 670b)

Aristotle uses this Pythagorean principle to explain why the spleen, which he says resides on the right side, is "watery." The relationship between "left and watery" also applies "dark," "bad," "women," and "crooked."

The presence of this list denotes a deep wish to overcome division not only in the cosmos but also within the psyche. By their nature, such lists represent an attempt to "unify" by fiat and declaration what their authors feel are antithetical and opposing entities. I call them "entities" for typically these authors do not distinguish between physical *characteristics,* like "hot" and "cold," and terms like "good" or "bad" that are defined in opposition to one another.

Nietzsche and Freud declared that Oedipus' "complex" and his titanic struggles against himself are relevant to us because we share similar struggles and similar self-understandings. By analyzing these antitheses, we discover that Oedipus' agony illuminates our own. If psychoanalysis were an *answer* to agonistic existence, as religion can be, then its formulations would not be interminable because its object, agon, would not be interminable. Psychoanalysis, the psychology par excellence of conflict, maintains that by giving up the urge to secure wholeness and cessation of conflict we will find a kind of peaceful recognition of our essential nature as self-conscious creatures whose struggles are unending.

Idealization, Nietzsche, and Freud

To idealize one set of opposites or to ascribe to it the grandeur that Nietzsche and Freud grant to the archaic Greeks is to engage in an agonistic event, for it entails denigrating another group. To be heirs to Nietzsche and Freud is to share their ideals and share their disdain. We love whom they love, despise whom they despise. To preserve culture, which is the task of art and psychoanalysis, is to replace "id" with ego; yet this is an unending, agonistic struggle. As Freud put it in a famous line: "The struggle which once raged in the deepest strata of the mind, and was not brought to an end by rapid sublimation and identification, is now continued in a higher region, like the Battle of the Huns in Kaulbach's painting."[23]

For Nietzsche and Freud, the noble response to agonistic struggle is that of Parmenides, Oedipus, Zeno, the archaic Greeks and themselves. The alternative responses, those of metaphysics, mysticism, the Hellenistic Greeks, and Christianity, are for them ignoble. Nietzsche and Freud raged against the deadliness of repression and the lies of "civilization." But by recognizing their tremendous influence, we grant to them our primary narcissism, our *élan vital,* and thereby erect a new barrier against *our* tasks. We may agree with them that metaphysical solutions, especially those offered by various kinds of institutionalized religion, are misguided, but we cannot then conclude that the task of confronting our interior struggles is now over. Nietzsche and Freud were not Christ-like persons who shouldered our deepest struggles and feelings. To repossess the vitality that we ascribe to the Greeks, to avoid modern neuroses, we must experience their own struggles with themselves. To regain feeling is to regain vitality: "One is free from depression when self-esteem is based on the authenticity of one's own feelings and not on the possession of certain qualities" (Miller 39).

The Greek, Nietzsche says, "is *envious* and perceives this quality not as a flaw but as a consequence of a *beneficent* deity: what a chasm of ethical judgment between us and him!" (HC 38). Envy, lust, rage, anger, and the wish to destroy are part of our essential nature and, at the same time, in conflict with another aspect of ourselves, the urge to unify and to resolve conflict. Ninety years later, Freud says these are fundamental aspects of our dual nature: "Our views have from the very first been *dualistic,* and today they are even more definitely dualistic than before—now that we describe the opposition as being, not between ego instincts and sexual instincts but between life instincts and death instincts" (SE 18: 53).

Finally, then, irrational numbers are not meaningless; they merely transcend reason. So too the unconscious mind, especially what Freud called the id, is irrational. It permits no easy formulation, no final listing of pairs gathered together in a balanced metaphysics, and no monistic solution: "The id . . . has no means of showing the ego either love or hate. It cannot say what it wants; it has achieved no unified will. Eros and the death instinct struggle within it" (SE 19: 59).

Notes

1. When Freud commented upon Nietzsche he did so with mixed feelings: he recognized his brilliance as an author and psychologist but also feared being too influenced by him. Peter Gay, in *Freud: A Life for Our Time* (New York, Norton, 1988), summarizes this well:

> Freud had read [Nietzsche] as a young student and spent good money on his collected works in early 1900, the year of Nietzsche's death. He hoped, he told his friend Fliess, "to find the words for much that remains mute in me." Yet Freud treated Nietzsche's writings as texts to be resisted far more than to be studied. It is symptomatic that after reporting the purchase of Nietzsche's works, he immediately added that he had not opened them: "For the time being too indolent." (45)

The question of Nietzsche's influence on Freud's ideas, especially the psychoanalytic theory of culture, is as old as psychoanalysis. Freud's early followers, especially Alfred Alder, Otto Rank, and Lou Andreas-Salomé, who knew Nietzsche well, "never tired of reminding Freud of the similarity between his and Nietzsche's thought, and ever since there has been a cacophony of voices available to call on Nietzsche's right of priority in the discovery of some part of psychoanalytic theory" (Kim R. Holmes, "Freud, Evolution, and the Tragedy of Man," *Journal of the American Psychoanalytic Association* 31 [1983]: 194–95).

2. "Analysis Terminable and Interminable" (1937), *The Standard Edition of the Complete Psychological Works of Sigmund Freud,* trans. & ed. James Strachey *et al.,* 24 vols. (London: Hogarth Press, 1953–1974), 23: 211–53. Abbreviated as SE in the text.

3. Translated by G. S. Kirk and J. E. Raven, *The Presocratic Philosophers: A Critical History with a Selection of Texts* (Cambridge: Cambridge Univ. Press, 1957), 343. They add: "Perception is due to an element (here including Love and Strife) in the body of the perceiver meeting with the same element outside."

4. Werner Wilhelm Jaeger, *The Theology of the Early Greek Philosophers* (London: Oxford Univ. Press, 1952; orig. 1947), 138.

5. Aristotle, *Metaphysica,* vol. 13 of *The Works of Aristotle: Translated in English,* ed. W. D. Ross, 2nd ed. (London: Oxford Univ. Press, 1960; orig. 1928), 1000b ff. Abbreviated in the text as W.

6. For example, Carl B. Boyer in *The Concepts of the Calculus and its Conceptual Development* (New York: Dover, 1959) makes no mention of Greek mystery religion or Greek mythology. In his history of Greek religion, *The Theology of the Early Greek Philosophers,* Jaeger does not mention Greek geometry or Zeno's famous paradoxes, generated out of a deep criticism of Greek number theory. Roy K. Hack's *God in Greek Philosophy to the Time of Socrates* (Princeton: Princeton Univ. Press, 1931) mentions Zeno only as student of Parmenides, the early Greek metaphysician. In his detailed monograph on Greek geometry and number theory, Wilbur R. Knorr in *The Evolution of the Euclidean Elements* (Boston: D. Reidel, 1975) argues that Zeno's paradoxes are not related directly to the "incommensurable" problem.

7. "The date and manner of the first discovery of incommensurability have not been preserved for us by any credible witness," Knorr states (21).

8. C. H. Edwards, *The Historical Development of the Calculus* (New York: Springer-Verlag, 1979), 10.

9. In contrast, Hindu mathematicians had no scruples against conceiving of "irrational" numbers. See Boyer, 61.

10. See Boyer, 23.

11. See *Physica* 6: 239b–240a; partially in *Metaphysica* 1001b; also *Analytica Priora* I: 65b18.

12. Friedrich Nietzsche, "Homer's Contest," this volume, 41. Abbreviated in the text as HC.

13. Nietzsche, *The Birth of Tragedy from the Spirit of Music,* trans. Clifton P. Fadiman, *The Philosophy of Nietzsche,* ed. W. H. Wright (New York: Modern Library, 1927), 992. Abbreviated in the text as BT.

14. Freud, *Beyond the Pleasure Principle* (SE 18: 61, n.1).

15. Freud did not call this "Thanatos" except in conversation. Later authors like Paul Federn employed it in written works. See Ernest Jones, *The Last Phase 1919–1939,* vol. 3 of *Sigmund Freud: Life and Work* (London: Hogarth, 1957), 297.

16. Ethelbert Stauffer, "Agon," *Theological Dictionary of the New Testament,* ed. Gerhard Kittel, trans. and ed. Geoffrey W. Bromiley (Grand Rapids, Mich.: Eerdmans, 1964), 1: 138. Stauffer summarizes Paul's theological transformation of the athletic or aesthetic "agon" into a supreme battle between the worldly and extra-worldly forces of evil and their opponents: "Where the Gospel is, there will be conflict and division" (139). Regarding Paul's text, Phillippians 1:30, he adds:

> Paul here uses the image of the agon along the lines of martyr theology of late Judaism. But he no longer thinks of the battle waged by the martyrs in the stadium to God's glory. He thinks of the conflicts and sufferings of the Christian life itself as a life which in its totality stands under the sign of the cross and in this sign carries the cause of Christ to victory. (139)

17. "The Spelling of Agon," *The New Yorker* (July 12, 1993): 84.

18. Philip Ellis Wheelwright, *The Presocratics* (New York: Odyssey Press, 1966), 207.

19. F. M. Cornford, "Mysticism and Science in the Pythagorean Tradition," *Classical Quarterly* (1922): 145. Cited by W. K. C. Guthrie, *A History of Greek Philosophy: The Earlier Presocratics and the Pythagoreans,* 6 vols. (Cambridge, UK: Cambridge Univ. Press, 1962–1981), 1: 248.

20. As Alice Miller explains, for a person prone to narcissism, "access to the 'true self' is thus only possible when [the individual] no longer has to be afraid of the intense 'psychotic' emotional world of his early childhood." *The Drama of the Gifted Child,* trans. Ruth Ward (New York: Basic Books, 1981), 57.

21. Carl Jung, "The Spirit Mercurius," *Alchemical Studies,* trans. R. F. C. Hull, vol. 13 of *The Collected Works of C. G. Jung,* ed. Sir Herbert Read *et al.* (London: Routledge & Kegan Paul, 1957).

22. Cf. W. K. C. Guthrie, *The Earlier Presocratics and the Pythagoreans,* vol. 1 of *A History of Greek Philosophy,* 245.

23. Freud, *The Ego and the Id* (SE 19: 39). Strachey informs us that this painting, by Wilhelm von Kaulbach (1805–1874), portrays the battle of Châlons in 451, in which Attila the Hun was defeated by the Romans and the Visigoths.

The Institutionalization of Conflict as an Interpretative Strategy in Freud's *The Interpretation of Dreams*

Lorna Martens

As the 1872 essay "Homer's Contest" attests, Nietzsche was fascinated by the aggressive instinct and the creative potential of the agon from his earliest writings. Freud, in contrast, felt no such immediate affinity for aggression. It took World War I for him to become seriously interested in what he called, in *Beyond the Pleasure Principle* (1920), the "death instinct," which was primarily identified by what he terms, in *Civilization and Its Discontents* (1930), the "aggressive instinct." Nevertheless, Freud was, from his earliest psychoanalytic writings on, attentive to the notion of internal mental conflict, which seems to have held superior explanatory potential for him. In his early writing on hysteria, Freud, along with his coauthor Josef Breuer, privileged wholeness and harmony as the ideal of health and pathologized conflict. Yet in Freud's next major work and magnum opus, *The Interpretation of Dreams* (1900), a striking reevaluation occurs. Here Freud elevates the idea of conflict within the mind to the very foundation of his metapsychology; he declares it normal, universal, and inevitable. This institutionalization of conflict as the essential mode of functioning of the mind's internal machinery is Freud's significant innovation vis-à-vis earlier authors, both those to whom he acknowledged a debt and those to whom, like Nietzsche, he refused one. The repressed unconscious is one of Freud's most perennial ideas, selling itself not only to the various post-Freudian psychoanalytic schools who have variously retheorized it but also to the popular imagination. We speak casually of the unconscious today, taking it for granted that it exists. Conversely, a persistent critical minority has pronounced the unconscious a trope.[1] This camp bases its skepticism principally on the unprovability of the unconscious' existence. Yet insufficient attention has been paid thus far to what strategic considerations may have motivated Freud to posit the unconscious precisely in the context in which he first introduces it, namely, that of dream interpretation. Through a reading of *Studies on Hysteria* and *The Interpretation of Dreams,* this essay will attempt to determine why Freud "discovered" the unconscious in the final chapter of the latter work.

From its inception, Freud's theoretical work pursues two distinct, if related goals: the interpretation of psychic phenomena and the formulation of a metapsychology. This twofold project is particularly evident in *The Interpretation of Dreams,* where six chapters dealing with dream interpretation lead up to a seventh, metapsychological chapter in which Freud formulates the famous "first topography" and also conjectures about the psyche as a dynamic and temporal entity. *Studies on Hysteria,* which Freud coauthored with Breuer in 1895 and which is usually considered his first psychoanalytic work, is a very different sort of book, insofar as it focuses on mental illness, concerns itself exclusively with female subjects, and, above all, bears the marks of a growing lack of consensus between the two authors, who finally found themselves obliged to write separate conclusions. But here too, hermeneutic questions are foregrounded. The doctors confront the riddle of the hysterical symptom; its interpretation serves as a point of departure for their joint and several theories of the etiology of hysteria. As any interpretation of psychic phenomena must necessarily be based on assumptions about how the psyche is composed and how it functions, both the jointly and the individually written theoretical essays contain various explicit and implicit metapsychological hypotheses. My thesis is that from *Studies on Hysteria* to *The Interpretation of Dreams* Freud modified his metapsychology at least in part with an eye to interpretative ends; that is, his new, more challenging hermeneutic object, the dream, demanded different metapsychological conditions for its interpretation. The dual psyche proposed in *The Interpretation of Dreams,* in which the "discovery of the unconscious" plays a crucial role, and the attendant notion of conflict psychology, appealed to Freud not least because they furnished him with an exceptionally versatile hermeneutic tool.

In the "Preliminary Communication" to *Studies on Hysteria,* published separately in 1893 or two years before the appearance of the book, Breuer and Freud situate hysteria within a framework of metapsychological assumptions that were entirely conventional in the cultural climate of the *fin-de-siècle.* The model of sickness and health that the authors invoke not only forms the backbone of the existing French theories on hysteria, to which Freud and Breuer refer, but also appears in one of Nietzsche's most popular works, *On the Advantage and Disadvantage of History for Life* (1874). Moreover, it was part of the stock-in-trade of the psychological novelist, forming the basis for the portraiture of the ubiquitous (literary) decadent antihero. The ideal, often figured by the image of the circle, is wholeness. Division, conflict, and disunity, whether provoked from without or issuing from within, signal ill health. Thus, in the opening chapter of *On the Advantage and Disadvantage of History for Life,* in the course of his polemic against memory and his plea for the vital importance of forgetfulness, Nietzsche posits the necessity of a "horizon" encircling the subject that will keep the clutter of historical learning from interfering with its development in its own present time. A "line" must divide an individual or a people from that which is distant, foreign, or past:

> And this is a general law: every living thing can become healthy, strong, and fruitful only within a horizon; if it is incapable of drawing a horizon around itself or, on the other hand, too selfish to restrict its vision to the limits of a horizon drawn by another, it will wither away feebly or overhastily to its early demise.[2]

Nietzsche continues:

> Cheerfulness, clear conscience, the carefree deed, faith in the future, all this depends, in the case of an individual as well as

of a people, on there being a line which distinguishes what is clear and in full view from the dark and unilluminable.

The "horizon" or "line" polarizes: it separates inner from outer, light from dark, known from unknown, and—by association with the main argument on forgetfulness to which these images are meant to serve as analogies—present from past. Health and happiness are identified with remaining firmly within one's own space or time, in the area that is "clear" and "in full view." The dark area on the other side of the "line" is dangerous: if the outside impinges on the inside, sickness or, in Nietzsche's formulation, the "historical malady" results.

In Freud and Breuer's "Preliminary Communication," we see a model for sickness and health remarkably similar to that found in Nietzsche's *On the Advantage and Disadvantage of History for Life* and *fin-de-siècle* literary texts.[3] The essential elements of the theory of hysteria proposed in the "Preliminary Communication" are the idea that the psyche can be split; the idea that the split has an external cause; and the notion that the split signifies mental illness.

The idea of the split consciousness or *double conscience* was in itself nothing new in psychiatric theory; Freud and Breuer refer to the work of Binet and Janet. Freud's later innovation in *The Interpretation of Dreams* is his declaration that the split in consciousness is a fundamental feature of every healthy psyche. The split becomes nonpathological, in fact, necessary; conflict becomes an intrinsic part of the psyche and psychic development. In *Studies on Hysteria,* however, it is taken for granted that a split consciousness is a sign of illness. The "other consciousness" manifests itself in hysterical seizures and symptoms.

According to Breuer and Freud, the cause of the split psyche is not itself psychic. Rather, the original, healthy wholeness of the psyche is disturbed by something foreign to it, something introduced from the outside. This "foreign body," as Breuer and Freud call it, is the memory of the trauma. Often the trauma took place far in the past, but its repressed memory nevertheless sits in the psyche, remarkably fresh. The discourse of bodily illness and health provides a language for speaking about trauma. Just as the integrity of a physical organism is disturbed when a "foreign body," say a splinter, invades it, the psyche is made ill by an external trauma that lodges itself in the mind in the form of a memory. Breuer and Freud conclude: *"Hysterics suffer mainly from reminiscences."*[4]

The authors thus propose a monistic conception of psychic health. The healthy psyche is perceived to be whole and unitary. "Illness" means that a boundary that should be inviolable, that between inside and outside, is transgressed. A similar boundary is presumed to exist between present and past. The pathogenic element is a piece of the outside and a piece of the past that interrupts the autonomy and also the presentness of the self. Breuer and Freud's model of health and illness is thus identical to Nietzsche's in *On the Advantage and Disadvantage of History for Life*. Both the temporal and the spatial versions of Nietzsche's line are implicit in Freud and Breuer's formulation of a "remembered trauma" as the cause of hysteria.

According to Breuer and Freud, the psyche's natural defense against unpleasant stimuli from the outside is abreaction. The organism reacts to the outside stimulus by producing an excess of affective excitation. In the normal healthy pattern, this excess excitation is expressed through the normal affective reaction, for example revenge or shouting. The memory to which the excitation is attached is expelled in the same process. When the subject is in a state of shock resulting from a trauma, abreaction fails to take place, so that the memory enters the psyche, causing a psychic split. The split-off part of the psyche in which the memory of the trauma resides is inaccessible to the subject's normal consciousness. The cure then takes place when this dark area is "brought to light," in Breuer and Freud's metaphor, or brought to consciousness in the psychoanalytic cure and expelled in words.

One of the tasks Freud and Breuer set for themselves in *Studies on Hysteria* is to explain how the sign is motivated, or in other words, why patients experience different symptoms. Why does one patient smell burnt pudding, while another has pains in her leg? The solution the authors propose in the "Preliminary Communication" is that the symptom is determined by the trauma. The trauma thus not only causes the hysteria but also provides the key to the interpretation of the symptom. "The most various symptoms . . . are . . . strictly related to the precipitating trauma"

(2: 4), they declare. Thus the symptom is determined by some element of the situation during which the trauma took place: if the trauma, i.e., an event that causes the subject to experience a painful affect, such as fright, fear, shame, or psychic pain, took place during a meal, for example, a patient might experience hysterical vomiting; if a patient's arm was asleep at the traumatic moment, she might suffer from hysterical paralysis of the arm. Freud's experience with the patient Cäcilie M. leads them, furthermore, to include another type of symptom determination, which they term "symbolic," so that moral disgust, for example, leads to the symptom of vomiting.

Freud writes all the case studies but one in *Studies on Hysteria*. In the course of these studies, he drifts away from the monistic conception of health he proposed along with Breuer in the "Preliminary Communication," so that by the end of the book, when he writes his separate theoretical conclusion, he has moved close to the theory of the dualistic psyche that he will announce in *The Interpretation of Dreams* and that will be fundamental to his thinking from that work onward. In his concluding remarks in "The Psychotherapy of Hysteria," he comes to see the trauma (coming from the outside) as less and less important in the etiology of hysteria; its place is taken by an affect coming from within, which is incompatible with other conscious ideas. The notion of a trauma is retained primarily as a way of explaining the onset of the symptom. At the same time, he deemphasizes the idea of mental illness. For if the psyche generates its own conflicts, conflict can no longer be thought of as unhealthy in itself.

Let us take as an example the case of Elisabeth von R., Freud's patient. In this case study, the trauma consists merely of the moment when the conflict between Elisabeth's erotic feelings and her moral ideas becomes apparent. Standing at her dead sister's bedside, she thinks about her brother-in-law: "Now I can become his wife." Freud designates this moment, and other comparable moments of Elisabeth's awareness of her love for her brother-in-law as the onset of hysterical conversion. Thereafter, Elisabeth experiences hysterical pains in the leg—pains that revive a preexisting somatic condition, but which the patient also associates symbolically with her unmarried state (she "stands alone," "cannot take a single step forward," etc.). There is no question of serious mental illness: Freud writes that "what she had in her consciousness was only a secret and not a foreign body" (2: 139).

The key concept in the shift in Freud's ideas is repression. Freud comes to the conclusion that repression is the *sine qua non* of hysteria. The earliest Freudian idea, repression, is a fascinating notion, which leads us to the idea of a dual psyche. Repression is allegedly the psyche's defense mechanism. The subject represses the incident with which the conflicting emotion is associated in order to protect itself from an unpleasant stimulus. But repression is an ambiguous defense. Let us compare it to abreaction, the forthright defense mentioned in the "Preliminary Communication." Abreaction allows the psyche to expel excitation along with the troublesome memory trace. Repression, in contrast, tucks the memory of the trauma away into the psyche. Consequently, it is itself the mechanism that creates the hysteria: it is simultaneously a defense and a capitulation, a wall and a gate. By virtue of its propensity to repress, the psyche becomes dualistic, the site of permanent conflict.

In his concluding remarks, Freud moves the split and the idea of conflict into the psyche. At the same time, the absoluteness of the split is undermined. Freud continues to believe that a boundary separates repressed (pathological) material from the rest of the psyche, but he begins to be interested in making the dividing line less definite:

> A foreign body does not enter into any relation with the layers of tissue that surround it, although it modifies them and necessitates a reactive inflammation in them. Our pathogenic psychical group, on the other hand, does not admit of being cleanly extirpated from the ego. Its external strata pass over in every direction into portions of the normal ego. . . . Nor does the treatment consist in extirpating something . . . but in causing the resistance to melt and in thus enabling the circulation to make its way into a region that has hitherto been cut off. (2: 290–91)

Why does Freud see things this way? I would suggest that he does so because his model opens the door to an exploration of the unknown with its attendant fascination. It enables him to recast the task and the role of the analyst and to turn him into a yet more powerful figure. A "foreign body" in the psyche demands a surgeon. The Freudian analyst is a detective-hero. On the one hand he is a clever, enormously patient sifter of clues, one who puts the pieces of the puzzle together—an investigator or interpreter. On the other, he is someone constantly struggling against resistances, an overcomer of defenses, a hero.

Freud's refashioning of the role of the analyst emerges in the metaphors he uses to describe the organization of pathological material in the psyche, metaphors that, he tells us, are not necessarily compatible with one another. Two crucial metaphors for the mind are the labyrinth and the archaeological site. Freud presents a threefold description of the psyche, as a temporal (chronological), a spatial, and a dynamic construct—a description that he will retain and elaborate on in the metapsychology in *The Interpretation of Dreams.* In the context of this discussion, he speaks of the "logical thread" that the analyst must follow—along an "irregular and twisting path" (2: 289), in "a zig-zag, twisted line" (2: 290). These images, implicitly, cast the mind as a labyrinth, the analyst as Theseus, the pathological material as the Minotaur. Concurrently, Freud repeatedly uses the word "strata" *(Schicht)* to refer to the mind. The patient finds "disconnected" things when she or he "clears up material lying within the same stratum" (2: 292). The analyst may "bury" *(verschütten)* things by accident (2: 292). This is the vocabulary of archaeology. The archaeological metaphor engages the ideas of outer/inner, light/dark, and surface/depth, and it also captures the temporal opposition present/past. Yet the earth is penetrable by the archaeologist—as the psyche is by the analyst. Like the labyrinth, it essentially provides an impediment that the analyst has to struggle with.

Both metaphors present a dual relation of the pathological kernel to the rest of the psyche: it is incompatible with it, yet potentially accessible. The archaeological metaphor subtly changes the significance of the "pathogenic kernel," for unlike the monster at the center of the labyrinth, there is nothing unnatural about something being buried below the earth. Hence, this metaphor will prove compatible with Freud's insight in the years following the publication of *Studies on Hysteria* that the normal psyche is dual, and it will prove more durable than the labyrinth metaphor. The analogy between archaeology and psychoanalysis is one that will continue to fascinate Freud. It dominates his interpretation of Wilhelm Jensen's novel *Gradiva* (1907), where the burial and excavation of Pompeii provide a model for the repression and unearthing of childhood memories.

Thus, with Freud's introduction of the concept of repression, we see an important shift in the way the antithetical configuration familiar from Nietzsche's history essay is regarded. The antithetical structure itself is retained, but humanity is no longer exhorted to stay in the light (the present, the known) and shun the dark (the past, the forgotten). No longer is conflict—the desire to be in two places at once—equated with being nowhere, with non-life. Instead, duality is elevated to the very explanatory mechanism that makes the psychic system work, and it therefore, despite the attachment of repression to the topic of mental illness in *Studies on Hysteria,* already takes on the appearance of a normal state.

In the years between the publication of *Studies on Hysteria* and *The Interpretation of Dreams,* Freud recognized that the traumas his patients related were not real but imaginary concretizations of the patients' own unacknowledged childhood desires. This insight was the basis for identifying the unconscious. With it, Freud institutionalized the dangerous area in the psyche on the other side of the line. Psychological conflict thus does not have an external cause but is purely internal and normal. "We must recognize," Freud insists, "that the psychical mechanism employed by neuroses is not created by the impact of a pathological disturbance upon the mind but is present already in the normal structure of the mental apparatus" (5: 607).

In *The Interpretation of Dreams,* psychic duality is firmly instituted. Freud establishes it, in the progressive stages of his argument, in hermeneutic, topographic, temporal, and dynamic modes. Ostensibly, the antithetical structure is ill-suited to a hermeneutics. By virtue of their very endeavor, hermeneutists assume the existence of motivated signs. The supposition that sign and meaning inhabit irreconcilable regions scarcely lightens the task of interpretation. Freud too aims to motivate the sign whenever possible. In *Studies on Hysteria,* he motivates the patient's symptom through the trauma, and in *The Interpretation of Dreams* he motivates the manifest content of the dream through the dream work and, even more so, through the symbol, which resembles what it signifies (stick: penis). Yet the antithetical structure, in a way that will presently become clear, will make it possible for Freud to insist on the certainty of interpretations based on extremely indirect, unapparent, or tenuous motivations.

In *Studies on Hysteria,* the formulation of repression afforded Freud a way out of an interpretative quandary. Through it, he found both a simpler and a more plausible motivation for hysteria than the trauma. Once he could posit repression, he no longer had to search for external traumas that motivated his patients' elaborate complaints—traumas that, once found, may well have struck him as disappointingly trivial compared to what he presumed to be their effects. In *Studies on Hysteria,* Freud confronted the perplexing symptom. Instead of focusing his efforts on finding an event in the patient's biography that corresponded to and hence explained it, he displaced the barrier between himself and it, between himself and the symptom's resistance to interpretation, onto the patient herself, in the form of a conflict between her conscious organization and the unacceptable affect.

In *The Interpretation of Dreams,* Freud employs the same strategy with the dream. He introduces his investigation with the following premise about the interpretability of dreams: "The aim which I have set before myself is to show that dreams are capable of being interpreted . . . 'interpreting' a dream implies assigning a 'meaning' to it—that is, replacing it by something which fits into the chain of our mental acts as a link having a validity and importance equal to the rest" (4: 96). By concluding that every dream has a "latent content," he decides that the incoherent material of the dream can be replaced by significant sentences that contain important revelations about the dreaming subject. Just as in *Studies on Hysteria,* but with greater confidence and daring, Freud starts with two things (the interpreter and the dream), and out of them fabricates three: the interpreter, the manifest content, and the latent content. His hermeneutic strategy, again, consists in relocating the barrier of incomprehension that exists between the interpreter and the phenomenon to be interpreted (interpreter//dream) to a new place within the phenomenon itself, between the dream and its hidden meaning (interpreter/manifest content of the dream//latent content). He thus displaces the inaccessibility of the dream to the place the dream comes from, which he names in the final chapter (7) the "unconscious."

In *Studies on Hysteria,* Freud, having identified repression as the cause of hysteria, still had to account for the specificity of the symptom. His solution was to retain the notion of the trauma precisely as an explanatory agent for the symptom (e.g., the patient's symptom is smelling burned pudding because pudding happened to be burning at a moment when the conflict in her feelings became apparent to her). In *The Interpretation of Dreams,* he confronts a similar problem. How can the particularity of the manifest content be explained? How may the interpreter link a particular dream with a particular meaning or latent content? His first step toward a solution is the ingenious notion of censorship. This barrier between the patient's unconscious (the site of latent meanings) and preconscious (whence the dream can proceed unproblematically into consciousness) does not merely divide antithetical psychic areas. The censorship inevitably distorts anything that passes it. Passage is, to Freud's mind, an exigency of the system viewed as dynamic. The presumption of distortion enables Freud greatly to simplify the task of interpretation. He narrows down the interpretative possibilities by making a generalization about dreams. Every dream, Freud claims, originates as a wish. In adults, the wishes are censored, distorted beyond recognition, so that the dream's manifest content bears little resemblance to what it represents.

Compared with *Studies on Hysteria,* his strategy in *The Interpretation of Dreams* is more daring because the conclusions he comes to cannot be objectively verified. In *Studies on Hysteria,* the success of therapy appears to validate his theory. Thus the last time he glimpses Elisabeth von R., a patient he cured of hysterical lameness, she is at a ball, and he sees her "whirl past in a lively dance" (2: 160).[5]

Freud's theory of interpretation opens out into a theory of the human psyche. This theory is in turn grounded in a theory of the psychic development of human beings, which in turn is grounded in their actual biological development. Freud will reiterate in later works what is implicit in *The Interpretation of Dreams:* the unconscious, consisting of wishful impulses, is present in infants from the start; the preconscious comes into being with language acquisition.[6] This ultimate grounding in what Freud sees as the uniform empirical human mode of being allows him to claim universality for his theory of interpretation: it is a theory that holds true for all cases.

In chapter 7, Freud institutionalizes the irreconcilable duality that informs his theory of interpretation in a mapping of the human psyche. The interpretative duality between the latent and the manifest content of the dream is reinforced by the metapsychology, such that the "latent" or hidden meaning in the hermeneutics becomes the "unconscious" of the metapsychology. The "unconscious" comprises two systems, the Ucs. (the substantive as opposed to merely adjectival unconscious) and the Pcs. (preconscious) : the Ucs. is designated as the source of the dream wish, while the Pcs. supplies the rational and verbal form of the "dream thoughts," which allows us to conceive of the hermeneutic object as consisting of significant sentences. Our task here will be to examine the process, purposes, and implications of this institutionalization.

In his description of the psyche, Freud asks us to think of the psyche in three ways: as topographic, dynamic, and temporal. The topography, which he discusses in the section "Regression," is the simplest and also most trivial representation. It may be seen as the last vestige of Freud's attempt to talk about brain anatomy in the *Project.* Here, however, it is wholly metaphoric. As a spatial representation, it is the system that connects most obviously with Freud's archaeological and labyrinth metaphors in *Studies on Hysteria.* Freud posits his "discovery," the Ucs., nonchalantly in this first reference, as a region or "system" in the mind. He observes briefly that it is the place that supplies "the motive force for producing dreams" (5: 541) and refers the reader to his section on the dynamic representation of the psyche (entitled "Wish-Fulfilment") for an explanation. "Wish-Fulfilment" and the following sections, where Freud presents his argument for the Ucs. conceived as dynamic, merit close scrutiny.

The most essential and serious representation of the psyche is the dynamic. Without energy, the psychic system would not be set in motion to begin with, and there would be no transitions from one so-called locality to the next. Hence, in the first section on the dynamic, "Wish-Fulfilment," Freud emphatically equates the dream-wish with energy: " . . . nothing but a wish can set our mental apparatus at work" (5: 567).

The dynamic involves three operative notions: excitation, energy, and quality. Excitation has to do with the body: the term presupposes that the mind operates at the service of the organism. Energy is another term for excitation, but energy leads Freud away from purely physical metaphors into economic ones: energy can be saved, squandered, budgeted, and so on. Quality, finally, is entirely psychic; it implies pleasure or unpleasure. The equation is as follows: excitation implies a build-up of energy; qualitatively, this build-up of quantity implies unpleasure. Conversely, the discharge of energy, initiated by wishing with an end to achieving satisfaction, is pleasurable. Freud retains the notion of the "Constancy Principle" or "Principle of Inertia" from his *Project* and contemporaneous letters to Wilhelm Fliess: the primitive psychic apparatus tries to keep itself so far as possible free from stimuli. Such stimuli may impinge on it from the outside, but they also arise internally, as somatic needs (5: 565). The notion of internal needs allows Freud to introduce an economic argument. In the case of a somatic need, the organism can no longer merely try to get rid of excess excitation as quickly as possible; it has to regard the excitation created by the need as energy with which to satisfy the need.

Freud formulates the primary and secondary processes as two different ways of budgeting energy. The primary process—where primary implies both chronologically prior and more primitive—tries to discharge the excitation arising from the stimulus as quickly as possible. Freud gives as an example a hungry baby: "A hungry baby screams or kicks helplessly" (5: 565). The infant discharges in motor activity the excitation aroused by its somatic need. Freud's second example is the hallucination, which, he asserts, is a close cousin of the dream. From the purely dynamic example of the baby, he moves to one that engages the psychic concept of wishing. Once the individual has had the "experience of satisfaction," a "psychical impulse" is created from the need, an impulse that seeks to "recathect the mnemic image of the perception [of satisfaction] and to re-evoke the perception itself" (5: 565–66). Freud calls such an impulse a "wish." The hallucination is its fulfillment.

The primary process, which Freud will eventually designate as the mode of operation of the unconscious (5: 599), follows what Freud calls the "unpleasure principle" (equivalent to the Constancy or Inertia Principle from the *Project* and letters to Fliess; later Freud would call it the pleasure principle). In short, the unconscious can do nothing but wish. Freud states: "As a result of the unpleasure principle, . . . the first ψ-system [i.e., the unconscious] is totally incapable of bringing anything disagreeable into the context of its thought. It is unable to do anything but wish" (5: 600). Consequently, the primary process squanders the energy derived from the stimulus by hallucinating an image of the satisfaction. But hallucinating is no real solution at all, for it does not remove the need. The primary process sacrifices true fulfillment to the pleasure of discharge.

The secondary process, which, as its name suggests, comes into being later (it will be identified as the mode of operation of the preconscious) (5: 599), involves a more efficient expenditure of energy. The secondary process inhibits the discharge of excitation; energy is converted to thought; and thought brings about the real fulfillment of the wish or removal of the need.

Freud's argument in chapter 7 inscribes a hermeneutic circle: his investigation of dreams beckons toward the grander project of formulating a metapsychology, while the metapsychology in turn promises to shed additional light on the mysteries of dreams. At the beginning of the "Wish-Fulfilment" section, Freud hypothesizes that adult dreams always involve an unconscious wish. He surrounds this hypothesis with many disclaimers: "I cannot offer any proof" (5: 552); "My supposition is . . . " (5: 553); "I am aware that this assertion cannot be proved to hold universally; but it can be proved to hold frequently, even in unsuspected cases, and it cannot be *contradicted* as a general proposition" (5: 554). Freud then moves from dreams to a discussion of the primary process. We are evidently meant, in turn, to apply the argument he presents in this discussion to dreams. Dreams, Freud implies, behave like hallucinations. By the end of the "Wish-Fulfilment" section, Freud believes that he has accumulated evidence to support his hypothesis that dreams always emanate from the unconscious, even though he will reiterate later that the unconscious genesis of dreams is unprovable. He states confidently: "...the reason why dreams are invariably wish-fulfilments is that they are products of the system *Ucs.,* whose activity knows no other aim than the fulfilment of wishes and which has at its command no other forces than wishful impulses" (5: 568).

In formulating the dynamic Ucs., Freud takes a leap. For dreams cannot be assimilated unproblematically to the model of hallucinations. Yet more disturbing, the primary process does not logically imply or "prove" the unconscious. We do not need the Ucs. to explain hallucinations, Freud's example of a manifestation of the primary process conceived as wishing. Three dislocations are necessary to move from the discussion of the primary process and the example of hallucinations to the case of dreams. Each one involves abandoning commonsensical ground—for Freud's argument about the primary and the secondary processes thus far, and the examples of the baby and the hallucination, are eminently plausible—and embarking into speculation.

First, unlike in the case of hallucinations, the "wishful impulses" that trigger dreams do not, for the most part, originate in somatic needs. Freud has covertly introduced the idea of purely psychic (and hence less provable) desires. Second, Freud needs to account for the fact that the dream, like the hallucination, takes place in the medium of visual images. In the case of the hallucination, he asserts that the primary process recathects the visual memory of the fulfillment of the need. But in the case of adult dreams, the infantile desires that motivate these dreams include "sexual wishful impulses from infancy" that were, we assume, never fulfilled in reality. Thus, despite Freud's references to unconscious memories, for example to "the memories on the basis of which the unconscious wish brings about the release of affect" (5: 604), there is no mnemic image of such wishes' fulfillment; or rather, there could only be a mnemic image of an imagined fulfillment. Paul Ricoeur, in *Freud and Philosophy,* explains this basing of dreams in the hallucinatory revival of perception, which he sees as a discrepancy, as a relic of Freud's belief in the reality of the childhood seduction scene.[7] Thus, in the case of an unconscious wish, we are dealing with something that was never either an objective need or, in many cases, a means of attaining real satisfaction—something, in short, for which there is no evidence, which Freud introduces *a priori,* yet something that ultimately will bear the weight of grounding his theory.[8]

Third, the psychic wishes harbored by the Ucs. are completely out of date. Fulfilling them today, as Freud states explicitly (5: 604), would create unpleasure. Freud's theory finds a way of dealing with this problem: these wishes, he contends, are unconscious, repressed, precisely because they are unacceptable to the adult consciousness. Yet the question remains, if one adopts a questioning attitude toward Freud's reasoning, why the organism bothers to preserve this archaic baggage.

In sum, the unconscious desires that give rise to dreams are purely psychic as opposed to somatic, archaic rather than contemporary, and they are never fulfilled in reality. Hence the dream does not relate to the generating wish the way a hallucination relates to a somatic need. It is not a perceptual recreation of a past fulfillment in response to a present need but the distorted expression of an unfulfilled desire, distorted because the wish is unacceptable. Dreams are intrinsically different from hallucinations. Consequently, the unconscious, the hypothesized repository of the desires that engender dreams, is not derivable from the dynamic description of the metapsychology. It is an addition to Freud's system of the primary and secondary processes. These processes would work perfectly well without the hypothesis of the Ucs. Indeed the primary process alone expresses the idea of the primacy of desire in the organism; the unconscious is not needed for that.

At this point, we might do well to examine why the Ucs., whose hermeneutic variant and precusor in the text—the latent content, which appeared to be an imaginative construct—is necessary in this system. Why not cross out the Ucs.? Why not reject the notion of infantile desires that, according to Freud, form the substance of the Ucs.? Why does Freud retain them and find a place for them in the psyche and then label it the most important place of all?

Let us consider what function the Ucs. performs in the context of Freud's theories. Freud first advanced a hermeneutic of dreams, whereby interpretation was facilitated by the assumption of hidden meanings that, moreover, possess a significant degree of uniformity in all cases: every dream is a wish. Freud then offered a dynamic description of the mind that posited desire as the organism's original motivating force. The Ucs. may be seen as a rapprochement of these projects, of Freud's hermeneutic enterprise and his dynamics. The dream's resistance to interpretation and Freud's consequent assumption of dream distortion and a latent meaning are compatible with the notion of a region harboring unacceptable wishes, wishes that live and demand discharge although we are not aware of them, wishes whose fulfillment today would be unpleasurable. The energy of the primary process may conveniently be located precisely in the same region, the Ucs. Indeed, Freud writes that the Ucs. is in possession of "the instinctual force which is at the disposal of the repressed wish" (5: 564).

In this fusion of the hermeneutic and the dynamic into a concept uniting both, the Ucs. (the temporal) plays a critical role. The dream wish must be unacceptable, hidden, yet alive: all these conditions are met, to Freud's mind, if the desire is conceived as an *infantile* sexual desire. The sexual nature of the desire fulfills the criterion of unacceptability. The genesis of the desire in the prehistoric period of early childhood, which is subject to amnesia, guarantees its hiddenness. The continued existence of the wish—indeed, its undiminished energy—remains to be explained. It is an article of faith for Freud that what is chronologically prior cannot be obliterated by what comes later. His belief in the importance and indestructibility of what is past is already evident in *Studies on Hysteria,* not so much in his theory of the pathogenic kernel as in his revision of that theory, by which pathogenic strata are perceived as being entangled with the normal mind. It was implicit in his archaeological metaphor for the mind of the analyst carefully removing layers of sediment to discover relics of the past. Decades later, in *Civilization and Its Discontents* (1930), Freud would affirm, again in the context of a lengthy archaeological analogy: "We are inclined to take the . . . view [*neigen zu der Annahme;* my translation] that in mental life nothing which has once been formed can perish" (21: 69).

What then is the significance of the Ucs.? Freud says that the Ucs. is "indestructible" (5: 577). It provides the absolute grounding of Freud's system—both the hermeneutics and the energetics. As we have already seen, Freud needed the Ucs.—supplemented by the Pcs. as the supplier of rational and verbal form—as a source of hidden meanings in his theory of interpretation. In his energetics, he needed it as an inexhaustible source of energy. In economic terms, it is a capitalist who cannot go broke. Its needs—unfulfillable because fulfilling them would contradict the pleasure principle—are permanent, not intermittent and fulfillable like physical needs. The Ucs. is a symbol for unfulfilled desire as the basis all energy and therefore of all life. Of the secondary process, Freud says, "Thought is after all nothing but a substitute for a hallucinatory wish" (5: 567). Alluding to the mythical Titans, Freud stresses both the power and the immortality of unconscious wishes:

> These wishes in our unconscious, ever on the alert and, so to say, immortal, remind one of the legendary Titans, weighed down since primaeval ages by the massive bulk of the mountains which were once hurled upon them by the victorious gods and which are still shaken from time to time by the convulsion of their limbs. (5: 553)

The status of the Ucs. as ground is made explicit by Freud: it is the "core of our being" (5: 603). Speaking of our unconscious as opposed to our conscious psychic life, Freud states: "The unconscious is the true psychical reality; *in its innermost nature it is as much unknown to us as the reality of the external world*" (5: 613).

While the Ucs. as a source of energy makes the system work, it also endangers it from the inside with its elemental, titanic force. Freud describes the psyche as a "citadel" that is constantly threatened by unconscious forces (5: 568). Given the status of the Ucs. as the unknown and as an indestructible source, what role does therapy play? Supposedly, its task is to extinguish the unconscious processes and bring the Ucs. under the domination of the Pcs.: the task of psychotherapy "is to make it possible for the unconscious processes to be dealt with finally and be forgotten. . . . What performs this work is the preconscious, and *psychotherapy can pursue no other course than to bring the Ucs. under the domination of the Pcs.*" (5: 578). Freud's celebrated statement that "*The interpretation of dreams is the royal road to a knowledge of the unconscious activities of the mind*" (5: 608) also suggests that the Ucs. is accessible. But in fact the analyst can only hold a candle into the darkness; it would undermine Freud's entire metapsychology if therapy could be complete. As Freud stresses, the structure of the mental apparatus as he has described it is normal, not pathological (5: 607–08). Freud finally circles back to the dream and writes it into this scenario of dangerous unconscious energy. The dream serves, precisely, as a safety valve for the organism (5: 579), which allows excitation to be expelled in a harmless fashion, for at night the door to motor activity is closed.

Let us recapitulate how the Ucs. comes into being. The hermeneutic endeavor imposes a hiddenness on wishes that, in the dynamic view, trigger the system. "Hidden" implies in dynamic terms an energy that cannot be leashed by the preconscious and is otherwise inaccessible. This energy is developed through desires that existed prior to the preconscious, namely earliest, or infantile, desires. Then, in a move back from the dynamic to the hermeneutic, Freud explains the existence of dreams as a "safety valve" for the discharge of this energy. Freud's argument comes full circle. His initial, perplexing insistence in chapter 2 that every dream is a wish—an assertion that flies in the face of common sense and makes the reader wonder why Freud is so intent on it—proves retrospectively to have its purpose: if *every* dream is a wish, dreams *may* be seen as safety valves for unconscious energy. And if one has such energy and such safety valves, the notion of an "indestructible" unconscious is validated.

At this point, it will be useful to compare Freud's system in *The Interpretation of Dreams* with the model we have derived from Nietzsche's *On the Advantage and Disadvantage of History for Life* and Freud and Breuer's "Preliminary Communication." First, it is essential for Freud that the two conflicting terms coexist. Gone is the identification of health with existence in the here and now. For Freud, to be human means to be where one is not, to be divided. Lending priority to the "dark," Freud chooses to emphasize a disruptive force rather than advocating the suppression of whatever might threaten self-contained plenitude. Nietzsche and Freud and Breuer had put the figure of opposition at the service of a system that was essentially static. Freud's system in *The Interpretation of Dreams* is dynamic. If desire triggers the system, conflict is its generative device, the mechanism that produces dreams and neurotic symptoms.

Second, for Nietzsche and Freud and Breuer the terms of the duality are firmly antithetical. Nietzsche and Freud and Breuer make no attempt to investigate the possibility of transition between the terms of their dualities; indeed, precisely the lack of such transition is imperative; it confirms the antithetical nature of the terms. For Freud in *The Interpretation of Dreams,* however, the very topics to which the dual structure is applied, the quest for meaning and the topic of energy/desire, imply movement between the terms. The hermeneutic endeavor necessarily posits that the relation between sign and meaning is motivated. Desire and energy, likewise, imply a processual movement between impulse and outcome. Thus, the terms of Freud's duality are subject to more complex demands than Nietzsche's or Freud and Breuer's. They must be antithetical—yet mutually accessible. The Ucs. must be hidden and yet not hidden. What this means for Freud is that he must forever balance two contradictory characteristics of the Ucs., allied with two different purposes of his theory: he must maintain both the penetrability and the impenetrability of the Ucs. Freud thereby introduces the issue of interaction between the two terms themselves. Inasmuch as his goal in interpretation, Freud is particularly interested in strategies of transition; to this end he devises the complex theory of the dream work, elaborated in chapter 6.

Nowhere more than in Freud's work is duality so richly exploited. Vis-à-vis earlier philosophical celebrations of the irrational, namely Schopenhauer's and Nietzsche's, Freud's decisive innovation is his insistence on *conflict* as the basis of life. The Freudian libido bears a remarkable and often noted resemblance to Schopenhauer's Will and to Nietzsche's will to power. All of them are perceived as the key to life. With the Will, Schopenhauer, who precedes Freud in overthrowing the Cartesian primacy of reason, makes desire the primary motivating cosmic force. The insatiable Will is characterized in terms of constant striving. True, "appearances" of the Will are forever coming into conflict with one another; true, one's intellect may sometimes tame one's Will;

but for Schopenhauer, nothing systematically opposes the Will. For Nietzsche likewise, the will to power is not systematically and permanently opposed by another force. On the contrary, Nietzsche is at pains to show how thorny problems of history—why the weak have prevailed over the strong, and why the ascetic ideal has seemingly won out over the will to power—are in fact reducible to the sole agency of the will to power.[9] By reading an exigency of the hermeneutic enterprise (hidden meanings) into the energetic enterprise (human energy needs an outlet, a mode of passage), Freud produces remarkably fruitful results. The ingenious notion of a barrier that distorts allows him to turn duality into conflict. Unconscious desire must be discharged, but it is opposed by the powerful censorship. While this desire is the primal motivating force, it does not motivate directly but, rather, always in a distorted or sublimated form. Its products, therefore, do not resemble itself. Hence, Freud can relate more than dreams and pathological symptoms to a far-flung latent content: in such later works as *Leonardo da Vinci and a Memory of his Childhood,* the genesis of art is explained according to the same model, as sublimated libido, and in *Totem and Taboo* and *Moses and Monotheism* Freud extends the model to the collective and accounts for the origin of religion in the same fashion, where taboo or morality takes the place of the censorship. Unconscious energy, libido, that must be discharged, yet must discharge itself through a powerful, distorting barrier, becomes responsible for the major products of human creativity.

Notes

Reprinted, with changes, from chapters 1 and 7 of Lorna Martens, *Shadow Lines: Austrian Literature from Freud to Kafka* (Lincoln: Univ. of Nebraska Press, 1996), by permission of the author and the publisher.

1. Philosophers of science have consistently been critical of Freud's ideas, including the unconscious. An extensive discussion is given in Adolf Grünbaum, *The Foundations of Psychoanalysis: A Philosophical Critique* (Berkeley: Univ. of California Press, 1984). Grünbaum himself attacks not Freud's metapsychology, which is avowedly speculative, but rather his clinical theory, which claims scientific status. He shows in particular that the concept of repression—the "cornerstone" of Freud's edifice—is poorly substantiated. From within the field of psychiatry Donald P. Spence, in *The Freudian Metaphor* (New York: Norton,

1987), argues that the substantive unconscious is a "metaphor" without "evidence of convergent effect or cross-validation" (19), hence an "empty construct" (23) which is "significantly unfalsifiable" (36). Among literary critics, Harold Bloom, "Freud and the Poetic Sublime: A Catastrophe Theory of Creativity" (1978), in *Freud: A Collection of Critical Essays,* ed. Perry Meisel (Englewood Cliffs, N.J.: Prentice-Hall, 1981), refers to Freud's "trope of the Unconscious" (213) and discusses poetic precursors like Coleridge (217). Perry Meisel, "Introduction: Freud as Literature," states that "Freud's characteristic trope or figure, the unconscious, is itself a literary rather than a scientific or philosophical achievement" (2).

2. Friedrich Nietzsche, *On the Advantage and Disadvantage of History for Life,* trans. Peter Preuss (Indianapolis: Hackett, 1980), 10.

3. An example that is closely contemporaneous with Freud and Breuer's "Preliminary Communication" and similarly Viennese is Hugo von Hofmannsthal's lyrical drama *Death and the Fool* (1893). The "Fool" Claudio is sick by virtue of his inability to conform to a monistic ideal of health, to draw the necessary "line" between self and other, present and past, and stay on his own side of it.

4. Sigmund Freud, *The Standard Edition of the Complete Psychological Works of Sigmund Freud,* trans. and ed. James Strachey *et al.,* 24 vols. (London: The Hogarth Press, 1953–1974), 2: 7. Further references to this edition will be given in the text.

5. Grünbaum shows that Freud based his claim for the scientific status of his clinical theory on his therapeutic achievements (93; cf. 167, 182). Thus, Freud substantiates the concept of repression (inadequately, in Grünbaum's opinion) through the success of therapy. I concur with Grünbaum, who views Freud's "theory of parapraxes and of dreams as *misextrapolations* of the generic repression etiology of neurotic symptoms, which had at least had prima facie therapeutic support" (193–94).

6. "The Unconscious," 14: 186–89; *The Ego and the Id,* 19: 20. Freud would supply further grounding in the child's social development when he formulated the relation of the metapsychology to the Oedipus complex in *The Ego and the Id.* In the Oedipus complex, which succeeds the stage of early infancy, the boy child hates his father as a rival for his mother's affections. The Oedipus complex is resolved when the boy identifies with his father; this identification constitutes the superego.

7. Paul Ricoeur, *Freud and Philosophy: An Essay in Interpretation* (New Haven: Yale Univ. Press, 1970), 95, 106–07.

8. Stan Draenos, in *Freud's Odyssey: Psychoanalysis and the End of Metaphysics* (New Haven: Yale Univ. Press, 1982), oversimplifies the situation in *The Interpretation of Dreams* when he asserts that in his "grounding operation," which establishes the priority of the Ucs., Freud makes the body, specifically the sexual instincts, the ground of the mind. In fact the "grounding operation" of the discovery of the Ucs. involves positing some much more tenuous entity than the body: an entity concocted to fit the requirements of

unacceptability, hiddenness, and immortality—i.e., infantile sexual desires, and ones moreover that are fixated on certain persons.

9. In *The Genealogy of Morals,* Nietzsche, in attempting to explain why the strong did not win out in human history, shows how the will to power turned dramatically against the self. The aggressive instincts were interiorized and the bad conscience born. Priests later put the bad conscience at the service of the ascetic ideal in order to demonstrate that the root of suffering lay in sinfulness. They thus denied all that was vital in man and attacked the health of Europe. But Nietzsche shows how, at each juncture in this development, an aspect of the will to power is really at work. Finally, by giving man an explanation for his suffering, indeed by ascribing it to him, the ascetic ideal in fact *saved* man's will. Even where the will wants nothingness, says Nietzsche, it is nevertheless still a will.

The Jewish Genius: Freud and the Jewishness of the Creative

Sander L. Gilman

The "intellectual attributes of the Jews," whether in the desert or in the banks of Europe, "have remained constant for thousands of years."[1] The qualities of the Jewish mind, of the "common mental constructions" that define the Jew, usually are understood in *fin-de-siècle* culture as negative and destructive.[2] The Jews "possess no imagination. . . . All who have any claim at all to speak, testify unanimously that lack—of let us say poverty—of imagination is a fundamental trait of the Semite."[3] The "Jewish mind does not have the power to produce even the tiniest flower or blade of grass that has grown in the soil of another's mind and to put it into a comprehensive picture."[4] "Hence the Jewish people, despite all apparent intellectual qualities, is without any true culture, and especially without any culture of its own. For what sham culture the Jew today possesses is the property of other peoples, and for the most part it is ruined in his hands."[5] Jewish scientists, such as the founder of the "sociology of the Jews," Arthur Ruppin, found it necessary to counter this view constantly: "It is incorrect to accuse the Jews of having talent but producing no geniuses. Genius is sown thinly among all peoples. . . . Certainly the number of highly gifted individuals among the Jews will increase as soon as the Jews are able to leave the merchant class in larger numbers, for it is clear that the education to acquisitiveness certainly hinders the creative gift."[6] This view was to be found as well within the medical literature of the age. Jews were neurasthenic or hysteric and evidenced the signs and symptoms of these debilitating diseases in terms of the language that they employed. Their aesthetic creations were therefore inherently flawed, as they reflected a diseased mind.

That the Jew could not produce transcendental works of aesthetic value was a commonplace in Germany from the Enlightenment on. That this inability was a psychological fault resulting from their Jewishness was a discovery of the medical science of the nineteenth century. This medicalization of the lack of true creativity on the part of the Jews became part of the discourse of degeneration. For the racial biologist of the *fin de siècle* the Jews could evidence no true genius and, therefore, their creations could have no true originality. Indeed, any seeming genius shown by the Jew was a mark of his degeneracy. Medical literature of the time tended to show that behind the Jews' supposed intellectual superiority was an inferior ability to perform measurable tasks, such as schoolwork.[7] It was the superficiality of the Jew, the Jew's mimicry of a world that he could never truly enter, that produced works that were felt to be creative but, in fact, were mere copies of the products of *truly* creative individuals. And this degenerate creativity was marked by the stigmata of disease, of madness.

But are "madness" and "creativity" necessarily linked? Aristotle believed that they were. In the *Problemata* he asked the question, "Why are men of genius melancholics?"[8] Melancholia, the dominance of one of the humors, the mythic black bile, was seen as the root of most mental illnesses from the ancient Greeks through the Renaissance. Aristotle saw figures such as Heracles as possessing a melancholic constitution but also saw "most of the poets" as being "clearly melancholics." "Creative" minds are diseased or, at least according to the ancients, are housed in a body dominated by black bile, the source of madness. The special role, closely associated with that of the priest, attributed to the artist and poet by the Greeks demanded a specific type of insight, an insight that was unique. Aristotle, who sought to determine the boundary between the "normal," observing member of society (defined by himself) and the "poet," employed a materialistic, strictly somatic definition of "creativity." For him, "creativity" is the product of the imbalance of the natural forces (the humors), forces that the Greeks believed created the stasis of daily life. "Creativity" is not the inspiration or punishment of the gods, but a product of the body and a sign of its pathology. The "creative" individual is thus "different" from the observer, diseased and productive.

This view of the relationship between "madness" and "creativity" has been sporadically accepted in Western culture since the Greeks. On one level or another, or at some remove, "creative" individuals are set apart from the normal not only by their actions but also by the source of these actions. The uniqueness of the "creative" individual is perceived as the result of some greater, overwhelming force that places the ordinary observer in a position removed from the wellspring of "creativity." This view is generally accepted throughout the nineteenth century and attains the status of a truism. Whether in the works of the Romantic psychiatrists of the early nineteenth century, who sought after a metaphysical answer to the idea of madness, or in the work of the biologically oriented psychiatrists who see mind (and, therefore, "creativity") as a simple product of the brain, the "creative" individual is labelled as drawing on resources (or errors) that are not present in the "normal" individual. And that "normal" individual is silently assumed to be the physician, scientist, or philosopher who is describing "creativity"! In framing the debates about the nature of "creativity" in the medical sciences of the twentieth century, we can see how the very object and meaning of the "creative" has shifted over time. "Creativity" is a universal category of Western thought, but what it means is historically and culturally determined in an absolute manner. Each age invents, to fulfill its own needs, what the truly "creative" is and each time constructs a working definition that satisfies its own need to place itself in relationship to the "creative."

The dominant theory of the relationship between creativity and disease in the late nineteenth century was that of Cesare Lombroso. Lombroso, in his first major work on the subject, *Genius and Madness* (1864), drew analogies between the products of genius and works made by the insane that he had seen during his practice in the Turin psychiatric clinic.[9] Lombroso's book, and his subsequent fame as the best-known medical champion of the concept of "degeneracy" as the central explanation of deviancy (from sociopathic and psychopathic to creative acts), moved this question into the center of the concerns of modern clinical and asylum psychiatry. It was only following Lombroso that the two questions were clearly separated: one line led to the examination of the "great" in order to find the psychopathological origin of their greatness; the other to examine the aesthetic products of the mentally ill to establish the nature of the creativity of the mad (and discover the "creativity" in their illness).

One issue that Lombroso addressed quite directly is the relationship between race, insanity, and genius. Jews, following the accepted wisdom of the age, evidenced a "curious" overabundance of "lunatics," "four or even six times . . . as [many as] the rest of the population." Lombroso was forced to separate this "fact" from its use: "This fatal privilege has not attracted the attention of the leaders of that anti-Semitic movement which is one of the shames of contemporary Germany. They would be less irritated at the success of this race if they had thought of all the sorrows that are the price of it, even at our epoch; for if the tragedies of the past were more bloody, the victims are not now less unhappy, struck at the source of their glory, and because of it deprived even of the consolation of being able, as formerly, to contribute to the most noble among the selections of species."[10] This is very much in line with Wilhelm Wundt's view that "care and tragedy can influence nutrition by limiting the entrance of air and blood" and can thus affect the psyche.[11] Jews evidence greater levels of genius because of "the bloody selection of medieval persecutions, and owing also to the influence of temperate climate, the Jews of Europe have risen above those of Africa and the East, and have often surpassed the Aryans" (Lombroso 133). At least one Jewish physician in Vienna agreed with Lombroso's claims. The young Arthur Schnitzler, writing in his father's medical journal in 1891, commented that Lombroso's information about the heightened risk of Jews for mental illness as the cost of the greater genius of the race is "of special interest for our times."[12]

Lombroso's statistical work relied on Joseph Jacobs, who attributed the Jews' talent to their religious traditions.[13] But Lombroso could not see any connection between "this rhythmical caterwauling and the sublime notes of Meyerbeer and Mendelssohn" (135). While Jews have a much higher rate of men of genius, they have yet to produce "men like Newton, Darwin, and Michelangelo . . . because they have not yet accomplished their ethnic evolution, as they show by the obstinacy with which they cling to their ancient beliefs" (136). In the work of Lombroso (himself an Italian Jew), the category of the creative was contaminated by the pathological, for him, "religious" identity (as for Mantegazza the practice of circumcision) contaminates the pure genius of the Jew. Lombroso expresses this attitude when he stresses that the genius of the Jew in its positive appearance brings a new level of creativity into the Aryan race.[14]

The question of the relationship between the idea of madness and the meaning of creativity was much discussed at the turn of the century. That Jews were active within the spheres of culture and science could not be contradicted—but was their activity to be understood as "creative?" The seemingly central role of Jews in culture was put into question by the argument that this type of art was superficial or perhaps even corrupting. Indeed, it was all too often argued that the "creativity" of the Jew was really a sign of his diseased, "mad" state. Thus, Lombroso's evocation of Heinrich Heine reflected a central motif in the work of *fin-de-siècle* scientists. For them, the ill Heine became the exemplary image of the diseased Jew. (According to Lombroso, Heine's illness was not madness per se, but a disease of the spinal cord, which "may have given a morbid character" to Heine's writing [152]. Arthur Schnitzler, in his review of Lombroso, countered with the claim that Lombroso was misreading Heine's "hatred" for Germany as a sign of his pathology; what Heine desired, according to Schnitzler, was to be healed of his love for Germany [236]. The impossibility of being both a Jew and a German led, in Schnitzler's reading, to a true madness.)

The debate about the nature of the Jews' creativity ran through the medical as well as the popular literature of the *fin de siècle.* Freud's younger Viennese contemporary, the self-hating Jew Otto Weininger, presented the dichotomy between the Jew and the Aryan in his *Sex and Character* (1903).[15] Otto Weininger had been a student of philosophy and biology at the University of Vienna at the *fin de siècle.* He published his revised dissertation, *Sex and Character,* in 1903 and killed himself shortly thereafter in the house in Vienna in which Beethoven had died.[16] Weininger was both a baptized Jew and a repressed homosexual.[17] His book became an immediate best-seller and established him as a serious contributor to the discourse about the relationship between race and gender at the beginning of the century.[18] This is a work of intensive self-hatred which, however, had an unprecedented influence on the scientific discourse about Jews and women at the turn of the century. Why, it might well be asked. Weininger's suicide shortly after the publication of this book helped to publicize his ideas, but they were hardly new ones to his contemporaries. The appeal of Weininger's work was not innovation but summation. To the end of a century he held up a polemical mirror that many found to contain truths of their times. (Read by Freud in an early draft, the book was fundamental in shaping at least some of his attitudes toward the nature of the body. And, indeed, it was seen as a serious work of science after its publication by radical thinkers of the time, such as the American arch-feminist Charlotte Perkins Gilman.[19] Ludwig Wittgenstein, confronted with his "Jewish" nature and his Catholic upbringing, accepted and incorporated aspects of Weininger's "philosophy" into his world view.[20] Its influence extended to the most original and influential work by Japan's leading *fin-de-siècle* philosopher Kitâro Nishida.)[21] What *Sex and Character* did was to restate in a scientific, i.e., biological context Arthur Schopenhauer's views on women and simply extend the category of the feminine to the Jew. It argued, within the rhetoric of contemporary science, that there is a psychological scale that runs from the Jewish mind on one end to the Aryan at the other. This scale is parallel to another, the "feminine" and the "masculine."

Weininger stressed that categories such as the "Jew" and the "Woman" were psychological states always found in tension with the "Christian" and the "Male." Weininger, the converted Jew, saw himself as less "Jewish" than the arch-anti-Semite Richard Wagner, whom he labels as "having an accretion of Jewishness in his art" (305). Jewishness is a "common mental construction." It does "not refer to a nation or to a race, to a creed or to a scripture. When I speak of the Jew I mean neither an individual nor the whole body, but mankind in general, in so far as it has a share in the platonic idea of Judaism" (306). Weininger constructs the image of the Jew like that of the woman as inherently negative, as necessarily to be transcended.

For Weininger, Jews and women have "no genius." He attacks Spinoza and Heinrich Heine as the representative Jewish thinkers who are viewed by his contemporaries as "creative" geniuses. They are for him incapable of true genius: "The philosopher Spinoza, about whose purely Jewish descent there can be no doubt, is incomparably the greatest Jew of the last nine hundred years, much greater than the poet Heine (who indeed was destitute of any quality of true greatness)" (216). Nevertheless, Spinoza lacks genius. What passes for genius in the Jew—and the woman—is but "exaggerated egotism" (317). Jewish creativity is inherently superficial.

What characterizes the woman is her language: "The impulse to lie is stronger in woman, because, unlike that of man, her memory is not continuous, whilst her life is discrete, unconnected, discontinuous, swayed by the sensations and perceptions of the moment instead of dominating them" (146). Women's language is lies; Jews' language is *Mauscheln,* speaking so distinctively that it marks the speaker as a Jew:

> Just as the acuteness of Jews has nothing to do with the true power of differentiating, so his shyness about singing or even about speaking in clear positive tones has nothing to do with real reserve. It is a kind of inverted pride; having no true sense of his own worth, he fears being made ridiculous by his singing or his speech. (324)

Jews and women, for example, have no "true humor," for true humor must be transcendent; Jews "are witty only at [their] own expense and on sexual things" (318). Jews are inherently more preoccupied by the sexual but less potent than Aryans (311). Their obsession is rooted in the fact that sex breaks down boundaries between individuals. Jews, like women, are "devoid of humor and addicted to mockery" (319). "The Jew who does not set out, like the humorist, from the transcendental, and does not move towards it, like the erotic, has no interest in depreciating what is called the actual world, and that never becomes for him the paraphernalia of a juggler or the nightmare of a mad-house" (319).

The Jews' supposed predilection for mockery became a leitmotif in the *fin de siècle,* one that was related to the very nature of the Jewish body. The psychoanalyst and first biographer of Freud, Fritz Wittels, argued, in reference to Freud's great opponent, the hunchbacked Karl Kraus, that Kraus's sense of satirical wit rested on his deformity: "Mockery seems to be linked with physical deformity, and in that way to be suitable as a special domain of the Jews," as Freud showed, "in the analysis of the phobia of a five-year-old boy [Little Hans] with its stress on castration and circumcision."[22] The "Kraus-neurosis" was supposedly the result of Kraus's deformity, but Wittels directly related this to the overall perception of the difference attributed to the body of the Jew. And the most evident reflex of these physical attributes, according to Wittels, is to be found in the nature of the Jew's language. It is the hidden language of the Jews, it is *Mauschel,* which is related to the physical nature of the Jews. They mock others because of their own physical infirmity, because of their circumcised penis.

Otto Rank reverses this view in his essay on "The Essence of Judaism" (1905), when he notes that "where the religion [of the Jews] is insufficient to do this [to maintain psychic balance], Jews resort to wit; for they do not have their own 'culture.' "[23] By "culture," Rank is adapting and reversing Weininger's theory of the centeredness of the Christian. "Culture," for Rank, is an advanced state of sexual repression. The Jews exist in a state much more "primitive" and "natural," in which this level of repression has not yet taken place. Humor becomes an atavistic sign of the sexuality of the Jews.

Continuing Weininger's argument, Jews are historically extremely adaptable, as can be shown by their talent for the superficial areas of "creativity" such as journalism. But in their essence they are truly unchangeable. They lack deep-rooted and original ideas (320). The Jews are the essential unbeliever; not even believing in themselves (321). The Jew has no center. He is critical, not a critic. He is not merely a materialistic; he doubts all and any truths. He is irreligious, indeed, his religion is not even a real religion. It is a reflection of the Jewish mind that always demands multiple choices. It is not the historical treatment of the Jews that has made them what they are: "Outward circumstances do not mould a race in one direction, unless there is in the race the innate tendency to respond" (308). And the Jewishness of the Jew is immutable. The Jew is a "parasite." He is a "different creature in every host and yet remains himself" (320). The Jew is the disease in the body politic.

It is in one arena that this immutability of mind and spirit, this moral "madness," most clearly manifests itself and that is within science, most specifically within the world of medicine. For the Jews there is no transcendentalism; everything is as flat and commonplace as possible. Their effort to understand everything robs the world of its mystery (314). Evolutionary theory ("the ridiculous notion that men are derived from monkeys" [314–15]), for example, is mere materialism.

The development of nineteenth-century medicine from its focus on bacteriology in the 1880s to its focus on biochemistry at the turn of the century meant a real shift of interest from the "organic" to the "inert" on the part of the medical scientist. For Weininger, Jews are natural chemists, which explains why medicine has become biochemistry: "The present turn of medical science is largely due to the influence of the Jews, who in such numbers have embraced the medical profession. From the earliest times, until the dominance of the Jews, medicine was closely allied with religion. But now they make it a matter of drugs, a mere administration of chemicals. . . . The chemical interpretation of organisms sets these on a level with their own dead ashes" (315). This Weininger interprets as a "Jewification" of medicine. For the Jews focus on the dead, the inert.

For Weininger, the turn of the century is the age of feminization, a corruption of society (including medicine) by the Jews: "This is the age which is most Jewish and most feminine. . . . It is a time when art is content with daubs and seeks its inspiration in the sports of animals; . . . a time for originality and yet with the most foolish craving for originality. The choice must be made between Judaism and Christianity, between business and culture, between male and female, between the race and the individual, between unworthiness and worth. . . . Mankind has the choice to make. There are only two poles, and there is no middle way" (329–30). Jewishness, like the feminine, is a state condemned to be "uncreative." This litany of hate places the Jew in an antithetical relationship to true "creativity." And as bearing a great risk for "madness." As we have seen elsewhere, Weininger's position is hardly unique. It reflects the general view of antisemitic racial science about the special nature of the Jew. Thus, "creativity" is linked to Jews, their "madness," and the ultimate source of their madness, their sexuality. Now we must try to imagine Freud confronted with this view. Of all of the topics he could have addressed about the nature of the psyche, why was it "creativity" that captured him? This choice seems as idiosyncratic as a means of discussing the normal structure of the psyche as those of dreams, or jokes, or slips of the tongue. One answer is that each of these can be linked to debates within the racial science of the late nineteenth century.[24]

Sigmund Freud's view was, on the surface, quite different from Lombroso's or Weininger's. In his writings from the close of the nineteenth century through the onset of World War I, he saw "creativity" (as he did dreams or slips of the tongue or neurotic symptoms) not as a set of formal processes or disease mechanisms in a subset of the population but as clues to the normal functioning of the unconscious in everyone. Where Lombroso saw the "mad" and their aesthetic productions as "throwbacks" to an earlier, more primitive state of development or as a sign of the diseased nature of the Jew, Freud saw all "creativity" as a sign of the universal, underlying forces that make all human beings human. He, too, saw it as pathological in that it was the result of deviation from "normal" psychological development, but as such, this pathology was a potential of all human beings, not merely a predestined subset. He studied the creative to understand the centrality of unconscious processes, especially the role of unconscious motivation in human action.

Freud, in his case studies of Leonardo (1910) and Michelangelo (1914), as well as in his critical readings of the creative works of Wilhelm Jensen (1907) and the strange autobiography of the "psychotic" Dr. Daniel Schreber (1911), looked at the "creative" work as a sign of the displacement of psychic (and for Freud that means sexual) energy into a different, seemingly unrelated undertaking.[25] The "creative" impulse is a form of displacement or repression analogous to the symptoms of the neurotic. The symptoms of the neurotic parallel the experiences or fantasies that underlie them but do not directly represent the underlying conflict that gives rise to them. For Freud, it is the sphere of the sexual in which these products (whether symptoms or works of art) always arise. For the "creative" individual is by Freud's definition one who *must* sublimate his sexual drive into the realm of fantasy. The truly creative individual represses all of his latent instinctual drives. Like the Jew in Viennese society, the creative figure must deny his essence to become what he can become. And like the Jew, that which is repressed in these creative individuals is the atavistic sexual drive. The reason for this sublimation, as in the case of the artists and authors listed above, is because of the socially unacceptable direction of the expression of their sexuality (from the homosexuality of Leonardo to the incestuous leanings of Jensen). All of these individuals represent sexuality on an earlier plane of development than the sexuality of the heterosexual.

In certain individuals, Freud argued, the active, social repression of these drives leads to the total sublimation of sexual curiosity and, thereby, to the creative process and the true work of art.[26] The "creative" object thus represents the fixed fantasies of the individual. The essential nature of the process of "creativity" is to mask the inherently objectionable (from the standpoint of society) nature of its origin. Works of art "conceal their personal origin and, by obeying the laws of beauty, bribe other people with a bonus of pleasure" (SE 23: 187).[27] The overarching "laws of beauty," the technique of the aesthetic, are the means by which the "creative" works. It is the universal mask that hides and manipulates. It is separate from the "creative" impulse and shapes how the observer sees the work of art. "Creativity" is seen in terms of the "creator" who produces a product, which is implicitly a commodity, as value is inherently attached to it. That product is cast in a form that is universal, and it manipulates the reader or viewer through its evocation of some universal law (the aesthetic). The "creativity" of the artist consists of placing a repressed aspect of the artist's psyche into the realm of the aesthetic. As Josef Breuer—focusing on the ultimate "creative" figure for nineteenth-century German culture—said in the *Studies in*

Hysteria (jointly authored with Freud in 1895): "Goethe did not feel he had dealt with an experience till he had discharged it in a creative artistic activity" (SE 2: 207).

But it is the act of seeing—the observer's act of seeing and responding to the creative product of the artist—which defines "creativity" for Freud. To use one of his examples, we—the naive viewer—look at Leonardo's image of the *Holy Family* and "see" the perfection and beauty of the work, but also are instructed in its "meaning" by the psychoanalyst. The psychoanalyst is able to see beneath the initial evocation of the aesthetic (which disguises the motivation of the author) and provide an interpretation of the work of art and of the psyche of the artist. The uninformed viewer's response is aesthetic; with the aide of the interpreter (Freud), we can understand the source of the artist's "creativity" and thus truly understand the "unseen" aspect of the work of art. Analogous to the psychoanalyst's explaining to the patient the typography of the dynamic unconscious, the critic explains to the viewer what he or she is observing. It is here that we learn to distrust the initial act of seeing and to link the act of seeing, not with a visceral response, but with the act of knowing. Freud's focus seems to be solely on the motivation that underlies "creativity." It is the discovery that the "creative" individual is "subject to the laws which govern both normal and pathological activity with equal cogency" that Freud illustrates (SE 11: 63). But his hidden agenda is to undermine our sense that we can see the world directly.

This is clearest in Freud's popular essay on "Creative Writers and Day-Dreaming," which was presented as a lecture to a lay (i.e., non-medical) audience in Vienna during 1907. Freud's overt intention is to present the parallels between "creativity" and childhood play. In this essay Freud defines "creativity" and the special status of the "creative" artist: "We laymen have always been intensely curious to know—like the Cardinal who put a similar question to Ariosto—from what sources that strange being, the creative writer, draws his material, and how he manages to make such an impression on us with it and to arouse in us emotions which, perhaps, we had not thought ourselves capable" (SE 9: 143). Freud places himself as a "layman" in opposition to the "creative" individual who makes a world that seems complete and who uses that world to manipulate our ("lay" or "non-creative") emotions. But it is a very special "lay" observer, one who has the insight to understand the underlying meaning as well as the immediate effect of the "creative." Freud's initial analogy is to the play of the child. Play is rooted in childhood fantasies of being able to control at least the immediate world of toys, in opposition to the real world which is beyond the manipulation of the child.[28] It is into this universe, in which uncontrollable realities are transmuted into manipulable fantasies, that the child escapes: "[F]or many things which, if they were real, could give no enjoyment, can do so in the play of phantasy" (SE 9: 144). It is "humor" that is for Freud the ultimate example of how the healthy adult can escape back into this world of playfulness: "[B]y equating his ostensibly serious occupations of to-day with his childhood games, he can throw off the too heavy burden imposed on him by life and win the high yield of pleasure afforded by *humor*" (SE 9: 145; Freud's emphasis).

Fantasy is like dreaming. It uses everyday impressions which are related to earlier (infantile) experience and "creates a situation relating to the future." Thus, the "creative" individual is like the playful child, but also like the neurotic in another central aspect.[29] Like the neurotic, the "creative" individual has the compulsion to tell (represent) his or her fantasies: "[T]here is a class of human beings upon whom, not a god, indeed, but a stern goddess—Necessity—has allotted the task of telling what they suffer and what things give them happiness. These are the victims of nervous illness, who are obliged to tell their fantasies" (SE 9: 146). In paraphrasing Goethe's *Torquato Tasso* in this passage ("and when a man falls silent in his torment / A god granted me to tell how I suffer"), Freud elides the artist as figure (Tasso) and the artist as author (Goethe) with the "mad person" as figure (Tasso) and the healer of the "mad" (Freud). The artificial line that Freud drew between the "creative" individual as neurotic on the one side and himself (and his listeners) on the other at the beginning of his essay is shown at its close to be a false dichotomy. The informed, psychoanalytically instructed observer "sees" below the surface. Freud joins the world of art as artifact and inspiration in his "creative" role as the psychoanalyst, but only in the most hidden and covert way.

In this essay of 1907 the "creative" individual is also not gender neutral. Young women have more erotic fantasies than do young men, who have in turn more fantasies of ambition. Both must learn to conceal and repress these drives, as they are unacceptable in polite society: "[T]he well-brought-up young woman is only allowed a minimum of erotic desire, and the young man has to learn to suppress the excess of self-regard which he brings with him from the spoilt days of his childhood, so that he may find his place in a society which is full of other individuals making equally strong demands" (SE 9: 147). Human sexuality, the wellspring of "creativity," is initially and more strongly present in the fantasy world of the female. And while these trends merge at some point early in the life cycle, the female is the gender whose fantasies are the more sexualized in their most primitive (i.e., earliest) form.

Thus Freud in this text provides a set of working hypotheses about "creativity." First, that "creativity" has to do with the representation of internal stories in a highly affective and effective manner; second, that "creativity" is parallel to the states of "childhood" and "neurosis," in that it is an attempt to gain control over the real world by creating a fantasy world over which one can have control (and "humor" is the prime example of this control); third, that there is a difference, but also a similarity, between the fantasy life (and therefore the "creativity") of men and of women. All of this is framed by a most ambiguous narrative voice, which claims that the "creative" artist is different than the author of the text that we are reading (this is made evident in the banality of the hypothetical novel that Freud outlines in his essay), yet which draws parallels between his experience and that of the artist both in reality and in the work of art.

Freud is, however, not interested in the problem of "creativity" for its own sake. He sees his explanation of the nature of "creativity" as one of the central proofs for the validity of his science, psychoanalysis. In the programmatic text of 1913, "The Claims of Psycho-Analysis to Scientific Interest," Freud outlines the theory of repression as the key not only to an understanding of the production of the "beautiful" but also as one of the substantial pieces of evidence of the explanatory power (read: scientific validity) of his views. The power of the aesthetic on the viewer is stressed. Freud, however, leaves the door open to yet further meaningful contributions to the understanding of the aesthetic through the science of psychoanalysis:

> Most of the problems of artistic creation and appreciation await further study, which will throw the light of analytic knowledge on them and assign them their place in the complex structure presented by the compensation for human wishes. Art is a conventionally accepted reality in which, thanks to artistic illusion, symbols and substitutes are able to provoke real emotions. Thus art constitutes a region half-way between a reality which frustrates wishes and the wish-fulfilling world of the imagination—a region in which, as it were, primitive man's strivings for omnipotence are still in force. (SE 23: 187–88)

Freud's reading of the work of art is clearly both within the paradigm of late nineteenth-century visual and literary art and, more importantly, still bound by Lombroso's association of the "creative" and the "primitive." But it is not the "primitive" localized in the inhabitants of the asylum or of the prison, the throwback, but the "primitive" within each and every human being. Freud seems to need to associate the "creative" with the universal and with a universal science, psychoanalysis.

What is clear is the basic difficulty of Freud's argument: if sexual repression is the key to "creativity," why are not all individuals who are sexually repressed "creative?" After World War I Freud himself became quite aware of this objection, as he later noted in his study of "Dostoevsky and Parricide" (1928): "Before the problem of the creative artist analysis must, alas, lay down its arms" (SE 21: 177). Or, as he states in his "Autobiographical Study" (1925): "[Psychoanalysis] can do nothing towards elucidating the nature of the artistic gift, not can it explain the means by which the artist works—artistic technique" (SE 20: 70). But I would rather ask the question in reverse. Why is it that Freud's early categories of "creativity" are so constructed to make all human beings potentially "creative?" Why does Freud need to universalize the question of the "creative?" Why does he need to place "creativity" within those sexual drives and psychic phenomena that are, according to Freud, present in all human beings, not merely the "insane?" Why is it the feminine that seems to have the closest relationship to the wellspring of the "creative?" What do "sexuality," "creativity," and "madness" have to do with one another at the turn of the century? Why must Freud still maintain that "creativity" is like "neurosis" in its inherent characteristic of repression?

The meaning of Freud's representation of the "creative," not as Lombroso's "throwback" or deviant but as a reflection of universal processes, can be understood in the context of Freud's role as a scientist and a Jew in *fin-de-siècle* Vienna. We can assume that the question of "creativity" had a special significance for Freud, especially during the period from 1903 to 1910, the period when Weininger's views were most widely circulated and discussed in the culture of Vienna. These views were being read against the more general debates within psychiatry about the special status of Jewish genius.[30] Freud needed to move the question of the Jew's "madness" and the Jew's "creativity" onto another level of debate. What he did was to take the special definition of these concepts and their relationship and make them part of his proof for the universality of the human psyche. Freud's stress on the sexual etiology of all neurosis led to his view that creativity is analogous to neurosis in its repression of conflicted sexual identity. The *fin-de-siècle* subtext which links the creative, the psychopathological, and the sexual to the portrait of the psyche of the Jew, is precisely what Freud was battling—covertly yet agonistically—in his work on the "creative."

Freud's response to this subtext was to separate the question of Jewish "madness" and Jewish "creativity" from the universal laws that he saw as causing psychopathology. These laws are parallel to the laws that determine the "creative." It is not surprising that Freud would focus so much attention on refashioning Lombroso's separate categories of the "normal" and the "abnormal." Unlike the Italian Jew Lombroso, Freud (according to his own account) only first began to sense his "racial" difference from everyone else when he began to study medicine. For him, science and race were linked experiences, and for him it would become a lifelong struggle to separate the two.[31] (Seen in this context, Weininger also offered Freud a major challenge in his view of "Jewish" medicine as a purely mechanistic, materialistic medicine, more chemistry than the art of healing. Jews are not "creative" in the realm of science, Weininger argued, but rather destructive.)

Freud first struggles to show how everyone who is creative or dreams or is "mad" responds to the same, universal rules of psychic organization. Freud's science, the science of psychoanalysis—which evolves over the closing decade of the nineteenth century, while rooted in a materialistic paradigm—self-consciously attempts to move medicine toward an understanding of the dynamic processes of the psyche, the immaterial aspect of the human being. Freud abandons "chemistry" for "metapsychology." This he is constrained to do because of his certainty that human sexuality—associated with the obsessive hypersexuality of the Jews, the very source of their perverse "madness"—lies at the center of human experience. Freud positions himself (more and more successfully as his thought develops after World War I) in opposition to the positivistic clinical gaze of Jean Martin Charcot and the materialistic brain mythology of Moriz Benedikt. His is not the "Jewish" medicine castigated by Weininger and has, therefore, at least the potential to claim a position as "creative." But Freud does not do this unambiguously, as we have seen in his 1907 essay on "creativity." For in openly labelling himself as "creative" he would be labelling himself as a Jew. He would be setting himself off from the universal role of the "layman" (to use his word) as the observer. But he is not the "layman," he is the scientist-physician. And his science must be universal, not particular, in its claims for "creativity." The scientist-physician lays claim to the universal gaze, unencumbered by national or racial perspective—especially in the arena of sexology, where the accusation is that Jews, by their very nature, are predisposed to seeing the sexual everywhere.

Freud thus has the "creative" operate as a reflex of that force which is present in all human beings—sexuality. As we have seen, it was this force that was used to label the Jew as different; for Freud, it now becomes the source of all human endeavors including the truly "creative." That this sexuality is present more in the feminine fantasy than in the masculine, is a reverse-mirror view of Weininger's dismissal of Jews' sexually contaminated "creativity." In fact, Freud reverses all of the poles of Weininger's antisemitic discourse on "creativity," and while he does maintain the link between "madness" and "creativity," he sees these tendencies as a product of universal rather than racial psychology. What is striking in all of Freud's discussions of "creativity" during the period from 1900 to 1919 is that he never cites any Jewish writer or painter—not his contemporary and neighbor, the playwright Arthur Schnitzler, or the best-known German artist of his day, the Impressionist Max Liebermann, or the classic examples of Jewish creativity, Spinoza and Heine—in his discussions of "creativity" and the nature of the "creative." "Creativity" is universal; Freud's examples are not. They self-consciously eliminate the "Jewish" component in European culture.[32]

Freud's work on "madness" and "creativity" in this period was limited by the antisemitic fantasies of *fin-de-siècle* medicine and culture. It was only with the political triumph of the German Nazis in 1933 that Freud openly praised the Jews as a superior people: "[W]hen one thinks that ten or twelve percent of the Nobel Prize winners are Jews and when thinks of their other great achievements in sciences and in the arts, one has every reason to think them superior."[33] In 1938, Freud, writing in a German emigré magazine, directly confronted the question of Jewish creativity. His answer to the rise of antisemitism is a paraphrase of a lost or invented essay reputedly by a non-Jew, in which the contributions of the Jews to the Diaspora are evaluated: "Nor can we call them [the Jews] in any sense inferior. Since we have allowed them to co-operate in our cultural tasks, they have acquired merit by valuable contributions in all the spheres of science, art, and technology, and they have richly repaid our tolerance" (SE 23: 292). "Science," such as psychoanalysis, and then "art" represent the Jews' "creative" contributions to German culture. But each is "creative" and each marks the positive presence of the Jew in European society. The ambiguity of "creativity" in the *fin de siècle* vanished in the harsh light of the Nazi realization of German culture's antisemitic fantasies. Against this terrible reality, Freud no longer spoke indirectly.

In the 1950s there was a continuation of the debate about the meaning of Jewish "creativity." After the Shoah, Silvano Arieti, certainly the most widely influential psychoanalyst after Freud to deal with the question of "creativity," reverses the process.[34] Arieti is fascinated by the relationship between "madness" in its mid-twentieth-century manifestation, schizophrenia, and the "creative."[35] Arieti's interest lies in examining the relationship between Freud's sense of "creativity" as stemming from the primary processes of psychic development, and reflected in the mechanisms of the dream, and the higher forms of psychic organization. For Arieti, the clue to the meaning of "creativity" lies in the psychopathological structures of the schizophrenic, who organizes the world along quite different structures than that of "normal" consciousness: "The seriously ill schizophrenic, although living in a state of utter confusion, tries to recapture some understanding and to give organization to his fragmented universe. This organization is, to a large extent, reached by connecting things that have similar parts in common. Many patients force themselves to see similarities everywhere. In their relentless search for such similarities they see strange coincidences; that is, similar elements occurring in two or more instances at the same time or at brief intervals. By considering these similarities as identities they attempt to find some clarity in the confusion of the world, a solution for the big jigsaw puzzle."[36] As one can see from this statement, Arieti is expanding upon but continuing Freud's model of the "creative."

But there is also an extraordinary subtext in Arieti's corollary to Freud's argument. For Arieti, an Italian Jew whose study *The Parnas* is one of the most moving accounts of the psychological destruction of Italian Jewry, the Jew becomes the prototypical creative individual.[37] Arieti creates a category that he labels the "creativogenic culture" which encourages the innovation of "creativity." Qualities such as the availability of cultural means, openness to cultural stimuli, emphasis on becoming, not just on being, tolerance for diverging views, freedom following repression all provide the matrix for the "creativity." It is of little surprise that for Arieti the exemplary "creative" individuals are the Jews. And the exemplary Jews whom Arieti chooses as his example of the truly creative are the scientists, especially the medical scientists. Like Freud, Arieti tabulates the relationship of "Jewish" Nobel Prizes to "German," "French," "Italian," and "Argentinian" Nobel Prizes and determines that "Jews exceed in all categories with the exception of the Peace Prize, where they are surpassed by the French and the Argentinians. If we examine the five fields in which prizes are assigned, we notice that the greatest Jewish contributions are in the fields of medicine and physics."[38] Of course, no working definition of the Jew can be offered by Arieti, as he rejects any biological definition of the Jew. What he does instead is to construct an ontological category quite similar to that of Weininger, simply reversing the poles of Weininger's argument. For Arieti, the "creative" becomes the Jewish state of mind and the Jew, "creativity" incorporated. But again, it is a specific form of the "creative": it is science and specifically the science of medicine, Arieti's own self-definition.

To contrast Freud and Arieti on the concept of "creativity" is to confront a world in which the question of Jewish particularism is repressed or qualified when "creativity" is addressed and one in which it is celebrated. Both views are answers to the charge that Jews, through their perverse sexuality, are different, "mad," and inherently "uncreative." Today, we have sufficient distance from the wellsprings of this turn-of-the-century debate about the "creative" and its sequels to see how Freud and his followers, such as Arieti, found themselves confronted with a need to provide a rationale for their own "creativity" in their construction of the world. What is the truly "creative" in this context becomes the writing of the scientist in his striving to define the "creative."

In the late twentieth century, "madness" and "creativity" are again closely linked within psychiatry as states that differentiate the voice of the observing scientist from the voice of the observed. But these concepts are now totally deracinated. The contemporary argument, like that of classical Greek or late nineteenth-century medicine, associates the two aspects of the mind through a definition that in some manner sees the mind as a reflex of the body. The most radical example of this epiphenomenalism views the mind simply as a product of the brain, much as bile is a product of the liver. (This parallel is the favorite one of the epiphenomenalists of the mid-nineteenth century, such as the French physician P. J. G. Cabanis.) "Creativity" is thus the state that results from some inherent error in the body of the "genius." Exemplary of the most radical position of this view is the work of Nancy Andreasen and I. D. Glick of the University of Iowa's College of Medicine.[39] In a review-essay published in 1988, they argue that there is a clear relationship between "creativity" and affective illness (particularly bipolar illness [manic-depression]). They do not argue a causal relationship between the act of creation and the presence of illness, indeed noting that creative individuals are most productive when their affective symptoms are under control. But they assume that the "creativity" of the artist is a parallel manifestation of the same underlying genetic error that they postulate as "causing" bipolar illness. Thus, the "creativity" of the artist is a reflex of his/her underlying biology and is closely linked to the simultaneous potential for illness. This view is qualified by K. R. Jamison of the Johns Hopkins School of Medicine.[40] Citing literature from both popular writing on creativity (such as the work of Arthur Koestler) as well as Nancy Andreasen's earlier essays on the relationship between bipolar disorder and "creativity," he sees the cognitive, perceptual, mood, and behavioral implications of "creativity" as analogous to "madness." Jamison's study focuses on a sample of "eminent British writers and artists" in order to study the differences of the experience of "madness" and "creativity" in self-designated "subgroups" (poets, novelists, playwrights, artists) as well as the overall structure of their "creative" experience. This sense of the "creative" is paralleled by him to the nature of the experience of individuals with bipolar illness, and he traces similarities as well as differences. Thus, Jamison sees the seasonal patterns of moods and productivity as potentially similar to but not identical with the hypomanic ("up") state of bipolar illness.[41] A third position is taken by A. M. Ludwig of the A. B. Chandler Medical Center of the University of Kentucky.[42] Unlike most medical writers on this question who are quite detailed in their definition of psychopathology but unable or unwilling to define "creativity," Ludwig attempts first to define "creativity." Relying on the assumptions of the psychoanalytic discourse about "creativity" (but not using it), he sees it tautologically as the structural relationship between the creative individual, the creative process, and the creative product. While he stresses the cultural context of any creative work, he too assumes that all cultures produce works that are "creative." And while not seeing "madness" as a prerequisite for "creativity,"

Ludwig argues that a touch of "madness" can enhance the "creative." All of these papers, had they been written at the end of the nineteenth century, would have evoked another variable in the discussion of genius—race. But to link pathology and race in late twentieth-century psychiatry is still a very tricky undertaking. A search of the medical literature for the past decade turned up no scientific studies with this variable. So we return to the age-old parallel between the creative and the mad, but today without any hint of the racial implications of this theme at the close of the last century.

Notes

Reprinted, with minor stylistic revisions, from Sander Gilman, *The Jew's Body* (New York: Routledge, 1991), chapter 5, by permission of the author and publisher.

1. Werner Sombart, *The Jews and Modern Capitalism,* trans. M. Epstein (Glencoe, Ill.: The Free Press, 1951), 320. On the meaning of the "genius" of the Jew see the detailed exposition by the French historian Anatole Leroy-Beaulieu, *Israel among the Nations: A Study of Jews and Antisemitism,* trans. Frances Hellman (New York: G. P. Putnam's Sons, 1895), 225–62. In refuting the claims about Jewish creativity, he manages to catalogue most of them.

2. Steven Beller, *Vienna and the Jews 1867–1938: A Cultural History* (New York: Cambridge Univ. Press, 1989), 78–83.

3. Houston Stewart Chamberlain, *Foundations of the Nineteenth Century,* trans. John Lees, 2 vols. (London: John Lane / The Bodley Head, 1913), 1: 418. On Freud's reading of Chamberlain see Sigmund Freud, *Gesammelte Werke,* 19 vols. (Frankfurt a. M.: Fischer, 1952–1987), Nachtragsband: 787.

4. Ludwig Wittgenstein, *Culture and Value,* ed. G. H. von Wright and Heikki Nyman (Oxford: Basil Blackwell, 1980), 19.

5. Adolf Hitler, *Mein Kampf,* trans. Ralph Mannheim (Boston: Houghton Mifflin, 1943), 302–03.

6. Arthur Ruppin, "Der Rassenstolz der Juden," *Zeitschrift für Demographie und Statistik der Juden* 6 (1910): 91.

7. Ruppin, "Begabungsunterschiede christlicher und jüdischer Kinder," *Zeitschrift für Demographie und Statistik der Juden* 2 (1906): 129–135. See also Irma Loeb Cohen, *The Intelligence of Jews as Compared with Non-Jews* (Columbus: Ohio State Univ. Press, 1927).

8. See the discussion in Bennett Simon, *Mind and Madness in Ancient Greece* (Ithaca: Cornell Univ. Press, 1978), 228–37.

9. Cesare Lombroso, *Genio e follia* (Milan: Chiusi, 1864).

10. Lombroso, *The Man of Genius* (London: Walter Scott, 1901), 136–37. The German translation, which Freud would have known, is *Der geniale Mensch,* trans. M. O. Fraenkel (Hamburg: Verlagsanstalt und Druckerei Actien-Gesellschaft, 1890).

11. Wilhelm Wundt, *Grundzüge der physiologischen Psychologie,* 4 vols. (Leipzig: Engelmann, 1887), 2: 457.

12. Arthur Schnitzler, *Medizinische Schriften,* ed. Horst Thomé (Vienna: Paul Zsolnay, 1988), 236.

13. Joseph Jacobs, "Distribution of the Comparative Ability of the Jews" (1886), reprinted in his *Studies in Jewish Statistics, Social, Vital, and Anthropometric* (London: D. Nutt, 1891), xlii–lxix.

14. Lombroso, *Der Antisemitismus und die Juden im Lichte der modernen Wissenschaft,* trans. H. Kurella (Leipzig: Georg H. Wiegand, 1894), 43–50.

15. All quotations are from the English translation, Otto Weininger, *Sex and Character* (London: William Heinemann, 1906).

16. On Weininger see my *Jewish Self-Hatred: Anti-Semitism and the Hidden Language of the Jews* (Baltimore: Johns Hopkins Univ. Press, 1986), 244–251; Jacques Le Rider, *Der Fall Otto Weininger: Wurzeln des Antifeminismus und Antisemitismus,* trans. Dieter Hornig (Vienna: Löcker Verlag, 1985); Le Rider and Norbert Leser, eds., *Otto Weininger: Werk und Wirkung* (Vienna: Österreichischer Bundesverlag, 1984); Peter Heller, "A Quarrel over Bisexuality," Gerald Chapple and Hans H. Schulte, eds., *The Turn of the Century: German Literature and Art, 1890–1915* (Bonn: Bouvier, 1978), 87–116; Franco Nicolino, *Indagini su Freud e sulla Psicoanalisi* (Naples: Liguori Editore, n.d.), 103–110; Le Rider, *Das Ende der Illusion: Die Wiener Moderne und die Krisen der Identität,* trans. Robert Fleck (Vienna: Österreichischer Bundesverlag, 1990), 229–58.

17. I am using the term "homosexual" throughout this and other discussions as a reflection of the debates about male and female gay identity within the medical literature of the period. While a number of different terms are used to represent male gay identity (including Homosexual and Uranist), it seemed clearest to reduce these to a single label. See in this context Richard Green, "Homosexuality as a Mental Illness," in Arthur L. Caplan *et al.,* eds., *Concepts of Health and Disease: Interdisciplinary Perspectives* (London: Addison-Wesley Publishing Company, 1981), 333–51; and G. Hekma, "Sodomites, Platonic Lovers, Contrary Lovers: The Backgrounds of the Modern Homosexual," *Journal of Homosexuality* 16 (1988): 433–55; as well as David F. Greenberg, *The Construction of Homosexuality* (Chicago: Univ. of Chicago Press, 1988).

18. See, for example, the discussion in Carl Dallago, *Otto Weininger und sein Werk* (Innsbruck: Brenner-Verlag, 1912); and Emil Lucka, *Otto Weininger: Sein Werk und seine Persönlichkeit* (Berlin: Schuster & Loeffler, 1921), 37–80.

19. Charlotte Perkins Gilman, "Review of Dr. Weininger's *Sex and Character,*" *The Critic* 12 (1906): 414.

20. Le Rider, "Wittgenstein et Weininger," *Wittgenstein et la Critique du Monde Moderne* (Brussels: La Lettre Volée, 1990), 43–65.

21. Kitâro Nishida, *An Inquiry into the Good,* trans. Masao Abe and Christopher Ives (New Haven: Yale Univ. Press, 1989).

22. *Protokolle der Wiener Psychoanalytischen Vereinigung,* ed. Herman Nunberg and Ernst Federn, 4 vols. (Frankfurt a. M.: Fischer, 1976–1981), 2: 351; translation from *Minutes of the Vienna Psychoanalytic Society,* trans. M. Nunberg, 4 vols. (New York: International Universities Press, 1962–1975), 2: 387.

23. All references to this hitherto unpublished essay is to the translation by Dennis Klein, published as Appendix C of his *Jewish Origins of the Psychoanalytic Movement* (New York: Praeger, 1981), here, 171.

24. See my discussion in my *Difference and Pathology: Stereotypes of Sexuality, Race, and Madness* (Ithaca: Cornell Univ. Press, 1986), 175–91.

25. On the question of the history of this tradition see John E. Gedo, *Portraits of the Artist: Psychoanalysis of Creativity and its Vicissitudes* (New York: Guilford Press, 1983); Edward Hare, "Creativity and Mental Illness," *British Medical Journal* 295 (1987): 1587–1589; John Hope Mason, "The Character of Creativity: Two Traditions," *History of European Ideas* 9 (1988): 697–715; Albert Rothenberg, *Creativity and Madness: New Findings and Old Stereotypes* (Baltimore: Johns Hopkins Univ. Press, 1990).

26. Freud, *Standard Edition of the Complete Psychological Works of Sigmund Freud,* ed. and trans. J. Strachey, A. Freud, A. Strachey, and A. Tyson, 24 vols. (London: Hogarth, 1955–1974), 9: 167–76. (Hereafter cited as SE in the text.)

27. In this context see C. M. Hanly, "Psychoanalytic Aesthetics: A Defense and an Elaboration," *Psychoanalytic Quarterly* 55 (1986): 1–22; and D. M. Kaplan, "The Psychoanalysis of Art: Some Ends, Some Means," *Journal of the American Psychoanalytic Association* 36 (1988): 259–93.

28. For a more extensive interpretation see Sarah Kofman, *The Childhood of Art: An Interpretation of Freud's Aesthetics,* trans. Winifred Woodhull (New York: Columbia Univ. Press, 1988).

29. See the discussion by Janine Chasseguet-Smirgel, *Creativity and Perversion* (New York: W. W. Norton, 1984) on the relationship between object relations theory and "creativity."

30. Wilhelm Hirsch, *Genie und Entartung: Eine psychologische Studie* (Berlin: Coblentz, 1894).

31. In this context see Maurice Olender, *Les Langues du Paradis: Aryens et Semites—un couple providentiel* (Paris: Gallimard, 1989).

32. See the discussion of Freud's idealization of non-Jewish intellectuals in Peter Homans, *The Ability to Mourn: Disillusionment and the Social Origins of Psychoanalysis* (Chicago: Univ. of Chicago Press, 1989), 88–95. The American-Jewish psychoanalyst Abraham Aron Roback did address this question in an early, popular paper, "The Jews and Genius," *American Hebrew* 40 (1919): 532, 576–78.

33. Joseph Wortis, *Fragments of an Analysis with Freud* (New York: Jason Aronson, 1984), 145.

34. Beginning with his essay "New Views on the Psychology and Psychopathology of Wit and the Comic," *Psychiatry* 13 (1950): 43–62, to his major study *Creativity: The Magic Synthesis* (New York: Basic Books, 1976), Silvano Arieti's work focused on this question and the, for him related, question of the nature and meaning of schizophrenia.

35. See my discussion of the history and meaning of schizophrenia in *Disease and Representation: Images of Illness from Madness to AIDS* (Ithaca: Cornell Univ. Press, 1988).

36. Arieti, *New Views of Creativity* (New York: Geigy, 1977), 7.

37. Arieti, *The Parnas* (New York: Basic Books, 1979).

38. Arieti, *Creativity: The Magic Synthesis,* p. 327–28. The slipperiness of this undertaking can be judged by examining Armin Hermann, ed., *Deutsche Nobelpreisträger* (Munich: Heinz Moos, 1978), where the "Jewish" prize winners are suddenly "German" prize winners. The ideology behind both of these categorizations is clear.

39. N. C. Andreasen and I. D. Glick, "Bipolar Affective Disorder and Creativity: Implications and Clinical Management," *Comprehensive Psychiatry* 29 (1988): 207–17.

40. K. R. Jamison, "Mood Disorders and Patterns of Creativity in British Writers and Artists," *Psychiatry* 52 (1988): 125–34.

41. There is a psychoanalytic parallel to these discussions: André Haynal, *Depression and Creativity* (New York: International Universities Press, 1985). On the present state of the discussion of the psychology of "creativity" see Robert J. Sternberg, *The Nature of Creativity: Contemporary Psychological Perspectives* (New York: Cambridge Univ. Press, 1988) and Albert Rothenberg, *Creativity and Madness: New Findings and Old Stereotypes* (Baltimore: Johns Hopkins Univ. Press, 1990).

42. A. M. Ludwig, "Reflections on Creativity and Madness," *American Journal of Psychotherapy* 43 (1989): 4–14.

Criminality and Poe's Orangutan: The Question of Race in Detection

Nancy A. Harrowitz

Edgar Allan Poe's "Murders in the Rue Morgue" is widely considered to be the first detective story: a kind of primal text. Millions of detective story aficionados have Poe to thank for the establishment of a fictional detective tradition through this story. It contains formal elements now widely recognized by critics as crucial to the genre: the discovery of a body, the search for the murderer, and the following up of clues as the abductive method behind that search. Poe's story is what is called a "locked room" type of mystery as well, as it is not clear how the killer could have escaped from the still-locked chambers where the murders took place.

This mystery is, however, much more than a combination of formal elements of a new genre. It establishes some important connections between a burgeoning literary genre of detection and the interest in the controlling of "dangerous elements" in society. These concerns are expressed in this same time period through the development of the discipline of criminology and through the development of biologically based theories about race. Dupin's "solution" to the mystery betrays, moreover, an important subtextual anxiety not only in reference to matters of race but also gender issues.

In his essay "Homer's Contest," Nietzsche analyzes the concept of struggle or agon and how it functioned for the early Greeks. At the beginning of the essay, he uses the contrast between "natural" and "human" as a way of addressing essential questions of civilization and how savagery is controlled in society. His valorization of the notion of the agon as the way in which the Greeks controlled baser impulses and encouraged poetic inspiration leads to a statement quite pertinent to an understanding of detective fiction. Nietzsche claims that just as "the concept of Greek rights evolved in truth from *murder* and from atonement for murder, so does the nobler culture also take its first victory wreath from the altar of atonement for murder."[1] The agon can be seen as the process that mediates between savage impulses (which can mean murder) and civilization (as the expiation of murder and the restoration of social order). Detective fiction is the text of the agon played out to its most extreme, requiring both a rupture in the social order (the murder) and its rectification (the solving of the crime). The binary opposition between civilization and savagery that Nietzsche develops through the agonistic concept can best be understood through an examination of the specific cultural context in which we find this struggle. Poe's first detective story gives us such a hermeneutic opportunity, both because of its primacy in the detective genre and because of the racial tensions often found in American Renaissance fiction.[2] The cultural scenario found in Poe's story, therefore, not only establishes a model for the agonistics of detective fiction as a budding genre but also invokes some specific historical tensions of America in the early 1840s.

In the story set in Paris, two women are found hideously murdered: one is partially dismembered, the other shoved up a chimney. The search for the perpetrator—a classical element in detective fiction for which this story is the progenitor—ends in a half-comical, half-serious discovery of an orangutan as the murderer. Is this somehow a parody of the genre before the genre even exists? Does this genre contain within itself the elements of its undoing? Is Poe teasing the mystery reader with his story and, if so, in how many ways?

Beginning with a long disquisition on the specific kind of analytical powers the detective must have in order to be able to "see" the evidence clearly and to put it into a meaningful framework, Dupin proclaims:

> But it is in matters beyond the limits of mere rule that the skill of the analyst is evinced. He makes, in silence, a host of observations and inferences. The necessary knowledge is that of *what* to observe. . . . The analytical power should not be confounded with simple ingenuity; for while the analyst is necessarily ingenious, the ingenious man is often remarkably incapable of analysis.[3]

The importance of the mind is unequivocally established through the hierarchy of analysis that Dupin postulates. The story places tremendous emphasis on the ability of the detective to use analytical powers, and its significance is carefully explicated by Dupin. In fact, we see in this section an outright intolerance and disdain for most detective methods because the reasoning behind them is not of the "right" kind, and Dupin obsessively returns to this point throughout the story. The rivalry between the prefect of the police and Dupin begins here and is played out in the famous "Purloined Letter," the second text in Poe's detective story trilogy.

Once all this has been established in the first part of "Murders in the Rue Morgue," we see just how high the stakes have become for "correct" reasoning on the part of the detective. The eventual unravelling of the mystery thus takes on that much more importance: can the *results* live up to the *reputation* of the *method?* Dupin's method appears highly serious: yet can the eventual identification of an orangutan as the perpetrator exist on this same plane of gravity?

Dupin's solving of the crime, that is, his identification of the orangutan as the murderer, is already significant for what it says about his method and for several other reasons as well. Let's look at how he actually solves the crime. Poe's eccentric detective conducts an investigation and discovers that all of the witnesses who overheard the crime as it took place are convinced that one of the languages they heard from the room was not their own: in other words, the Spaniard thought it was French, the Frenchman thought it was Russian, and so on. Part of Dupin's ratiocination regarding his hypothesis as to the killer's identity is based on the linguistic assumptions made by the witnesses:

> The witnesses, as you remark, agreed about the gruff voice; they were here unanimous. But in regard to the shrill voice, the peculiarity is—not that they disagreed—but that, while an Italian, an Englishman, a Spaniard, a Hollander, and a Frenchman attempted to describe it, each one spoke of it as that *of a foreigner*. Each is sure that it was not the voice of one of his own countrymen. Each likens it—not to a voice of an individual of any nation with whose language he is conversant—but the converse. . . . Now, how strangely unusual must that voice have really been, about which such testimony as this *could* have been elicited! (Poe 211–12)

Largely from this bit of linguistic information, Dupin theorizes that a non-human, an animal, must have done the killing, as its speech was not recognizable, was not, in other words, indigenous to Europe. Dupin entertains the possibility that the killer could have been a non-European in the following way: "You will say that it might have been the voice of an Asiatic—an African. Neither Asiatics nor Africans abound in Paris; but, without denying the inference, I will now merely call your attention to three points. The voice is termed by one witness as 'harsh rather than shrill.' " It is represented by two others to have been "quick and *unequal*.' No words—no sounds resembling words—were by any witness mentioned as distinguishable" (Poe 212).

Based on his analysis of the witnesses' reaction to what they heard, Dupin comes up with the hypothesis that a particular kind of orangutan has committed the crime. He believes as well that this animal is owned by a visiting sailor from a Maltese ship, and that the animal is still on the lam. In order to flush out the sailor, discover more about the crime, and prove his hypothesis, he places a notice in the paper advertising a found orangutan, meets the sailor and elicits from him a full confession that corresponds in every detail to Dupin's hypothesis. A perfect example of ratiocination or abductive reasoning that Dupin demonstrates in the first part of the story? Not exactly, for the question of foreign language is still unresolved. Those three points, cited above, that Dupin mentions as responses to his interlocutor's presumed objection regarding the possibility of the presence of an Asiatic or African, do not in fact answer that objection; there is no reason to suppose that the witnesses would have been able to recognize words from either an Asiatic or African language. The fact that these utterances seemed quick, unequal, and harsh does not exclude the possibility that they belonged to a language with which the witnesses were not familiar; indeed, this is precisely the supposition of the witnesses themselves!

The evidence that Dupin considers in his solving of the crime can be divided into two categories: linguistic, based on the reports of witnesses who tell what they heard, and material. Once Dupin has decided that the first category of evidence leads him to a non-human perpetrator, the linguistic is left behind in the story and a search for empirical information on the animal-like nature of the beast is undertaken. The material evidence is considered by Dupin in ways that continue to reveal his cultural agenda. He examines the bodies and discovers fingerprints and a tuft of fur upon one of them. Dupin uses the work of the naturalist Cuvier to narrow down his animal suspects, as he employs Cuvier's description of the digits of the orangutan. The narrator, serving as Dupin's foil, confirms Dupin's hypothesis regarding the animal identity of the murderer.[4] The narrator relates:

> It was a minute anatomical and generally descriptive account of the large fulvous Ourang-Outang of the East Indian Islands. The gigantic stature, the prodigious strength and activity, the wild ferocity, and the imitative propensities of these mammalia are sufficiently well known to all. "The description of the digits," said I, as I made an end of the reading, "is in exact accordance with this drawing. I see that no animal but an Ourang-Outang, of the species here mentioned, could have impressed the indentations as you have traced them. This tuft of tawny hair, too, is identical in character with that of the beast of Cuvier." (Poe 218)

This primitive form of fingerprinting, fifty years before Francis Galton's work on the subject, demonstrates the importance of the material clue and shows as well a link between the animal and monstrosity because the very size of the ape's paws and "fingers" intimidates Dupin's interlocutor. Dupin uses this pseudo-fingerprinting technique to test his hypothesis about the identity of the perpetrator further.

In examining the importance of fingerprinting, we should remember that detective fiction developed partially as a result of a concern regarding the new phenomenon of larger urban areas that were undergoing a process of refinement and topographical categorization when, for example, street addresses were beginning to be used for the first time. Works such as Baudelaire's essay on the figure of the *flâneur* and Poe's story "The Man of the Crowd" demonstrate the increasing anxiety generated by large uncontrolled urban areas. Criminology was in part an attempt to understand what happened to certain individuals living in the city setting and how their crimes could be understood. And the capacity for tracking and thus containing these criminals became of the utmost importance. The tracking itself takes place within the realm of both the hereditary (e.g., Cesare Lombroso, the influential Italian criminologist, and his theory of the born criminal) and the physiological, in other words the capacity to read material bodily clues such as fingerprints. Lombroso's attempts to pinpoint physically the born criminal, to identify an anatomically defined human type, represent these anxieties regarding the importance of recognizing and potentially containing the criminal. In the work of Francis Galton, however, we see these interrelated issues come together.

Galton, who was Darwin's first cousin, coined the term *eugenics,* which he defines in the following way: "Eugenics is the science which deals with all influences that improve the inborn qualities of a race; also with those that develop them to the utmost advantage."[5] He believed that hereditary factors were of the utmost importance in determining the future direction of a society, and so the control of heredity was a task that society should take on.

Although not the first to come up with the idea of fingerprints, Galton was responsible for developing a systematic study of fingerprints (1892) that made them potentially useful to police forces. His reasons for developing fingerprinting as a science were, however, linked to his eugenics program: he hoped to show a connection between individuals and their race and possibly the inferiority of certain races. Eventually, however, Galton had to admit defeat because even though, as he says, "the impressions from Negroes betray the general clumsiness of their fingers, their patterns are not, so far as I can find, different from those of others." We do not have to look very closely at this statement to see that Galton's logic is suspect. If in fact the impressions "betray the general clumsiness of their fingers," Galton would have evidence of the racial difference that he sought; yet Galton admits that the patterns do not demonstrate any such difference. Impressions and patterns are not the same: impressions, as Galton uses the term, refer to the marks left by the fingers when pressed onto the surface, and the patterns are the resulting whorls and swirls. Because Galton cannot connect the patterns with racial differences, he displaces the difference he is convinced must exist onto impressions. His observation about the impressions from Negroes is a racist assertion, a culturally informed belief, generated by his own conclusions about difference where none exists; and in fact, it is one not borne out by his own research.

The issue of presuppositions in scientific research is crucial in the concerns about identity that Galton raises in his analysis of why fingerprints are useful. Galton quotes from an abstract of remarks made by M. Herbette, Director of the Penitentiary Department of the French Ministry of the Interior: " 'To fix the human personality, to give to each human being an identity, an individuality that can be depended upon with certainty, lasting, unchangeable, always recognisable and easily adduced, this appears to be in the largest sense the aim of the new method.' "[6] In her analysis of the role that Galton's fingerprinting plays in Mark Twain's novel *Pudd'nhead Wilson,* Susan Gillman claims that "like any other 'natural' index of the self—race or gender, for example—fingerprints point toward the culture that appropriates nature as the basis of socially constructed identities."[7] The question of cultural identity is played out in the digits of the orangutan in Poe's story as well: even though Poe's story was written a generation before the work of Lombroso and Galton, it nevertheless resonates with the culture of criminology developing at the time. In fact the cultural knowledge possessed by the detective informs the abductive reasoning that takes place in the story. Charles Sanders Peirce's logical category of abduction, which is essentially the method Dupin uses in the first "mindreading" scene of the story and later in his creation of the hypothesis, is based upon the notion that a consideration of general truths, laws of nature, or personal experience can lead to the formation of a hypothesis.[8] In the mind of Dupin, who is influenced by cultural attitudes and stereotypes, the homicides were the work of an exotic monster; yet his clues (large hands and a tuft of fur) do not necessarily point to an orangutan from the East Indian Islands. In reading this story and pondering the concerns Poe raises regarding nature and civilization, we must keep reminding ourselves that this story was written more than a decade before the appearance of Darwin's evolutionary theories: a reminder that literary culture and science inform one another. The notion of a "socially constructed" identity furnishes perhaps the first real clue in understanding what Poe's story is all about, as we examine carefully the jumps in Dupin's logic, from unrecognized language (which then becomes a nonhuman monstrous utterance) to a tuft of fur and large digits (which are transformed into an orangutan).

Before the "real" identity of the perpetrator can become clear, however, we must examine the significance of the ape more closely because it is what the orangutan ultimately represents that provides another clue about the *cultural,* as opposed to "natural," identity of the monster.[9] He is described as tawny, furry (some fur he leaves behind provides one of the clues), violent, and, it would seem, he possesses a sense of craftiness, as he leads his master on a wild chase through the streets, pausing long enough so that the sailor almost catches up, then taking off again.

But this is only the beginning of the story of the representation of the animal. "Aping" as a cultural strategy is called into question in the simultaneously humorous and grotesque scene—*serio ludere*—the sailor narrates of discovering the "ape" aping his master shaving: he finds the orangutan with his face lathered up and a razor in one paw. This aping is monstrous because it is through this action that the orangutan discovers the razor-as-weapon he will later use to murder the two women. Moreover, the act invites us to consider whom the "ape" is aping when he kills and dismembers the two women. Dupin's explanation falls short. The orangutan swings boldly through the window, attempts to shave one of the women, and goes into a murderous rage when she resists. The bodies are discovered in unnatural positions, which emphasizes the horror of the act and the horrible agent of the act of murder, the perpetrator. And there is another important element present here: the ape is certainly aping by attempting to shave, but *whom* is he trying to shave and ultimately murder? A woman. The first victim protests against being shaved; and at this point, the orangutan, imitating a human act, slits her throat: "[W]ith one determined sweep of its muscular arm it nearly severed her head from her body." The orangutan takes on distinctly human characteristics when the sailor discovers him at the murder scene: "The fury of the beast, who no doubt bore still in mind the dread whip, was instantly converted into fear. Conscious of having deserved punishment, it seemed desirous of concealing its bloody deeds, and skipped about the chamber in an agony of nervous agitation" (Poe 222).[10] The orangutan's "fury" presents him as an emotional, sentient, and calculating creature. The pun fury/furry associated with the description of the ape leads us to ask not only *whom* is the ape aping but *what* it is aping.[11] Is he aping murderous activity directed toward a female, an activity that is singularly human, or is he imitating a random and banal human action gone awry because he is aping imperfectly? The very anthropomorphizing of the ape that takes place in the story leads us in the direction of the former, even while Dupin addresses the latter. The imitative act of shaving emphasizes the ape's human qualities; but what separates beast from man is excessive hair—fur, in the case of the ape, who tries to remove it through shaving. This raises the possibility that the beast is not only trying to imitate his master but in some sense *become* his master as well.[12] When we consider the orangutan as a double for his master, the sailor in port, the meaning of Poe's choice of an orangutan as the perpetrator becomes clearer.[13]

The name orangutan itself means "wild man of the forest in Malay,"[14] and it is certainly the wildness of this strange "man" that Poe is after, whether or not he was conscious of this etymology. The nature of the crime points to a hidden story within this story, one about which Dupin seems blissfully ignorant but about which the reader becomes increasingly aware. Leo Lemay claims that a clue to the meaning of the story is found in three tropes at the end that refer to a mind/body dichotomy, suggested by Poe throughout the story. Lemay postulates that the reader interprets the account as a sex crime:

> The narrator does not use our modern terminology and say that the murderer must have been a psychotic sex maniac—but that is clearly what he (and every one reading the story for the first time) must think. Poe deliberately creates this impression. . . . Dupin repeatedly suggests that the crime must have been committed by a sex maniac. He asks the narrator if he "had observed anything *'peculiar'* at the scene of the atrocity." The narrator finds "something in his manner of emphasizing the word *peculiar* which caused me to shudder." When we read the narrator's reaction, we too shudder at the peculiarity of the crime. (Lemay 177)

Lemay's convincing argument does not, however, take into account the foreign-language question, nor does it fully engage the question of the perpetrator's "cultural" identity. Let us take another look at the foreign language issue, which will provide more clues about the identity of and meaning behind this perpetrator.[15]

What is compelling about Dupin's emphasis on the importance of foreign language in his investigation is his simultaneous refusal to consider the importance of his *own* indigenous language, namely, the clues furnished by the crime journal accounts of the murders. Lemay points out that the recurrence of the word "drawers" in the account of the story encourages the reader to suspect a far different type of crime than the one that the seemingly innocent Dupin wildly imagines. In one instance "drawers" is mentioned three times in a single paragraph, ostensibly to refer to a chest of drawers that had been rifled through in the women's apartment. By paranomastic association, however, their underwear is conjured up at the same time through this repetition. Dupin himself is complicitous in the setting up of the paranomastic structure: "drawers" is repeated three times as he recounts his hypothesis to the narrator. He has, seemingly unwittingly, picked up and simultaneously ignored this clue found in the journal narrative.

The story identifies difficulties inherent in language (specifically foreign language) in another way, through a purported difficulty of translation. At a certain point, the narrator says: "I have said that the whims of my friend were manifold, and that *je les ménageais:*—for this phrase there is no English equivalent"

(Poe 210). Yet there is an English equivalent ("I indulged [his whims]"): so why is an essentially false translation problem set up? At another moment in the text, the narrator interjects an editorial remark in the middle of the newspaper account of the crime: "Many individuals have been examined in relation to this most extraordinary and frightful affair. [The word 'affaire' has not yet, in France, that levity of import which it conveys with us]" (Poe 204). Stephen Peithman informs us: "Affair as a romantic intrigue dates back to 1702. The French prefer *affaire du coeur*" (Poe 204, n. 54). Once again, a translation is imagined where none exists: the wordplay between "affair" and *affaire* draws the reader's attention to the sexual undertones addressed by Lemay. The wordplay emphasizes the thorniness and semantic unreliability of foreign language. A structure of linguistic impediments has been created in support of Dupin's linguistic itinerary. His hypothesis about foreign language thus constitutes a crucial part of his theory about the murders.

Information about the crimes is presented in two ways: through Dupin's own investigation and through journal accounts of the crimes. Dupin misses or suppresses the clues found in the journal rendition and pays attention only to his own evidence, a symptom of the systemic blindness that allows him to ignore the very details that disturb the reader. One of his prime pieces of evidence supporting the hypothesis that the monkey did it lies in Dupin's discovery of a broken nail embedded in the window sill of the crime scene. The police had seen this nail as a whole nail. The broken nail gives the appearance of being whole and of serving its function of keeping the window shut. By all appearances, the orangutan could not have used the window as a means of egress. The locked room is, however, not really locked: the solution to the crime lies in the discovery of this broken nail, duly embedded in the window but unable to keep it shut. The false nail and the false translation problem function as red herrings in the story, diverting attention from more serious questions about the identity of the perpetrator, questions that the reader senses but does not fully understand.

The blindness that causes Dupin to conclude that orangutans abound on the streets of Paris more than their racially suspect counterparts, Africans or Asians, is compatible with another logic:

one that shuns the possibility that this is not a geographically exotic and logically impractical perpetrator that we are dealing with but instead the garden variety white male pervert easily found at home. This perpetrator would rifle through dresser drawers, looking for another kind of drawers, and would commit atrocities against women. Language therefore both *does* and *does not* furnish evidence for Dupin: or rather it is the narratology of language that he willfully ignores. Language is thus reduced to a marker of difference, and is seen as exotic and potentially out of control, rather than recognized for its ability to convey information through subtleties such as syntax and structure. The story presents the conflict between our view of different civilizations and our desire to identify scapegoats. It is far easier for Dupin to imagine a runaway orangutan, a wild man of the forest, than face the truth about "sexual" relations at home: the agonistics of violence against women. His approach is really rather childlike in its naiveté: the theory of the monstrous ape he develops is the product of a child's imagination.

Dupin's assumptions shed light on the "second story," the untold account of the two women victims, who are not allowed to speak for themselves but are instead represented solely through this hideous crime.[16] Dupin's apparent blindness to the sexual implications of the crime reveals another subtext that has become the focus of intense critical concern since Lacan's "Seminar on the Purloined Letter." Blindness and vision, the hidden and the open, are of utmost concern in this story, the second of Poe's detective trilogy; the two Dupin stories need to be read against each other in order to appreciate fully the ramifications of blindness suggested by the story. Dupin theorizes about the detective method once more before he begins his investigation, and describes it in terms of visual ability: "Vidocq, for example, was a good guesser, and a persevering man. But, without educated thought, he erred continually by the very intensity of his investigations. He impaired his vision by holding the object too close" (Poe 209). Dupin further hypothesizes about the importance of peripheral vision as the vision that sees the most. The use of Dupin's oblique, sidelong vision leads him to a marginalized, farfetched conclusion regarding the perpetrator. What John T. Irwin calls "the paradox of analytic self-inclusion, of absolute self-consciousness, that lies at the heart of Poe's detective stories" (13), together with Dupin's false structures of linguistic and visual knowledge, calls attention to an essential problem here: Dupin's unshakeable belief that he is in full control of the information available to him and that the itinerary of his thought is one that unfailingly heads in the right direction. "Murders in the Rue Morgue," while simultaneously theorizing the precise nature of this analytical power in the first part of the story, undoes the effectiveness of analysis through the creation of a subtext over which Dupin lacks vision or control. It is through the strategy of suppressed knowledge that this subtext functions.

This strategy tends, as Lemay's discussion of drawers suggests, to operate through linguistic clues that the reader is able to see but Dupin is not. Let us, for instance, ponder the significance of the words "advert," "convert," and "pervert." Dupin uses the word "advert" when describing his own mental processes in putting together clues and "solving" the mystery: "Let me now advert—not the whole testimony respecting these voices—but to what was *peculiar* in that testimony. Did you observe anything *peculiar* about it?" (Poe 211) "Advert," or to "turn one's attention to," is intimately related to "convert," or *convertere,* to turn about, turn in character or nature. This process can be used to describe the colonialist's attempt to overcome difference by converting the subjected other. And finally "pervert," a relation of the first two, is derived from *pervertere,* to turn round or about, turn the wrong way, overturn, turn to error or ruin. Dupin adverts to what was "peculiar," the conversion of difference, while failing to discover the pervert, who turns out to be among or even part of our very selves, in other words, indigenous.

Dupin's reasoning in the story is not only highly suspect but blind as well to its own shortcomings. He claims that Asiatics and Africans "do not abound in Paris," as a response to the narrator's query regarding the possibility that the perpetrator speaks a non-European language. Dupin assumes that there has to be some sort of population of the group in question to make their purported presence a logical possibility. Now, this assumption of course throws into some question Dupin's own hypothesis about the orangutan as perpetrator since it then suggests that orangutans *do* abound in Paris; this notion is implicitly behind his belief that the crime was committed by an orangutan. So we are still left with a puzzle after Dupin has answered so quick-wittedly the main puzzle of the text, i.e., the whodunit. The puzzle is, instead, "whosaidit" or "whydunit." Why does Poe choose an orangutan as the "perp," to use modern police lingo? Why an enormous orangutan, after setting up so well the conditions under which members of other races or religions (or gender) were understood in the xenophobic culture of the nineteenth century? And why would an orangutan commit a crime like this? Could it be that Poe is transferring a cultural anxiety regarding the perceived murderous, monstrous capacities of "foreigners" onto a naturalistic anxiety regarding ferocious animals? And what would the stakes be in such a displacement? It might be tempting to write off Dupin's faulty reasoning as yet another example of farfetched detective fiction, but, as we have seen, clues in the story itself point to a far more complex scenario.

A further examination of both sailor and pet and their relationship, elucidates some of the questions that this tale generates. We are told that the sailor is from a Maltese vessel. Dupin makes this observation even before the sailor's arrival on the scene through the discovery of the sailor's hair ribbon left at the scene of the crime, which was knotted in a fashion peculiar to the Maltese. The threat of the exotic that the orangutan represents is further explored in the account of his owner, the sailor. The sailor is both French and emphatically not French, as he comes from a Maltese vessel. The significance of this last fact becomes clear in looking at the history of Malta and its relationship to colonizers, both actual and would-be.[17] The Maltese islands have a long history of domination by various European powers. They were historically perceived as on the way to the far-off lands of Asia and Africa, yet belonged at the same time to the Europeans. While marginal in geographic terms, they were considered centrally and strategically located by various powers because of their usefulness as a military base in the Mediterranean. The Maltese islands do not include French as one of their indigenous languages: in fact, the absolute contrary is true, as the Maltese successfully rose up against Napoleon when he tried to impose French as the official language after his takeover in 1798. The sailor thus becomes a figure for a kind of reverse colonization: he speaks

French, yet is employed on a Maltese vessel, where French would not have been spoken. As a sailor, he is in a subordinate position on this ship which suggests the failed colonization of Malta by the French. This last point is emphasized by the fact that his hair ribbon is knotted in a Maltese way: his dress has to a certain degree conformed to the dominant culture aboard ship.

But there is another, perhaps more burning linguistic question regarding the sailor, whose French (the "gruff" voice) was recognized as such by most of the witnesses. Why does the sailor speak French to the orangutan? This too is a clue regarding the special identity of this ape: it is as if the sailor believes the orangutan understands French, is himself indigenous. In fact, their linguistic interaction is described as "two voices in loud and angry contention" in the journal account. The sailor and the ape thus share a simultaneous indigenous/nonindigenous status: both exotic and Other, both familiar and at home. Both are identified with the indigenous pervert to whom the murders are attributed. They also share a propensity to mimic. The sailor apes the fashions of the Maltese in his hair ribbon, and the ape apes the "master" shaving, and the darker side of human behavior that this shaving ultimately signifies. There is a connection between them as well in the very clues they leave behind: the sailor's ribbon is used to contain his hair, and this ribbon is left behind at the scene of the crime; and the orangutan leaves behind fur that he attempted to shave off in order to mimic the civility of his master.

The fact that the ape's master is a sailor has an importance beyond the sailor's association with geographical slippage. While sailors were often treated as slaves themselves, this particular sailor is a would-be master who, however, cannot control his property. His would-be slave, his uncontrollable exotic pet, first apes his shaving and then takes complete possession of the razor. Traces of the nineteenth-century Gothic obsession with the exotic and with monsters are evident in the portrait attributed to Cuvier of the violent, ferocious, enormous ape whose "imitative propensities" are well known. The text provides evidence of another nineteenth-century preoccupation: the concern with containing those elements of society that seem to defy control—whether they are criminals, women, or members of another race or religion. Or murderous orangutans, for that matter, who are figures for xenophobic fear of the outsider: the Asian or African. "Asiatics or Africans" exist in the story as a subtextual set of imaginary perpetrators; they nevertheless represent a real danger. A link between the orangutan and the imaginary perpetrators, who are characterized by racial otherness, is suggested by the narrator's description: "This tuft of tawny hair, too, is identical in character with that of the beast of Cuvier." The word "tawny" was used to refer to brown-skinned people throughout the nineteenth century.[18]

Dupin's point, made in the story through his own incoherence on the subject of foreign language and through his own inability to read journalistic clues, is that homicidal orangutans, Asiatics, and Africans are in some way interchangeable. They all speak the language of difference—unrecognizable to "civilized" Europeans. Dupin sets up geographical boundaries for his concept of what civilized language is, and these boundaries do not extend farther east than Russia or farther south than Spain. He excludes all other human possibilities beyond these geographical limits, as if they did not and could not exist in the fictive world he has created. Geography works as another kind of marker in this text: just as the orangutan stands in for the absent, yet present threat to society by the racial other, Paris is made to stand in for Baltimore. The text includes another displacement: the not completely French sailor stands in for the French.

Poe's specific choice of an orangutan is a surrogate, an imitation of those all-too-human "foreign" groups who, because they live among us, are potentially more threatening than the unrestrained orangutan. Evidence of the orangutan's association with cultural difference, as opposed to just "wildness," lies in its "imitative propensities." The "ape" is able to ape not only the shaving action of his master but also violent human behavior through the act of murder. His aping brings to the surface cultural anxieties about the incomprehensible behavior of the "foreigner"—who is often portrayed as mimicking the behavior of the society in which he or she lives.[19] He is able to stand in for his human master and serves as a vehicle of displacement for the stereotype of the oversexualized Other, in this case the African or Asian. The ape is also the atavistic model for the human, although Darwin's model of evolution appears years after Poe's story.

The orangutan's exotic language alienates him further from the larger European community. The marginalization of a criminal is achieved by exposing his difference from the community. The non-indigenous condition of the orangutan shows a broader concern with cultural difference, even while Poe undermines this by having the sailor speak French to him. The language of difference, in this case displaced onto the animal "language" of the orangutan, is thus found in what is akin to a "primal scene" story of the detective genre. The language of the indigene underscores the potential threat that this outsider, found at home and purportedly able to understand the language of home, represents.[20]

Another tale by Poe, "The Narrative of Arthur Gordon Pym," sheds further light on his view of race relations and how these relations might be figured in his fiction. In that story, the dichotomy between "natives" and "white men" is set up in such a way that their respective physical environments mirror the irreconcilable split between the worlds of the native and the would-be colonist. Poe takes here the black/white dichotomy to absurd extremes: the notion of white or black as a cultural and physical threat is found to reside not only in human beings but in objects themselves. In "Murders in the Rue Morgue," where Poe refuses to refer directly to a race crisis, he instead displaces this tension from species to species, rather than from race to race. And his mechanism for doing so consists of the virtual suppression of knowledge, both sexual and racial, by the detective whose method claims the contrary. The orangutan, according to Lemay's analysis, is a stand-in for violent sexuality, but what Lemay does not take into account is another side of the orangutan's cultural identity, a racial one.

"The Murders in the Rue Morgue" can thus be read as paradigmatic on several levels. Not only is it ostensibly the first "true" detective story, but it introduces some chilling concerns about difference and its perceived perniciousness that become a subtext in the genre of detection because of this genre's close affiliation with the development of criminology. It is not only the threat of a sexual crime that Poe is covering up here, nor only the untold story of the two women. Through his figuring of the orangutan as criminal, Poe is also alluding to a crime of racial proportions and a culturally defined perpetrator. The sexual dimensions of the story only highlight the prevalent stereotype of the oversexualized criminal, especially the one associated with racial alterity. By setting up duplicitous structures of understanding for the detective, which cover up the racial tensions I have discussed, the story unsettles the same epistemology of detection that it establishes as reliable and which has been adopted ever since as indispensable to the detective genre. The exploration of the relationship between the savage and the civilized in Poe's story is, then, representative of agonistic conflicts on several fronts. Detective fiction, as we see in the case of Poe's story, can function as a testing ground for theories regarding race, sexuality, and the interactions of these two categories through a displacement of "reason" onto xenophobia.

Notes

1. Friedrich Nietzsche, "Homer's Contest," this volume, 37.

2. For a discussion of ideological issues within American Renaissance fiction, see Sacvan Bercovitch and Myra Jehlen, eds., *Ideology and Classic American Literature* (New York: Cambridge Univ. Press, 1986).

3. Edgar Allan Poe, *Annotated Tales,* ed. Stephen Peithman (Garden City, N.Y.: Doubleday, 1981), 199.

4. Peithman points out how incorrect this portrait that Poe gives of the orangutan is: "The male orangutan stands about four-and-one-half feet tall and weighs about one hundred fifty pounds. It has long arms, used for swinging from tree to tree, and is a shy, peaceful vegetarian—a most unlikely candidate for the violent perpetrator of the two murders" (Poe 218, n. 92).

5. Francis Galton, "Eugenics: Its Definition, Scope and Aims," *Essays in Eugenics* (New York: Garland, 1985), 35.

6. Galton, *Finger Prints* (New York: Da Capo, 1966), 169.

7. Susan Gillman, " 'Sure Identifiers': Race, Science and the Law in *Pudd'nhead Wilson,*" *Mark Twain's Pudd'nhead Wilson: Race, Conflict, and Culture,* ed. Susan Gillman and Forrest G. Robinson (Durham: Duke Univ. Press, 1990), 100.

8. For a discussion of the role of Peircean abduction in detection and more specifically in the first part of "Murders in the Rue Morgue," see Nancy Harrowitz, "The Body of the Detective Model: Charles S. Peirce and Edgar Allan Poe," *The Sign of Three: Dupin, Holmes, Peirce,* ed. Umberto Eco and Thomas A. Sebeok (Bloomington: Indiana Univ. Press, 1983), 179–97.

9. Orangutans are not, biologically speaking, apes. My use of the word "ape" to refer to Poe's orangutan underscores the similarity in the figurative usage of both. Poe himself uses the two terms interchangeably in the story.

10. J. A. Leo Lemay, "The Psychology of 'The Murders in the Rue Morgue,' " *American Literature* 54.2 (1982): 165–88, has also noted this superimposition of human traits onto the animal.

11. My thanks go to Alan Rosen for pointing out this pun to me and for his thoughtful suggestions and comments on my reading of this story.

12. I am grateful to Virginia Jewiss at Dartmouth College for discussing this point with me.

13. See Lemay for further discussion of the orangutan as a double for the sailor.

14. John T. Irwin, *The Mystery to a Solution: Poe, Borges and the Analytic Detective Story* (Baltimore: Johns Hopkins Univ. Press, 1994), 65.

15. Lemay concludes that the two women have created the chimera of the sex pervert murderer through their own fear of sexuality. This conclusion seems to me not only off-base but in fact undermines his entire analysis of the women as a lesbian couple.

16. Cynthia Jordon, "Poe's Re-Vision: The Recovery of the Second Story," *American Literature* 59.1 (1987): 1–19.

17. For more information on this topic, see Brian Blouet, *The Story of Malta* (London: Faber & Faber, 1967), and Sir Harry Charles Joseph Luke, *Malta: An Account and an Appreciation* (London: Harrap, 1960).

18. See the Oxford English Dictionary.

19. For example, one of the principal arguments against the assimilation of Jews in Germany in the late nineteenth century was the perceived impossibility of this enterprise, based on the notion that Jews could not assimilate fully, could never become "real" Germans as their differences (posited as both "racial" and cultural) were too great. If complete assimilation was not achievable, then the uncomfortableness of difference would still be felt; ergo, it was better to have the Jews move away and leave Germany to the *Volk*.

20. For a discussion of how language works to identify and isolate, albeit in a different context, see Sander L. Gilman, *Jewish Self-Hatred: Antisemitism and the Hidden Language of the Jews* (Baltimore: Johns Hopkins Univ. Press, 1986). One of the points that Gilman makes is that Jewish language was seen as reflective of cultural behavior as well.

III Agonal Aesthetics and Narrative Theory

> What a problem unfolds for us here, when we ask about the relation of contest to the conception of a work of art!
>
> Nietzsche, "Homer's Contest"

"A Chain of Utmost Potency": On the Agon and the Creative Impulse

John A. McCarthy

> Is it reasonable to assume a purposiveness in all the parts of nature and to deny it to the whole?
>
> —Immanuel Kant, *Idea for a Universal History*

I. Unitary Science

The role of human creativity within the "morphogenetic" framework provided by the dynamic, ever-changeful universe in which humankind exists stands at the center of the following reflections. This chapter also deals with metascientific efforts to establish a unity of science, not just in terms of a unity of idiom shared by the disciplines but in more encompassing terms of a unity of laws in the sciences and humanities, in natural and social phenomena. This broad perspective thus contributes to the development of an ideal, all-encompassing system that has been labelled "unitary science."[1] Critical to the concept of unitary science is the feasibility of an interconnected, universal set of laws running through the various subsets of disciplinary knowledge. Central to my present argument, therefore, are: 1) the acceptance of the notion of unitary science as a *working hypothesis;* and 2) the viability of microreduction.[2] To see my argument as a contribution to the literature on the hierarchical "Great Chain of Being" would be a mistake. The difference between the "Great Chain of Being" and a "most potent chain" is analogous to the difference between classical Euclidean geometry with its principle of periodicity and Benoît Mandelbrot's fractals with their asymmetricality.

This paper draws upon the arguments of Paul Oppenheim and Hilary Putnam for the unity of science as "an alternative to the view that it will eventually be necessary to *bifurcate* the conceptual system of science by the postulation of new entities or new attributes unrelated to those needed for the study of inanimate phenomena" (411). Oppenheim and Putnam present evidence that would suggest that it is not at all necessary to separate the life sciences from the physical sciences. Using their argument of structural uniformities within the natural sciences, I argue that there are infrastructural similarities between the sciences and the humanities. The point of convergence is the notion of agonistic creativity.

While Oppenheim and Putnam posit unitary science as the ultimate goal of cumulative microreduction, "complete microreduction"—which involves identifying empirically the lowest common denominator of existence (417)—is of little concern here. Concepts of virtual particles or DNA are of limited use as analogies of creativity, if they are seen as mere products of nature. However, if the focus is on the dynamics of interaction within elementary particles or strings of DNA (or for that matter, superstrings), the value of the model increases exponentially. Oppenheim and Putnam's interest in microreduction as a tool for understanding what holds the nucleus together and how DNA passes genetic codes on is comparable to the aesthetician's or philosopher's interest in the workings of creativity itself.[3] The shift in focus, therefore, is from the ordered *natura naturata* to the dynamically evolving *natura naturans*.

It would be misleading to conceive of this paradigm in terms of the standard universe-as-clock-metaphor, which has dominated scientific thinking since the sixteenth century. Oppenheim and Putnam's cumulative microreduction might bear resemblance to Pierre Simon de Laplace's belief that a single mathematical formula will eventually be able to explain the workings of the universe, but they do not seem as confident as he was of finding rational order at the end of their own reductionist journey. For present purposes it is important to note their belief in an evolutionary connection between inorganic and organic matter, such that any discontinuity between the two spheres is essentially superficial (Oppenheim and Putnam 418–20).

A corrolary between the questions of scientists and those of philosophers readily presents itself. The philosopher's "what is truth?" is echoed by the physicist's fascination with what holds the universe together and the biologist's query, "when does life emerge from inorganic matter?" While the question is formulated differently in the two camps, each group has set itself the goal of fathoming the essence of reality. That essence would appear to be the nature of creativity itself. Problematic for both scientist and philosopher is the nature of the relationship between subject and object, between experience and imagination. They have not always been able to agree upon what is real. Thus, Werner Heisenberg concludes that the old Platonic question of what is real presents itself to the biologist eyeing desoxyribonucleic acid: is the double-stringed bundle of information contained in DNA really the living organism, or is it only the form of inner chemical reactions?[4] A similar question arises for the physicist working in elementary particle theory who wonders: "Are these smallest units really the building blocks of matter or are they only mathematical representations of symmetrical groupings according to which all matter is constructed?" (Heisenberg 324). Such queries point beyond the entropic conception of the universe as a clock by inviting us to consider how the cosmos functions without loss of energy.[5] These responses, resultant of precisely controlled research in the natural sciences, prompted Heisenberg to see a parallel between the scientist's and the philosopher's or poet's quest for an understanding of reality. Consequently, the journey into the inner world of appearance has disclosed "a chain of utmost potency" rather than a hierarchical chain of being for scientist and humanist alike. The cultures of hard science and moral science are bound together in a common search for the fundamentals of creative activity. The quotation in the title of this paper is designed to underscore the agonal tension as fundamental to creativity both in the scientific and the artistic realms.

II. Expanded Middles

Quite tellingly, the "Prologue in Heaven," which provides the metaphysical framework for Faust's adventures, opens with dominant metaphors of light and sound in reference to the workings of creation:

> The sun sings as it sang of old
> With brother spheres in rival sound,
> In thunderous motion onward rolled
> Completing its appointed round.
> The angels draw strength from the sight,
> Though fathom it no angel may;
> The great works of surpassing might
> Are grand as on Creation day.[6]

Traditionally, the image has been interpreted as a reference to the Pythagorean notion of spheric harmony resulting in a kind of divine music that has accompanied Platonic thought through the ages. Yet Goethe seems to emphasize more the contentious nature of the interaction rather than any harmonic confluence. (Perhaps because he is also following the Book of Job?) The revolutions of the sun and its kindred stars create a din of sounds in contention with one another, a competition repeated with each new day as if each day were a new beginning. While the sight is awesome, not even the higher intelligence of angelic beings is capable of fathoming these "incomprehensibly grand works" *(unbegreiflich hohen Werke)* that are as impressive as on Creation day. In other words, the periodic rotations of the sun and stars, while apparently mirroring the previous day's rounds, might be seen as a code for agonistic creativity itself, since the movement is caused by contending forces and gives rise to a "din" of sounds rather than to harmonic chords. From self-duplicating movement a whole cacophony of divergencies results. Dare one think in this regard of the infinite variety that results from the self-duplication of desoxyribonucleic acid in living organisms or from elementary particles in inorganic matter?

The allusion to agonistic motion on the grand scale of things (as well as in microreductionism) is brought out more clearly in the lines:

And swift beyond conception flies
The turning earth, now dark, now bright,
With clarity of paradise
Succeeding deep and dreadful night;
The sea in foam from its broad source
Against the base of cliffs is hurled,
And down the sphere's eternal course
Both cliff and sea are onward whirled.
And storms a roaring battle wage
From sea to land, from land to sea,
And forge a chain amid their rage,
A chain of utmost potency. (F 1. 251–62)

An image of the earth turning on its axis, alternating between brilliant light and deepest night, is followed by a picture of the incessant assault of the raging sea on the brazen cliffs impeding its path. Both potent images are bundled together as the entire scene is rendered as a projectile hurtling through endless space, caught up in eternal combat with the elements. The extraterrestrial as well as the terrestrial mirror and condition one another involuntarily in a process of mutual (re)creation. They constitute, as the final line indicates, "a chain of utmost potency." It is a potency that emphasizes the interconnection of the cosmic and the human; each movement is not an isolated instance but a part of an evolutionary whole.[7] Goethe would thus appear to shift the emphasis from harmonic interplay to agonistic contention.

It is a potency for self-creation, that is, for "becoming what one is," whether one thinks of mountains rising from the plains driven by elemental forces, the growth of the oak tree from the acorn, or the development of the human being. More generally: it is the potency for the world to evolve even if the outcome of the evolution is uncertain. Heisenberg answered his own query about the goals of science and art by suggesting "that at the conclusion of the trip neither life nor the world is to be found but rather understanding and clarity concerning the ideas which order the world" (325).[8]

By endeavoring to force his forming will on the formless and wily sea, Faust constructs his coastal empire along the interface of that which is (formed) and that which is not yet (formed). Ultimately he comprehends the nature of that chain of utmost potency, envisioning a ceaseless struggle of a bonded yet free people through the ages. The insight into the agonistic quality of human existence in ceaseless contest with elemental forces causes him to remark that if he could experience such a chain of free yet enslaved activity, he would experience ultimate satisfaction. The conditional nature of the remark escapes Mephisto, who believes their contract now concluded.

However, the attentive reader does not overlook the ambivalence inherent in the prospect of a race of people seeking to exert control over the controlling forces of nature in an endless sequence of action and reaction *(Wirkung, Gegenwirkung).* The agonistic forces evident in creation would appear to be identical to the agonistic creativity prerequisite to the land reclamation project envisioned by Faust. The final scenes of *Faust II* continue the imagery of this dynamic interplay. Their mystical flavor has long fascinated Goethe scholars, who have wondered how Faust's heaven could ever be a state of rest? Goethe's God would have to be the eternal self-realization of the fundamental energy of the universe in localized time and space, or what Alfred North Whitehead calls the "eternal accident of creativity" (Böhm 38–39, 59). The deity at the end of Faust's journey into the inner realm would thus appear to be self-creative "actual entity" and simultaneously self-creative "actual event" (Böhm 46), that is, both individuated instance and process.

Despite all the evidence of struggle, however, it seems inappropriate to define agonistic creativity solely in terms of *agonistikos,* that is, as the art of winning or prevailing, even if Faust's actions seem to fit this model. Of relevance in this regard is Goethe's own assessment of natural forces in his essay, "Nature" ("Die Natur"), penned in 1783 for the *Tiefurter Journal:* "One abides by her [nature's] laws even when one resists them; one cooperates *with* her, even when one desires to act *contrary to her*" (SA 11: 8; Goethe's emphasis). Harold Bloom, on the other hand, sees the creative agonist as locked in a struggle for dominance through usurpation and displacement.[9]

While the agonist denotes a competitive or "divergent" individual, it also connotes cooperation or "convergence." For example, in the field of medicine, "agonist" refers to one of a pair of coordinated muscles that together give rise to a movement counterpoint to that of the antagonist. Thus cooperative effort between two muscles counteracts the intruding, "antagonistic" force (much like the chain of humans cooperatively challenging the assaults of the sea in *Faust*). Moreover, "agonist" is etymologically related to *agonos,* the designation of a non-angular line (*a-gonia* = without angle) as well as one of two lines on the earth's surface, along which the direction of the magnetic needle is truly north and south—in other words, that point at which opposites are conjoined and arbitrarily labelled north and south (or in the moral realm: good and evil).

Equally striking is the fact that "agnostic" belongs to the same word family as *agon, agone,* and *agonistikos.* Originally used to designate an opponent of the official Christian church in North Africa in late antiquity, "agnostic" now also incorporates the sense of not knowing and not being able to know last things. Thus "agonist" would specify a particular intellectual attitude that is not strictly and merely oppositional in the sense of "antagonistic" nor in the sense of lines at right angles to one another, nor in the simple sense of a straight line without variation to either side. Rather "agonist" implies a kind of mirroring and convergence of overall movement without reduction into mere mechanical repetitive motion. While the agonist "thrives" on tension, it is an effort to coordinate dissonant structures rather than to dominate through displacement or usurpation.

An analogy to the processes observable in high-speed accelerators presents itself here: colliding particles give rise to other particles that are not necessarily smaller than the ones smashed. What in reality occurs is not the microreduction of the smashed particles but rather the creation of new particles from the kinetic energy of the particles thrown into direct "combat." In this connection, the notion of separation or of dominance loses its conceptual value and calls for "a new, broader way of thinking" (Heisenberg 324–25). Modern chaos theory offers such a "new" way of conceptualizing, although it really is a throwback to a point prior to the rise of reductionist science with Kepler, Galilei, Descartes, and Newton. *Agonos* and *agonistikos* might then be likened to the phenomena of unpredictability and strange attractors as posited in contemporary chaos theory. But more about that later.

III. Thinking Aside

Goethe addressed this new, broader way of thinking in *Faust* as well. Along with the metaphor of creation in the "Prologue in Heaven," great significance is attached to the game of numbers in the play. In the scene between Mephisto and the prospective scholar, traditional logic is mocked as a mechanical, fruitless exercise:

> Then comes the philosopher to have his way
> And proves things have to be his way:
> The first being so, the second so,
> The third and fourth are so-and-so;
> If first and second were absent, neither
> Would third and fourth be present either. (F 1. 1928–32)

Such thinking will produce no great insights since self-absorption can hardly spark creative associations.

In the scene, "Witch's Kitchen," this notion of sterility is expanded upon when the witch recites her "one-times-one":

> This must ye ken!
> From one take ten;
> Skip two; and then
> Even up three,
> And rich you'll be.
> Leave out the four.
> From five and six,
> Thus says the witch,
> Make seven and eight,
> And all is straight.
> And nine is one,
> And ten is none.
> This is the witch's one-times-one! (F 1. 2540–52)

Such mathematical wizardry has puzzled readers for centuries, causing many to respond with Faust: "I think the hag's in fever and delirium" (F 1. 2553). Faust, of course, assumes that words uttered are framed by referentiality. Mephisto refers to this human penchant when he remarks: "Man has a way of thinking, when he hears a word, / That certainly behind it lies some thought or other" (F 1. 2565–66). Yet Faust fails to grasp the witch's meaning because he discerns no frame of reference. If one exists, it is radically different from his accustomed one. His is a language of human self-consciousness (a recent innovation in the total history of the universe), whereas hers seems primordial in its lack of discernible referentiality.[10] The witch's chaotic world transcends the linear logic of Faust's thinking up to that point, even as the image of the ever-agonistic struggle along the irregular sea coast metaphorically anticipates the creative agonism of the rejuvenation scene with its turbulent bubbling of heated fluids, wild activity, smashed globes and crown (symbols of order), and mirroring of Faust's inner turmoil in the spectral image of a seductive woman. Each symbol externalizes the transformation Faust is undergoing in the scene. Thus it marks a significant paradigm shift in Faust's conception of the world; it is the temporal and spatial point at which he begins to live life fully.

With the absence of a ready frame of reference, disciplinary logic is transformed into gibberish for the conservative or "convergent" thinker. The witch remarks to Faust who is as much perplexed by the various actions in the room as by her words:

> The lofty force
> Of wisdom's source
> Is from the whole world hidden.
> Once give up thinking,
> And in a twinkling
> It's granted you unbidden. (F 1. 2567–72)

These lines express the core of Faust's conversion from mechanistic Newtonian science to a new tension-filled way of thinking. The straight flow of mechanical energy through pulleys, ropes, and gears is replaced by the untidy turbulence of the thermal energy of eros and heated ambition. Faust's previously methodical inquiry becomes free flowing, seemingly random. In his subsequent experiences, Faust learns of the need to reorient radically his thinking. Instead of laboring further under the delusion that he can achieve ultimate knowledge through orderly self-directed microreduction, he allows himself to be moved by the deep structures of existence themselves, i.e., by the impulses common to the internal and external worlds. While Faust earlier sensed the limitations of traditional means of scientific inquiry, his mental reorientation is fully effected in the "deconstructive" witch's kitchen, itself a powerful metaphor of creativity. The scene is necessary for the dangerous game the Lord and Mephistopheles had earlier agreed upon to be played out. While the Lord functions as a kind of *agonarch* (that is, a judge or overseer), Mephisto assumes the role of an *agonothete* (or supervisor in the games of contest). Not simple binary logic but the complex agonistic forces beyond the conventional dualism of "good" (the Lord) and "evil" (Mephisto), subject and object, mind and body, become the key factors in Faust's development. Faust is, of course, unaware of these contending impulses and the wager between the Lord and Mephisto as he undergoes the creative process of "deconstructing" and "reconstructing" his being.

The contending forces metaphorically present in *Faust* are equally manifest in Goethe's scientific and philosophical thinking throughout the gestation period of the play. Agonal dialectics are at the heart of his theoretical musings on the nature of scientific investigation as well as of his world view in general. His theoretical "The Experiment as Mediator between Object and Subject" ("Der Versuch als Vermittler von Objekt und Subjekt" [1797]) distinguishes, for example, between two essential methods of inquiry. One he labels mathematical, the other—which he says is "of a higher art"—requires a different way of thinking (SA 11: 33). Because the latter bears resemblance to an open, inquiring stance, I will label it "essayistic."[11]

The mathematical method Goethe criticizes is an iterative, self-referential system of inquiry, which focuses on individual phenomena and trusts implicitly in an objective and reliable relationship between the perceiving subject and the analyzed object. It is a closed system of individually identifiable parts that the perceiving subject pieces together like an erector set so that its demonstrations of evidence are really just "recapitulations" of a theorem rather than brand new arguments (SA 11: 34). Of greater interest to Goethe in this essay are "the more fundamental forces and elements" of nature *(die gemeinern Kräfte und Elemente)* that are caught up in an eternal struggle between action and reaction *(Wirkung und Gegenwirkung)*. It is the interweaving of these fundamental agonal forces that gives rise to the whole, for "in living nature nothing occurs which is not bound by the whole" (SA 11: 31–32). Goethe's sympathy lies with this latter method of inquiry, for it seeks to understand how individual phenomena interrelate in a dynamic system. Human observations, however, are limited to surface phenomenon. This is especially true of living organisms, whose vital operations occur beneath the surface and, in fact, require a covering (which is forever changing) in order to be vital. That appears to Goethe to be a fundamental "principle of organization."[12] Thus, Goethe is not confident that the search for the inner secrets of reality can be comprehended because, as he adds, "the disproportion between human understanding and the nature of things reminds us in timely fashion that no individual is capable enough of bringing any endeavor to closure" (SA 11: 33).

The thought is reminiscent of Goethe's notion in "Oration on Shakespeare's Name Day" ("Rede zum Shakespear-Tag" [1771]) of the mysterious middle-point that holds all phenomena together and gives the human as well as the cosmic world a sense of unity while constantly evading the piercing gaze of the inquiring mind. Obviously, there is also a parallel here to Faust's search for the fulcral point of the universe in the sign of the macrocosm or its unifying energy in the Earth Spirit. In order to approach a measurement of that unity in the biological realm, for example, Goethe recommended taking a protracted, polyperspective view to assess the nature of organic development (SA 11: 22f.). Goethe clearly preferred the "essayistic" method of analysis to the "mathematical" one, whether in literature or in scientific inquiry.

In a response to critics of his *Theory of Color* entitled "On Mathematics and its Misuse" ("Über Mathematik und deren Mißbrauch" [1826]), Goethe underscores what he considered to be the misuse of mathematical inquiry as practiced in his day. He laments the tendency to reduce mathematical inquiry to exact calculations and disavows the equally dominant tendency to overspecialize, which leads to a distortion of the true relationship of the parts to the whole. Citing d'Lambert, Goethe asks: "Is that person who states that 2 × 2 is 4 more knowledgable than the person who is content to say that 2 × 2 is 2 × 2?" (SA 11: 79–80). The latter equation summarizes precisely Goethe's criticism of the growing, self-absorbed disciplinarity of the mathematical sciences that privilege the part over the whole.[13] Advances in mathematics have led to an abuse of the method of inquiry itself; namely, the loss of a sense of the whole and the estrangement of the part through a process of self-referentiality (SA 11: 85).

To Goethe's mind, mathematics is essentially a guild system (SA 11: 92) that expresses a simple idea in an increasingly complicated manner, to no other purpose than to underscore the growing complexity of the formulations themselves. The complexity takes on a life of its own, so to speak, and surface play displaces the essential unity of the whole. Because of the loss of an encompassing view, he is skeptical that any real advance has been made. $2 \times 2 = 2 \times 2$ is essentially Goethe's way of saying that $(12,4 + 3,4) + \times = 24,2 - 2$ or that $27 \overset{=}{<} 3^x \overset{=}{>} 81$ (and these are, of course, still very simple equations). What this self-referentiality does is to obscure the reality of multiple perspectives in constant flux. Using the analogy of intertwining and expanding geometric figures each of which contains an endless series of points on the circumference, Goethe argues against the paucity of perspective in the mathematical sciences of his day (SA 11: 88–89). For his part, he claims the "right to observe, study, and understand nature without the aid of mathematics in its simplest, most secret impulses as well as in its most striking phenomena" (SA 11: 78). This he has chosen to do from his earliest youth. He thus eschews the self-referentiality of mathematical thinking as an abuse. In fact, anything that becomes an end in itself *(Selbstzweck)* is an abuse. In a companion piece, "More on Mathematics and Mathematicians" ("Ferneres über Mathematik und Mathematiker"), Goethe describes mathematicians as "strange people" who "promoted themselves as a universal guild and refuse to acknowledge anything that is not calculable within their system" (SA 11: 100; cf. 11: 252). There would appear to be a parallel between Goethe's critique of the mathematician's self-satisfied arrogance, the perplexing witch's "One-Times-One," the exhortation: "Once give up thinking, it's granted you unbidden," and Nietzsche's later rejection of the Cartesian episteme *(cogito ergo sum)* with its incumbent notion of a single, self-contained, and directive thinking subject.

Without wishing to push the comparison between two such unlikely partners as Goethe and Nietzsche too far, I might chance another parallel between the dangerous game involving Faust and Nietzsche's own perception of life on the edge as the "most dangerous game."[14] Both would seem to concur, moreover, that the accurate assessment of any "truth" would have to factor in the relative time-spatial coordinates. And certainly Nietzsche was not unsympathetic to the Goethean view that the "kinetics of life," as Karl J. Fink recently stated, are to be found in the "intensified middle, on the borders between opposition . . . [and] at the joints of nature."[15] One is reminded here of Nietzsche's insistence on a "total economy of life" (BGE #23) and his skepticism toward a "continual falsification of the world by means of numbers" (BGE #4).

IV. Quanta of Energy

While Goethe never relinquished his optimism in the teleological movement of nature and humankind's participation in that evolution, Nietzsche reacted sometimes desperately in promoting the self as a means of warding off the emptiness of a purely chaotic universe. This difference is perhaps best captured by the two thinkers' divergent conceptions of the individual psyche. Goethe considered it to be wholly natural that the perceiving subject relates all experiences of the external world to him/herself, because individual self-consciousness is produced by the encounters with the world.[16] For Nietzsche, the self and the notion of self-consciousness became problematic. He doubted that the individual is the " 'measure of all things' " and mistrusted the value of self-consciousness, suggesting that even the reflective thinking of philosophers is secretly driven by instincts (BGE #3). The individual is no longer seen naively as unified and in control of his/her perceptions, Nietzsche contended curtly: the individual is a mini-chaos of instincts and emotions that follow no preset pattern. The rejection of classical epistemology with its clear-cut relationship between self-directing subject and reified object proved immensely liberating for Nietzsche. But even for Goethe the problematizing of the assumed separateness of subject and object meant that human potential would evolve more fully, precisely because of that collision of natural and moral forces. For Nietzsche, the denial of a telos and its incumbent apparatus of moral directives forced the individual even more dramatically into taking responsibility for creating her/his own value systems. In the human being Nietzsche saw emphatically an uneasy union of the created and the creator (BGE #225). For Nietzsche, "only a philosophically skeptical life allows that degree of freedom required for great artistic work."[17] Here, Nietzsche's dictum easily comes to mind: " 'I no longer believe in anything'—that is the correct way of thinking for a *creative person.*"[18] Goethe, of course, continued to believe in nature.

Nietzsche's " 'I no longer believe in anything' " seems to be an echo of the witch's "Once give up thinking, / And in a twinkling / It's granted you unbidden" (F 1. 2570–72). What might that connection be? On the one hand, the loss of theological belief, on the other, the seeming demise of any fixed, enduring center of referentiality. Trust in a universal telos has vanished. Not believing in anything would thus translate into an absence of predictability and specific goal orientation beyond that of the individual will. Faust gives up science for the full experience of life unfettered by inherited presuppositions of what must be; he shuns pedantic scientific analysis in favor of intuitive, creative energy. Nietzsche's free spirit renounces all attachments (BGE #41, #44).

Ultimately, Nietzsche valued art as the full expression of life, rejecting art when it declined into mere iterative self-deception designed to make life and knowledge bearable.[19] While its therapeutic value remains intact—e.g., "Art exists *so that the bow shall not break*"[20]—the real significance of art lies much deeper. That profundity resides in its essentiality as cipher or code. Nietzsche saw the world as a text (BGE #34, #38, #47). And all attempts to interpret that essential text of life, whether philosophically or artistically, reproduce the ciphers in altered fashion. They recreate the text, albeit not in the same iterative way as the mathematicians satirized by Goethe. Nietzsche even claims in his writing that each interpretation tends to obscure the original "text" of life by imposing human order on it. Humans, in other words, recreate the world in their own image.

In *The Gay Science,* Nietzsche reformulates the fundamental mathematical equation of 2 × 2 as follows: "*One times one.—*

One is always wrong, but with two, truth begins.—*One* cannot prove itself, but two cannot be disproved" (GW 12: 196, #260). The reformulation occasions a shift from the notion of static monism to that of a productive dialectic. In this context, artistic creativity might then be equated to the agonistic vitality of organelles, that is, of biological life processes themselves, since they are iterative, but not exactly so. The scientific paradigm shift could then be expressed in artistic terms: Prometheus Bound is displaced by Chaos Bound.[21] In either context, the strongest entities (ideas, sentiments) survive in a combative system of natural selection.

The key to Nietzsche's activity as philosopher-poet is the effort to constitute his own self repeatedly by controlling and perhaps converging the large number of powerful and conflicting tendencies evident in the human being. Style, for Nietzsche, as Alexander Nehamas suggests, "involves controlled multiplicity and resolved conflict."[22] Nietzsche himself spoke of "contention" *(Kampf)* as the "father of everything good." Even polished prose is possible only as a result of the ceaselessly contending forces between the poetic and the prosaic (GW 12: 120, #92). The goal of all that effort and the stamp of one's particular creative style is essentially becoming what one is. "Becoming what one is" is due in part to the delusion of self-determination, in part to external circumstances beyond the individual's (or artist's) control. Here, Nietzsche seemingly gestures at the need to conflate those evolutionary and cataclysmic forces of creation that Goethe had ascribed respectively to Thales and Anaxagoras (*Faust II* 1. 7855–56).

Central to Nietzsche's notion of creativity is the concept of energy. He wrote, for example, "A quantum of energy is just such a quantum of instinct, will, action: more, it is nothing other than exactly this instinct, will, action" (GW 15: 304, #13). In his notes for the project *The Will to Power,* he urges us to imagine the "world as a certain measure of energy" and as containing a "certain number of energy points" (GW 19: 373, #1066). The world runs through an innumerable number of possible combinations of these points of energy in a process of eternal return of absolutely identical series. Yet Nietzsche resisted the notion of eternal return as something purely mechanical; if it were mechanistic, the process would come to a state of final rest *(Finalzustand)*

and this, he argues, has not happened. Thus he stresses that his concept is incomplete and hypothetical.

The scientific reductionist would have us believe that the world is not simply mechanical because of the ability of each "point of energy—and not just man—" to construct the world from its own point of view. That individual perspective provides a variable that prevents exact periodicity (GW 19: 106, #636). The full expression of this *Kraftcentrum* is the will to power in all its manifestations that are opposed to a mechanical interpretation of cosmic and psychic movement. In *The Will to Power,* Nietzsche uses the term *Machtquanta* to expand upon his critique of a mechanistic world view, arguing that there are no natural laws, no causal relationships, just ventings of energy that carry their own consequences with them. Then he explains:

> A quantum of energy is characterized by the effect that it has and the resistance it encounters. Moral indifference plays no role here, although it might be conceivable. In essence, it is the impulse to coerce others and to defend itself against coercion. It is not a matter of individual survival, for every atom impacts upon the entirety of existence. Existence disappears when this emanation of will to power is eliminated from the concept. That is why I call it a quantum of "will to power," for it embodies that trait which is essential to the mechanical order which it characterizes. (GW 19: 103–04, #634)

Nietzsche's metaphorical language saliently expresses the nature of the agonistic forces at play in the universe. The essence of organic and inorganic matter is the energy that dances about each individual element, binding all together in a tense union of opposites, each opposing force seeking to exert its strength. Again in *The Will to Power* he states:

> And do you know what the "universe" is to my mind? Shall I show it to you in my mirror? This universe is a monster of energy, without beginning or end; a fixed and brazen quantity of energy that grows neither bigger nor smaller, does not consume itself, but only alters its face. . . . It is . . . energy everywhere, the play of forces and force-waves, at the same time one and many, agglomerating here and diminishing there, a sea of forces storming and raging in itself, forever changing, forever

> rolling back over incalculable ages to recurrence with an ebb and flow of its forms, producing the most complicated things out of the most simple structures; producing the most ardent, most savage, and most contradictory things out of the quietest, most rigid, and most frozen material, and then returning from multifariousness to uniformity, from the play of contradictions back into the delight of consonance. . . . this, my Dionysian world of eternal self-creation, of eternal self-destruction, this mysterious world of twofold voluptuousness; this is my "Beyond Good and Evil," without aim, unless there is an aim in the bliss of the circle. (GW 19: 373–74, #1067)

The dominant image in this passage—which could easily have drawn its inspiration from the opening image in Goethe's *Faust*—is striking as a succinct summary of the various aspects of the agonistic forces that make creativity possible. Nietzsche locates those self-sustaining and constant forces, moreover, at the center of the universe. Turbulent energy appears here as that which holds the universe together, that which causes life, and gives rise to the ever-changing forms of existence. Consequently, Nietzsche's quantum-universe and mankind's actions in it take place beyond "good and evil"; that is, beyond human value judgments and outside the pale of traditional binary thinking. Nietzsche's universe, then, is the product of a new way of thinking advocated by Goethe, by Heisenberg, and by anyone desirous of breaking through the bonds of disciplinary, compartmentalized thinking to a quasi-mystical view of the interconnection of all existence. Only on the surface are the disciplines of physics, biology, ethics, etc. individuated. Underlying everything is vibrant energy, itself an artistic process. What Nietzsche suspects of chemical transformations in inorganic nature, would seem to be applicable to other manifestations of quanta: "Chemical transformations in inorganic nature are perhaps artistic processes as well" (GW 6: 19).

V. Autopoietic Chaos

The grand union of the multiple contending and coexistent tendencies addressed in the preceding can be explained further in terms of deterministic chaos.[23] The term itself, "deterministic chaos," is oxymoric: "deterministic" means controlled to the nth degree; "chaos" means totally unpredictable. Conjointly they describe the operations both of the universe and of the creative mind: out of the hidden structures of chaos new order emerges. Regulated chaos in this sense would thus seem to define the relationship between the agon and creative activity.[24]

The connection between creativity and chaos or the relationship between absolute freedom and absolute determinism also seems evident in the function of human memory. Gregor Morfill and Herbert Scheingraber ask rhetorically why would humans have memory if the world were absolutely deterministic, unresponsive to human input? Human memory allows us to change the sequence of events. And if humans did not have this ability to provide "feed-back" to the cosmos, then having memory would be useless. Consequently, the world is neither deterministic (that is, absolutely predictable); nor is it purely chaotic (that is, totally unpredictable). "Could it not be," they ask, "that the human brain is the way it is because the world is chaotic?" (55). Their meaning is that human beings do not appear to be mere playthings of chance. Humans are capable of actions and reactions just like other interactive forces within the universe, but with one distinctive difference: humans do it (supposedly) consciously and willfully. Perhaps human beings are like the unstable neutrinos released in particle smashing that are apparently not yet realigned?

The single, fundamental assumption underlying modern chaos theory is that each and every individual phenomenon "is most decidedly part of a collective process" (Briggs and Peat 231). It is a process of continual recreation, of *autopoiesis* (self-creation), or, if you will, of becoming what one is. (The faint allusion to eighteenth-century notions of *Bildung* a là Goethe, Herder, and Kant is intended.) The wholeness of the individual parts is mirrored in the appearance of so-called "strange attractors," deep structures that coordinate aperiodically the agonistic forces in the universe.[25] At the heart of chaos theory is thus the notion of the essential creativity of biological, ecological, and cosmological energy, apparently unlimited in its potential, but not wholly accessible to the searching mind because its reproductions are never exact.[26] Scientists no longer assume the direction of development and are uncertain of the future, since present circumstances are an unreliable basis for prediction (Morfill and Scheingraber 55). Instead, Werner Heisenberg's Uncertainty Principle now tends to hold away.[27] If God plays dice, humankind would not know it. And it does not really matter.[28]

In *Does God Play Dice?* (1990), Ian Stewart rightfully warns his reader about going overboard and seeing in chaos the grand theory to end all theories. He does not believe in grand theories that solve everything. Yet he does believe in the importance of intuition as a helpful tool in the hands of the scientist (310–13), and scientists seem to be moving intuitively toward unitary science. It does not matter that the intuitive feeling is subjective, since the subject is also part of the entire scheme. Moreover, Stewart stresses the role of mathematics as the mother of modern chaos theory, averring: "Chaos came out of Mathematical Imagination, sired by Physics" (292). The physics part refers to quantum mechanics as advanced by Werner Heisenberg and Max Planck; the mathematical part refers to Poincaré's differential equations rather than to arithmetic iteration. Each arose in reluctant opposition to the dominant view of the day.

In keeping with the metaphor of scientific revolutions as earthquakes, one might say that chaos theory is not a sudden reshaping of topography, but rather the gradual accumulation of tension that eventually destablizes the terrain. Thus chaos theory was present long before it was recognized as a revolutionary paradigm. Similarly, Henri Poincaré's calculations lay fallow for fifty years until Edward Lorenz rediscovered him. Someone somewhere in the distant past knew about the hot topics (of science) today in one sense or another (Stewart 297).

This notion of dynamic complexity is a long way from the concept of a stable "great chain of being." The geometry advanced now is not the linear kind of mathematics to which Goethe strongly objected. Rather it is a non-linear means of measuring complex, multi-dimensional phenomena. Ernst Cassirer argued that a movement originated with Leibniz, leading "from mere geometry to a dynamic philosophy of nature, from mechanism to organism, from the principle of identity to that of infinity, from continuity to harmony."[29] Principles of non-linear dynamics evolved that ultimately led to Arnold Mandell's notion of the "flowing geometries that sustain complex systems like the mind."[30]

Aperiodicity, randomness, dissipation, and nonequilibrium phenomena are commonplace in our physical surroundings and physical beings. The recognition of that fact should prove as exhilarating and frightening as the "death of God" for Nietzsche. The physical and moral worlds have become equally problematic or, perhaps more accurately: disequilibrious. Yet disequilibrious states are not unhealthy, for equilibrium is the point of absolute rest; in the biological realm it spells death. The sense of being "out of control" does not mean that one really is out of control. It just means that one is unaware of any controlling device or energy. One might access that deeper controlling instance if one were to let go of linear logic as the witch had exhorted Faust. Letting go of the consciously ordered is as frightening as it is invigorating. Both Goethe's Faust and Nietzsche's free spirit were conscious of the dangers of the "games" they played.

The essence of chaos seems related to the essence of agonistic creativity, for both are marked by a sense of abandonment in the interplay of dissonant forces. If chaos can be defined as the "delicate balance between forces of stability and forces of instability" (Gleick 309), then agonistic creativity can be seen as the trend toward creation of new order(s) through dominance, that is, through *autopoiesis* or "becoming what one is" in a decentered universe. The universe exists in a state of tension between stability and instability; similarly, the aesthetic is equally dependent on a state of suspended tension.

An analogy might serve to underscore the inner rhythms inherent in the world of chaos, rhythms which become evident in the work of art as a state of balanced tensions. The opening lines of the "Prologue in Heaven" make clear reference to the sounds of creation resultant of terrestial and extraterrestial movement. And Goethe had drawn an analogy between the outer ear that is attuned to air-borne sound waves and a presumed "inner ear" attuned to cosmic vibrations. Goethe's analogy is essentially a variation of his suggestion that humankind is subject to the laws of nature even when willfully contesting those laws. To Nietzsche's mind, musical texts, whether the cacophonous Dionysian or harmonic Apollonian brand, were more authentic than literature, for the world of words is removed from the realm of immediacy. Consequently, the logocentrism of literature cannot easily reflect the pulsations of life, as music can. The artist and her art might be likened to a tuning fork that immediately reproduces the hidden rhythms of a non-verbal, chthonian world. Appropriate is the analogy of Chladny's figures; that is, the regular geometric lines produced in grains of fine sand spread out on a thin board when a violin bow is drawn across its edge. The sympathetic vibrations of the tuning fork and the self-rearrangement of the grains of sand in response to an external stimulus might be viewed as "metaphorical representations of music," i.e., "metaphors of a metaphor" (Stern 184). The poet, the musician, the artist are media through which the cosmic symphony is expressed.

The world behind the original metaphor that J. P. Stern labels "chthonian" is not without tension and strife. Perhaps one could see a parallel between Chladny's figures as "metaphors of a metaphor" and the constantly shifting masks to which profound spirits are partial. Nietzsche wrote in *Beyond Good and Evil:* "Every profound spirit needs a mask: more, around every profound spirit a mask is continually growing, thanks to the constantly false, that is to say *shallow* interpretation of every word he speaks, every step he takes, every sign of life he gives" (BGE #40). Apparently, the only way to fathom the essentiality behind the mask is to experience all the voluntary and involuntary masks. This stereoscopic view would counteract the superficiality of one-dimensional interpretive acts, while hinting at the wholeness of the stereophonic fullness of the hidden creative force itself. Thus, while Nietzsche's insistence that the self is not unified in a simple way is insightful, it does not necessarily follow that the death of man and the ultimate destruction of the self are inevitable. "Becoming what one is" suggests a complex unity of forces shaped by that which one is becoming through the interaction of creatively agonistic tendencies.[31]

In Faust's case, the conflict is generated by the tension between being and non-being, between the something and the nothing, between regulated movement and turbulence, between the alteration of light and dark, ultimately between Faust's affirmation of life ("But I am set on it" *[Allein ich will!]* F 1. 1785) and Mephisto's attempts to negate life. In this agonistic alteration between the forces of expansion and contraction, between ordered individuation and dissolution, a parallel to the phenomenon of revelation and masking addressed by Nietzsche becomes apparent. Goethe concluded one of his early reflections on the nature of morphology by stating that all surface phenomena are destined to individuation, displacement, and decay in an endless process of renewal by creative forces within.[32]

The creative antagonisms of Faust's struggles were surely the product of loaded dice. While he could not know the projectory of his own movement, the Lord knew it. The readers of the text, of course, do not have a prologue in Heaven to predict their future. But humans seem subject to similar agonistic forces that are somehow shaped into recurring, non-iterative patterns. The scientific paradigm shift toward these strange attractors, which defy disciplinary logic, force themselves on human consciousness and impact upon creative activities. The deep structures of chaos would appear to affect the symmetrical asymmetricality of human genetic coding like some eradicable virus that is passed on from generation to generation, so that humans remain bound yet creative, like Prometheus. DNA is forever reproducing, reconstructing itself according to a creative principle that appears as feedback loops in a long, drawn-out evolutionary process. At first sight these might look like agonistic forces in Bloom's sense rather than converging ones.

Chaologists are now questioning the accuracy of Darwinian observations, proposing instead a theory of coevolution, of mutual impact and conditioning. According to that view, one must consider the effect of the emergence of one gene or trait or species to dominance on the development of every other gene or trait or species that is in contact with the isolated phenomenon. There is hardly a linear progression in the dissolution of one order and the emergence of another; stability and instability are interactive. Yet the "joints" of nature or the saddle of balanced tensions between opposing impulses bring into view a "third territory that lies between order and disorder" (Hayles 15).[33] That third order is the "space" of the aesthetic. It evolves through the feedback of orderly and disorderly states. "Evolution," Ford said, "is chaos with feedback" (Gleick 314).

If evolution is taken to mean "producing new forms," then the operations of chaos are similar to those of creativity. It is a combination of the agon and autopoiesis. The agon might now be seen as the dynamic flux of energy that promotes networkings with similar as well as dissimilar properties, combining and recombining them in a new collective process. Whereas the agon tends to be a contained, definable contest, autopoiesis suggests a very complex and open system. Autopoietic structures appear to be cybernetic, being marked by a spontaneous ability to recognize similarities and differences in rapid fashion to bring about new combinations. While each autopoietic structure has its boundaries, the boundaries themselves are more like permeable membranes than protective walls. Consequently, the dynamics of one structure has almost ready access to the inner workings of another autopoietic structure. There would appear to be a kind of coordinated movement going on, one that avoids periodicity and is self-propelling. It all sounds very much like Nietzsche's description of the universe as a bundle of energy, or like Goethe's metaphor of existence in the "Prologue in Heaven." Goethe the poet-philosopher and Nietzsche the philosopher-poet seemed to recognize intuitively such feedback loops as a basic principle of the creative impulse.

In sum, creativity is always agonistic (e.g., as with birthing) but one need not conclude that it is purely human. For both Goethe and Nietzsche there was an additional, indeterminable factor in the equation of creativity. For Goethe, it was the conviction that the whole is greater than the sum of its parts, or more specifically that the relationship between the creating subject and the envisioned object was by no means a simple linear and rational one; rather $2 \times 2 = 5$ not 4. Creative persons know only too well that the end product is usually quite different from what they originally imagined. The suggestion that the relationship between subject and object is dominated neither by the subject nor by the object might prove troubling for those who see the artist creating by force of her/his own willful genius.[34] The mysterious ordering principle that coordinates the interaction of creator and created would itself appear to be the source of creative activity.[35] If one eliminates, as Nietzsche suggested, categories of quantification, the concept of the self, and the notions of time and space, then nothing except quanta of energy would remain (GW 19: 105, #635). In effect, creativity would appear to be an expression of the release of energy within the total context of the dynamic universe. Creativity, then, would be tantamount to "becoming what one is," whether in Goethe's sense or Nietzsche's. It would also be "divine" in Whitehead's meaning in *Process and Reality*.[36]

This study intentionally draws upon thinkers and evidence from divergent disciplines and epochs, in order to underscore through the confrontation of apparent opposites a commonality of underlying assumptions. A comparison of the obviously similar would hardly have been fruitful. Precisely in this regard, Thomas Kuhn has noted that "enterprises need not be similar in order to influence one another; the case for intrinsic similarity would profit from a less systematically selected group of examples."[37] Nor was the focus of this analysis on external aesthetic criteria, for definitions of the beautiful are culturally and historically relative. Moreover, in the arts the aesthetic is the goal, while in the sciences it is a tool or a mere by-product (Kuhn 342).[38] Fractals are a case in point. The example of such nonconformist thinkers as Goethe and Nietzsche from the heyday of microreduction demonstrates that their very opposition to the dominant scientific convictions of their day was itself creative. Confronting Goethe with Nietzsche and the natural sciences with the moral sciences is perhaps a bit like particle smashing: one is surprised when neither loses any mass. Instead, the kinetic energy seems to duplicate the original particles. The explosive instrusion of the one into the other creates "a chain of utmost potency" that is not about to end.

Notes

1. Cf. Hans Blumenberg, *Die Lesbarkeit der Welt* (Frankfurt a.M.: Suhrkamp, 1986); Arthur Koestler, *The Act of Creation* (New York: Macmillan, 1964); and Thomas Kuhn, *The Structure of Scientific Revolutions,* 2nd ed. (Chicago: Univ. of Chicago Press, 1972).

2. Paul Oppenheim and Hilary Putnam, "Unity of Science as a Working Hypothesis," *The Philosophy of Science,* ed. Richard Boyd, Philip Gasper, and J. D. Trout (Cambridge: MIT Press, 1991), 405–10.

3. See, e.g., in addition to Koestler, also Peter Böhm, "Energie—Kreativität—Gott. Anmerkungen zur Metaphysik Alfred North Whiteheads," *Perspektiven der Philosophie. Neues Jahrbuch* 17 (1991): 37–75. Each draws upon advances

in the natural sciences for his respective discipline and presents unusual arguments. While Koestler's work is older, it is far from outdated.

4. Werner Heisenberg, "Gedanken zur 'Reise der Kunst ins Innere,' " *Versuche zu Goethe. Festschrift für Erich Heller. Zum 65. Geburtstag am 27.3.1976,* ed. Volker Dürr and Géza von Molnár (Heidelberg: Stiehm, 1976), 323.

5. In an effort to preserve the Newtonian universe of essential order, modern chaos theory presents a notion of "positive chaos" in opposition to the entropy-based "negative chaos" propounded by Ludwig Boltzmann in the late nineteenth century. See John Briggs and F. David Peat, *Die Entdeckung des Chaos. Eine Reise durch die Chaos Theorie* (München: Hanser, 1990), 26–29. Originally published in English as *Turbulent Mirror. An Illustrated Guide to Chaos Theory and the Science of Wholeness* (New York: Harper & Row, 1989).

6. Johann Wolfgang von Goethe, *Faust, Parts I and II,* trans. Charles Passage (Indianapolis: Bobbs-Merrill, 1965), lines 243–50; abbreviated in the text as F with line number. For the original German, see the Sophienausgabe: *Werke* (hrsg. im Auftrage der Großherzogin Sophie von Sachsen), vol. 14 & 15, ed. Erich Schmidt *et al.* (Weimar: Böhlau, 1887–1919); abbreviated in the text as SA.

7. Cf. Thomas Kuhn's reevaluation of the concept of dynamism in Aristotelian physics, which emphasizes the context of motion. According to that theory, motion is possible only in terms of changing attributes attached to matter *(Urstoff),* but not in terms of any essential change in the *Urstoff* such as transition from non-existence to existence or vice-versa. Kuhn, *Was sind wissenschaftliche Revolutionen?,* trans. Horst Dieter Rosacker (Munich: Carl Friedrich von Siemens Stiftung, 1984), 12–14, 42–43.

8. All translations are my own, unless otherwise noted.

9. Harold Bloom, *Agon: Towards a Theory of Revisionism* (New York: Oxford Univ. Press, 1982), 16ff.

10. On the history of human consciousness see Richard Bucke, *Cosmic Consciousness: A Study in the Evolution of the Human Mind* (New York: Innes & Sons, 1901).

11. On essayism, see John A. McCarthy, *Crossing Boundaries: A History and Theory of Essay Writing in Germany, 1680–1815* (Philadelphia: Pennsylvania Univ. Press, 1989), 27–65.

12. Goethe, "Die Absicht Eingeleitet" (1807), first published in *Zur Morphologie I* 1 (1817). See Hamburger Ausgabe: *Werke,* ed. Erich Trunz *et al.,* 14 vols. (Hamburg: C. Wegner, 1955–1960), 13: 58–59.

13. Here I disagree with the accents set by John Neubauer in his reading of Goethe's argument in "Über Mathematik und deren Mißbrauch." Neubauer sees Goethe expressing his rejection of "mathematical physics" (311), stating his preference for "all knowledge on the basis of its usefulness for mankind" (312), and airing his loathing of abstraction (316, 318). Each of those points would seem to miss the main thrust of Goethe's irritated response. Goethe criticizes the tendency toward microreduction without consideration of the total context of

each particular part. Goethe laments the lack of "feed-back loops" of other bits of information. See John Neubauer, " 'Die Abstraktion, vor der wir uns fürchten.' Goethes Auffassung der Mathematik und das Goethebild in der Geschichte der Naturwissenschaft," *Versuche zu Goethe,* ed. Dürr and von Molnár.

14. Friedrich Nietzsche, *Beyond Good and Evil,* trans. R. J. Hollingdale (New York: Penguin, 1981), #41. Abbreviated in the text as BGE with aphorism number.

15. Karl J. Fink, *Goethe's History of Science* (Cambridge: Cambridge Univ. Press, 1991), 153.

16. Goethe, "Über die Mathematik und deren Mißbrauch": "Es liegt in jedem Menschen und ist ihm von Natur gegeben, sich als Mittelpunct der Welt zu betrachten, weil doch alle Radien von seinem Bewußtsein ausgehen und dahin wieder zurückkehren" (SA 11: 87); see also the beginning of "Versuch als Vermittler" (SA 11: 21).

17. Leslie Paul Thiele, *Friedrich Nietzsche and the Politics of the Soul: A Study of Heroic Individualism* (Princeton: Princeton Univ. Press, 1990), 119–20.

18. Nietzsche, *Gesammelte Werke* (Musarionausgabe), ed. Dr. Richard Oehler *et al.,* 23 vols. (Munich: Musarion Verlag, 1920–1929), 14: 15. Abbreviated in the text as GW.

19. Cf. Thiele, 120–30.

20. Nietzsche, *Untimely Meditations* (1873–1876), trans. R. J. Hollingdale (Cambridge: Cambridge Univ. Press, 1983), 213.

21. See J. P. Stern, *A Study of Nietzsche* (Cambridge: Cambridge Univ. Press, 1979), 176. To be sure, Stern does not consider a physiological or biopsychological explanation of Nietzsche's aesthetics to be adequate. "Prometheus Bound" is obviously a reference to Aeschylus' tragedy of conflicting free will and fate, while "Chaos Bound" is an allusion to N. Katherine Hayles, *Chaos Bound: Orderly Disorder in Contemporary Literature and Science* (Ithaca: Cornell Univ. Press, 1990).

22. Alexander Nehamas, *Nietzsche: Life as Literature* (Cambridge: Harvard Univ. Press, 1985), 7.

23. In defining "deterministic chaos," Gregor Morfill and Herbert Scheingraber use the analogy of traffic flow. Sometimes the cars crawl along bumper to bumper, sometimes they pass by in groups, then individually, then not at all. And all this in no discernible order. "Chaos" refers to the unpredictability of the individual configurations of traffic passing a given point, while "deterministic" refers to traffic signals, stop signs, and other kinds of unplanned disruptions which "regulate" the flow of vehicles (*Chaos ist überall . . . und es funktioniert. Eine neue Weltsicht* [Frankfurt a.M.: Ullstein, 1991], 9–10).

24. Cf. Briggs and Peat, 225–31.

25. Cf. Hayles, 146–52.

26. Hayles writes: "Because the orbits [of Lorenz's phase space model] 'wandered' in complex and unpredictable ways, knowing the starting point for a given run did not help one to know where the system would be at any future moment" (149).

27. Ian Stewart, *Does God Play Dice? The Mathematics of Chaos* (Cambridge: Basil Blackwell, 1989), 285ff. See also Arkady Plotnitsky, *Complementarity: Anti-Epistemology After Bohr and Derrida* (Durham: Duke Univ. Press, 1994).

28. "God does play dice with the universe," Joseph Ford stated in reply to Einstein's famous remark to Max Born who had suggested the future of the universe was unpredictable. Einstein believed in complete law and order in the universe. "But they're loaded dice," Ford concluded. More recently, Stewart concluded: "If God played dice . . . He'd win" (qtd. in Stewart, 331).

29. Ernst Cassirer, *The Philosophy of the Enlightenment,* trans. Fritz C. A. Koelln and James P. Pettegrove (Boston: Beacon Press, 1955), 36 *et passim.*

30. James Gleick, *Chaos. Making a New Science* (New York: Penguin, 1987), 299.

31. See Michael Morton, *The Critical Turn: Studies in Kant, Herder, Wittgenstein, and Contemporary Theory* (College Park: Penn State Univ. Press, 1993), 241–276.

32. See Goethe, "Die Absicht Eingeleitet" (HA 13: 59).

33. Nietzsche spoke of this dialectical process in chemical terms. Two elements "vie" with one another in a contest of force until a third element arises from their union: "In der Chemie zeigt sich, daß jeder Stoff seine Kraft so weit treibt, als er kann: da entsteht etwas Drittes" (GW 16: 302).

34. Goethe, a chief representative of the creative genius, noted the convergence of "willful" subject and "passive" object when he wrote in "Über Naturwissenschaft im Allgemeinen": "Es ist etwas unbekanntes Gesetzliches im Object, welches dem unbekannten Gesetzlichen im Subject entspricht" (SA 11: 154), later adding: "Alles was im Subject ist, ist im Object und noch etwas mehr. Alles was im Object ist, ist im Subject und noch etwas mehr" (SA 11: 162).

35. See Paul Davies, *The Cosmic Blueprint* (London: Heinemann, 1987), 138–51.

36. Alfred North Whitehead, *Process and Reality. An Essay in Cosmology,* ed. David Ray Griffin and Donald W. Sherburne (New York: Free Press, 1969; orig. 1929), 286; cf. Böhm, 59–68.

37. Kuhn, *The Essential Tension: Selected Studies in Scientific Tradition and Change* (Chicago: Univ. of Chicago Press, 1977), 341–42. Friedrich Cramer, *Chaos und Ordnung. Die komplexe Struktur des Lebendigen* (Frankfurt a.M.: Insel, 1993), 12, endeavors to close the gap between the two "cultures" as well.

38. On the aesthetics of nature in its micro and macro dimensions, see Anthony Zee, *Fearful Symmetry: The Search for Beauty in Modern Physics* (New York: Macmillan, 1986). The relationship between the aesthetics of science and of the arts is not yet fully fathomed.

The Partial Song of Satanic Anti-Creation: Milton's Discourses of the Divided Self

Elizabeth Sauer

The official historical and epic narratives are constantly intercepted by the multiple narrators in *Paradise Lost,* who all present their own genesis accounts. In each case the narrative act comes unsolicited and is characterized as morally ambiguous or dangerous. The presentation of the individual autobiographical accounts is likewise complicated, and in their attempts at remembering their personal histories the speakers of *Paradise Lost* continually draw attention to the limitations of language that impede self-representation. In fact, few characters in non-dramatic texts written prior to *Paradise Lost* have as much opportunity to tell their own stories and are, at the same time, plagued by as many difficulties with narration as Milton's characters. In this chapter I examine the "Sad task" of narration and of historical interpretation in which Satan and the poet-narrator participate. This "Sad task," identified by Raphael prior to the account of the war in heaven,[1] refers not only, like Aeneas's "sad remembrance," to the recollection of tragic historical events,[2] but also to the problems of verbal and self-representation. Referential insecurity, subjective expression, and heightened self-awareness in the accounts of Satan and the poet-narrator are concentrated in the soliloquy and monologue—primary sites of internalized agonistic strife in the tragic epic.[3] The complex attempts at self-representation in the monologues challenge the hegemony of cultural and literary expression established in the traditional epic and tragedy and, more specifically, destroy "that naive wholeness of one's notions about the self that lies at the heart of the lyric, epic, and tragic image of man."[4] The monologic speeches, which are very much dialogized throughout the poem, expose the composite, contradictory nature of identity.

The speeches of Satan and the poet-narrator, who both undertake the difficult task of recounting tragic events, exhibit, like Raphael's preface to the war in heaven, an ambiguous, intertextual, and multivocal quality. Despite the apparent opposition between the two characters, the poem develops out of the ambivalent relationship between these two voices and, in particular, between the poet's language and both the monological discourse and the wandering signification of the devil's speeches.[5] "Opposition is not necessarily emnity; it is merely misused and made an *occasion* for emnity," Freud contends.[6] A psychoanalytic approach to the relationship between the epic poets in *Paradise Lost* challenges our assumptions about the poet-narrator's dominance and the politics of voice in the text. In a Freudian context, aggression is antithetical to civilization, and at the same time strife and competition are the bases for human activity as well as creativity. Freud applies his account of the evolution of civilization to personal development in locating the origin both of the "super-ego of an epoch of civilization" and of an individual in guilt, aggression, and fear of and resistance to authority (78). Hailing Freud as the prophet of the agon and of its ambivalences,[7] Harold Bloom adopts the model developed by his precursor for his theories about poetic interpretation and criticism. *Kairos,* the "fusion/defusion of the fundamental drives, love and death," is the heart of poetry, even the figuration for poetry itself. Bloom defines *kairos* as "image of voice," "crossing," "poetic stance," or primal ambivalence in the Freudian sense (36; 38). The example in *Paradise Lost* of Satan's rebellion against divine authority, cited throughout *The Anxiety of Influence*[8] and *Agon: Towards a Theory of Revisionism,* supports Bloom's contention that the mind cannot conceive of interpretive power without the demigod or king whose power must be usurped.

After examining the narrative and oratorical strategies of Satan in the monological speeches of the tragic epic, I focus on the poet-narrator's dialogized voice and his negotiation between "barbarous dissonance" and multivocality in the official narrative. Bloom's hierarchical model of interpretation[9] effectively illuminates Milton's account of Satan's agonistic struggle with God. This contest leads eventually to Satan's misreading of history and to the devil's retreat into both willful narcissism and incessant autobiography. In my discussion of the poet-narrator's role in *Paradise Lost,* the Bloomian theory of the agon is placed in a constructive tension with the Bakhtinian definition of authority, in which power is dispersed among multiple voices to create a plurality of centers of consciousness, displacing the "single and unified authorial consciousness."[10] Implicit in the tenuous signified-signifier association in the tragic accounts of both poets—and also represented by the hierarchical and heretical relationship between the Father and the Son—is both a sense of anxiety and loss as well as the possibility for greater interaction among the other *characters.* The accommodation in the poem of concepts, such as contending interpretive voices and narrations, mixed genres, and—particularly in the scenes involving Satan—comedy, parody, and irony, tells us something about the poem's agonistic composition and the conditions that informed its creation.

I

The epic begins not with the Genesis creation story, but with Satan's own tragic history, from which Milton struggles to dissociate his own poetic origin and creativity.[11] At the beginning of the poem, the vision of the Muse from whose view "Heav'n hides nothing" (1.27) is displaced by the perspective of Satan, who comments on the change he sees in Beelzebub:

> If thou beest hee; But O how fall'n! how chang'd
> From him, who in the happy Realms of Light
> Cloth'd with transcendent brightness didst outshine
> Myriads though bright. (1.84–87)

Here Milton recalls Aeneas's encounter with Hector's ghost,[12] who in the classical epic represents the defeated warrior Hector, but who also acts as a prophet of Aeneas's triumph (2.381–82). Satan is interested in his companion's countenance and words, both because Beelzebub reminds him of his own tragic past and fallen condition and because Beelzebub, as a prophet (1.143–55), inspires Satan to author the devils' destiny (1.157–91). Satan, then, is the modern poet who misreads and rewrites the past.[13] The resulting anxiety produces a satanic counter-epic, one imitated by the devils, and one that recounts the demonic poets' "Heroic deeds and hapless fall" (2.549). Satan's own darkened vision is thereby inscribed as a comedy and as comic revelry in the official tragedy.[14]

Having suppressed his past and all contending voices from the start, Satan, the dictator of Pandemonium, "dwells within his abstract potential and cannot confront situations at all."[15] The narrative that the mock-author develops expresses the forms by which consciousness "both constitutes and colonizes the world it seeks to inhabit comfortably"[16] and also exposes the Sin-ful consequences of the imaginative act of colonization.[17] Satan's misreading of his story produces the anxiety from which the satanic epic and the devils' destiny are made. The fall of Satan and the devils is continually rehearsed in their literal reenactment of the original temptation to which they themselves fall prey in Book 10. The script they write later in the poem is a chapter of the "partial"—partisan and fragmented—song identified in Book 2 (552). The satanic literary creation is the heathen, mythological, and comic counterpart to the tragic Genesis story of original sin. Again the fruit proves bitter, for the myth of the Titans Ophion and Eurynome ends with the expulsion of these Olympian rulers by Saturn and Rhea (10.578–84).

The authoritative position that Satan assumes in revising the past is one he adopts in the first public address to his cohorts after their fall. The poet-narrator represents Satan as a tragic classical hero, who succeeds in enchanting his followers by his splendor, though he is darkened like the eclipsed sun.[18] The sun in eclipse perplexes monarchs (and royalist censors)[19] with fear of change, according to the narrator (1.594–98). In his Book 4 mock invocation, Satan will find himself similarly overshadowed by the sun, "the God / Of this new World" (4.33–34). A fallen monarch who conceals his defeat, Satan holds his audience mute in anticipation of his oration: "Thrice he assay'd and thrice in spite of scorn / Tears such as Angels weep, burst forth: at last / Words interwove with sighs found out thir way" (1.619–21). Satan uses rhetoric and gestures to smooth over any signs of conflict or self-contradiction, as the narrator reveals in his critique of Satan's stage-work. Still, the relationship between the poet and the devil he portrays is not simply oppositional but is built as well as on identification and a shared interest in contest and performance, including verbal performance. The poem in fact develops out of the struggle inspired by the equal pressures of the poet's fascination with the ancients, his allegiance to the scriptural tradition, and his desire to assert his own voice. The description of Satan as a hero who, though fallen, possesses a form that has "yet not lost / All her Original brightness" (1.591–92) testifies to his nobility and the poet's muted admiration for the classical antihero. The characterization of Satan as an actor, deceiver, and simultaneously, a champion—the meanings of the epithet *agonistes*—heightens the tension between the carnivalesque and the tragic in this portrait,[20] which anticipates the same in the dramatic representation of Samson's agonistes.

Drawing on classical and Renaissance sources for the above description (1.619–21), Milton appropriates an epic formula—conventionally used in accounts of military combat and ceremonial action—to represent the Periclean orator at the point of addressing his audience in a mode that is at once formal and confessional.[21] For his portrait of Satan as a statesman, orator, and tragedian in Book 1, Milton is indebted to Virgil's descriptions of Aeneas[22] and, more immediately, to Thomas Sackville's portrait of Henry, Duke of Buckingham, in *The Mirror for Magistrates:*

> Thryse he began to tell his doleful tale,
> And thrise the sighes did swalowe up his voyce,
> At eche of which he shryked so wythal
> As though the heavens rived with the noyse:
> Tyll at the last recovering his voyce,
> Supping the teares that all his brest beraynde
> On cruel Fortune weping thus he playnde.[23]

The account of the fallen monarch in *Paradise Lost* fragments and parodies the instructive histories that make up *A Mirror for*

Magistrates. The agonistic interplay of the two tragic scenes heightens the parodic character of the satanic performance. Buckingham's and Satan's sad task of recounting the narratives complements the tragic subject matter of the histories. However, while Buckingham confronts his experience, offering it as an example by which readers might learn to check their own actions and political ambitions, Satan deliberately misreads the tragedy of his rebellion to deny its relevance. The devil's first public speech, to which he refers in Book 4 as one of his "vain boasts," presents a resolved argument. His deliberative rhetoric—rhetoric addressed to a political assembly or ruler to persuade the addressee to some course of action on a public issue—is directed at an audience of one; it renders its listeners mute prior to its presentation and makes no mention of them afterwards. The dialogues between Satan and the fallen angels are equally ineffective and take on the character of manipulative rhetoric because Satan suppresses resistance to authority.[24] Satan's control of the outcome of the infernal council in Book 2 is a primary example of his censorship of dissenting voices and of the devils' own epic history.

In his first soliloquy, Satan's memory is awoken first by conscience, then by the Sun's beams, which brought "to [his] remembrance from what state / [He] fell" (4.38–39), and finally by his recognition of his difference from the creator. The acknowledgment of a higher authority is potentially liberating, thus revealing a dialectical relationship between obedience and freedom. "A grateful mind / By owing owes not, but still pays, at once / Indebted and discharg'd; what burden then?" (4.55–57), Satan admits, recognizing that unmerited advancement leads only to further decline (89–92). Plunging ever deeper into his *self*-made hell, however, he eventually shuts out all memories and creates for himself an identity that resists interrogation and is allegedly immune to difference and alteration—the projection of "A mind not to be chang'd by Place or Time" (1.253). By repressing the history of the fall, Satan evades all responsibility; his rhetoric is filled with passive constructions and suppositional statements. The fragmentation of the past is represented by the truncated lament and parodic consolation that bring the soliloquy to its abrupt conclusion.[25] The devil ends his self-confrontation, silences the voices that speak of his relationship to God and history, and announces unambiguously in a statement of anti-creation: "So farewell Hope, and with Hope farewell Fear, / Farewell Remorse: all Good to me is lost; / Evil be thou my Good" (4.108–10).

Temporarily suspending the related events, Satan's five soliloquies offer a particular point of view on the action, one that replaces the choric commentary in the early plans for the tragedy. Satan here is a choral character who distances himself from the action while providing the spectator-reader with an alternative, though largely distorted or ironic, reading of events. Interrupting the narrative, the soliloquies project a will-to-sameness and allow for only a singular perspective.[26] Their meditational mode and psychological content make them resistant to other viewpoints. Yet the language of the soliloquies inevitably splinters, thus taking revenge on those who would use it to suggest that there are no alternatives to a given thought or action.

In the first soliloquy of Book 9, Satan again declares his plan for anticreation: "only in destroying I find ease / To my relentless thoughts" (129–30). His language anticipates his perverse metamorphosis or demonic incarnation (9.166) into the serpent; the temptation scene is signalled by the alliterative "s" sound of Satan's words used to address Eve thereafter:

> Revenge, at first though sweet,
> Bitter ere long back on itself recoils;
> Let it; I reck not, so it light well aim'd,
> Since higher I fall short, on him who next
> Provokes my envy, this new Favorite
> Of Heav'n, this Man of Clay, Son of despite,
> Whom us the more to spite his Maker rais'd
> From dust: spite then with spite is best repaid. (171–78)

The speech recounts the act of the divine creation that culminates in the fashioning of Adam and Eve, an event that proves to be the devil's greatest source of torment. Satan turns his spite on Adam, whose creation by God he reduces to an act of vengeance against himself; he thus misreads the historical event, returning Adam—"this Man of Clay, Son of despite," "rais'd / From dust"—to the clay and dust from which God originally created him. In the fifth soliloquy—Satan's most solipsistic speech addressed to his own thoughts, one that best reflects his own divided mind (9.473–93)—the devil provides an impressive portrait of Adam which contradicts his previous description. As Satan himself realizes, however, revenge, like language, "ere long back on itself recoils." Satan later is literally transformed into the serpent that consumes and becomes dust (10.566; 208). Moreover, he is reduced to uttering spite through his hissing (10.543), which recalls the dire "noise / Of conflict" produced by the warring angels (6.211–12) and the "dismal universal hiss" from the serpents' "innumerable tongues" (10.507–8). The language of the soliloquy also imitates the cannon fire: the diction "recoils," "well aim'd," and "fall short" characterizes the temptation speech as a militant action.

Satan is described prior to his first speech as standing above his cohorts in a shape and gesture proudly eminent "like a Tow'r" (1.591). The tower, a traditional emblem for the Son, is here representative of Babel. The numerous creaturely disguises that the harlequin adopts throughout the narrative ridicule his once stately form and performances. Likewise, the meaning of his eloquent speech multiplies; the many conflicting significances conveyed by his words flame out defiantly toward heaven (1.663–69) only to "recoil" and wound the speaker himself. Both the militant language and the past return to haunt and mock him. Satan's soliloquies, particularly the two in Book 9, suppress all contesting voices and perspectives and gradually become more inwardly directed. At once recounting and participating in Satan's fall and humanity's original sin in Book 9, the poet-narrator exposes the dialogic nature of his speaking voice, which also moves between the postlapsarian soliloquy and the restorative dialogue.

II

The demonic bacchic dissonance that his poetry attempts to evade endangers the song of Milton's Orphic poet—the dominant voice of the official narrative:

> But drive far off the barbarous dissonance
> Of *Bacchus* and his Revellers, the Race

> Of that wild Rout that tore the *Thracian* Bard
> In *Rhodope,* where Woods and Rocks had Ears
> To rapture, till the savage clamor drown'd
> Both Harp and Voice. (7.32–37)

The poet-narrator's resistance to the demonic bacchic revelry in composing his "great Argument," his genesis account, becomes one of the primary sources of agonistic strife in the poem at large. The problems of expression, which register even in lofty verse, are particularly evident in the lyrical moments of Milton's epic. The poet-narrator's awareness of the distinction between name and signification in the third proem, in which he invokes the "Voice divine" (7.2), opens into this highly self-conscious scene. In the same proem, however, the poet-narrator, who is confined to the "Native Element" (7.16), associates himself with Orpheus, fearing "the barbarous dissonance" that is a product both of the fallen satanic discourse that pervades and threatens the tragic epic and of the historical political conditions to which its style is answerable. In the *Memoirs of Thomas Hollis,* we hear: "Could the character of Charles the Second, with his rabble rout of riotous courtiers, or the cavalier spirit and party just after the Restoration, be marked stronger and plainer than in the beginning of the seventh book?"[27] The reference in *The Readie and Easie Way* to the diabolical royal pamphleteers "[creeping] out of thir holes, thir hell"—pamphleteers whom Milton identifies as the "tigers of Bacchus . . . inspir'd with nothing holier then the Venereal pox" (*Prose,* 7: 452–53)—provides one possible gloss for Bacchus and his Revellers. Here, Milton's images recall not only the feminized royalist confusion—which "fatally stupifi'd and bewitch'd" the people (*Prose,* 3: 347)—but as well the "language of [the Tory scribblers'] infernal pamphlets" (*Prose,* 7: 452), which maligned the poet-revolutionary himself.

The authority of the official narrative voice is threatened in a variety of other ways in *Paradise Lost.* The poet-narrator proposes in the fourth proem to replace the descriptions of epic wars and battles—the kind that fill the classics and, ironically, Book 6 of *Paradise Lost*—with illustrations of "the better fortitude / Of Patience and Heroic Martyrdom / Unsung" (9.31–33). The psychological rewriting of the traditionally heroic subject matter to compose a poem that is even more heroic depends, according to the narrator, on his being inspired by the Muse. Indeed, we are led to believe that the voices of the Muse and the poet have already merged; thus, the final proem becomes the only one of the four that is not an invocation. Ironically, the threat of univocality inspires thoughts of uncertainty:

> Mee of these
> Nor skill'd nor studious, higher Argument
> Remains, sufficient of itself to raise
> That name, unless an age too late, or cold
> Climate, or Years damp my intended wing
> Deprest; and much they may, if all be mine,
> Not Hers who brings it nightly to my Ear. (9.41–47)

The poet-narrator's primary concern is not the possibility of being muted; he is more threatened by the tyrannical imposition of a single perspective and by the possibility that "all be mine / Not Hers." Presumption and failed dialogue render him potentially more vulnerable to "an age too late, or cold / Climate, or Years."[28]

The suggestion that the "mortal voice" of the poet may be speaking alone affords the possibility of meaninglessness or bacchic cacophony: "[I]f the speaker depends solely on himself, his 'evil days' will be read as the expression of 'evil tongues,' a reminder of the confusion of tongues in Babel and an expression of disorder."[29] The soliloquy, monologue, apostrophe, and even the invocation in *Paradise Lost* are postlapsarian modes of discourse that reveal the conflicted nature of the speakers. The consequences of soliloquizing are repressed by the internally divided Satan, who, as we have seen, tyrannizes over the other voices in the poem. The reformation of the soliloquy begins, paradoxically, in the more self-conscious moments of the poet-narrator's invocations and leads eventually to creation of the elegies, laments, and dramatic exchanges in *Paradise Lost.*

If, as Joan Webber argues, the seventeenth-century cosmic personality probably gave rise to the future omniscient first-person author,[30] then the presentation of this consciousness simultaneously contains within it the seeds of its own undoing. The eventual disappearance of the omniscient, controlling narrative voice, which comments on the lives of all characters and knows their secrets, coincided with the breakdown of colonialism.[31] If we argue for the complete autonomy and equality of all the represented voices of the poem, the results, however, differ little. The modernist and postmodern transformation of fiction is characteristically multivocal, as Bakhtin has shown, and encouraging of ambivalence and multiplicity. The contest of voices must, nevertheless, continue; the equalization of voice that denies all difference is socially and politically oppressive rather than liberating, offering no grounds for fighting domination and effecting change, or even addressing the need and possibility thereof.

Out of the conflict between dissonance and multivocality, the poem emerges. Milton includes in the poem's linguistic range not only the competing voices of Satan and the primary speaker but also a chorus of narrators—Sin, Eve, Raphael, Adam, and Michael—who all serve as interpreters and relaters of their own histories. Through the dialogue between God and Christ, in which the latter is elevated on the basis of merit, the rebellion of one-third of the angels is precipitated. In reaction to the uprising, Abdiel finds a voice and acknowledges in reference to Christ:

> how far from thought
> To make us less, bent rather to exalt
> Our happy state under one Head more near
> United. (5.828–31).

The narration of the war in heaven and the creation account by Raphael, who makes a disclaimer to knowledge (8.229), inspires Adam's relation of his own creation story. Similarly, Eve, who has the last word in the poem—excluding the narrator's description of the departure from Eden—is born out of the dialogue between God and Adam, and borne out of the chaos of her own imaginary sphere, from which she is, however, never wholly dissociated. These conversations of the speakers in the poem connect the oral histories of the individual characters to each other and to the poem's official narrative. At the same time, the exchanges among the diverse voices are often not easily distinguishable from the poet-narrator's preoccupation with self-legitimization.

By foregrounding the poet-narrator's words while simultaneously accommodating multiple interpreters and creation accounts, the text reflects and endorses the establishment of a socio-political system based on hierarchically structured relationships in which contributory elements nevertheless interact. Privilege becomes a function not primarily of the narrator's dominating presence and claims to inspiration—which the poem in fact problematizes—but of his relationship to the poem's other narrators. In composing *Paradise Lost,* then, Milton creates a self-conscious text that reflects the motivations for and methods of the poet's complex orchestration of voices. If the poem on the one hand is concerned with contesting various kinds of authority, including the privileged status affixed to the single voice as the guarantor of truth, it is, on the other, deeply involved in the representation and justification of an alternative means of orchestrating voices and discourses.

Notes

Permission to reprint selections from chapter 3 of my book *Barbarous Dissonance and Images of Voice in Milton's Epics* (1996) has been granted by McGill-Queen's University Press.

1. *Paradise Lost, John Milton: Complete Poems and Major Prose,* ed. Merritt Y. Hughes (New York: Odyssey, 1957), 5.564. All citations of the poem are to this edition. Citations of Milton's prose are from the *Complete Prose Works of John Milton,* ed. Don Wolfe *et al.,* 8 vols. (New Haven: Yale Univ. Press, 1953–1982).

2. Virgil, *The Aeneid,* trans. John Dryden, ed. Robert Fitzgerald (New York: Macmillan, 1965), 2.3–6.

3. On the soliloquy and monologue as fallen discourses, see John Barclay Broadbent, *Some Graver Subject: An Essay on* Paradise Lost (New York: Schocken Books, 1967), 80; Barbara K. Lewalski, Paradise Lost *and the Rhetoric of Literary Forms* (Princeton: Princeton Univ. Press, 1985), 97–105; Christopher Kendrick, *Milton: A Study in Ideology and Form* (New York: Methuen, 1986), 158; Marshall Grossman, *"Authors to Themselves": Milton and the Revelation of History* (Cambridge, UK: Cambridge Univ. Press, 1987), 71; Catherine Belsey, *John Milton: Language, Gender and Power* (New York: Blackwell, 1988), 89. For a recent alternative reading of the soliloquy's purpose as a vehicle for the re-creation of selfhood, see David Robertson, "Soliloquy and Self in Milton's Major Poems," *Of Poetry and Politics: New Essays on Milton and His World,* ed. P. G. Stanwood (Binghamton, N.Y.: Medieval & Renaissance Texts and Studies, 1995).

4. M. M. Bakhtin, *Problems of Dostoevsky's Poetics,* ed. & trans. Caryl Emerson (Minneapolis: Univ. of Minnesota Press, 1984), 120.

5. The relationship between the poet-narrator and Satan has been extensively examined since Dryden. For some recent studies, see John Carey, "Milton's

Satan," *The Cambridge Companion to Milton,* ed. Dennis Danielson (Cambridge, UK: Cambridge Univ. Press, 1989); Kenneth Gross, "Satan and the Romantic Satan: A Notebook," *Re-membering Milton: Essays on the Texts and Traditions,* ed. Mary Nyquist and Margaret W. Ferguson (New York: Methuen, 1987); and Hye-Joon Yoon, " 'The Fiend Who Came Thir Bane': Satan's Gift to *Paradise Lost,*" *Milton Studies* 29 (1992): 3–19. I will consider the relationship between the narrative strategies adopted by both characters.

6. Sigmund Freud, *Civilization and Its Discontents,* ed. James Strachey, trans. Joan Riviere (London: Hogarth Press, 1975), 49.

7. Harold Bloom, *Agon: Towards a Theory of Revisionism* (New York: Oxford Univ. Press, 1982), viii.

8. Bloom, *The Anxiety of Influence: A Theory of Poetry* (New York: Oxford Univ. Press, 1973).

9. Bloom, *Agon,* 43.

10. Bakhtin, *Problems of Dostoevsky's Poetics,* 6.

11. Various critics have attempted to account for Milton's decision to begin the poem with Satan's history and then degrade Satan during the course of the narrative. According to Stanley Fish, the reader undergoes a moral reorientation (*Surprised By Sin: The Reader in* Paradise Lost [New York: St. Martin's Press, 1967], 38–56); Edward W. Tayler claims that the reader experiences a progressive unveiling of an essence there from the beginning (*Milton's Poetry: Its Development in Time* [Pittsburgh: Duquesne Univ. Press, 1979], 66–68). William Kerrigan argues that Satan represents the "origin, the original original sin, *Milton* turns away from" (*The Sacred Complex: On the Psychogenesis of* Paradise Lost [Cambridge: Harvard Univ. Press, 1983], 170). For a more recent psychological-biographical study of Milton, see John Shawcross's prizewinning *John Milton: The Self and the World* (Lexington: Univ. Press of Kentucky, 1993).

12. Virgil, 2.358–59.

13. Cf. Bloom, *Anxiety,* 20–21.

14. Comedy is based on a word meaning "revel": Gr. *komoida; komos.*

15. Grossman, 37.

16. Hayden White, *Tropics of Discourse: Essays in Cultural Criticism* (Baltimore: Johns Hopkins Univ. Press, 1978), 99.

17. See the Sin-Satan-Death confrontation in 2.648 ff.

18. See William Blake, *The Marriage of Heaven and Hell,* in *The Complete Poetry and Prose of William Blake,* ed. David Erdman (Berkeley: Univ. of California Press, 1982), 33–45. Cf. also Percy Bysshe Shelley, "On the Devil, and Devils" and *A Defence of Poetry,* in *The Complete Works of Percy Bysshe Shelley,* ed. Roger Ingpen and Walter E. Peck, 10 vols. (New York: Gordian Press, 1965), 7: 91–92 and 7: 29–30. The Romantics were not the first to address the controversy of Satan's heroism; see, for example, Joseph Addison's criticism of "Mr. *Dryden*'s Reflection, that the Devil was in reality *Milton*'s Hero" (*Criticism on Milton's* Paradise Lost, ed. Edward Arber [London, 1868], 44).

19. The first edition of *Paradise Lost* was nearly suppressed, according to John Toland, *The Life of John Milton . . . with Amyntor . . . and Various Notes Now Added* (London, 1761; rpt. Folcroft Press, 1969), 121.

20. See Paul R. Sellin, "Milton's Epithet Agonistes" *SEL* 4 (1964): 157. Bakhtin defines the Carnival as a second life or counter culture which opposes the official or high culture in literature and in public life, adding elements of indeterminacy, incivility, inversion, and comedy. Bakhtin, *Rabelais and His World,* trans. Helene Iswolsky (Cambridge: MIT Press, 1968).

21. Cf. Homer, *Iliad,* trans. Martin Hammond (Harmondsworth: Penguin, 1987), 21.176–77; *Odyssey,* trans. E. V. Rieu (London: Penguin, 1991), 11.206–207; Virgil, 6.700–701; Edmund Spenser, *Faerie Queene,* ed. Thomas Roche (New Haven: Archon Books, 1984), 1.11.41.

22. Virgil, 2.1–6; 6.949–52.

23. Sackville, "The Induction," *The Mirror for Magistrates,* ed. Lily B. Campbell (Cambridge, UK: Cambridge Univ. Press, 1938; rpt. Barnes & Noble, 1960), 547–553.

24. Lewalski, 80–84.

25. Lewalski, 99.

26. Satan's five soliloquies are found in: 4.32–113, 4.358–92, 4.505–35, 9.99–178, 9.473–93. The orientation of the soliloquy and apostrophe toward an object world that cannot respond marks the change in emphasis from auditory to visual perception that suspends dialogue altogether. The vocative, thereby, is reduced to the descriptive, "eliminating that which attempts to be an event"; what is at stake is "the power of poetry to make something happen" (Jonathan D. Culler, *The Pursuit of Signs: Semiotics, Literature, Deconstruction* [Ithaca: Cornell Univ. Press, 1981], 140).

27. Francis Blackburne, comp., *Memoirs of Thomas Hollis, Esq.,* 2 vols. (London: Printed by J. Nichols, 1780), 2: 623.

28. Kerrigan lists interpretations of the phrase "an age too late" that include political explanations (*The Prophetic Milton* [Charlottesville: Virginia Univ. Press, 1974], 78–80). For Milton, Bacchus serves as a poetic muse; see, for example, "Elegia" 6, "Familiarum Epistolarum" 25. By calling on the meaning rather than the name of Urania in *Paradise Lost,* the poet, however, distinguishes the pagan Urania from the Christian Muse. Still, his inspired poetic creation continues to be threatened by (pagan) royalist bacchic dissonance and by the possibility that "all be mine, / Not Hers who brings it nightly to my Ear" (9.46–47).

29. Donald F. Bouchard, *Milton: A Structural Reading* (Montreal: McGill-Queen's Univ. Press, 1974), 109–10.

30. Joan Webber, *The Eloquent "I": Style and Self in Seventeenth-Century Prose* (Madison: Univ. of Wisconsin Press, 1968), 256.

31. Frances E. Mascia-Lees, Patricia Sharpe, and Colleen Ballerino Cohen, "The Postmodern Turn in Anthropology: Cautions from a Feminist Perspective," *Signs* 15.1 (1989): 30.

The Penman and the Postal-Carrier: Preordained Rivalry in Joyce's *Finnegans Wake*

Andrew Schmitz

Finnegans Wake is figuratively fuelled with voices *a latere*. It celebrates "marryvoising,"[1] a delirious dance of competing phrases in a strange celebration of strife, conflict, and struggle. All names are surface phenomena and all are interchangeable. Left and right become variable: "Lefty takes the cherubcake while Rights cloves his hoof" (FW 175). Through the interchange of names, *Finnegans Wake* appears both to invite and repulse meaning. "And one of these fine days," *Finnegans Wake* tells us, "man dear, when the mood is on me, that I may willhap cut my throat with my tongue tonight but I will be ormuzd moved to . . . introvent it . . . [and] open your pucktricker's ops for you" (FW 425). Like a tongue cutting its own throat, the text humorously undercuts itself, impelling us toward one of at least two different possibilities. We can either express confidence in its postponed promise to open itself "one fine day" to our eyes (Greek: *ôps*), to make sense, and to become legible, or we can assume the role of this text's curious postman: we can impatiently "introvent" (intervene, invert, invent) the procedure of reading by opening the letter (suggested by the postscriptum in "o*ps*") before it has even had time to arrive properly. Both possibilities are presented in *Finnegans Wake*. And as usual, through a "terrible mastering signature,"[2] it includes them among its own list of options, thereby registering countless secret self-parodies—both legitimating and delegitimating.

These secret self-parodies result in a curious inversion. At the extreme, the mastering gesture transcends its own authority. The unintentional "oops" of these moments presents *Finnegans Wake* as a self-infatuated text without a self. Like a contagious outbreak of foot "in" mouth disease,[3] the bumptious and funny malapropisms and self-parodies contain a stylistic skepticism glimpsed as well in the attitude Joyce adopted toward the very theoretical trellises he used in *Finnegans Wake,* like that of Giambattista Vico's *Principi di Scienza Nuova* and Bruno of Nolan's heretical writings.[4] The figures of Lefty and Rights (of Shem and Shaun) in *Finnegans Wake*'s "gipsy's bar" (FW 177) are central examples of the intervening and inverting indeterminacy that ultimately produces the figure of the "*Primum opifex*" (FW 185) or first artificer; this "shining keyman" (FW 186) is the key figure of agonistic fabrication in *Finnegans Wake.* Critics maintain that Shem and Shaun are names for the warring brethren in *Finnegans Wake.* Their relationship is one of intimacy and of conflict; they are brothers and opposites. Like the biblical twins, Jacob and Esau, they are ultimately battling for the position of preeminence in the family. As halves of each other or "opprobro[s]" (FW 188), Shem and Shaun articulate in opposition whatever it is that each is said to represent individually (they constitute "polar andthisishis" [FW 177]).[5] Insofar as each implies the other, they constitute an important theme of interchange and exchange in *Finnegans Wake.*[6] The brothers exchange a fake currency symptomatic of an overheated economy—perhaps the "savage economy of hieroglyphics" Samuel Beckett (15) exhorted us to see in *Finnegans Wake,* inaugurating a cycle of inflationary practices: forgeries, counterfeits, and overinvestments—in short, an "epical forged cheque" in the work's hyperinflated marketplace (FW 181).

At the same time, the agonistic play of the brothers in *Finnegans Wake* is interlaced with the theoretical vocabulary of opposition, thesis, and antithesis. One can say that this language of opposition always risks the movement toward a single figure. And ultimately, as some critics have argued, all the siblings constitute a unitary consciousness, various sides of a human mind striving to come together.[7] The relationship between Shem and Shaun in *Finnegans Wake,* the argument runs, is made possible by and produces a structural "livingmeansuniumgetherum" (FW 186). Out of the twins' incredulous, disbelieving struggles arises a theoretical constant: the notion of the final unity of all opposition. As Jean-Michel Rabaté has insightfully remarked, such a reading is useful because it structurally "squares" the serial "circle"[8] of *Finnegans Wake*—thereby allowing us a fundamental geometrical schema so that readers may at least sketch the space between the perpetually "sloothering" (FW 195) vocabularies of *Finnegans Wake.*

If we stop, though, after squaring the serial "circle" of *Finnegans Wake,* we have not yet seen the distorting activity and concurrent indeterminacy of elements of Joyce's parodic machinations in the text. On its broadest level, there is evidence that Joyce envisioned *Finnegans Wake* to tempt and then undo whatever literary analysis prefers to posit as the basic units in a consequent configuration.[9] Joyce's desire both to tempt and dismiss analysis suggests a playful mastering impulse. Joyce once allowed that while *Finnegans Wake* was outside a historically determined moment of literature, "its future is inside literature."[10] The gesture is identified with an element in literature which is, so to speak, involved in a permanent revolution. As Jean-Francois Lyotard, for instance, has indicated, the avant-garde work is in a perpetual future anterior in which the laws organizing and articulating the text are in the process of being produced. For here the artist or writer appears to be producing works that are without familiar categories and rules:

> Those rules and categories are what the work of art itself is looking for. The artist and writer, then, are working without rules in order to formulate the rules of what *will have been done.* Hence the fact that work and text have the character of an *event.*[11]

The *Finnegans Wake* will, then, be permanently opening literature to a mode of writing for which it presently lacks expression, but at the same time the work will accomplish a change in what we will call literature so that the retroactive inclusion of *Finnegans*

Wake is assured. In any case, one wonders if *Finnegans Wake* wants either to be in literature or to be literature's future. If the latter is true, then *Finnegans Wake* disappears as soon as it is in literature. Joyce's poetics is, to use Jean-Michel Rabaté's term, "extinctive" (215) in the sense that with every rule it will have formulated, there arises a native instinct to denaturalize, to go back over its own code, a disposition toward a preordained rivalry with itself. This preordained rivalry will not appear as such within the confines of the work's squares, but in the distortion of those squares. To paraphrase a remark of Beckett's: the work of *A Work in Progress*[12] is not about rivalry; it is that rivalry itself.[13]

In the example of the voice that "may willhap cut my throat with my tongue" (FW 425), a polyvalent and complex "message" disbelieves the very code it implies, and tends to make the code the (abject) object of a humorous and wry parody. If this is not only the expression of brilliant style but also a form of stylistic skepticism, may we not borrow from the insecurity that has traditionally attended the position of a certain philosophical skepticism to elucidate it further? The skeptic advances what s/he simultaneously wishes to subvert. The refutation of skepticism argues from the mere law of non-contradiction that since one cannot undermine what one is concurrently presupposing, skepticism creates the conditions for its subsequent refutation. Skepticism could be called the only inadvertent self-refuting position, and philosophy has never stopped being amused by this. The skeptic is inadvertently divided from within, like a malapropism of the intellect, accidentally saying too much even in the most rigorous of formulations. The skeptic's own voice is therefore not one voice, but presupposes two—bickering—voices.[14]

In order to spell out the connection between the double voice of the skeptic and the preordained conflict it exemplifies, it is important to return to question the *Finnegan* in the title and another counter-title, "Faunagon" (FW 337). "Again," which is heard in *Finn-egan,* and "agon," which is heard in *"Faun-agon,"* suggest a link between the parodic self-doubting of the text and a certain violent element of desire expressed in the *agon.*

In an 1872 essay, "Homer's Contest," Nietzsche spoke of the agon as a "tiger-like pleasure in destruction *[Vernichtungslust],*" which tempts and incites men to engage in contest.[15] The seemingly natural links between the beautiful and the victorious find a darker and colder reference in Hesiod's theogonic lore: "A life that is swayed only by the *children of the night:* strife, lust, deceit, old age, and death" (HC 36). The geometrical purity of lines in the Homeric world implies the exultant step out of Hesiod's "stifling air" (HC 36); but it is as well a justification of it, as the Homeric player is incited to return again to usurp the concept of a pleasure in destruction from the immediacy of desire. So there is no final mediating formula for arriving at the truth of the Homeric "world of myth *[Mythenwelt]*" extorted from us by a pre-Homeric "reality *[Wirklichkeit]*"; mediation and unity belong to the mythic world, and the pre-Homeric world would "*extort [erpressen]*" this unity without being of this orderly world (HC 36). From Plato, for example, Nietzsche admires nothing so much as the agonistic extortion of every artifice, discursive form, and art he ultimately comes to reject:

> With Plato, for example, that which is of particular artistic significance in his dialogues is mostly the result of a rivalry with the art of the orators, sophists, and dramatists of his time, invented with the aim of being able to say in the end: "Behold, that which my great competitors can do, I can do, too; yes, I can do it better than they. No Protagoras has written such beautiful myths as I; no dramatist such an animated and captivating entirety as the *Symposium;* no orator has composed such orations as I set down in the *Gorgias*—and now I discard it all together and condemn all imitative art! Only contest made me a poet, a sophist, an orator!" (HC 41)

Attending for the moment only to the "now" of Plato's famous rejection of art, we see that the rejection of "imitative art *[nachbildende Kunst]*" involves for Plato gathering it "all together" one more time. The moment of the "now" of "now I discard" is woven at the same time with what it wishes to undermine. Like the inadvertency of skepticism, the "now" of the agon is humorously revealed through its other. How the past comes toward us, reappearing in our agonistic emulation, is answered through the inadvertent affirmation, the "yes" offered to those we wish to reject.

The moment of the violent "now" of agonistic struggle in *Finnegans Wake* echoes in the "again" and the "agon." Joyce seizes upon many different registers to make the point that literary mastery is a beautiful and inadvertent plagiarism, the creative act of forging is, at its best, a forgery, and innovation is a relentless intertextuality. In *Finnegans Wake,* the reign of the sovereign, free artist swoons and wakes a figure sharing itself through its work.

The preordained rivalry and "dividual chaos" of *Finnegans Wake* require us to invert and invent again even the simplest rules of reading. That is, they disclose agonistic production to be both the gathering together of a past and an act of gesturing beyond it. If the past includes the valorization of the free artist/subject, this agonistic future being constructed in *Finnegans Wake* will in general confront and reject the security of the artist-subject. In such a world, authorship becomes synonymous with plagiarism. The *Wake* offers us at least two hyperbolic intensifications of the meaningfulness of writing—Shem and Shaun. Shaun formalizes the principle of a curious postman who impatiently "introvents" (intervenes, inverts) the supposedly neutral delivery of the mail by opening the letter and forever redirecting its contents. Shem represents the figure of the writer in dire need: there a dark, dirty sin results from an act of writing reduced to an act of slavish transcription, a form of writing so insignificant that it is only the most blind act of reading. The extremes of postal redirection and writerly transcription are in themselves the material through which Joyce has defined two battling brothers.

Shaun argues that his brother Shem is a low sham intellectual, "Herr Studiosus" (FW 193), an "outlex" (FW 169) or outlaw, a vegetarian pervert, who lives the life of a madman / heretic in a "Haunted Inkbottle" (FW 182) armed with a "pelagiarist pen" (FW 182); he begs the world to support him and yet is indifferent to the turmoil of "this two easter island" (FW 188), and is therefore an "egoarch," simply shifting his bitter theology from a proper object to himself ("Monsieur Abgott" [FW 188]). The callous inertia and flatness of Shaun's invective displays an important shift in the *Wake.* Set against the tumultuous ego-inversion of the nearly private language of "Shemish" (FW 422), Shaun, who is "self-exiled in upon his ego" (FW 184), is a "chum of the angelets" (FW 191), one who accompanies the messengers. As "chum" stems from a foreshortening of "chambre-fellow," Shaun spatially extends Shem's silent intensity. Joyce formulates Shaun as a principle of extension. The important shift is away from personal, psychological description and toward an indifferent mathematical functioning. Shaun is the principle of basic mathematics. Shaun can add (lose something in profusion) and subtract (expurgate dangerous messages), but he cannot control figures; nor can he find an unknown variable. The text suggests these Shaunian operations by endlessly adding address onto address as Shaun obscures the letters he is charged with delivering:

> 12 Norse Richmound . . . 92 Windsewer. Ave . . . Exbelled from 1014 d. Pulldown. Fearview. Opened by Miss Tate . . . 8 Royal Terrors. (FW 420)

The letter's sudden disappearance (subtraction) is the result:

> Letter, carried of Shaun, son of Hek, written of Shem, brother of Shaun, uttered for Alp, mother of Shem, for Hek, father of Shaun. Initialled. Gee. Gone. (FW 420)

This mathematical function (or disfunction) is one of the essential disseminating logics of self-betrayal. At the end of the address, Shaun has initialled the letter he claims not to have read. As his style inadvertently slips out his secret urges ("ops" [FW 425]), he begins the inversions through which Shemish is made, however torturously, intelligible.

Now let us follow some of the transcription scenes *Finnegans Wake* offers us of Shem in the act of writing. Literally in the crib, while still a "cribibber":

> . . . after lying out his litterery bed, for two days she kept squealing down . . . and bawling out to her jameymock farceson in Shemish . . . huw Ananymus pinched her tights and about the Balt with the markshaire parawag . . . and him, the cribibber like an *ambitrickster* . . . making his pillgrimace of Childe Horrid, engrossing to his ganderpan what the *idioglossary* he invented under hicks hyssop! Hock! Ickick gav him that toock, imitator! (FW 422–23; *emphasis mine*)

This account of writing is associated with the violent pleasures of an agonist. The Balt, wearing a periwig and in disguise, merges with the term "Ananymus." The fact that "Ananymus" stands for a scribe's self-effacing non-signature indicates that what Shaun fears is more than a motherly favoritism for Shem. The "ambitrickster" is an interlocutory trickster, an *ambigere,* one who "wanders about," who is both the sultry hero of Alp's confession and its scurrilous author. When "Hock!" is read quite literally as the joint of the hind leg of a four-footed beast, the meaning of the series begins to unravel. We hear a possible rhythm in "hicks, hyssop! Hock! Ickick . . . toock," the measured sound of a clock mechanism (tick-tick-tock). The fourth word after the three strikes of the clock is "Imitator!" Referring us to the three cycles of Vico, Shem constructs an "idioglossary," or a private lexicon that can also prompt the recorso term from Shaun—"Imitator!" Furthermore, if "Ananymus" refers us to Shem (or even if Shem is effacing a name and constructing a variable name, a fill-in name), then the passage moves from Alp's art of recounting a narrative of sexual come-ons to Shem's transcription. From the narrative of Alp told to Shem (which might not be a narrative but the act itself), Shem creates an "idioglossary."

Shem is an ambitrickster, therefore, able to stray between the narrative and the event in the narrative. Shem hears Alp's confession and participates in the misdeeds identified in the written confession. Shem is both in the story, in the sense of being the participant in the sensual event the story is narrating (pinching Alp's tights), and in simultaneously narrating the events of "Ananymus" after the event occurred.

But who or what is this so-called "Ananymus"? An unnamed man, certainly, but also an image of the unsigned writing. Why is it, as Shaun says, written into an "idioglossary?" As we know from the study period section of the *Wake* (Book II, Section 2), Shem is particularly adept at constructing figures and calculating mathematical equations with variables. Shem can project unknown factors and construct sensual figures ("construct ann aquilittoral dryankle Probe loom!" [FW 286]). Just as he makes variables from the figures of Alp's sexual confession, he leaves open the place of the father or lover through the "Ananymus." While he looks like he is working ("making his pillgrimace of Childe

Horrid" [FW 423]), he is constructing an "idioglossary."[16] The fabrication of an imaginary and self-consistent jargon is one of the central themes of agonistics in the *Wake*. Certainly we must also note that the writing contains an act of rebellion against authority, if only because it displaces a name with variables.

Since it is a transcription, this writing-rebellion ultimately remains idioglossic. Joyce will be accused of having created in the *Wake* the ultimate private language, represented in part by the *primum opifex* figure. Curiously, this writing resists the rule of "imaginative inspiration" in literature, namely the organic trope of spontaneous genius and a harmony of associated natural forms. Stephen Dedalus, in *A Portrait of the Artist as a Young Man,* addresses this former model which, as we shall see, is one of the targets of *Finnegans Wake*'s parodic dislocations. Stephen's theory of art amounts to an "applied Aquinas,"[17] holding open an aesthetic model.[18] The concept of inspired genius is clearly satirized when Shaun bitterly complains that his brother stands in general "defiance of the Uncontrollable Birth and Preservativation (Game and Poultry) Act" (FW 184). The defiance is worked into a series of signifying chains in order to combine the activity of "idioglossing" and the usurpation of authorship with a hilarious predilection for canned, processed food:

> [H]e preferred Gibsen's teatime salmon tinned, as inexpensive as pleasing, to the plumpest roeheavy lax or the friskiest parr or smolt troutlet that ever was gaffed between Leixlip and Island Bridge. . . . None of your inchthick blueblooded Balaclava fried-at-belief-stakes or . . . greasilygristly grunters. (FW 170)

These culinary preferences are complemented by his interest in foreign literature (Ibsen in "Gibsen"), his unwillingness to burn heretics (fried for their beliefs at the stake), and his sexual impotence ("none of your . . . greasilygristly grunters"). As such he is a traitor, a follower of a false religion, and chaste.

Ironically, the indictment of usurping meaning in the idioglossary is identified with Shem's "condign satisfactions." In turn, the text at once brings to the surface the resistance to literary deference and raises the charge of plagiarism—the erasure of one authorial name, and the substitution with another.

These constitute, as it were, at least two vying vocabularies in the *Wake;* at one point the *Wake* appears to affirm the point of view associated with that of Stephen Dedalus, and at another point the text presents a rather unsanitary resistance to it. The affirmation of Dedalus is knitted into a bitter condemnation made by Shaun of Shem:

> [Y]ou have become of twosome twiminds forenenst gods, hidden and discovered, nay, condemned fool, anarch, egoarch, hiresiarch, you have reared your disunited kingdom on the vacuum of your own most intensely doubtful soul. Do you hold yourself then for some god in the manger, Shehohem, *that you will neither serve nor let serve, pray nor let pray?* (FW 188; *my emphasis*)

These principles lead to a refusal to "serve." In *Portrait,* not to mention *Ulysses,* the writer in general is connected to the fallen Lucifer through the desire not to serve.[19] In *A Portrait of the Artist as a Young Man,* Cranly asks Stephen whether Stephen could ever bring himself to make his "easter duty" for his mother. The latter quickly replies:

> —I will not, Stephen said.
> —Why not? Cranly said.
> —I will not serve, answered Stephen.
> —That remark was made before, Cranly said calmly.
> —It is made behind now, said Stephen hotly. (PA 239)

The reply states precisely the difficulty of assigning the agonist's usurpation of the name with that of the skeptic's inadvertent disarticulation. Cranly's remark is the briefest possible restatement of the refutation of skepticism here written into a theological register of Lucifer's fall. Not serving assumes service no matter how minimally and that law of the "falling body" (and "fallen body"), whose scientific formulation gives Bloom so much difficulty in *Ulysses,*[20] will be given yet another self-parodic twist. If "it is made behind now," as Stephen reports, he cannot quote it without inadvertently having served. Stephen's snap answer to Cranly is that "not to serve" is to exhibit luciferian pride. The anterior implicated in the citation has become a spatial posterior.

But then what could Stephen's remark actually mean? Is he speculating that, behind both past, present, and future, the *Non Serviam* presents itself without appearing as such? The spatial trope of behind and not before essentializes the relationship because it suggests the world of appearance expressing what never as such appears. In all events, Stephen does not appear to believe his own retort or to be able to control it completely.[21]

But unlike the *Portrait* and *Ulysses* which feature ego-centric figures, the *Wake* moves from any controlling ego. The gesture the *Wake* offers us leaves itself open to reworkings. That is, the *Wake* is never prior to the always densely layered event of its transcription. The *Wake*'s fundamental experiment may be to construct a writing that is able to undo itself. One of the finest and most brutally humorous moments of this writing is the *primum opifex,* or first artificer, whose production is, as we shall see, predicated on a temporal model: not exactly forgetfulness but the consciousness of the corrosiveness of memory. Up to this point, we have seen that Shem converts into variables literature's erotic scenes, encoding himself in an "idioglossary" in which "Ananymus" can serve to enjoy the position occupied by other male figures. This activity is boundless in that it surpasses the dread and anxiety of trespassing upon the holy inanimate "spacest sublime" (FW 419) of literature by not respecting its original. For an idioglosser in this expanded sense, the terrible weight of memory is rewired into action.[22]

Shem's writing passes from his "wit's waste" (FW 185) through his own body and beyond his "epical forged cheque" (FW 181) toward the limit the passing of waste suggests: the association of idioglossaries with feces. According to Patrick McCarthy, this is "the most sophisticated discussion in all of Joyce's books of the relationship of the artist to his works" (FW 602).[23] The following passage treats Shem's "making of synthetic ink":

> Weeping and groaning *(flens et gemens)* he evacuated *(evacuavit)* himself into his hand. Afterwards, disburdened *(exoneratus)* of the black brute . . . he placed his own dung *(stercus proprium),* that he called his purgings *(deiectiones),* in a once-honored vessel of sadness *(in vas olim honorabile tristitiae posuit)* . . . He then pissed into it. . . . Finally out of the faul dung, mixed with the good offices of divine Orion, cooked and exposed *(exposito)* to

> the cold, he made indelible ink for himself *(encaustum sibi fecit indelible).* (FW 185; *my translation*)

Joyce mocks censorship practices by having Shaun report these events in Latin.[24] But once "cloaked" in Latin—from a safe corner, as it were—Shaun carefully describes Shem collecting his own excrement and urine, mixing them in a vessel of sadness and producing an indelible ink.

Considering this more closely, we should first point out that the vessel *(vas)* was changed by Joyce from *poculum,* a cup, to the second draft's altered form. Joyce could have made this change to give the vessel a sexual significance, as Robert Boyle has noted (11). The desecration transforms the vessel into an ink bottle and effectively sets it to work. Perhaps the process of creating ink and paper can be read as a mock-eucharistic act (EXP 4). The sadness of this vessel is left unclarified, though. Why, if it is an inkbottle, is it a "once-honored" vessel? Could it be referring to another vessel of sadness? An urn? The funeral urn is suggested by the sense of the passage as a whole. The extreme isolation of the artist forces him to return to his own waste in order to continue producing ink and paper. The funeral urn draws a link between the body of the dead ancestor and the feces of the artist. In extremes, the *primum opifex* puts his feces in a funeral urn and thereby wrongs or dishonors the urn. The indelible ink, which cannot be cleansed or erased, represents a palimpsest in which the artist is re-membered. The change of a "once honored" urn to an "stinksome inkenstink" (FW 183) also suggests a deliberate self-parody.[25] This refers us to a famous passage from *Portrait.* Dedalus meditates on his name; is it, among other things: "[A] symbol of the artist forging anew in his workshop out of the sluggish matter of the earth a new soaring impalpable imperishable being?" (PA 169).[26] Clearly the family name will become a "symbol of the artist forging anew." The reference to the "new soaring impalpable imperishable being" of *Portrait* is subject to a biting reevaluation in the *Wake*'s eternally recreative and "unasyllabled" destiny (FW 183). Dedalus speaks of an artistic forging that arises directly from the name of the father. In the *opifex* figure, the artificer does not create "anew"; he can merely produce on the basis of the desecration of the urn. If he can only write Dedalus again, his writing will always have been nothing but the parody itself.

Shortly after the description of the desecration of the urn and the production of ink, we are told of what the *primum opifex* actually does with his ink:

> [T]he first and last alshemist wrote over *every square inch* of the only foolscap available, his own body, till by its corrosive sublimation one continuous present tense integument slowly unfolded all marryvoising moodmoulding cyclewheeling history (thereby, he said, reflecting from his own individual person life unlivable, transaccidented through the slow fires of consciousness into a dividual chaos, perilous, potent, common to allflesh, human only, mortal). (FW 185–86; *emphasis mine*)

The writer figured in this passage writes over his little square inches until the "corrosive" sublimation has burned the ink into the flesh and transformed the body black. The *Wake* seems to linger on this point, adopting an ornate "corrosive sublimation" when the past participle "burned" would have sufficed. Once again, this passage refers us to an earlier text. In the "retreat" section of *Portrait,* a feverish Jesuit priest, attempting to scare schoolboys, explains that the fires of hell are to be felt eternally: " . . . though it rages with incredible intensity it rages for ever" (PA 121). He then contrasts divine fire with mortal fire. Mortal fire "destroys at the same time as it burns so that the more intense it is the shorter is its duration" (PA 121). The "consciousness" of this slow fire is only formed through ("transaccidented" [FW 186]) the *Wake*'s corrosive inkfires. The sanctity of the "dead" Dedalus, the prior formulas of authorship and mastery, have begun to transcend themselves.

In the *opifex* section, this idioglossary has turned in on itself. It is a writing that marks the corrosiveness of a finite and mortal "fire of consciousness." Such idioglossic writing is never new. As such it configures the *Wake* as a whole. Richard Ellman, Joyce's biographer, remarked that the *Wake* is a "wholly new book based upon the premise that there is nothing new under the sun" (545). Ellman's remark suggests an active, agonistic act of forgetting which involves a violent usurpation of all prior proper names, including the writer's own: Joyce, Dedalus, even Shem. The work of the *primum opifex* is ultimately never innovative. With a self-inverting idioglossary, do we see a self-subverting work of art? Certainly. But this subversion must be placed against the theme of mastery it is meant to transcend.

Notes

1. James Joyce, *Finnegans Wake* (New York: Viking, 1963), 186. Abbreviated in the text as FW.

2. Jacques Derrida, contribution to panel "Deconstructive Criticism of Joyce," at the Ninth International James Joyce Symposium (Frankfurt a.M.: June 1984), qtd. by Ellen Carol Jones, "The Letter Selfpenned to One's Other: Joyce's Writing, Deconstruction, Feminism," *Coping With Joyce: Essays From the Copenhagen Symposium,* ed. Morris Beja and Shari Benstock (Columbus: Ohio State Univ. Press, 1989), 186.

3. The letter ridiculed by Stephen Dedalus in *Ulysses* concerns the infectious "foot and mouth disease" that Mr. Deasy is worried will infect horses. Joyce, *Ulysses,* ed. Hans Walter Gabler *et al.* (New York: Random House, 1986), 26–27. Abbreviated as U.

4. See Samuel Beckett, "Dante . . . Bruno. Vico . . . Joyce," *Our Exagmination Round His Factification For Incamination of Work in Progress,* Samuel Beckett *et al.* (London: Faber & Faber, 1961), 5; and William York Tindall, *A Reader's Guide to James Joyce* (New York: Noonday Press, 1959), 244ff.; and James S. Atherton, *The Books at the Wake: A Study of Literary Allusions in James Joyce's Finnegans Wake* (New York: Viking, 1960), 36–37.

5. These issues have been addressed extensively by Joyce scholars. See, for example, Father Robert Boyle, "*Finnegans Wake,* Page 185: An Explication," *James Joyce Quarterly* 4 (1966): 3–16; and Boyle's essay in *A Conceptual Guide to Finnegans Wake,* ed. Michael H. Begnal and Fritz Senn (University Park: Pennsylvania State Univ. Press, 1974). Robert M. Polhemus devotes the chapter "Joyce's *Finnegans Wake* (1924–39): The Comic Gospel of Shem" to the Penman section, in *Comic Faith: The Great Tradition from Austen to Joyce* (Chicago: Univ. of Chicago Press, 1980), 294–337. The final chapter in *Alchemy and Finnegans Wake* (Albany: State Univ. of New York Press, 1980) by Barbara DiBernard focuses on the "Penman" section as well.

6. At one point Shemish and Shaunish voices haggle over and finally exchange "sylvan coyne" (FW 16), wooden nickels, in a deal to sell each other Ireland, configured as a rubbish heap. The theme of counterfeits appears frequently thereafter—especially in the Shem the Penman section (FW 169–95).

7. Kimberly Devlin argues Shem and Shaun are conflict within a single dreaming self in "Self and Other in *Finnegans Wake:* A Framework for Analyzing Versions of Shem and Shaun," *James Joyce Quarterly* 21.1 (1983): 31–50.

8. In what follows, I am paraphrasing Jean-Michel Rabaté's argument. Rabaté compares Lévi-Strauss' structuralist approach to Umberto Eco's notion

of serial thought. See Rabaté, "Lapsus ex Machina," *Joyce upon the Void: The Genesis of Doubt* (Basingstoke, UK: Macmillan, 1991), 115–18. Also see Claude Lévi-Strauss, "Overture," *The Raw and the Cooked: Introduction to a Science of Mythology: I,* trans. John and Doreen Weightman (New York: Harper & Row, 1975); and Umberto Eco, "Pensée structurale et pensée sérielle," *Musique en jeu* 5 (November 1974): 45–56.

9. As in the image of the "collideorscape" (FW 143), the text combines certain recurrent atomic elements into complex wholes, and then breaks these down into certain recurrent elements. But the process of creation and destruction does not always end or begin with the *same* "atomic" elements. Rabaté has discussed this "anti-etymological movement" (115).

10. Mary and Padraic Colum, *Our Friend James Joyce* (New York: Doubleday, 1958), 130. Qtd. in Richard Ellman, *James Joyce: New and Revised Edition* (New York: Oxford Univ. Press, 1982), 634.

11. Jean-François Lyotard, *The Postmodern Condition: A Report on Knowledge,* trans. Geoff Bennington and Brian Massumi (Minneapolis: Univ. of Minnesota Press, 1984), 81.

12. This was Joyce's operative title for *Finnegans Wake* during the years preceding the *Wake*'s official publication.

13. Beckett is criticizing literary critics for their formalism in reading *Finnegans Wake* when he makes the following remark: "Here form *is* content, content *is* form. You complain that this stuff is not written in English. It is not written at all. It is not to be read—or rather it is not only to be read. It is to be looked at and listened to. His writing is not *about* something; *it is that something itself*. . . . When the sense is sleep, the words go to sleep. . . . When the sense is dancing, the words dance" (14).

14. This bifurcating, doubling discourse of the skeptic is the grounds for its dismissal. An example of this dismissal is offered by G. W. F. Hegel: Skepticism's "talk is in fact like the squabbling of self-willed children, one of whom says *A* if the other says *B,* and in turn says *B* if the other says *A,* and who by contradicting *themselves* buy for themselves the pleasure of continually contradicting *one another*" (*Hegel's Phenomenology of Spirit,* trans. A. V. Miller [Oxford: Clarendon, 1977], 126).

15. Friedrich Nietzsche, "Homer's Wettkampf," *Sämtliche Werke. Kritische Studienausgabe,* ed. Giorgio Colli and Mazzino Montinari, 15 vols. (Berlin & New York: de Gruyter, 1967–1977), 1: 783; "Homer's Contest," this volume, 35. Abbreviated in the main text as HW and HC, respectively.

16. See Rabaté for his fascinating reading of the idioglossary: "Idiolects, Idiolex," *James Joyce, Authorized Reader* (Baltimore: Johns Hopkins Univ. Press, 1991), 122–24.

17. Joyce, *A Portrait of the Artist as a Young Man* (New York: Penguin Books, 1976), 209. Abbreviated in the main text as PA.

18. Lyotard argues in "The Sublime and the Avant-Garde" that once the concept of genius gained acceptance, the posts of *sender - addressee* fundamentally alter. It is no longer a question of an artist's copying masters but one of an attentive inspiration. Hence aesthetics supplants poetics and rhetoric, "which

are didactic forms, of and by the understanding, intended for the artist as sender. No longer 'How does one make a work of art,' but 'what is it to experience an affect proper to art?' " See *The Lyotard Reader,* ed. Andrew Benjamin (New York: Blackwell, 1989), 203.

19. The line is from Jeremiah 2:20:

> For long ago you broke your yoke
> and burst your bonds,
> and you said, "I will not serve!"
> On every high hill
> and under every green tree
> you sprawled and played the
> whore.

Holy Bible: New Revised Standard (New York: Oxford Univ. Press, 1989).

20. See *Ulysses,* "Lotus Eaters" episode (U 59).

21. Appearances deceive. By the time we reach the "Circe" episode in *Ulysses,* Stephen's rebellion has become a mode of internalized distress and guilt, as the nightmarish vision of his mother's ghost ends with her pointing a cancerous crab in the direction of Stephen's heart (U 475).

22. Margot Norris makes this point also: "This paradox is clearly the crux of the philosophical problem which Joyce set out to solve technically in *Finnegans Wake*" (*Critical Essays on James Joyce,* ed. Bernard Benstock [Boston: G. K. Hall, 1985], 216). See also Hugh Kenner, *Dublin's Joyce* (Boston: Beacon Press, 1956), 301.

23. Patrick A. McCarthy, "The Structure and Meaning of *Finnegans Wake,*" *A Companion to Joyce Studies,* ed. Zack Bowen and James F. Carens (Westport, Conn.: Greenwood Press, 1984), 602.

24. One of the titles borrowed in this section is from Wyndham Lewis's "Cantelman's Spring-Mate," which first appeared in *The Little Review* (1917). The American post office refused to handle the issue, alleging obscenity. See the editors' preface in *Unlucky for Pringle: Unpublished and Other Stories,* ed. C. J. Fox and R. Chapman (London: Vision Press, 1973), 84. The reference in *Finnegans Wake* is: "You will enjoy cattlemen's spring meat" (FW 172). See also the description of Joyce's legal battles with U.S. obscenity laws in Ellman's biography of Joyce (497, 502–4).

25. See Danis Rose and John O'Hanlon, *Understanding Finnegans Wake: A Guide to the Narrative of James Joyce's Masterpiece* (New York: Garland Publishing, 1982), 105.

26. The entire passage runs thus: "What did it mean? Was it a quaint device opening a page of some medieval book of prophecies and symbols, a hawklike man flying sunward above the sea, a prophecy of the end he had been born to serve and had been following through the mists of childhood and boyhood, a symbol of the artist forging anew in his workshop out of the sluggish matter of the earth a new soaring impalpable imperishable being?" (PA 169).

The Gender of Fiction: Henry James's "Backward Glance" at the Agon of Composition

Cecile Mazzucco-Than

> What lives longest to his backward vision . . . is not the variable question of the "success," but the inveterate romance of the labour.
>
> —Henry James, "Daisy Miller"

The arenas of creative contest in Henry James are found in his critical essays on other authors and their works, published in magazines and collected in volumes throughout his life, and particularly in "the story of [James's] story itself,"[1] the Prefaces to the New York Edition of his works, and his unfinished autobiographical works, *A Small Boy and Others* and *Notes of a Son and Brother*. The Prefaces retrace the growth of the works contained in each volume of the New York Edition and wittingly or unwittingly foreground James's creative agon. They convey his desire for self-mastery and an attempt to contain the conflict that produced his art: namely his own representations of writing as masculine or feminine. Through the act of writing the Prefaces, James is in fact his own overanxious precursor, as well as his own engendered, perfect Other. He approaches his texts as a (re)reader and (re)writer who struggles for mastery over his own works and searches for complementarity in his competing artistic drives.

Perhaps the writing of the Prefaces was James's way of mastering his own texts and the creative contest that produced them by attempting to fix their origins in a new theory of his own making, a theory developed through hindsight, the artist's "backward vision" (2: 1286). As James looks back at his works in the Prefaces, the author encounters an Other he does his best to come to terms with. The creative contest raises several important issues: the first is the question of the gender of fiction, which is related to what could be termed the gender of authorship (that is, whether a masculine or feminine "hand" wrote a work).[2] The second is the question of subjectivity, the encounter between author and Other illustrated in part by the gendered metaphors James uses to describe his art, namely fiction as building and dominance, corresponding to the masculine, and fiction as embroidery and subversion, corresponding to the feminine. Finally, there is the question of fiction as an art, and, more specifically, James's attempt to elevate the genre of the novel to a work of art by redefining it, especially in the Prefaces. James struggles with the crises in gender identity and construction that work their way into the aesthetic discourses of the late nineteenth-century and early twentieth-century fiction writers and into the network of meanings, associations, and relations in his own texts. The tension between gendered opposites identified in James's nonfiction results in texts that convey the pleasure of process while calling for closure, product, and success.

These three issues correspond to various aspects of the creative contest as presented in Harold Bloom's *Agon,* which depends on an Oedipal model of usurpation. The question of subjectivity and the question of authorship (the latter suggested by Bloom's own anxiety of influence as well as Sandra Gilbert and Susan Gubar's gendered reconstruction of it as the anxiety of authorship)[3] address what Bloom sees as the author's need to slay the father or precursor, as found in anterior texts by the author himself or different authors, and set up one's own text in their place. The question of fiction as an art, or James's struggles to master his genre, seems directed toward the ultimate end described in Bloom's *Agon* as the power to will texts, to be in full control of the abyss of creation,[4] the void or foremother in opposition to and prior to *the place of the father* (245). However, while the Oedipal subject searches for a transcendent, paternal signifier that promises union, wholeness, and cultural privilege—associated with control and frugality instead of the maternal or pre-Oedipal outside of the cultural order, which is associated with a lack of control, multiplicity, infinity, and waste—James's texts sustain a perpetual struggle between gendered opposites. The strong attraction to the paternal power to master texts never overcomes the equally strong attraction to an *écriture féminine,* a writing from the body, a fluidity and identity with the maternal.

In James's early essays, especially the reviews of popular novels, the precursors with whom James struggles are writers of texts that predated his own and helped to define the novelistic form in which he intended to work. These precursors were predominantly female, and James both despised them for what he saw as their prolific, workmanlike products, yet envied the writers for the popularity of their texts. In discrediting his precursors, James could set himself up as forefather of the novel as work of art; yet in confronting them, James may have glimpsed the abyss of his own creation, the fluidity and love of digression that constantly tempts him. In James's early review articles, especially those written about Anglo-American authors and their work, he seems determined to identify the "feminine as distinguished from the masculine hand" (1: 646). Two observations can be made: first, the masculine hand belongs to a male author and the feminine hand to a female author, and second, the feminine/female hand is destructive while the masculine/male hand is constructive. In addition to identifying a direct relationship between the sex of the author and the gender of his or her fiction, James makes a direct connection between the gender of fiction and the style of the work or the techniques the author uses to produce the work.

In his 1876 review of Frank Lee Benedict's *St. Simon's Niece,* James dismisses this novel as "the work of a young woman of tawdry imagination" because the "style is inimitably feminine. 'So they talked on until Fanny worked herself into one of her nervous states, and was absurdly gay.' I am sure the reader will agree these simple words were not written by a masculine hand" (1: 36). He also states that he is not misled by the "name on the title-page (which may easily be a pseudonym)" (1: 36). James does not confuse the *nom de plume* with the *nom-du-père*. He is canny in his alliance yet separation of sex and gender. From a single sentence typical of the style of the work, James deduces the sex of the author. James makes a similar identification in his 1865 review of Harriet P. Spofford's *Azarian:* "Like the majority of female writers . . . she possesses in excess the fatal gift of fluency" (1: 610). James describes language as "the stamped and authorized coinage which expresses the value of thought" and in this context, Spofford's verbose work is "incoherent and meaningless" (1: 604). She cannot compare to Guy de Maupassant who wrote in a style of "masculine firmness . . . in which every phrase is a close sequence, every epithet a paying piece" (2: 534).

Examples of masculine/male hand are more difficult to locate. As suggested by the essay on Guy de Maupassant, the most outstanding and valuable characteristic of masculine writing is its trenchancy and its structure. In his 1866 essay on Alexander Dumas, the younger, James writes that "he has driven in his stake at the end as well as at the beginning. Such writing is reading for men" (2: 280). In his 1868 review of Octave Feuillet's latest novel, James defends the novelist against the charge that he is a "feminine writer" despite the "light and unsubstantial character of his materials and superficial action of his mind," by drawing attention to his "thoroughly masculine quality," that is, his mastery of the dramatic form (2: 282). Feuillet's work may seem as "simple" as Benedict's, but his experience as a dramatist gives it a masculine substance, weight, complexity. James writes: "Women assuredly have no turn for writing plays. A play is action, movement, decision; the female mind is contemplation, repose, suspense" (2: 282). Even George Sand, whose life may have problematized gender for James, is reduced to her sex, the female mind/feminine hand that determines her work.[5] In his 1876 article on Ernest Renan's latest work, James refuses to entertain his own idea of a comparison between Renan and George Sand: "Mme. Sand's style is, after all (with all respect) a woman's style" (2: 633).

James does not link the female mind with a specific genre, although he certainly recognized the women writers' dominance in the tradition of novel writing, in which he attempted to clear a space for himself. Although James's conflict with the popular women writers does not disappear by the time he writes the

Prefaces and some of the later reviews, the link between the gender of fiction and the sex of the author becomes less obvious and is displaced onto the gendered metaphors James uses to characterize fiction, especially his own. He internalizes the debate begun in his reviews of the conflict with the Other in his own art.

In a 1917 *Atlantic Monthly* essay celebrating W. D. Howells, Helen Thomas Follett and Wilson Follett chasten Henry James for "withdraw[ing] further and further from the America we know, into the queer world of his own intensely self-conscious art."[6] "Queer," "self-conscious," and "art" are key words separating James from popular, contemporary novelists like Howells. In linking Howells to "the America we know," the Folletts are not referring to the novelistic style made popular by the female writers of the 1850s, but the masculinization of the novel that followed when authors like Howells showed their muscle in social problem novels and a journalistic style.[7] Yet James is no longer even part of the novel of manners of the "feminine fifties" to which his early fiction most closely corresponded. The Folletts' play on the sociocultural stereotypes underlies "the American abroad" theme of James's novels—the puritanical, masculine American culture confronting the decadent, effeminate European. "Queer" not only suggests effeminacy and homosexuality, but also uncomfortableness, awkwardness.[8] James's work does not fit in existing categories. He is trying to elevate the novel to the status of art through his own theories of the novelistic form. His work is highly self-conscious, aware of itself as art, and problematically gendered. The Folletts' comments reinforce the legend of the late James as high artist, *Cher Maître,* The Master, impenetrable to all but an elite group. As early as 1882, Howells's essay "Henry James, Jr." describes James's work as an acquired taste: "they [the reading public, critics, etc.] would have liked him better if he had been a worse artist."[9] James's own letters support these reports; James's 1890 letter to Robert Louis Stevenson, for example, congratulates him on *The Master of Ballantrae:* "Somehow a miracle has been wrought for you (for you they are) and . . . the most unlikely number of people have discerned *the Master* is 'well written.' "[10] Similar remarks surface in the Prefaces, such as James's lament that, like the phoenix, "the reader with the idea or the suspicion of a structural centre is the rarest of friends and of critics" (2: 1108).

The Prefaces, then, are James's most self-conscious look at his art and near-final effort to set up his theory of the novel as forefather of future novels. The levels of subjectivity in the Prefaces are difficult to distinguish. In *Agon,* Bloom points out three "Whitmans" in *Song of Myself,* two of them distinctively gendered. Although James also wrestles with gender, a more useful example in identifying the "Jameses" of the Prefaces is Lacan's "talking" desk placed with a human observer between two mirrors:

> Thus by being placed with one of us between two parallel mirrors, it would be seen to be reflected to infinity, which means that it will be much more like the observer than one might think, since in seeing one's image represented in the same way, it too is seen by the eyes of another when it looks at itself, since without this other that is its image, it would not see itself seeing itself.[11]

With the exception of the observer, this scene is very like Lacan's description of the mirror stage, where the subject confronts its Other and passes into the Symbolic. In her study of James, Donna Przybylowicz posits a mirror stage in James's Prefaces and autobiographical works, a struggle between the "Other" of the Symbolic and the "other" of the Imaginary, where the subject wishes to be simultaneously subject and object.[12] Keeping Przybylowicz's statement of this wish in mind, the presence of the observer is for me the most important aspect of this trope because this presence turns looking at one's own reflection into an acutely self-conscious act.

Suppose James, like the desk, stood in front of two parallel mirrors with a human observer. The result might have been similar to the following passage from the preface to *The Golden Bowl,* where James becomes (re)reader and (re)writer coming face to face with himself as his own muse:

> To re-read in their order my final things, all of comparatively recent date, has been to . . . become aware in other words that the march of my present attention coincides sufficiently with the march of my original expression. As the historian of the matter sees and speaks, so my intelligence of it, as reader, meets

> him halfway, passive, receptive, appreciative. Into his very footprints the responsive, the imaginative steps of the docile reader that I consentingly become for him all comfortably sink. . . . This truth throws into relief for me the very different dance that the taking in hand of my earlier productions was to lead me. It was, all sensibly, as if the clear matter being still there, spread over a plain, my exploring tread for application to it, had quite unlearned the old pace and found itself naturally falling into another, which might sometimes more or less agree with the original tracks, but might most often, or very nearly, break the surface in other places. (2: 1329–30)

James is his own best reader, and as he looks into the mirror he sees himself as his own precursor. Two Others stand out in the anxiety of influence produced by his multiple reflections. The first represents James's "final things, all of comparatively recent date" such as *The Golden Bowl* (1904), and the second represents James's "earlier productions" (2: 1329). In the first, James finds the perfect Other, Lacan's good listener sought after by every speaker (*Ecrits* 140). James, the (re)reader and (re)writer of the 1906–1908 Prefaces, usurps this first Other—James, the original reader and writer of the *Golden Bowl*—by merging with him. James so identifies with "the historian of the matter"—the center of consciousness of his most recent works—that he ceases to be the aggressive critic who differs with his past work and becomes "passive," allowing his feet to sink into the footsteps of the historian. In the second, James finds a mirror image, an opposite he attempts to usurp by diverging from "the original tracks" to the point that he "very nearly break[s] the surface in other places" (2: 1330). James's backward glance at his "earlier productions" (2: 1329) reveals the difference between his early and his final methods, tracks that diverge rather than coincide.

Przybylowicz presents James's "anxiety concerning the way writing splits his existence and produces an ego ideal and not a reflection of the true subject" (277). In Przybylowicz's model, James would gladly escape the Symbolic to enter the Imaginary which, for James, is a realm of pure art (238). The Prefaces represent the power of art to impose form on an unruly creation and evade social or cultural restrictions to achieve Imaginary union with the "specular image . . . free of the contradictions and oppositions of the external world" (238). Przybylowicz links this external world with the social or cultural changes that make James long for former ways of life and retreat into his art to create the perfect past (11–14).

However, Przybylowicz's model presents a Henry James much too self-contained. James is always conscious of the observer(s) standing with him at the mirror. He is supremely conscious of himself not only as (re)reader and (re)writer of his own works, but also as an author and writer whose works will be published and distributed to readers of James's era and future ages. While he looks at himself, he also sees those who will look at him as he regards himself. James seeks other good listeners by addressing unnamed observers. No matter how much he retreats into his "palace of art" (Przybylowicz 14), James wishes to influence the external world. He will make the present and future observers who stand with him at the mirror more conscious of how they and others practice the art of the novel.

In the Preface to *The Golden Bowl,* James certainly states that his later work presents the best, the fullest use of his talent; but beyond suggesting that his later work needs less revision to bring it up to his current standards, this Preface offers another dimension to James's mirror images, the masculine and feminine duality that forms a large part of the discussion of the art of fiction in and for James. The ever-spreading snow-covered plain suggests the endless expanse of canvas that terrifies the young artist in the preface to *Roderick Hudson* and the fatal fluidity of the feminine. The masculine trenchancy is represented in James's attempts to frame his work, to "break the surface" with a stamp of his boots despite the endless surface that leads him on and on.

The feminine and masculine qualities of fiction extracted from James's early review essays on female and male novelists are examined in James's 1880 essay on Sainte-Beuve's *Correspondence* and embodied in the striking metaphor from the Preface to *Roderick Hudson:*

> [A] young embroiderer of the canvas of life soon began to work in terror, fairly, of the vast expanse of that surface, of the boundless number of its distinct perforations for the needle and of the tendency inherent in his many-coloured flowers and figures

> to cover and consume as many as possible of the little holes. The development of the flower, of the figure, involved thus an immense counting of holes and a careful selection among them. That would have been, it seemed to him, a brave enough process, were it not the very nature of the holes so to invite, to solicit, to persuade, to practise positively a thousand lures and deceits. The prime effect of so sustained a system, so prepared a surface, is to lead on and on; while the fascination of following resides, by the same token, in the presumability *somewhere* of a convenient, of a visibly-appointed stopping place. (2: 1041)

The artist works "in terror" of the tension between the gendered elements of his own art. The feminine elements of the young embroiderer's art are identified with fluidity, "pliability," "subtlety," and mystery as they are in the essay on Sainte-Beuve (2: 681). Similarly, the masculine elements aim to contain and control the feminine Sainte-Beuve's "faculties of the masculine stamp" such as "completeness," "solid sense," "passion for exactitude" (2: 681). The gendered qualities can be associated to a great extent with the sexually charged images of the hole and the needle. The holes embody many feminine characteristics. They are "boundless" in number and create a "vast expanse" of surface whose seeming infinity lures, invites, and solicits the artist. The artist feels somewhat safe in following this unknown, frighteningly compelling, limitless expansion and overabundance, not only because he wields the needle—the masculine force that counts and selects among the holes to produce a flower or figure that will "cover and consume as many as possible of the little holes" (2: 1041)—but also because the artist presumes somewhere the infinity must be contained and this "stopping-place" will be "convenient" and "visibly-appointed."

However, James redefines the oppositional relationship of masculine and feminine in his own metaphor and undercuts a possible Oedipal interpretation of it as well. Although covering a limitless and fluid expanse, the holes form "distinct perforations," a "sustained" "system" and a "prepared surface." Their organization reveals a masculine element in an otherwise feminine subversion of patriarchal order—holes that run beneath and threaten the flowers and figures intended to cover and consume them. The embroidery itself suggests both feminine and masculine qualities. The flowers and figures are produced through a masculine system of careful counting and selecting, yet like the holes themselves, once grafted on the canvas, the embroidery takes on the characteristics of its ground, spreading "as many as possible of the little holes." Each image representing a masculine or feminine characteristic can be further subdivided into masculine and feminine characteristics of its own. The work of art is less the product of integration or assimilation than of the tension between masculine and feminine characteristics that depend on each other for their own definition.

The ever-spreading canvas finds a powerful and subversive parallel in James's architectural metaphors. In the Prefaces, James refers to a "plot of ground" upon which he will build a "literary monument" (2: 1080). In the Preface to *The Portrait of a Lady,* James boasts that when he built his house of fiction he "would leave no pretext for saying that anything is out of line, scale or perspective. I would . . . never let it appear that the chequered pavement, the ground under the reader's feet, fails to stretch at every point to the base of the walls" (2: 1080). In the Preface to *Roderick Hudson,* James reveals a similar "anxiety"; he worries that "the ground has not been laid for it, and when that is the case one builds vainly in the air: one patches up one's superstructure . . . the building none the less totters and refuses to stand square" (2: 1051). The characteristics of the literary monument correspond to what I have previously identified as masculine characteristics. It is "neat and careful and proportioned" and displays "technical rigour" (2: 1080). However, the checkered ground suggests the embroidery canvas that solicits and entices and seems to behave independently of the needleworker who attempts to frame and contain it. Here, instead of endless expansion, there is endless contraction or shifting, but the result is still an undermining of closure where the stopping-place, be it the embroidery hoop, frame, end of the canvas, or the wall of the house of fiction constructed upon the checkered ground, is as illusory as the horizon. The ground undermines the structures James constructs upon it as if his literary monuments or houses of fiction were sandcastles on the beach.

James swerves even more from the Oedipal model in a passage from *Notes of a Son and Brother* when he describes his relationship with his mother:

> She lived in ourselves so exclusively . . . that I think we almost contested her being separate enough to be proud of us—it was too like our being proud of ourselves. We were delightedly derisive with her even about pride in our father . . . for what really could exceed the tenderness of our fastening on her that she *was* he, *was* each of us . . . the very canvas itself on which we were floridly embroidered?[13]

This passage seems to recount a pre-Oedipal union with the mother, a rejection of the Symbolic, a peek at the abyss of James's own creation. James, like Bloom's Freud (*Agon* 118), seems to be searching for a final position. In his 1908 letter to Howells, he proposes a preface to introduce the proposed volume of his collected Prefaces[14] and the autobiographical works may be the cap for his struggle to articulate the history or source of his own art. James begins the above passage from his autobiography by using plural pronouns, then qualifies them by speaking of "what she seemed to do for her second son in especial" (NSB 344), singling himself out as feeling most intensely this unique relation. He writes that she "*was* each of us," as if in being so closely identified with her children, even her pride in each of them was each child's self-love. Yet the narcissistic relationship is not complete. The mother retains her separate identity, the children "almost complain" of the slight separation created by motherly pride, but their displeasure is not voiced. She forces them to establish their own identity. Thus she is an ambivalent figure, the so desired mother that is one with each child and a symbol of the phallocentrism that demands separation from the mother: " . . . she *was* he [the father]" too. James uses an equally complex metaphor in his notebooks to describe the relationship between his mother and her children: "She was our life, she was the house, she was the keystone of the arch. . . . She was patience, she was wisdom, she was exquisite maternity."[15] In speaking of his mother, James is drawing on the complex contradictory tension between masculine and feminine elements that make up his art. He struggles with abyss and forefather, Imaginary and Symbolic, unable to fix his art entirely in either one.

James's Preface to *The Lesson of the Master* proposes a "new life" for fiction, one in which "[i]ts final savour has been constituted, but its prime identity destroyed," and in which there is "as little as possible about its 'being' Mr. This or Mrs. That" (2: 1237). However, James recants, saying his "recommemorative" mood has reminded him of some quite different significance of the story:

> A marked example of the possible scope, at once, and the possible neatness of the *nouvelle,* . . . is the effort to do the complicated thing with a strong brevity and lucidity—to arrive on behalf of the multiplicity, at a certain science of control. Infinitely attractive—though I risk here again doubtless an effect of reiteration—the question of how to exert this control in accepted conditions and how yet to sacrifice no real value; problem ever dearest to any economic soul desirous to keep renewing, and with a frugal splendor, its ideal of economy. (2: 1237)

In each sentence of the above-quoted passage, two opposing concepts struggle for mastery. The concepts again fall into two groups, each representing one of the two genders, prime identities of faction, masculine or feminine, which allow fiction to "be" "Mr. This or Mrs. That." Words like "scope," "complicated," "multiplicity," "splendor," and "infinitely" signal the feminine characteristics of James's works, and words like "neatness," "brevity" and "lucidity," "science of control," "frugal" and "economic" refer to the masculine. James's oxymorons such as "frugal splendor"; an "economic soul" which desires; and "the question of . . . control" as being "infinitely attractive" (2: 1237), embody tension between and within each gendered group. The *nouvelle* could be James's name for the "new relations" he had outlined in previous paragraphs, marked by tentativeness and a tension between opposites.[16]

In a letter to Robert Louis Stevenson written around the time James was completing *The Tragic Muse* (1888), James proposes "for a longish period, to do nothing but short lengths" (Smith 175). He describes these works in an image that calls to mind his metaphors for fiction: "a multitude of pictures of my time, projecting my small circular frame upon as many different spots as possible and going in for number as well as quality" (175), one last attempt to beat popular writers, male and female, at their own game. The resulting *nouvelles* present pictures more of James's own artistic dilemma than his "time," and strain the small circular frame to produce James's long, fluid final novels. Marcia Jacobson associates these tales with James's attempts to enter the popular magazine market of the 1890s, especially after the failure of his play, *Guy Domville.*[17] However, instead of open attacks on the popular novelists, especially women like Spofford, designed to clear a space for himself as forefather of the novel, James sets himself up as the underdog, the unrecognized artist of a form superior to "the hard and fast rule of the 'from six to eight thousand words' " that governed the short story (2: 1228).

James offers two images that convey the importance of the *nouvelle.* One image is of himself "after so many years astride the silver-shod . . . but oh so hugely nosing . . . grey mule of the 'few thousand words,' ridiculously back where I had started" (2: 1268). He insists that only in "clutch[ing] at the claim in question," his artistic handling of the tale, can he present himself as a Don Quixote, a figure noble and triumphant, at least in his own eyes and those of a few sympathizers, despite the "thankless bruises" from a public unappreciative of his attempts to raise the novel to the status of art (2: 1268). Another occurs in his Preface to *Daisy Miller.* James recognizes *Daisy Miller* as "essentially and pre-eminently a *nouvelle*" (2: 1270) and the only one to come close to success. However, he also declares himself too afraid to "ride the *nouvelle* down-town, to prance and curvet and caracole with it there" (2: 1275), because he might fall off and disgrace himself on Wall St., the world of successful and masculine bankers. James, so long uptown among "music masters, french pastry cooks, ladies and children" (2: 1274), doomed to write of "international young ladies" (2: 1277) and embarrassed by his "attested predilection for poor sensitive gentlemen" (1: 1250), is more comfortable in his role as Don Quixote.

When I imagined James standing between the two parallel mirrors, seeing himself reflected into infinity, before and behind, I also posited an observer who could see him or herself reflected into infinity. The observer(s), the popular female and the popular male writers, such as Spofford or Howells, gave way to Edith Wharton, who stood beside James in the last years of The Master's life and described him as "build[ing] intellectual houses for the next generation."[18] That next generation included Dorothy

Richardson, who hails James and his center of consciousness technique as "pathfinder"[19] for herself, and other stream of consciousness writers such as Virginia Woolf, daughter of James's friend Leslie Stephens. In a sense, James is coopted by the literary descendants of the very women he sought to avoid and credited with beginning a novelistic style based on the feminine fatal gift of fluency or "the terrible *fluidity* of self-revelation" (2: 1316) he fought so hard to contain. In her autobiography, Wharton recalls sending James a "copy of *Du Côté de chez Swann* on its first appearance."[20] Although unsure if James really read the book, Wharton speculates "all his principles and prejudices went down like straws in the free wind of Proust's genius" (235).

James's house of fiction is fragile, easily blown about by critics who catch hold of only one aspect of his agon such as the Folletts, or more recently F. W. Dupee, who termed him the "great feminine novelist of a feminine age in letters,"[21] or feminist critics like Sandra Gilbert or Susan Gubar who see him as part of the "male critical establishment" (110). James's art is built on tension between the masculine and feminine elements of his fiction, most often attempts at closure undermined by the attractiveness of digression. Even the Prefaces, which attempt to explain his life's work, to elevate it to the status of art, and to give it closure, are littered with digressions and attempts to cut off digressions—the spreading canvas struggling against its frame. For every sentence in which James resists digressions, such as "*that* story—by which I mean the story *of* it—would take us much too far" (2: 1286), there are apologies for digressions: "I have lost myself once more, I confess, in the curiosity of analysing the structure" (2: 1077). In the preface to *The Golden Bowl,* which deals with revision, James describes his struggle as if he were looking into Lacan's parallel mirrors. Similarly, he speaks of tracing the "growth of the immense array of terms, perceptional and expressional, that . . . in sentence, passage and page, simply looked over the heads of the standing terms—or perhaps rather, like alert winged creatures, perched on those diminished summits and aspired to cleaner air" (2: 1332–33). The Prefaces present a James perpetually struggling between masculine and feminine, precursor and ephebe, Imaginary and Symbolic, in an agon that is never-ending yet always generative.

Notes

1. Henry James, *Literary Criticism: French Writers, Other European Writers, The Prefaces to the New York Edition,* vol. 2 of *Literary Criticism* by Henry James, ed. Leon Edel (New York: Library of America, 1984), 1309. James's essays are henceforth quoted in parenthesis with volume number.

2. James, "Constance Fenimore Woolson," *Literary Criticism: Essays on Literature, American Writers, English Writers,* vol. 1 of *Literary Criticism,* 646. Henceforth quoted in parenthesis with volume number.

3. See Harold Bloom, *The Anxiety of Influence* (New York: Oxford Univ. Press, 1973), and Sandra Gilbert and Susan Gubar, *The Madwoman in the Attic: The Woman Writer and the Nineteenth-Century Literary Imagination* (New Haven: Yale Univ. Press, 1979), 46–53.

4. Bloom, *Agon: Towards a Theory of Revisionism* (New York: Oxford Univ. Press, 1982), 29.

5. See Leland Person, Jr., "Henry James, George Sand, and the Suspense of Masculinity," *PMLA* 106.3 (1991): 515–28.

6. *Critical Essays on W. D. Howells 1866–1920,* comp. Edwin H. Cady and Norma W. Cady (Boston: G. K. Hall & Co., 1983), 249.

7. See Alfred Habegger, *Gender, Fantasy and Realism in American Literature* (New York: Columbia Univ. Press, 1982), for an account of Howells's eventual mastery of his femininity, something James never accomplished.

8. I rely on a clue from Alan Sinfield's *The Wilde Century: Space, Effeminacy, Oscar Wilde and the Queer Moment* (New York: Columbia Univ. Press, 1994) to place the Folletts' 1917 article at a time when "queer" was just beginning to take on connotations of effeminacy and homosexuality and, in the United States, an association with European decadence seen as un-American (155). Although the 1982 supplement to the Oxford English Dictionary gives 1932 as the earliest date for such associations and Sinfield seems to support this (134), Sinfield also cites a 1919 Naval investigation of homosexual practices that uses the word "queer" to label the man who played the " 'woman's part' " (154).

9. *Discovery of a Genius: William Dean Howells and Henry James,* ed. Albert Mordell (New York: Twayne, 1961), 114. Similarly, in an 1897 letter to his publisher Edward Garnett, Joseph Conrad writes that although he enjoyed the artistry of James's *The Spoils of Poynton,* he could "imagine with pain the man in the street trying to read it." See *Joseph Conrad on Fiction,* ed. Walter F. Wright (Lincoln: Univ. of Nebraska Press, 1964), 7.

10. *Henry James and Robert Louis Stevenson: A Record of Friendship and Criticism,* ed. Janet Adam Smith (London: Hart-Davis, 1948), 188.

11. Jacques Lacan, *Ecrits: A Selection,* trans. Alan Sheridan (New York: Norton, 1977), 134.

12. Donna Przybylowicz, *Desire and Repression: The Dialectic of Self and Other in the Late Works of Henry James* (Alabama: Univ. of Alabama Press, 1986), 15–16.

13. James, *Notes of a Son and Brother, Autobiography,* ed. Frederick W. Dupee (Princeton: Princeton Univ. Press, 1983), 343–44. This text is abbreviated as NSB in the essay.

14. Richard P. Blackmur, "Introduction," *The Art of the Novel: Critical Prefaces,* Henry James (New York: Scribner, 1962), viii.

15. James, *The Complete Notebooks of Henry James: The Authoritative and Definitive Edition,* ed. Leon Edel and Lyall H. Powers (New York: Oxford Univ. Press, 1987), 229.

16. For a discussion of origin and application of James's *nouvelle,* see Lauren T. Cowdery, *The Nouvelle of Henry James in Theory and Practice* (Ann Arbor: UMI Research Press, 1986).

17. Marcia Ann Jacobson, *Henry James and the Mass Market* (Alabama: Univ. of Alabama Press, 1983).

18. Edith Wharton, *The Writing of Fiction* (New York: Charles Scribner's Sons, 1925), 117.

19. Dorothy M. Richardson, *Pilgrimage,* intro. by Walter Allen, 4 vols. (New York: Knopf, 1967), 1: 11.

20. Edith Wharton, *A Backward Glance* (Philadelphia: Curtis Publishing Co., 1933; rpt. New York: Scribner, 1964), 235.

21. F. W. Dupee, *Henry James* (New York: Doubleday Anchor Books, 1951; 1956), 97.

IV Agons of Gender and the Body

Man, in the highest and noblest of his strengths, is wholly Nature, and carries her uncanny dual character within him.
—Nietzsche, "Homer's Contest"

The Muse Abused

Lisabeth During

Orpheus at a Loss: Aesthetic Negligence and the Missing Woman

Gayatri Spivak, in a paper on "Displacement and the Discourse of Woman," asks about the relations between a "certain metaphor of woman" and the discourse of truth in philosophy, a discourse which, as she puts it, "we are obliged 'historically' to call the discourse of man."[1] Under the influence of Nietzsche and Freud, philosophers have lately moved the woman-metaphor from the periphery to the center.[2] In so doing they have discovered that the feminine is a useful term for possibilities and forms of play otherwise denied them. Their discovery, in my language, is called envy of the Muse.

Contemporary French theory has been marked by its attentions to the question of the feminine. Spivak has Derrida in mind, but other names could be added. Deleuze and Guattari demand a stage of "becoming-woman" from all, even women, who desire to escape the molar and majoritarian discourses; Lacan jokingly identifies himself, God, the Real, and death with the *jouissance* of the woman. Spivak observes much to be grateful for in deconstructive readings, which she thinks show a " 'feminization' of the practice of philosophy." But she also finds there (as do I) the creation of a new fetish: woman as a name for agonistic strife and radical alterity, the mark of difference from the law. Not so long ago, and in a not dissimilar fashion, the avant-garde had discovered the subversive possibilities of a feminine mode of imagining and writing. The parallels are worth examining.

For the avant-garde, as for the Symbolists in the 1890s, the visitation of the feminine represented the artist's acquisition of an interior paramour. Where the ego could go only so far into the anarchic world of the imaginary, the artist-seer could invoke a muse who was undeterred by the threat to order and control. In the psycho-mythology of the *fin-de-siècle,* the imaginary feminine was the artist's other self, his own Beatrice beckoning him to experiments beyond the borders of the conscious mind and guarding him against its dangers. The modern sibyl has undergone a certain amount of naturalization since the heady days of nineteenth-century spiritualism. In contemporary invocations of the feminine, the mythology is less explicit, the Muse more fully interiorized. Those who write under her inspiration, to her dictation, see their adventures as a form of becoming "feminine."

This puts us, women readers, in an awkward position indeed. Are we to be flattered? Grateful? Does not our uneasiness in the face of this attention leave us looking a bit sulky, humorless, and ungallant, even gauche? But there are reasons for not playing along. It is interesting to note that, with the exception of Derrida, the French tend to dissociate "becoming-feminine" from feminism. Like their mentor Nietzsche (who saw feminists as failed men), they find these two positions incompatible. There may indeed be mythologies of the feminine worth salvaging, and even some theologies of the feminine that deserve a place in the history of aesthetic ideas. But the story of the feminine birth of the artist—or philosopher—has to be first recognized for what it is: a murder masquerading as an act of love.

I want to tell several stories in this chapter, stories that raise the question of woman as medium. They tell of women who inspire, empower, enchant, and suffer, in order that the cause of art might triumph. Their backgrounds are Romantic and exotic, but their lesson austere. They teach that art demands renunciation; beauty has a price. The artist's imagination is refined through death or at the least madness. Rereading Greek mythology, we can see that Eurydice, a mortal nymph, becomes the perfect Muse, the ever-reliable inspiration, only when left for dead.

Orpheus is, of course, not incidental to Modernism. Many of our best images of the Modernist mystique are icons of Orpheus. Jean Cocteau made cinema out of Orpheus' adventures, and it is rash to attempt an analysis of the psychosexual meanings of Orphic Modernism without consulting the director of *Blood of a Poet.* Rilke named his poet-self Orpheus, and understood a great deal about the relations between death, idealized womanhood, and the poet's desire. Mallarmé refined the Muse to a state of almost inhuman ethereality. Though I cannot here address the entire tradition of the Orpheus myth, I will use aspects of it to suggest a counter-agonistic myth to the Oedipal drama, described by Harold Bloom. Where Bloom sees Oedipus everywhere, I see a surprising number of episodes that have Orpheus' name on them. Where Bloom's family romances focus on the conflict between fathers and sons (women, except for the "virtual" Mother, being notoriously absent), mine find the conflict, and the violence, in the relationship between the male subject and the female love or muse.

In *Das Buch der Könige,*[3] the second installment of his extraordinary, shamanistic project, Klaus Theweleit proposes the Orpheus-Eurydice relationship as a key to the sexual ambivalence of Modernist writing. Orpheus, who for Theweleit reappears most centrally in Gottfried Benn, is a Narcissus who requires an other. He cannot create without Eurydice, at least not without her response and investment. Disconsolate, he storms the underworld. His mourning for her is a song more powerful than any he had ever produced. Even the inanimate world is moved. But is it the woman he loves who is essential to his rich lament? Orpheus' fatal turn on the road back from Hades has normally been interpreted as a failure of trust. Theweleit wonders at just how convenient it may have been. Reciprocated passion has rarely been a blessing for the artist. In the history of the Eurydice theme that Theweleit investigates, the semi-divine Muses and oracular priestesses give way to human lovers. But it seems essential to their power and artistic usefulness that something of their early inaccessibility remain.

The Eurydice story is part of a Romantic strain in Western myth-making and love-making of which the clearest example is Poe, and not far behind, Dante Gabriel Rossetti.[4] Poe wrote its epigraph: the death of a beautiful woman is the most poetical topic in the world. The death of the beloved may fruitfully be wept over; while her loss is tragic it is also a useful stimulus. What if it is, in fact, desired? Orpheus' victory over death and separation is through song, although his song in turn leads to madness. We have been told that the artist is sacrificial, that Dionysus himself must die for passion to flow into image, for the artist's longing to reach the ears and eyes of others. Why then do we see so many female cadavers on the artistic path to the ideal?

If Theweleit levels a certain accusation against the murderous, or at least negligent, egoism of the Modernist, Catherine Clément has an even gorier story to tell.[5] In the history of Romantic art, which not coincidentally overlaps with the history of grand opera, murder and mayhem are the order of the day. Romantic genres get much of their energy from the vigor with which they dispatch, harass, de-materialize, and generally bury women alive.[6] Clément's detective work reveals an Orphic intention everywhere. In the operas whose feverish plots she summarizes with relish, a sacrificial exchange takes place whereby a woman must die in order that love be eternal. The heroine can be poisoned by a snake or by her own hand, carried off by consumption, crushed under a pyramid, murdered in error, destroyed by love or by leaping out of a tower, killed by a Spanish knife or by singing too much, buried by her lover or ravished by sinister gods. But whatever happens she is unlikely to make it into the finale. All this is occasion for much lament and great enjoyment. Clément's account of the birth of tragedy makes us wonder if music did not in fact arise earlier in the Orphic story than previously imagined: not in the Bacchic frenzy that the demigod inspired but in the mourning for Eurydice.

Orpheus, as we know, was a divine man, center of a festival of cruelty, whose seductive song and dance led to his own death at the hands of enraged women. In the light of his earlier surrender of his wife, are we to see the maenads' act as an early example of feminist reader-response criticism? Can we picture a future for art that permits the survival of the artist? There is another scene of origins for poetry, where a man mourning for a woman escapes dismemberment and lives to make a tale of it. Some of our Orpheuses are canny. One, whose pseudo-biography is my main cautionary tale, was André Breton.

The Anxiety of Surrealist Romance

> The lady, in esoteric love, matters least. So, too, for Breton.
> —Walter Benjamin

In one curious allegorical rendering of the Orpheus-Eurydice legend, the fifth-century *Mythologiae* of Fulgentius, Orpheus is represented as a mere performer, a musical wizard of dazzling but merely human gifts. Spontaneous eloquence is not the whole truth about art, Fulgentius warns. Orpheus is the power of sound, mysterious in its effects, its ability to move and charm. Eurydice, on the other hand, is the reflective thought, the theory; hers are the intellectual secrets of the art of music. Once these two were joined. Now, the allegory suggests, the practice and theory of music fall into disunity just as the lovers are made to part. Orpheus is forbidden to look upon Eurydice and loses her when he does so. The secrets of the magical effects of music do better to remain a mystery. Eurydice, as esoteric knowledge, is placed at a haunting distance. All the better to permit the expressiveness of the artist?

The philosophic tradition into which Fulgentius's allegory fits is not sure about this point. Is Orpheus the figure for sound alone? Does Eurydice represent word or sense, increasingly irrelevant to "pure" or absolute music?[7] Does the myth suggest that Orpheus, whose song speaks intimately to beasts and stones, was too crude to serve as the faithful spouse of speculative theory? Or is it saying that his creativity requires protection from a cerebral metaphysic of musical numbers and proportions? The medieval musical treatises that followed Fulgentius decided that Eurydice represented that hermetic aspect of musical knowledge, never to be fully revealed; we glimpse it only in fleeting appearances. The true musician cannot help but desire such secrets, which could link him to the harmonies of the spheres. But in wishing to see them face to face, body pressed to body, as it were, he risks losing the fragile balance of sensuality and spirit. A ghostly beloved becomes the less threatening muse.[8]

One modern tradition corrects both Hellenism (not much interested in Eurydice) and the pious Platonists of the Middle Ages. Romanticism, as we saw before, chooses not between Death and the bride, but Death as the bride. In Jean Cocteau's classic film, Orphée knows the earthly lover is a bind. Supportive, sacrificial, but finally domestic, Cocteau's Eurydice cannot compete with the charms of a leather-clad mistress from the underworld. By the time he reaches the screen, Orpheus has undergone several transformations. From a Dionysian devotee he has become a philosopher, a Christ-figure, and a precursor of the chivalric lover. Eurydice, who was for Fulgentius "profound thought" or knowledge, has become increasingly superfluous, an abstraction. What does Orpheus sacrifice when he sacrifices her? Not his connection to his work: the death that claims her leaves him free. Few mortal women would choose to share this fate. Cocteau's Orphée pursues a muse who is a sublime technological fantasy: the cool and elegant Death casts an unflattering light on the anxious pastoral of Eurydice's world. With Cocteau the poet returns to mythology. Despite the distractions of a suitor from the underworld, Eurydice knows she has lost. It is not difficult to sympathize with the frustrations of the Bacchantes, for Orpheus could hardly wait until his wife's body was cold to trade in eros for narcissus.

Surrealism repeats Orpheus' act when it makes a fetish out of the eternal feminine. One of its critics, Rudolf Kuenzli, shares Theweleit's suspicions of Modernist sexual politics:

> Surrealist art and poetry are addressed to men: women are only means to bring about these works. Woman is seen by the male Surrealists only in terms of what she can do for them. She is their muse—who also happens to know how to type, as in Man Ray's photograph of 1924 entitled *Waking Dream Séance*. The woman (here, actually Simone Breton) becomes the medium, the hands, through which the dreams of the Surrealists are preserved on paper. She is, so to speak, a recording machine. She of course has no dreams of her own, but faithfully encodes male dreams. Women are to the male Surrealists . . . servants, helpers in the form of child muse, virgin, *femme-enfant,* doll.[9]

Surrealism was never less than explicit about its investments in a certain kind of woman as mediator. She is the door into an unknown where she is not welcome, the instrument on which the imagination plays. Created according to the parameters of male fantasy, she is subject to his desire or its lack. Surrealist desire repeats that of its Romantic precursors in its fondness for the dead or mad female object. Pursued as a second soul for the male artist, an internal sibyl, the mysterious woman finds that his dream, which has required her appealing stupor, can become a nightmare. Breton, in his romance *Nadja,* mistakes his mistress for a ouija board.[10]

Nadja is a waif, a woman poor to the point of misery whose only peace is found drifting through the streets of Paris. Her appearance is dishevelled and her movements unpredictable. She keeps herself alive through casual prostitution and occasional favors. Although her grasp on reality is tenuous, she has talents that intrigue Breton: she has a knack for inspired remarks, she can read minds, and, sometimes, she can foretell events. A wayward, outwardly passive Cassandra, she moves as if in a dream, and in her wake appear impossible coincidences, random and unconditional intensities. In every sense she is outside the law. Breton is presumably the narrator and hero of the tale. Although it bears her name, it is he who frames the story. Addressed to himself, the question that begins the book, "Who am I?," is the autobiographer's token. In a culture familiar with Montaigne's essays, "Who am I?" is a tease, a way of introducing the contemplative mode, holding out the possibility of truth and disclosure. This promise is both kept and not kept in Breton's text. As an opening to *Nadja,* the question is a self-regarding intrusion. Breton lets us know that the reason for this tale is not the mystery, the unsolved question of Nadja, or even Nadja and him, but the all-engrossing enigma of the writer's self.[11]

For Symbolism and Surrealism, which I am taking as exemplary of the Orphic tradition, woman has a well-defined part to play. She is not herself a creator. Rather she is the mystery, the truth, the excess of art. Julia Kristeva puts it like this:

> If a woman cannot be part of the temporal symbolic order except by identifying with the father ["the law"], it is clear that

> as soon as she shows any signs of that which, in herself, escapes such identification and acts differently, resembling the dream or the maternal body, she evolves into this "truth" in question. It is thus that female specificity defines itself in patrilineal society: woman is a specialist in the unconscious, a witch, a bacchanalian, taking her *jouissance* in an anti-Apollonian, Dionysian orgy.[12]

Nadja is the name for Breton's specialist in the unconscious, a name that is the beginning of the word for hope in Russian but only the beginning, and also, although Nadja herself does not make the connection, a name for "nothing." Nadja came as Breton's lesson. She instructed him in a code of Surrealist practice that he is described as still too clumsy to fathom. Her drawings provided the models for Surrealist art; her occult genius never failed to produce the inexplicable coincidences that Surrealist writing will repeat relentlessly. But an image is just as good in its absence.

The madness of Nadja allows transgression to be placed at a distance. Breton, "in his defense," as he says, adds only the words that turn her into an internal presence: is she there? Or is it only me? The story of Nadja and Breton is not a love affair. It involves an agonistic transfer between woman and man, castaway and survivor, medium and seeker. In the end there is a selective metempsychosis. Her powers of poetic fantasy, her vacillations between play and torment, migrate to him. Banished beyond the gates of limbo is all the violence, humiliation, confusion that darkened Nadja's life. Breton covers this up with a certain amount of bluster. The wandering soul that he conjures up and copies from will bequeath him a language for poetry. But legacies, as Eurydice's story emphasizes, are only passed on after death.

Writing it up, Breton turns his romance into a case study. Nadja hovers between mad seer, privileged oracle, and modern psychiatric problem. Before his Surrealist career, Breton was a psychiatric intern; he worked under Babinsky, who was in turn the assistant of Charcot. Like his teachers, Breton has the idea of accompanying his text with photographs: these, he writes after the fact, will corroborate its tone of "medical, above all neuropsychiatric, observation." Yet the photographs are as bizarre and banal as Nadja's deliverances. They evade all explanatory or illustrative connection to the text.[13] Indeed, Breton will not explain Nadja or his possible moral irresponsibility with her. Unlike Freud, he is not interested in justifying his relations with an intriguing but unstable young woman by discovering the dangers of unrecognized counter-transference. It is enough to prove that a madwoman cannot be the object of the poet's transfiguring desire.

At the end of the tale Breton repudiates his agonal Muse. He no longer needs her. The woman herself is exiled to the "beyond" from which she sends out haunting and inaudible messages to him. He, on the other hand, decides not to visit her. Her solicitation had accomplished its purpose. It was not necessary for him to go as far, to risk the place where she ends up, a place where, as he says, hope and terror are indistinguishable. The masculine artist—now an author instead of a visionary vagrant—steps back from the horror implicit in *jouissance.* Nadja—frail, sexually abused, ignored—retreats, leaving a space for Breton to occupy with a new figure. This one, he promises himself, will be something more than a threshold into "surreal" alterity. She, named only X, is the signifier for a convulsive beauty, electrically registering every move of the human mind. Dispensing with the need for a woman whose identity might extend beyond that of the artist, Breton's new muse, heralded at the end of *Nadja,* is less a person than a combination of words.

Tradition and the Masculine Talent

In a program otherwise committed to destroying the very motive for sublimation, Surrealism preserves the appearance of renunciation. Surrealism has a peculiar relation with the poetic tradition. It has forgotten nothing; it is, at face value, ignorant of repression. Can it fit into the literary canon at all? Over the last thirty years, we have been accustomed to hearing that the struggle to inherit tradition, to win its recognition, and then to surpass it is Oedipal. Each epoch fights to define itself against the past. Harold Bloom sees in the English poetic tradition from Milton to Ashbery a band of brothers competing and murdering the father. Listening to the struggles of each poet to acquire a voice, we are forced to confront the outrages committed in the name of tradition by its devotees. Bloom's theory revels in its aggression, though his post-Miltonic agonists do not commit real violence, going only so far as rigorous misreading, deluded fidelity.

Freud, the acknowledged father of Bloom's theorizing, had represented the crimes of male children against their precursors as a quasi-religious form of cannibalistic incest. The band of brothers are true to a sacred trust, even though their acts are defiant and destructive. The ritual act of patricide preserves the sacred substance of the paternal body. Dismembered, it is absorbed as an empowering sacrament. For Bloom, the strong poet, and only he, has a virile inheritance. The Olympian revolt against the Titans turns out to be a form of filial piety: the precursor's work is challenged, rejected, but reappears subliminally. Often, it must be said, that return is crippling. The fathers do not lightly give up. It has taken years for German literature to recover from the magnitude of Goethe. For his young followers, like Hölderlin, Kleist, Heine, the patrilineal genealogy was literally unbearable. When the father refused to die—or to pass on his blessing—a destructive desire turned back on the poetic self. Heine tried to ward it off with a fantasy of revenge and castration. In an uncanny tale, he dreamt about Goethe in lustful pursuit of a beautiful marble statue. At last the inexhaustible creator is doomed to surrender to frustration and sterility. No hot kisses can make these frozen beauties respond.

Because the past cannot be erased, even the most iconoclastic rebellion reveals traces of its forebears. There is no first time, no way of occupying a place of origin.[14] One is always already spoken for. Bloom meditates in the following way on the insemination of poetry: "Influence, as I conceive it, means that there are *no* texts, but only relationships *between* texts" (3). Poems are made up by other poems. Poetic signature is produced by a long struggle with the words of the past, a struggle that fails. Milton fights with the Bible and the Classical epic. Blake with Milton, Kierkegaard with Hegel, Freud with science and Jewishness, Wittgenstein with metaphysics and skepticism. The lamp of creative power is passed on not through a god but through rivalry and willful profanation. The gods themselves acquire their power in this way.

Bloom's model of tradition is compelling. But it succeeds only by virtue of what it leaves out. Gilbert and Gubar come straight to the point, asking where such an implicitly or explicitly patriarchal theory of literature leaves literary women. If the pen is a metaphorical penis, with what organ can females generate texts? If the poetic process is a sexual encounter between a male poet and his female muse, "[w]here, then, does the female poet fit in? Does she want to annihilate a 'forefather' or a 'foremother?' What if she can find no models, no precursors? Does she have a muse, and what is its sex?"[15] Bloom's fantasy fails to engage the desires of women. The family romance and the image of manic possession need to be revised. Only with a lot of maneuvering will it explain persuasively the position of the female poet in relation to an archive of names, tributes, and sexual innuendos, an archive that was, it seems clear, established on the assumption that *she* would be somewhere else. I cannot begin to suggest what such a revision might look like. But I can propose an agonistic counter-example to Bloom's mythology of the agon. And here I want to offer in the last section of the chapter some speculations on the "psychosexual context" that I think distinguishes an avant-garde movement like Surrealism from the canon of poets Bloom recognizes. For the avant-garde, the anxiety of influence has a different sexual etiology. Orpheus and his more playful Dionysian companions seem to live in a world without fathers. We hear little about vengeful patriarchal gods. Nor are incest taboos and sibling rivalries relevant in a context of interchangeable demigods and metamorphoses. The demand for recognition here does not address a defeated father, but an artistically dispatched, poignantly remembered, female ghost. Feminist revisionists, in their critique of the patriarchal authoritarianism of the literary canon, should not neglect to note the designs of Modernism on women.

The Orphic tradition is not patrilineal or matrilineal. It also involves a sacrificial act of origin. But the body under the knife is female. As Bloom argued, the Oedipal model of inheritance is based on a fear of incest, with the concomitant threat of castration. The artist's self-assertion is plagued with fears of the father's intervention. Yet this sense of working under the shadow of an all-powerful rival has been productive, Bloom would have it, for the history of art: the more monumental the acts of repression, the more imaginative the strategies poets have used to deflect internal censorship. In *A Map of Misreading,* he writes: "The glory of repression, poetically speaking, is that memory and desire, driven down, have no place to go *in language* except onto the heights of sublimity" (100).

The Orphic or Dionysian poet, on the other hand, does not repress enough. He is ludic rather than sublime in the Bloomian sense. For Freud this would mean that the masculine artist has not completely separated himself from the mother. This has its consequences not only for language but, as I tried to show with Breton, for love. Freud argues that the passage through the Oedipal passion and horror is essential: the male child must confront his own part in idealizing and debasing the mother in order properly to love those who replace her. The fear of castration is the beginning of idealization. And Medusa's head triggered that horror. The memory of mother's missing genitalia lingers, Freud believes, in the unconscious of the males among us. Because men want a better resolution to the Oedipal disappointment, they have created art. For what is beauty but a compensation? In Freud we can detect an explanation for the cult of the female nude as signifier for beauty: in art, the nude accomplishes what passion cannot. It overwhelms our senses with an image of the whole, the perfect, the more-than-complete, and thus the fetishized body.

Freud has a way, let us call it patronizing, of making the grown-up masculine artist into a dutiful child. If you continue to uphold your part of the bargain, he says, to cover over the pain of repression with the fantasmatic pleasures of ideal harmonies, then you will escape the knife as well. Your envy will not be held against you; rather it will be admired as the sign of your glorious ambition. Freud has not yet learned that you should not make bargains with children. The Surrealists, knowing Freud as well as they deem useful, want to give up this part of the game. They want to stay children, but not to be dutiful. They will not join the discredited religion of beauty, even for the rewards that Freud and Bloom think attend the heroes of repression. And the first stage in their campaign is precisely the onslaught on the sublimity of the female nude.

In Surrealist art, female bodies return in bits and pieces, not idealized and made whole, but incoherent, discontinuous, diffused by the wayward movements of desire, like the pre-Oedipal space that the "artistic" nude replaces. Women in Surrealism are less signifiers than analogies for everything from the mechanical world to the world of the stomach, the bowels, the tomb. The woman in Surrealism is a link in a chain of succession, a single and interchangeable part of an endless semiosis without depth, an *objet trouvé* displayed in a new montage. She is the entrails consulted by these apprentice sorcerers. In the Surrealist objects of Hans Bellmer, Max Ernst, and Marcel Duchamp, the category "woman" is finally cancelled. Woman is represented neither as discourse nor as nature. She has, at least, ceased to play an analogical function: she no longer signifies otherness or fertility or vice. But woman as sex object, as sex alphabet, gets a new lease on life. The sexual geography of woman's anatomy, from a man's point of view, has become for Surrealism a magical technology. It is the female body, obsessively fetishized and dissociated, that is the Surrealists' instrument of ecstasy. As Freud and Deleuze remind us, the Surrealist's body in bits and pieces is the signifying body of the paranoiac. Its last incarnation is in the mechanical dolls and demented automatons of Bellmer. It is aggressively, indifferently female. Even the phalluses are sewn together out of random breasts, buttocks, and vaginas.

The disintegration of the idealized female body is perhaps the most striking effect of the Surrealist rejection of the Oedipal code. Mayhem in language and logic is another. For those artists who believe themselves to be working outside the world of the fathers, different strategies and different uses of language have been necessary. Yet one does not need to be an anti-Modernist to notice that anarchic play has a way of running down with time. Although I do not want to end with an apology for authority, the law, or castration, I do think that one needs to point out a certain superficiality in the Surrealist rebellion. There are, after all, only so many things one can do with a dismembered mannequin. Even chance has a habit of turning up repetitions and regularities. Surrealism is an Orphic tradition that refuses to take seriously the cost of the Orphic sacrifice, the sacred exchange. It desires its muse without the experience of loss and mourning. I see the story of Orpheus and Eurydice as a warning: Romantic inspiration involves renunciation, a certain transfer between the poet and death, or sometimes, between the poet and madness. In the Orphic account of how one becomes a poet, the generating fathers are displaced in favor of the divine women, the visionary objects, the "specialists in the unconscious" whom Kristeva identifies. They, it seems, are even more readily expendable.

Orpheus cannot create on his own. He lacks a father and his mother, Calliope, the muse of epic, is not in sight. A wife is necessary for his emergence as artist. Eurydice is not just part of the Orphic account of poetic influence and inspiration. She *is* it. The Orphic tradition is composed of those who see themselves outside a patrilineal succession. They want to declare breaks, ruptures, inversions of the past. They do not want to repress it and relive it between the lines. I have associated them with one of the contemporary avant-garde movements, but their finest instances were as the "dark" Romantics, the Gothics, perverts, melancholics like Poe, Hoffmann, Baudelaire. They are connected by their sense of themselves as martyrs of art. Their dream is to be self-begetting. This is also their problem, because even Satanic rebels realized that inversions have to start from somewhere. If inspiration cannot be passed on from the words of others, then a wall must be constructed powerful enough to keep out those haunting and compromising voices of the fathers. In Freudian terms this technique is called disavowal, denegation, acting as if it did not take place.

The Modernist suppression of the immediate past—a suppression that often, as in Baudelaire, looks to the archaic past or to occult traditions for its sources—involves yet another swerve. The disavowal of Oedipal conflict has its price. Too strong a defense against influence can be crippling, even trivializing. Maurice Blanchot invites us to think of Odysseus strapped to a mast so that he can hear the song of the Sirens without succumbing to it. Inspired but helpless, childishly immobilized, he cannot move in any direction because the slightest response may drown him in the music already there, the Sirens' music. The Orphic artist in Surrealism is in a similar position. He thinks he can evade disintegration, escape madness or the spell of "art" by appealing to the Siren herself. Surely she can save him, if she is willing to be turned into a real woman. The husband of Melusina made a similar request. Drawn onto the land by love, the mermaid-muse, like Nadja drifting into Breton's life from a shadowy background, gives the artist what she knows. As his muse she can empower without being powerful. But the deal is that the domesticated muse is wedded to mortality. Sooner or later, the beloved must be abandoned or die. The artist cannot be dependent on her. Beatrice in Dante's poem was already dead when she told Dante that he must lose her in order to find that to which she leads. Blanchot is our most reliable translator of Modernist desires. He interprets the Beatrice event, here called Eurydice, in the desexualized language of avant-garde purity:

> He is only Orpheus in his song, he could have no relationship with Eurydice except within the hymn, he has life and actuality only after the poem and through the poem, and Eurydice represents nothing more than that magical dependence which makes him into a shade when he is not singing and only allows him to be free, alive, and powerful within the space of the Orphic measure. . . . [I]n the song Eurydice is already lost and Orpheus himself is the scattered Orpheus, the "infinitely dead" Orpheus into which the power of the song transforms him from then on.[16]

It is an unexpected revelation from a woman's glance that frees the artist from paralysis and from dependence on others. She draws him away from the compromising contracts of the law and the Oedipal pact, from the false idealizations of the aesthetic. In her he can touch the beyond of language, the beyond of sense. She is the place that his tale must reach and into which it must disappear. Hers is the death, the madness, the silence; his the memory, the survival, the voice.

Notes

1. In Mark Krupnick, ed., *Displacement: Derrida and After* (Bloomington: Indiana Univ. Press, 1983), 169.

2. That the gendered language of some major philosophical arguments is more than a metaphysical conceit is persuasively demonstrated by recent feminist critiques of the history of philosophy, for example, Genevieve Lloyd, *The Man of Reason: "Male" and "Female" in Western Philosophy* (London: Methuen, 1984).

3. Klaus Theweleit, *Orpheus und Eurydike,* vol. 1 of *Buch der Könige* (Basel: Stroemfeld / Roter Stern, 1989).

4. The classic account of this Dark Romantic tradition is Mario Praz, *The Romantic Agony,* 2nd ed., trans. Angus Davidson (London: Oxford Univ. Press, 1970).

5. Catherine Clément, *Opera, or the Undoing of Women,* trans. Betsy Wing (Minneapolis: Univ. of Minnesota Press, 1988).

6. Elisabeth Bronfen, in her brilliant study, *Over Her Dead Body: Death, Femininity, and the Aesthetic* (New York: Routledge, 1992), casts her net wider than the usual suspects. She discusses *Lolita, The House of Mirth, Vertigo* (whose repetitions of Orpheus are also confirmed by Theweleit), as well as work by women artists. Yet Poe is also indispensable to Bronfen's thesis. For Poe, the exemplary poet of the Dark Romantic tradition, only the dead beloved can be the muse. Like Orpheus, he creates to fill the vacuum, but unlike Orpheus he needs the (departed) woman as medium for his relation to death, his true object of fascination. Bronfen argues to a general principle: "[D]eath transforms the body of woman into the source of poetic inspiration precisely because it creates and gives corporality to a loss or absence" (362). The beloved's absence is necessary to the poet's renewal of force, not just through the dynamic of a purifying sacrifice but because, frankly, she is in the way. Only in death, etherealized into muse, can she "take possession" of him without the interference that her physical presence represents.

While I find Bronfen's interpretations never less than persuasive and her material dazzling, my focus is narrower. She wants to press harder than I have done here the problem of our cultural investment in femininity as the "acceptable face" of death. It is a point we have learned from Freud, among others: death the ultimate alterity, death which is unrepresentable and at once feared and desired, is transferred as if by proxy to the feminine body which, however difficult to handle in life, becomes nicely indeterminate beyond the grave. A woman's death, argues Bronfen, permits her passage into figurality; like Beatrice, then, she can be both fetish and medium (see her chapter 15, "Risky resemblances"). By contrast, my invocation of femininity and death does not implicate the culture as a whole, as Bronfen's more comprehensively psychoanalytic reading does. I identify the Orpheus-Eurydice theory of art with Modernism and, specifically, with the avant-garde. The bad conscience of the Surrealist artist toward his own origins is as much my theme as the dangerous exchanges between men, women, and death. Murder is one crime; being derivative is another.

7. This may be it. Listen to Clément on the sexual difference between word and music, vulgarians and purists, in an imaginary dialogue ("Duets on the Golden Calf") with several of the male clan of musicologists:

> I am going to commit the sacrilege of listening to the words . . . I am determined to pay attention to the language, the forgotten part of opera. . . . He says . . . the words of language are an unacceptable interference in music that cannot be permitted. It should be possible to

> banish them all. They prevent one's really hearing. They are parasites. . . . He loves to say that the music is what provides the meaning, which is false; because, although it accompanies, completes, provokes, or slows it down, it does not give meaning to words, which have their own power and their own internal sense. He loves to say that the charm of opera is that nothing is understood and that it is better that way. Silence. I wonder about that. . . . The dead part of opera, language, is *my* problem. . . . Women again. In opera, the forgetting of words, the forgetting of women, have the same deep roots. Reading the texts, more than in listening at the mercy of an adored voice, I found to my fear and horror, words that killed, words that told every time of women's undoing. (Clément 12–22)

8. My account of Orpheus in the Middle Ages comes from Elizabeth A. Newby, *A Portrait of the Artist: The Legends of Orpheus and their use in Medieval and Renaissance Aesthetics* (New York: Garland, 1987), 73–128.

9. "Surrealism and Misogyny," *Surrealism and Women,* ed. Mary Ann Caws, Rudolf E. Kuenzli, and Gwen Raaberg (Cambridge: MIT Press, 1990), 18–19.

10. André Breton, *Nadja,* rev. ed. (Paris: Gallimard, 1974).

11. In my reading of *Nadja,* I have benefited from Susan Rubin Suleiman's inspired juxtaposition of three heroines: Duras' Lol von Stein, Freud's Dora, and Breton's Nadja. They form an uncanny trio. See Suleiman's rewarding book, *Subversive Intent: Gender, Politics and the Avant-Garde* (Cambridge: Harvard Univ. Press, 1990).

12. Julia Kristeva, *About Chinese Women,* trans. Anita Barrows (London: Marion Boyars, 1986), 35.

13. Rosalind Krauss, in a brilliant and perhaps perverse essay on Surrealism, points to Breton's stress on an antimony between perception and representation. Automatist writing and drawing, and also photography in its clinical efforts to avoid the hand of the conscious agent, are praised by Breton as means to surreality, while representation bears the old Platonic scars, suspected of cheating and deceit. To avoid mimesis in favor of vision meant for Breton something close to the quirky materialism of the dream. Photographic evidence, used in the way Breton planned to use the photographs commissioned from J.-A. Boiffard for *Nadja,* is not doing the job of illustration. It is an independent testimony with no claim to be confirming or substantiating the text. Krauss puts it like this: "Within the high oneric atmosphere of these books, the presence of the photographs strikes one as extremely eccentric—an appendage to the text that is as mysterious in its motivation as the images themselves are banal" (Krauss, "The Photographic Conditions of Surrealism," *October* 19 [Winter 1981]). Reprinted in her *The Originality of the Avant-Garde and Other Modernist Myths* (Cambridge: MIT Press, 1985), 98.

14. "But who, what is the poetic father? The voice of the other, of the *daimon,* is always speaking in one; the voice that cannot die because it has survived death—*the dead poet lives in one*. . . . A poet, I argue in consequence,

is not so much a man speaking to men as a man rebelling against being spoken to by a dead man (the precursor) outrageously more alive than himself" (Harold Bloom, *A Map of Misreading* [New York: Oxford Univ. Press, 1975], 19).

15. Sandra Gilbert and Susan Gubar, *The Madwoman in the Attic: The Woman Writer and the Nineteenth Century Literary Imagination* (New Haven: Yale Univ. Press, 1979), 6, 47.

16. Maurice Blanchot, *The Gaze of Orpheus and other Literary Essays*, trans. Lydia Davis (Barrytown, N.Y.: Station Hill Press, 1981), 101.

The Sportive Agon in Ancient and Modern Times

John Hoberman

Supreme athletic effort drawing upon the strength of mind and body is a hallmark of both ancient Greek and modern Western civilization. Yet despite this shared obsession and the successful restoration of the ancient Olympic games in modern form over the past century, we must recognize that these physical cultures represent profoundly different cultural worlds that assign different meanings to competitive athletic acts as well as to regulated athletic competition. For this reason we must assume that the meaning of the sportive agon[1] (or test of body and will) has changed in a fundamental way. Because ancient Greek sport was embedded in political, religious, and theatrical dimensions unique to that culture, the athlete occupied roles that do not have modern counterparts other than in a superficial sense. He competed—as Nietzsche points out in his early essay, "Homer's Contest" (1872)—in the service of the state and in the shadow of the gods, and the overall spectacle in which his performance took place assumed a cultural significance for which the modern world has no genuine equivalent. Today, the sportive agon acquires its meaning in a world that has been transformed by a profound cultural development: competition against quantitative norms and the increasing scientization of the athlete's body. Ancient Greeks could not experience the physiological self-consciousness that permeates our own sense of high-performance sport. There is, however, a theme that unifies the athletics of ancients and moderns: removal of virtually all restraints on the development of athletic powers—physical culture's version of Promethean ambition itself.

The legacy of Winkelmann's interpretation of the ancient Greeks has concealed the absence of restraint that characterized their athletic ethos. "A common modern myth about the ancient Greeks," notes Waldo E. Sweet, "is that they were 'moderate,' that is, they did not go to extremes. This is demonstrably false: the ancient Greeks were in fact very immoderate, even impulsive."[2] Like their modern counterparts, ancient Greek athletes subjected themselves to extreme physical and mental exertion and reaped large—indeed, sometimes enormous—financial rewards and prestige as a result of their accomplishments in athletic competitions. Then, as now, these incentives encouraged a sportive ethos of toughness that caused grotesque injuries and even deaths in training and competition.

Our conception of ancient Greek sport does not, however, assign primary importance to material incentives. It is more satisfying—and, one hopes, more accurate—to find the wellspring of athletic ambition in an ideal that transcends the pursuit of wealth. Nietzsche's "Homer's Contest" offers a suitably idealistic portrait of the contest or competitive struggle *(Wettkampf)* that went on inside the stadium and, on a larger scale, suffused the lives of the Athenian cultural elite. Struggle *(Kampf)* itself, he claims, was nothing less than the "well-being and salvation" of the polis, while the cruelty of victory was "the peak of life's glories" *(die Spitze des Lebensjubels).*[3] Nietzsche uses the athletic metaphor of a relay race to convey this competitive ethos: "Every great Hellene passes on the torch of the contest; with every great virtue a new greatness is kindled" (HW 788; HC 39). From a modern standpoint, a surprising aspect of this culture of achievement is that it was a collective process that suppressed the cult of the solitary and extraordinary talent:

> The original sense of this extraordinary device is, however, not one of an outlet, rather one of a stimulant: one does away with an outstanding individual, so that once again the competing game of strengths may awake: a concept that is hostile to the "exclusivity" of genius in the modern sense, but presup-

> poses that in the natural order of things there are always *several* geniuses, who mutually incite each other to act, as they also mutually hold themselves within the bounds of moderation. That is the core of the Hellenic concept of contest: it abhors sovereign mastery, and fears its dangers; it desires, as *protection* against the one genius—a second genius. (HW 789; HC 39–40)

The entire "popular pedagogy" *(Volkspädagogik)* of the Greeks is based on this ideal of "agonal education" (HW 789; HC 40). Every citizen dreamed of serving his city-state by achieving success in competitive activity.

One of Nietzsche's primary concerns in this essay is to differentiate between the ancient agonal ethos that he clearly respects and the modern ambition of which he just as clearly disapproves. One crucial distinction separates the profoundly civic-minded focus of the Athenian's ambition from the limitless and unfocused aspirations of modern man. Modern ambition, says Nietzsche, aims at the "unmeasured" and the "unmeasurable" (*in's Ungemessene und Unzumessende* [HW 789; HC 40]), so that this fixation on the infinite actually confines the modern man who dreams of limitless achievement. Here he compares the futility of modern striving to the swift-footed Achilles' vain attempt to catch the tortoise in Zeno's parable (HW 790; HC 40). This rather abstract distinction between ancient and modern ambitions does not, however, convey the full measure of Nietzsche's contempt for the weakness of modern humanitarian ideals. In addition to its status as a civic virtue, the ancient ideal of competitive struggle possessed, in Nietzsche's view, an element of ferocity that modern people cannot contemplate without dread. "I am afraid," he says, "that we do not understand these things in a sufficiently 'Greek' way; indeed, that we would shudder were we ever to understand them from a Greek perspective" (HW 784; HC 36).

Nietzsche takes evident pleasure in extolling in the Greeks a ruthless exuberance that is, he claims, accessible to the modern sensibility only in its capacity to chill the souls of effete humanitarians. (This exuberant Nietzschean version of *épater le bourgeois* anticipates the mannered *froideur* cultivated over many years by Ernst Jünger.) A corollary of this fundamental dichotomy between ancient and modern sensibilities would distinguish as well between their respective athletic agons. Did the physical culture of ancient Greece include that element of ferocity so admired by Nietzsche? The philosopher Gunter Gebauer has pursued this dichotomy in the context of examining attempts to ground a sportive ethics that can accommodate the unrestrained ambitions of athletic competitions whether ancient or modern.

Gebauer's dichotomy distinguishes between the *oral* culture of ancient Greece and the modern *written* culture that promulgates the modern Olympic ideal of *citius altius fortius* (faster, higher, stronger) and inscribes quantifiable record performances in documents that constitute a written history of athletic achievement. Yet the purpose of Gebauer's inquiry is much less to distinguish between ancients and moderns than it is to establish the uncommunicability of the elite athlete's "internal perspective" and its fundamental immunity to the normative rule making so dear to ethics.[4] The subjective experience of the athlete, he implies, is "oral" in precisely this sense, and this orality precludes a "moral" interpretation of the athlete's actions in the heat of competition. Hence a "different level of discourse would be useful in the discussion of the morals of today's athletes." The key to this interpretation of the athlete's experience lies in the nature of competition itself: "We will see that the way in which competition is engaged in is characterized by the fact that it is not distinct, that it cannot be pinned down to concepts, and furthermore that it is ambiguous by nature and constantly changing. Competition in sport is absolutely no realm in which morals can flourish, let alone ethics."

This interpretation of the athletic agon emphasizes the competitor's search for almost any kind of advantage over his rival and his mobilization of both physical and mental capabilities in the pursuit of victory. The "spirit" or "essence" of the game that corresponds to this agon cannot appropriately be governed by the "rules" of a game, since the proscriptions inherent in such regulations will damage the scope and spontaneity of the creative agon. Gebauer must therefore reject an "essentialism of rules that ostensibly would guide the actions of all athletes. It is unfair and intellectually dishonest to hold up to athletes today a rigid code of virtues. Athletes, confronted with many competitors who are nearly their equals, are increasingly called upon to optimize their mental possibilities" (470).

This version of the athletic agon focuses on intelligence rather than the conventional image of brute strength carrying the day. Detienne and Vernant, Gebauer notes, "have described in classical Greek thought a 'great category of mind' that also subsumes the quest of the ancient athletes for the 'advantage.' It is a 'game of social and intellectual practices' that are bound to the conditions of place and time, embedded into conduct, and inseparable from it." This form of athletic cunning was called *Mètis* ("wits") and is defined as "the category in which thinking, knowledge, and recognition are melded into a complex whole that is applied to a fleeting and ambiguous reality that cannot be grasped by logic, concepts, and argumentation. *Mètis* appears particularly in situations of confrontation and competition" and "makes it appear as though one's physical abilities transcend human powers and attain the quality of the unique" (471). Gebauer's purpose here is to stress the role of intelligence in competition and thereby challenge the "rules of the game," rooted in ethical thinking, that claim an authoritative role within the "fleeting and ambiguous reality" of the competitive struggle.

How should we respond to this attempt to create a kind of "teleological suspension of the ethical" (Kierkegaard) within the experiential realm of competition? How, we might ask, can ethics exercise *any* authority within such a transitory and ambiguous sphere? Gebauer's position appears to be romantic and even Nietzschean in its vision of the unfettered athletic imagination and the performances it makes possible. "It is the aspiration of athletes themselves to act according to their imaginations, internal scenarios, and wishes for immortality," he writes. "This goes beyond a mere desire for perfection or excellence. It deals with the individualistic morals of achieving distinction through action." The problem here is that an individualistic morality that expresses the wishes and imagination of the athlete may have nothing to do with shared norms and may, therefore, be no morality at all. As Gebauer himself points out, "Such egocentric morals can create cultural values but can also threaten them" (471). Gebauer's interpretation of the sportive agon thus leaves unresolved the problem of regulating the imaginative strategies and desires that it produces. As we shall see, the fertile imaginations and burning desires of today's elite athletes have created an "egocentric morality" that has imperilled high-performance sport as we know it.

To what extent is this "Nietzschean" interpretation of the sportive agon rooted in the thinking of the master himself? Can Nietzsche's thought serve as an intellectual pedigree for an agonistic ideal based on the athlete's ambition to achieve self-transcendence through high performance? While "Homer's Contest" makes it clear that Nietzsche saw unbridled competition as an essential vital principle, this interest in the stimulating effects of intense rivalry does not address the self-transformation achieved by many modern athletes through scientific training methods and the use of proscribed drugs. In this respect, Nietzsche's extraordinary interest in the body and its physiological mysteries can be seen as a transitional phase between two epochs in the history of thinking about the athletic potential of the human organism. Nietzsche lost his sanity at a time (1890) when scientific interest in the physiology of the athlete was still in a nascent state.[5] Interest in the physiology of athletic stress blossomed in Europe during the 1890s as Nietzsche declined prior to his death in 1900. The same period saw the rise to popularity of the intrepid (and drug-ingesting) six-day cyclists who pedalled themselves to exhaustion before excited crowds in the velodromes of Europe. Nietzsche's chance to adopt the elite athlete as an exemplar of the "great health" he celebrated in the ancient Greeks was thus destroyed by his illness.

This is not the place to explore the richness of Nietzsche's (primarily metaphorical) thinking about physiological processes.[6] While we should note that his exaltation of physical vitality seems to have grown (in a rather perversely overcompensating way) out of his own medical martyrdom—the dysentery, diphtheria, headaches, and digestive disorders that made him "thirst for the end" (1880)—our task here is to assess his role as a thinker about physical strength and judge to what degree it foreshadowed the athletic ambition to break records and thus transcend human limits. The fact is that Nietzsche's interest in gymnastic exercises and horseback riding as conducive to health, or his enthusiasm about the "primeval physicality *[physischen Urwald-Leiblichkeit]* of barbarian peoples," are not the same thing as an interest in record-breaking sport (Schipperges 57).[7] Similarly, it is interesting that Nietzsche wondered about the morality of changing the body by altering its chemistry with drugs; but his substantial interest in pharmacology, including stimulants, did not envision performance-enhancing drugs.[8] After a century of high-performance athletics, and a quarter-century of anabolic steroid abuse by elite athletes, it may be difficult for us to recognize that the exaltation of physiological vitality is not always synonymous with the exaltation of prodigious athletic feats.

The "athleticizing" of Nietzsche's meditations on human physiology was accomplished by the medical historian Georges Canguilhem in *The Normal and the Pathological* (1943). Canguilhem borrowed from Nietzsche (who had borrowed from the physiologist Claude Bernard) the idea that the distinction between "normal" and "pathological" physiology was an illusion, and that the disease process is a natural stimulant to health. "Diseases are new ways of life," Canguilhem remarks with Nietzschean boldness, without which the healthy organism cannot be tested and physiology cannot progress. Abolishing the distinction between the normal and the pathological prepares the way for man to "compel nature and bend it to his normative desires," that is, to modify the human organism as he sees fit. The prospect of such modifications raises in turn the problem of defining what is normal and what is abnormal: "To the extent that living beings diverge from the specific type, are they abnormal in that they endanger the specific form or are they inventors on the road to new forms?"[9] This sort of thinking points toward biological experiments on the human organism that even Nietzsche could not have imagined.

The idea of normal human physiology is for Canguilhem "not static or peaceful, but a dynamic and polemical concept" that points toward a defiance of human limits. His own polemic on human biology is rooted in the Nietzschean ideal of "great health" and finds its fulfillment in that image of human transcendence through athletic achievement Nietzsche did not live to see. His idea of "health in the absolute sense" implies nothing less than a "boundless capacity to institute new biological norms," and supreme athletic achievement is the most dramatic representation of expanding human powers. He thus quotes approvingly "Thibaudet's witty remark": "It is the record figures, not physiology, that answers the question: how many meters can a man jump." Our "seduction" by "the image of the athlete" is thus rooted in the fact that health is an "establisher of vital norms."[10]

Having destabilized the very concept of health, Canguilhem is free to violate health in the service of a dynamic ideal by arguing that "the possible abuse of health is part of health" (200), and here we may note that our acceptance of the inhuman stresses of high-performance sport is a perfect fulfillment of Canguilhem's physiological bravado. (Twenty-five years earlier, the pioneering French sportsphysician Philippe Tissié had pointed out that "sportive fatigue produces a kind of experimental disease in the healthy man."[11]) "If we can speak of normal man as determined by the physiologist," Canguilhem writes, "it is because normative men exist for whom it is normal to break norms and establish new ones" (164). The development of this ethos over the past century has coincided with the scientizing of high-performance sports such as long-distance cycling (the Tour de France) and the track and field events, whose best practitioners are now routinely served by teams composed of physicians, physiologists, biomechanicians, psychologists, and nutritionists in addition to trainers and coaches. The role of medical science in this "gigantic experiment carried out on the human organism"[12] is curiously ambiguous, in that it preserves the viability of the athlete's body for the purpose of enabling it to deal with the ever-greater degrees of stress that are associated with record-breaking performances. This is, truly, a Nietzschean sportsmedicine in the service of an athletic agon that will not end until the resources of the human body are utterly exhausted or the psychological toll of training becomes too great for most athletes to bear.

Modern high-performance sport fulfills Canguilhem's expectations by threatening the health of athletes rather than preserving or improving it.[13] Sports physicians have made periodic announcements to the effect that certain training regimens or events have pushed the human body to its limits. Many elite athletes live with the constant risk of injury, and some coaches take steps to minimize possible damage. Thus in 1992 a German trainer noted that she assigned cross-training exercises to her (female) shotputters so that they would not wind up as "orthopedic scrap-metal."[14] At the same time, there are sporting events such as the Tour de France cycling race that are by their very nature literally "inhuman" in the demands they make on the human organism. A five-time winner of the Tour, the Spaniard Miguel Induráin could not on one occasion recognize the video image of his own pain-distorted face—a stress-induced (if temporary) loss of identity in the midst of his agon. Small wonder that another winner of the Tour, the American Greg Lemond, has commented that all of the riders are "pedalling in the red zone" where the threat of physiological breakdown is always near.[15] This is why the Tour has been a drug-soaked event for the past hundred years. "Everyone," Lemond said in 1992, "believes that his competitor is taking some sort of wonder drug."[16] Here as elsewhere in elite sport, the use of drugs tends to extend the agon rather than relieve the agony. Anabolic-androgenic steroids, which are synthetic variants of the male hormone testosterone, have made it possible for many athletes, both male and female, to intensify their training and thus improve their performances. (The fact that these drugs are banned has not stopped their use by athletes.)

The scientizing and pharmacologizing of elite sport have complicated the athletic agon in various ways. Some athletes have reported an intuitive sense that certain of their competitors are in a supernormal state that gives them a special advantage. A few have reported abnormal states of mind and body suggesting they had been drugged without their knowledge for the purpose of boosting their performances.[17] The idea that many top performances are no longer possible without a sophisticated sportsmedical establishment is likely to discourage those lacking such resources. On the other hand, the world-record-setting Kenyan runner Yobes Ondieki once refused to submit to Western-style physiological monitoring on the grounds that knowledge of such data would amount to a form of psychological imprisonment that would inhibit his performance.[18] Indeed, sports science has come to be seen by some Europeans as the white athlete's last hope against the superior performances of African athletes.[19] One result of these uncertainties and anxieties is the fact that, in addition to the traditional agonistic relationship with one's competitors, there is now for many elite athletes a less dramatic but no less real physiological agon that is acted out in the form of laboratory tests and training norms that are pitiless in their demands for greater fitness and greater suffering as the price of progress. The physical and emotional costs of these agonizing training ordeals are seldom conveyed to the sporting publics that consume the resulting performances as entertainment.

An extreme development within the agonistic physical culture of the late twentieth century is the advent of "ultra-sports" such as triathlon competitions, which combine long swims, cycling races, and marathon runs, and foot races that can cover distances up to 100 miles over difficult terrain. The difference between traditional high-performance sport and these ultra-events can transcend any quantitative measure of physical exertion. For while the traditional elite athlete manages stress in order to produce a performance, the ultra-athlete is more likely to produce a performance in order to seek out stress as a kind of total experience. One example of such an ordeal is the Swiss Alpine Marathon, a 67-kilometer race over rugged mountain terrain a mile and a half above sea level. In 1995, this event attracted 1652 participants who took anywhere from five to twelve hours to complete the course. The attending physician described participation in such an event as a physiological paradox: "The run itself is medical idiocy, whereas the training sessions that lead up to it do promote good health." The most interesting feature of such agons is the transformation of a quantitative performance into a state of mind that is more important than objective performance norms. As one observer puts it: "Everyone experiences 'his' run in his own way; often in a state of exaltation *[im Rausch]* in which a mental high compensates for the physical pain."[20] This ostensibly solitary agon thus creates a comradeship of suffering that deemphasizes athletic competition in favor of celebrating a shared ordeal. The deepest agon thus pits the group as a whole against the human limits that are inherent in all of them.

Implicit in this culture of exertion and suffering is the possibility of revolt against its terrible demands. "You murderers! You damned murderers!" the exhausted French rider Octave Lapine screamed at the organizers of the Tour de France in 1910 as he arrived at the top of a long mountain climb.[21] The apparent naïveté of Lapine's outrage is a measure of our own desensitizing to the self-inflicted physiological violence that we take for granted. "The athlete is a sick person *[un malade]*," Philippe Tissié bluntly stated in 1919, as if seconding Lapine's protest, and he warned that the increasing demands of the performance principle would put athletes at medical risk (155). At the end of the twentieth century it is clear that the cautionary response to stress that is so evident in Tissié's writings must now compete with an embracing of medically supervised stress that makes the body in pain a privileged site of human striving and thus human identity itself. The ostensible masochism of these "extreme" experiences can be understood as a defensive response to a gradual loss of the body in an increasingly electronic environment. For in a world in which "virtual reality" threatens to displace the experiential primacy of blood, sweat, and tears, the corporeal agon may appear as a last defense against the evaporation of life as we have known it.

Notes

1. The Oxford English Dictionary defines the word *agon* as "the contest for the prize at the games," and by extension, "any contest or struggle. *Gr. Antig.* A public celebration of games, a contest for the prize at those games."

2. Waldo E. Sweet, *Sport and Recreation in Ancient Greece: A Sourcebook with Translations* (New York: Oxford Univ. Press, 1987), 118.

3. Friedrich Nietzsche, "Homers Wettkampf," *Sämtliche Werke: Kritische Studienausgabe,* ed. Giorgio Colli and Mazzino Montinari, 15 vols. (Berlin: de Gruyter, 1967–1977), 1: 785. "Homer's Contest," this volume, 37. Abbreviated in the text as HW and HC, respectively.

4. Gunter Gebauer, "Citius—Altius—Fortius and the Problem of Sport Ethics: a Philosopher's Viewpoint," *Sport, the Third Millennium: Proceedings of the International Symposium, Quebec City, Canada, May 21–25, 1990,* ed. Fernand Landry, Marc Landry, and Magdeleine Yerlès (Sainte-Foy: Les presses de l'Université Laval, 1991), 468.

5. See John Hoberman, *Mortal Engines: The Science of Performance and the Dehumanization of Sport* (New York: The Free Press, 1992): 62–99.

6. See Heinrich Schipperges, *Am Leitfaden des Leibes: Zur Anthropologik und Therapeutik Friedrich Nietzsches* (Stuttgart: E. Klett, 1975).

7. See also Schipperges 148, 167, 169. Translations are my own, unless otherwise noted. Nietzsche's interest in the health of the (male) body is aesthetic rather than athletic. For example: "Personal *manly virtù, virtù* of the body, is regaining value, estimation becomes more physical, nutrition meatier. Beautiful

men are again becoming possible." Nietzsche, *The Will to Power,* trans. Walter Kaufmann and R. J. Hollingdale, ed. Walter Kaufmann (New York: Vintage, 1968), 78.

8. See Schipperges (129); and Malcolm Pasley, "Nietzsche's Use of Medical Terms," *Nietzsche: Imagery and Thought: A Collection of Essays* (Berkeley: Univ. of California Press, 1978), 128.

9. Georges Canguilhem, *The Normal and the Pathological,* trans. Carolyn R. Fawcett and Robert S. Cohen, intro. by Michel Foucault (New York: Zone Books, 1989), 100, 41, 141.

10. See Canguilhem (239, 196, 164, 201), and especially: "But perhaps human physiology is always more or less applied physiology, physiology of work, of sport, of leisure, of life at high altitudes, etc." (271).

11. Philippe Tissié, *L'Education physique et la Race* (Paris: Flammarion, 1919), 156–57.

12. W[ildor] Hollmann, "Risikofaktoren in der Entwicklung des Hochleistungssports," *Sportmedizin-Kursbestimmung* (Deutscher Sportärztekongreß, Kiel, 16–19. Oktober, 1986), ed. H. Rieckert (Berlin: Springer, 1987), 15.

13. See, for example, Hoberman (1–32).

14. "Der schwierige Versuch, den Obelixen zu trotzen," *Süddeutsche Zeitung* (December 31 / January 1, 1992).

15. See "Atemzug für zwei," *Der Spiegel* (July 20, 1992): 191–92.

16. "Die Akte Telekom," *Der Spiegel* (April 18, 1994): 223–24.

17. See, for example, "Die Akte Telekom" (222).

18. "Das Laufen ist ihre zweite Natur," *Süddeutsche Zeitung* (September 3, 1991).

19. As the president of the German Track and Field Federation *(Deutscher Leichtathletikverband)* stated in 1993: "In the developed countries track and field are caught up in a deep crisis: the athletes see the superiority of the Africans in the distance races, and many simply give up. No young person is going to train for the title of 'the world's fastest white man.' TT " "Die Profis abkopplen" (Interview with Dr. Helmut Digel), *Der Spiegel* (August 23, 1993): 144. On the failure of Western sports science to boost the performances of white athletes, see "Die Springflut der schwarzen Sieger," *Süddeutsche Zeitung* (September 16, 1988): 56.

20. "Extreme Ausdauerleistungen und die Frage nach dem Sinn," *Neue Zürcher Zeitung* (July 31, 1995): 25.

21. "Atemzug für zwei" (191).

Baudrillard, *After Hours*, and the Postmodern Suppression of Socio-Sexual Conflict

Cynthia Willett

There was a time when Hollywood films could end happily and yet make a socially progressive contribution to conflicts that afflict American culture. This, however, is not the prevailing view about the classical Hollywood films. Most critics argue that the screwball comedies of the '30s and '40s, or what Stanley Cavell terms the "comedies of remarriage," concoct a magical escape from very real class and gender struggles of the Depression.[1] My claim is that, on the contrary, screwball comedies such as Howard Hawks's *Bringing Up Baby* (1938), George Cukor's *The Philadelphia Story* (1940), Preston Sturges's *The Lady Eve* (1941), and Frank Capra's *It Happened One Night* (1934) educate their audiences to reinterpret the liberal American definition of the "pursuit of happiness."

The contemporary suspicions about the former claim arise predominantly from postmodernist critiques of classical structures of plot and character development. In this chapter, I shall focus on the postmodern theory of French sociologist Jean Baudrillard and an exemplary postmodern film, Martin Scorsese's *After Hours* (1985), in order to argue that postmodern culture does not so much critique as suppress the socio-sexual *agons* (i.e., the conflicts that instigate plot and character development) of classical Hollywood comedy and, with these *agons*, the possibility for progressive social change.

Screwball comedy exhibits a dialectic that can be dubbed "Neo-Aristotelian." Films of this genre account for middle-class America's cultural debt to a classical ethical principle that has become known as "the golden mean." The Hollywood films portray heterosexual marriage as a unity of two extreme characters (often drawn from upper and lower classes, while also representing contrasting roles of artist and yuppie, jock and intellectual, scientist and artist, etc.). Cast in such roles, each character moderates some dimension of his or her personality in order to learn to communicate with a prospective mate. Most typically, the comic film juxtaposes the values of the practical but rigid to the free but irresponsible. This type of comedy emphasizes that each of the contrasting characters learns from the other and that it is this mutual education that justifies the happy ending.

Bringing Up Baby, for example, opposes a rigid and excessively rationalistic[2] scientist played by Cary Grant to the screwball, or, to use the postmodernist language of Deleuze and Guattari, the "schizophrenic"[3] Katharine Hepburn. Both Grant and Hepburn are comic characters precisely to the degree that they verge from an ethics of moderation, originally conceptualized by Aristotle as necessary to the happiness of the human being *qua* social animal. The comedy ends happily only when the hyper-rationalist Grant learns to become more flexible, that is, more open to the surprises as well as the pleasures of erotic desire, and Hepburn's "feminine negativity" (as Julia Kristeva terms the transgressive pleasures of "schizoid subversion") yields to a certain measure of social responsibility.[4]

This mutual transformation is evident in the final scene of *Bringing Up Baby.* Hepburn approaches Grant in his laboratory, where he is piecing together the skeletal remains of a brontosaurus. While throughout most of the film Hepburn gleefully displaces one thing after another, at last she returns something, namely, the missing tail-bone of the brontosaurus, to its rightful place. Grant, on the other hand, allows the rather phallic bone to fall and the entire lifeless structure of the dinosaur to collapse in order to embrace the fully living Hepburn. The rigor mortis of a masculine rationalism, no less than the transgressive eroticism of "feminine negativity," give way before a renewed vision of community. The two contrasting characters learn something.[5] It is this mutual education, that is, this way of "being brought up," that produces a non-hierarchical vision of social exchange, or what Northrop Frye in his discussion of comedy terms a "pragmatically free society," and that thereby legitimates an otherwise unearned happy ending.[6]

My defense of screwball comedy is not motivated by a simple nostalgia for traditional films. The '30s and '40s films clearly contain images that are regressive by contemporary standards. An example of the limitations of classical screwball comedy is found in *The Philadelphia Story*. This film centers on a haughty heiress (played by Katharine Hepburn) and her alcoholic ex-husband (played by Cary Grant). The final scene of the film has Grant standing behind Hepburn, who, in puppet-like fashion, repeats the words that Grant gives her to say before an audience expecting a wedding ceremony. The image of a woman who has become what the film depicts as "easy to handle" and therefore "ready for marriage" is not what the contemporary feminist would want to associate with a happy ending. My interest in classical screwball comedy is in the agonal dialectic that animates the plot. In *The Philadelphia Story,* the overly rigid Katharine Hepburn recognizes her own imperfections and forgives those of others while Cary Grant learns to moderate his frivolity and accept his various social responsibilities.

The mutual transformation of contrasting characters provides a basis for a pragmatic model of community. Much of the laughter of screwball comedy is caused by misunderstandings between eccentric main characters. As the characters confront those vices that are destructive both to themselves and to others, they engender necessary conditions for communication. At the same time, the end of the screwball film does not typically show these characters as having lost their distinctive differences. The comedy in the film's final scene usually develops through the affirmation of those idiosyncracies of character that are products of a pluralistic community. For example, in the last scene of *Bringing Up Baby,* the ever-exuberant Hepburn returns the missing bone only in order to pull down the entire skeletal remains of the brontosaurus. The resolution of the film's main conflict does not require that Hepburn transform her eccentric self. Nor does comic resolution require that Grant and Hepburn adopt the same styles of self-expression. On the contrary, the final scene celebrates residual differences between Grant and Hepburn and thereby suggests that comic dialectic does not anchor communication or community in shared concepts, or otherwise in what postmodern critics term the logic of the same, but in shared laughter over the playful exchanges between idiosyncratic human beings.

Hollywood screwball comedy restages the agons of dialectic derived from a fundamentally tragic conception of social change that originates in Hegel and is appropriated by Marxist philosophies.[7] The constant ironies and eventual revelations that characterize Hegelian dialectic grow out of Hegel's reinterpretation of classical Greek tragedy. Hegel argued that classical tragedy should not be viewed as a static and one-sided human transgression against transcendent law but as a fully human struggle between partial and intertwined perspectives of a dynamic ethical society. According to Hegelian dialectic, the struggle between opposed perspectives leads to tragic violence until each side recognizes its interdependence on the other. The reversals and acts of recognition identified with German idealism, however, subordinate human claims for happiness to an abstract notion of truth. Notoriously, Hegelian dialectic leaves behind social and political spheres in order to locate truth tentatively in a cathartic art (that is, art whose function is the purgation of the spectator's emotions) and finally in a purely concept-based philosophy.

My suggestion is that dialectic, as redefined by way of classical American film comedy (rather than classical European tragedy), promotes the struggles and reconciliations required of an ethical society without finally sacrificing human desire to a cathartic or otherwise overly abstract truth. The contrasting characters that make up the comic dialectic grow in the American comedies as in the classical tragedies to recognize both their own limitations and the virtues of those who are different. In this sense, comic dialectic parts from what Northrop Frye identifies as the traditional principle of comedy, namely, "unincremental repetition, the literary imitation of ritual bondage" (Frye 168). The audience does not so much laugh at inferior types who fail to transform themselves as laugh with idiosyncratic characters who learn to moderate precisely those eccentricities that are destructive to self and Other before these differences escalate into all-out war.

Comic dialectic works only when social differences are mediated rather than polarized as they are in the classical tragic agon. This distinction between the approaches to social differences can in part be accounted for by way of the diverse aims that inform comic and tragic dialectics. Comic dialectic aims towards the horizontal interrelation of individuals in a pragmatically free community and not the vertical subordination of individual happiness for the sake of a more abstract concept of truth. On the contrary, a typical comic plot transforms the life of the socially and sexually repressed thinker into the less predictable but more liberated life of the lover. *Bringing Up Baby* presents such a transformation. The nerdy Cary Grant first appears before the camera alone and in the pose of Rodin's "The Thinker," while the final scene brings together Grant and Hepburn for an embrace that mimes Rodin's "The Kiss."

My argument is that if comic dialectic breaks down in postmodern film it is not because classical Hollywood films create "fairy tale" illusions of happiness and therefore are not credible, but because they invoke an ethical dynamic that is overlooked by postmodern critics. Scorsese's *After Hours* depicts what happens *after* the dialectic (that is, the plot progression) of Hollywood comedy *no longer works*. The film sets up the same oppositions between male rationality and female irony that animate *Bringing Up Baby*. However, while in the screwball comedy an agonistic encounter between male and female values leads to mutual transformation for both male and female characters, *After Hours* preempts any dialectical exchange between the so-called "opposite sexes." With the breakdown of dialectic, the American postmodern scene is literally "after hours."

Baudrillard accounts for the failure of postmodern culture to generate social progress in terms of the rise of new forms of power. His argument is based on a premise that he shares with a broad range of post–World War II European and American philosophers (including poststructuralists and Wittgensteinians). According to this view, subjectivity is an effect of language. The implication is that meanings are grounded in external communication networks and not in personal or private subjective experiences. These networks are made up of a web of external signifying relations or matrices whose endpoint, as Bill Martin points out in

Matrix and Line, can be an "asocial 'textualism.' "[8] For Baudrillard, in postmodern culture these matrices of power take the form of the global information net, which reaches into every aspect of our personal lives. Not emotion-laden language games but emotionless computer chips store memory and determine subjectivity. Power is no longer experienced as repressive of subconscious desire and, therefore, does not lead to agonistic opposition. In Baudrillard's terms, the agonistic scenes of classical drama reverberate in postmodern "obscene" or the visual equivalent of postmodern noise, which fails to produce a vision for social change.[9]

Scorsese's *After Hours* exemplifies the "hi-tech postmodernism" of Baudrillard and so too can be interpreted as a direct attack on the emancipatory claims implicit within comic dialectic. Paul Hackett (played by Griffin Dunne) presents a postmodern version of the classic comic role of the bore, in this case a computer hack (hence, Hackett's name) with a banal desk job in upper Manhattan. Just as the opening shot in *Bringing Up Baby* fixes the nerdy paleontologist behind an elaborate matrix of skeletal remains, so the first shot of Paul Hackett locates him within an equally lifeless maze of office desks topped with computer monitors. In both films, male characters are positioned within structures of power that are indifferent to social and expressive dimensions of the self. Also in both films, the plot is set in motion by the machinations of a female character. But if in the end Hepburn transforms the stiff Grant into a flesh and blood human being, the female characters that Dunne encounters only serve to harden the defenses of an ever more paranoid male subject. In screwball comedy, an encounter with an Other brings about the emancipation, or, I am arguing, the redefinition, of desire. For the narcissistic subject defined by postmodernism as an effect of power, an encounter with an Other outside that system of power can only pose a threat.

Paul Hackett's nightmarish encounters with the series of threatening women occur in downtown Soho. After work, Hackett encounters a seemingly innocent and seductive blonde named Marcy (played by Rosanna Arquette). The two characters discover a mutual interest in Henry Miller's *Tropic of Cancer.* After briefly discussing the book, which is taken to be stating something to the effect that art is dead, Marcy mentions that she shares a loft with an authentic Soho artist whose specialty is bagel and cream cheese paper weights. Hackett uses the bagel and cream cheese sculpture as a ploy for pursuing his more obvious interest in Marcy. Later that night he shows up at her loft and finds her roommate, the kinky sculptress Kiki Bridges. Kiki is at work on a papier-maché figure that recasts Edvard Munch's expressionistic "The Scream" in the style of George Segal's bland and expressionless mummies. The papier-maché sculpture serves as a central figure in the film, immediately suggesting a central difference between dialectical and postmodern experiences of alienation. The blank postmodern figure, unlike its expressionistic predecessor, exhibits a subjectivity that is not so much repressed as socially and sexually empty.

The almost obligatory flirtation between Hackett and Kiki leads nowhere, Kiki falling asleep just as Hackett is about to seduce her. Meanwhile, Marcy returns to the loft to discover Kiki asleep in Hackett's arms. After Marcy is satisfied that nothing happened between Hackett and Kiki, she promises Hackett an evening of wild fun, all the while intimating that because of some kind of accident her body may be covered with burn marks. The image of burn marks not only turns Hackett off but solicits his worst fears of mutilation.

Hackett runs out on Marcy, who has no one to listen to her and thus commits suicide. Meanwhile, Hackett finds himself without money and trapped in Soho for the night. Hackett makes his way to a bar where the bartender offers a subway fare if Hackett retrieves a key for the cash register from the bartender's apartment. However, the apartment residents mistake Hackett for a thief and he finds himself chased through the streets of Soho by a mob of vigilantes threatening either to burn him alive or tear him to shreds. During the chase, Hackett encounters three more blond women, a waitress at the bar, a driver of an ice cream truck, and an old customer of a music club, "Club Berlin," where he also seeks a haven from the threatening mob. However, Hackett's escape from the mob to the Club turns out to be yet one more trap. The older blonde at the Club saves Hackett from the mob only by wrapping him in a papier maché figure that exactly resembles Kiki's version of "The Scream."

The fact that the bouncer at Club Berlin recalls the doorkeeper in Kafka's "Before the Law" emphasizes that Hackett has fallen into a Kafkaesque style maze of paranoid proportions but with a difference. In Yuppie America there is one way out of terror, namely to return to work, as I discuss below. By chance, the real thieves in the film mistake the papier-maché Hackett for Kiki's sculpture, and cart Hackett away. Hackett falls out of the thieves' van in front of the gates of his company the next morning.

Classic Hollywood oppositions reappear in the film in the descriptions of uptown and downtown Manhattan. *After Hours* plays on Soho's reputation as a free-zone for avant-garde art and unsanctioned sexual encounters.[10] If upper Manhattan represents what dialectical thinkers would diagnose as the appropriation of libido to the productive tasks of instrumental reasoning, the Lower East Side promises to desublimate desire and liberate the imagination. In classic screwball comedy, an agonistic encounter between the two worlds would have been *both* productive *and* liberating. But while Dunne seeks a liberating reversal in his life, the ironies in Soho escalate without end. The result is a nightmare of repetitions and reversals without dialectical advance until Dunne is by chance returned home (for the yuppie, work is home) exactly on schedule for work.

After Hours parodies the nightmare of leaving home in *The Wizard of Oz.* For example, Dunne's dizzying fast taxi ride to Soho simulates tornado-like winds. More significantly, like *The Wizard of Oz,* Scorsese's film solicits the conservative sentiment that there is no place like home. In *After Hours,* however, the discovery that there is no place like home turns out to be the parody of a real discovery. Dunne finds himself anxious to return to a home that is no place, or no *real* place, but rather an abstract work space. Even the minimalist decor of his apartment duplicates the sterile, geometric style of his office building. In sharp contrast to the existential black of Soho, uptown interiors come in blank industrial white. Both work space and living space in upper Manhattan center on modern technologies of communication: computer, telephone, cable television. But Dunne's inability to converse with his new colleague at work or to resist grazing the TV with the remote control suggests that upper Manhattan may offer security, but it cannot offer the playful dialogue that screwball films taught viewers to demand from what they would call home.

As a postmodernist, Baudrillard argues in terms more devastating for dialectical progression than do, for example, even the most pessimistic critical theorists. According to Baudrillard, the new devices for exchanging information do not block the human potential for self-expression and social exchange in the reified object of the commercial system, but rather they substitute the simulacra. Since the simulacra of communication do not frustrate but instead pacify desire, they prevent any impetus for personal or political change and preempt any interchange between dialectically opposed characters or positions. As a typically postmodern film, *After Hours* preserves and even intensifies two of the traditional elements of dialectical development: ironic reversal and repetition. But because the film cancels the communication of opposites, of the "opposite sexes" for example, it also denies opportunities for self-discovery and mutual recognition that enable dialectical advance and a happy ending.[11]

Repeatedly, Griffin Dunne finds himself staring before a mirror and yet unable to pull himself together or otherwise discover a cogent sense of self. At the end of the film, Dunne is the same narcissistic bore that he was in the beginning. The adventures of the yuppie do not lead to new powers of self-expression or mutual understanding. In effect, scenes are repeated and reversed; tensions mount but nothing happens. If classical dialectic measures the advance of plot by way of reversals and moments of recognition, *After Hours* deconstructs plot and cancels the linear component of temporal advance.

But then if postmodern America stands at the end of time, *After Hours* demonstrates that it is not because the United States has attained the final goals of history.[12] Nor, if Baudrillard is right, can we mourn the "failure" of historical progress. For failure, like progress, presupposes the possibility of human goals, purposes, or desires, whereas the postmodern screen displays instead scintillating electron beams. The power of these scintillations redefines subjectivity as an effect of electronic communication networks and abstract information systems that paralyzes dramatic progression and dissipates historical dialectic.[13]

After Hours depicts the inescapable networks of power that displace modern dialectic as boring, lifeless, and emasculating. The occupation of computer operator identifies Dunne with what Baudrillard has characterized in his "Ecstasy of Communication" as a "pure screen, a switching center for . . . networks of influences" (133). The paradigmatic postmodern subject exists as a node in circuits of information, of endless connections that relay information and process knowledge. Hi-tech postmodernity transforms the first premise of modernism, knowledge is power, from the "hot universe" of passion, desire, and will, into what Baudrillard deciphers as a "cold universe," or one that optimizes the "smooth operational surface of communication" (127). The pathos that moves dialectical history or even the will that impels Nietzschean-style genealogies of power have disappeared, and seemingly without a trace.

Unlike "true" power, Baudrillard explains, the power of the cold universe produces not a strategy or a stake, but simulations created from mass consumption. Politicians are transformed into media stars. The political as such no longer exists: "Likewise with work. The spark of production, the violence of its stake no longer exists."[14] If the Enlightenment and the Industrial Revolution locate the origin of value in labor, Baudrillard argues that postmodern capitalism has not redefined but disavowed both labor and value.[15] There are only simulacra, "dedicated exclusively," writes Baudrillard, "to their recurrence as signs, and no longer to their 'real' goal at all" (S 41).

If Baudrillard is right, the unsatisfying relation between characters and values of Soho and Upper Manhattan does not illustrate implacable forces resistant to mutual accommodation. *After Hours* does not leave erotic impulses repressed and resistent to the demands of labor in a stalled dialectic. Baudrillard explains: "No so long ago sex and work were savagely opposed terms: today both are dissolved into the same type of demand" (S 36). It is because Griffin Dunne is not libidinally repressed that Soho can provide no cure for him. The classic polarities re-emerge, intensify, and then disperse; for "only capital," Baudrillard writes, "takes pleasure" (S 35).

After Hours ends by returning an unemancipated Dunne to his solitary post at the computer terminal. Although Dunne's position is solitary, the character is not alienated in the classical sense. Computer networking deletes the agonistic difference between self and Other. For example, Griffin Dunne's work place shows no evidence of the traditionally oppressive hierarchy in relations of power. There is no struggle for recognition between employer and employee. Dunne answers to no one. The only encounter between employees occurs in the opening scene, where Dunne instructs a new trainee. But the trainee's attempt to communicate to Dunne his fantasies of becoming a writer meets neither with sympathy nor hostility. Art is dead, and neither dreams nor fantasies register in postmodern memory banks. The new trainee must realize what Griffin Dunne already accepts: dramatic encounters have no place on what Baudrillard unveils as the "empty stage of the social" (S 48).

In a critique of Marxist dialectic, Baudrillard argues:

> [The transmissions of the communication industry are] . . . anti-mediatory. . . . They fabricate non-communication—this is what characterizes them, if one agrees to define communication as an exchange, as a reciprocal space of a speech and a response, and thus of a *responsibility . . . they are what always prevent response,* making all processes of exchange impossible (except in the various forms of response *simulation,* themselves integrated in the transmission process, thus leaving the unilateral nature of communication intact). This is the real abstraction of the media. And the system of social control and power is rooted in it.[16]

Once the communication industry infiltrates social discourse, the mechanism of pre-programmed response emerges. Thoughts count for no more than what can be recorded on the computer-read data sheets of the opinion poll. Emotions reduce to electrical discharges. Between the sexes, person-to-person connection is not possible.[17] For example, a disinterested Dunne accepts the six digits that the lonely Soho barmaid (Teri Garr) gives out as her telephone number even though he realizes that the number is incomplete. Meanwhile, the barmaid, who is, so to speak, not quite "properly wired," insists that those six digits comprise her complete telephone number. Postindustrial networks put out of play the elements of reciprocal exchange necessary for ethical comedy.

A social nexus without reciprocal exchange is not a society deprived of information. On the contrary, Baudrillard portrays postmodern society as a society without secrets. From census takers, poll takers, data collectors of all kinds, the sheer quantity of information accumulated today is "obscene." Baudrillard describes this state of positive communication as a place where "all secrets [are] abolished in a single dimension of information . . . [and where there is] an extermination of interstitial and protective spaces" (E 131). Whatever postindustrial communication would fail to register has no status as fact and therefore cannot be a secret. In the opening scene, Dunne is demonstrating to the new trainee the steps required for storing files in the computer memory. Whatever fails to make it into the file is irretrievably lost. But just as the new trainee finds no register (in Dunne, in his new occupation) for his dreams of being a writer, Dunne will find that the electron beams that wrap his daylight world cannot record his nightmare in Soho. The final scene of the film returns Dunne from his nightmare in Soho to a pre-programmed greeting on his computer screen. The programmed greeting is indifferent to viewer response. The information systems of postmodernism cannot register traces of the secret night, "after hours."

Yet another premise of postmodern culture, at least as it is represented in the ethical context of Derridean deconstruction, leads the postmodern critic to suspect that no system of power is total. As Derrida argues, every system is haunted by the residues of what it would exclude. And so a deconstructive reading of *After Hours* yields what the theories and programs of Jean Baudrillard would elide. In the final scene, Dunne appears at work with the telltale traces of the other world of Soho still on him. The plaster dust that speckles his suit and tie suggests what otherwise the film would erase. There is a remainder of secret desire that is not neatly channelled into the sterile networks of technological power. Not all pleasures belong, as Baudrillard hypothesizes, to capital and its simulacra. The expression of a desire outside of the demands of the new institutions of power can and does occur.

So too the sense of distraction or irony that characterizes Griffin Dunne's performance at work reveals hidden pockets of friction in the system. This friction—this difference within the interstices of any conglomeration of the same—enables dialectical critique and accounts for the possibility of resistance to capitalist forms of power.[18] The redefinition of the human being beyond interiority into terms that are operational is never clean.

Thus, a deconstructive interpretation of *After Hours* could serve to rehabilitate avant-garde efforts to oppose and even overcome the debilitating effects of institutions of power. Of course, Derrida poses dialectic as a primary target for deconstructive practices. Nonetheless, deconstructive theory would locate a basis for difference in the margins of what Baudrillard theorizes as the totalizing power of the new technology. The remainder depicted, for example, in *After Hours,* between power and its other could serve to reengender dialectical change.

Scorsese's film, however, presents a second stumbling block for ethical advance. For even if a deconstructive interpretation of the film would in theory provide a basis for radical difference, Scorsese's film succeeds in frightening its yuppie viewer away from any kind of an encounter with extreme difference. If *After Hours* reveals the emptiness of the culture of information, it also represents the impulses of the avant-garde as pathological and bizarre. Dunne's escape from the culture of information to the culture of expression is represented as a relapse into a nightmare of sado-masochistic violence. If Baudrillard on occasion romanticizes graffiti-art and the speech of the streets as the only surviving forms of reciprocal, agonistic communication, *After Hours* demythologizes that dream as insipid fantasy (CS 176). The pervasive evidence of the commercialization or otherwise the death of art, as well as the castration images that characterize the graffiti of Soho, support Douglas Kellner's claim that the so-called free "communication [of the street] can be just as manipulative, distorted, reified as the rest as media communication" (67).

The Soho of *After Hours* recalls in part the Paris of Henry Miller's *Tropic of Cancer,* the book that Dunne is reading in the first scene in Soho, and that initially attracts the attention of Rosanna Arquette. But if, as I have argued, the streets of Miller's Paris—the city that Miller describes as a whore—"flow with the healthy fluids of life,"[19] the series of women who appear in Scorsese's Soho tease and frustrate and finally cancel the desire that they promise to set free. *After Hours* may not succeed in erasing all traces of libidinal communication outside of systems of power, but it does succeed in conjuring up fear for what is alien.

This paranoia may be justified if indeed unrepressed desire—at least as it is exhibited in the manipulative behavior of Griffin Dunne in *After Hours* or in the characters of Henry Miller's *Tropic of Cancer*—is without responsibility, that is, without the possibility of reciprocal exchange.[20] Throughout the film any interest that Dunne shows in the "opposite sex," not to mention in the value of art (e.g., the bagel and cream cheese paper weights), only fuels narcissistic sexual gratification. Dunne journeys to Soho not, as he pretends, in order to admire the work of a Soho artist but to pursue the artist's attractive if strangely troubled roommate, Rosanna Arquette. Dunne interprets Arquette's desire for a heart-to-heart discussion of her problems as a block to his advances. Throughout the various chase scenes of the film, Dunne shows that he is incapable of caring for another person.

Arquette finally stops stalling when she mistakes Dunne's sexual interest for sympathy. But just at the point where Arquette is open to Dunne's advances, he convinces himself that her anxiety comes from attempting to conceal a badly burned body. A phobia of burn scars prompts Dunne to leave and anticipates the hell-like night to follow. If Dunne appears in Soho on the prowl, the pursuer becomes the pursued. He is chased first by women who seem only to seek some understanding and finally by an almost bacchanalian mob led by the driver of the ice cream truck. The mob mistakes him for a thief and, more appropriately, an intruder, and threatens in Dionysian fashion to tear him to bits.

Dunne's encounters with a weird series of demanding women, emasculated gays, and thieving latinos reinforce middle-class male phobias of life outside of the "normal" channels of success. The central focus of the film is on the series of blondes, all of whom fit stereotypes in a misogynist culture. The move from uptown to downtown is also a move from a world centered on men to one that is depicted as female. The series of blondes range from Arquette, whose attractiveness is tied to the presentation of herself as victim, to the clinging but also nagging, wifely barmaid, to the bitchy driver of the ice cream truck, and finally, at Club Berlin, to the cradling arms of the overprotective mother-type.

Moreover, each blonde comes from an older generation than the former, thus invoking yet another object of repulsion, that of the aging woman. Numerous castration images, for example, bathroom graffiti exposing a penis to the jaws of a shark and the mousetraps surrounding Teri Garr's netted bed, emphasize the clear danger that women with power evoke.

Dunne survives the mob of vigilantes only with the help of the last woman, the motherly one, who shelters him within a papier-maché figure in her womb-like salon. The fact that the figure resembles the sculpture of the artist whose work he originally sought to purchase satirizes the countercultural drive to transform life into a work of art. The figure represents Dunne's regression from active consumer to passive object. Wrapped in shreds of newsprint, the emasculated Dunne literally vanishes into the bits of information that comprise the communications networks. The stiff, fetal figure pulled from the dark subterranean world of Soho suggests that the muted Dunne is about to be not reborn but stillborn to the labor force, or what Baudrillard terms "the deep-frozen infantile world" once known as the real (S 24).

Dunne does not escape from his nightmare intact. Near the end, while Dunne is dancing with the last of the blondes and as the words of the musical refrain repeat, "Is that all there is?," he mumbles that all he wants is to live. In effect, this allegedly advanced society at the end of history reduces the human being to a most elemental impulse: drained of speech and desire, it seems that the *animal laborans* wants to subsist.[21] Nothing more is at stake.

After Hours evokes a sense of uneasiness with the system and yet mocks the yuppie's failure to change it. The film promises and frustrates and finally paralyzes a paranoid male subject before webs of power that are depicted as castrating, all-consuming, and female. The aging motherly blonde saves Dunne from the Dionysian mob by virtually suffocating him in shredded newspaper. The resulting figure of the muted Dunne aptly anticipates, not his recovery as a speaking subject, but his return to the suffocating matrices of the postmodern communication networks. That the paralyzing arms of the communications network extend into Soho art suggests that Dunne, like the character of Dorothy in *The*

Wizard of Oz, never really left home to begin with (home being, for Dunne, the labyrinthine systems of power).

In its contemporary usage, the word "matrix" signifies a network of intersections between input and output leads in a computer that is also sometimes referred to as the "motherboard." This contemporary figuration of the switchboard of the computer as maternal is linked to the identification of the etymological root of the postmodern term "matrix" with the Latin *matrix.* The Latin term signifies womb and stems from *mater* or mother. *After Hours* has Dunne returned to the security of his computer station as to a kind of womb. But if Baudrillard is right, the matrices of postmodern power lack the "secret pockets," that is, the interstices of either existential desire or interpersonal alterity, that might resist dominant sources of power and engender narratives of subversion and social change. As long as postmodernists like Baudrillard and Scorsese project images of power as castrating and castrated matrices, as though of a maternal origin missing—not a penis but the folds of a womb—no tale of ethical and political change is possible. The disfiguring and disenabling "hysterectomy" performed by hi-tech postmodernism does not so much re-envision as remove the sources of desire.

Baudrillardian theory would suggest that Dunne is no more a passive object than his Soho female tormentors are aggressive subjects. There is no agon of classical polarities because there are no more poles. The "pacification" that characterizes postindustrial societies stems from the fact that "the two differential poles [of classic dialectic] implode into each other . . . [producing] a simultaneity of contradictions that is both the parody and the end of all dialectic" (S 70). If comic dialectic moderates rigid characters by way of encounters with their equally excessive opposites, postmodern farce dismantles the free zone that exceeds the grids of power and engenders dialectical advance. No longer free, Soho appears as the product of the reactionary imagination, stereotypes constructed out of regressive narcissistic middle-class phobias. The final diminution of Griffin Dunne to an image of fetal passivity represents his domination by power structures that are depicted not in terms of a masculine economy of mastery but rather as emasculating matrices of pre-programmed technology. In postmodernity, power is not phallic: it is maternal. This new image of power, however, is not friendly to women, at least not as long as major artists and theorists like Scorsese and Baudrillard schematize power by relying on reactionary images of the feminine.

I suspect, however, that the web of emasculating and emasculated powers envisioned in *After Hours* is not real. If Oz turns out to be nothing but a dream and Dorothy had never left Kansas, so Soho is woven out of the paranoid projections of the yuppie male imagination. Dialectic requires some minimal opening to a flesh and blood Other. For Dunne's character there is none. In *Bringing Up Baby,* Cary Grant encounters a woman beyond his imagination and outside of the projections of male phobia. *After Hours* locates Dunne before castrated victims or castrating powers but never outside of paranoid projections of female power. Scorsese's film should be interpreted as an indictment of the hardened narcissism that, Baudrillard admits, characterizes postmodernism. Once the "opposite sex" is approached as a person and not a barren object, power—especially as Baudrillard theorizes the matrices of power in the postmodern era—would no longer be figured as a woman without secret pockets. It is not, as Derrida argues, radical alterity that obstructs dialectical movement—at least not in this case. Rather, postmodernism seems to have deconstructed the happy endings of comic dialectic when in fact it has fallen short of those classic scenes.

Notes

Reprinted, with changes, from *Cultural Critique* 34 (Fall 1996), with permission of the publisher. I am grateful to Julie-Olin Ammentorp, Robert Frodeman, and Janet Lungstrum for their comments on earlier versions of the chapter.

1. See my "Hollywood Comedy and Aristotelian Ethics: Reconciling Differences," *Sexual Politics and Popular Culture,* ed. Diane Raymond (Bowling Green: Popular Press, 1990), 15–24. Cf. Stanley Cavell, *Pursuits of Happiness: The Hollywood Comedy of Marriage* (Cambridge: Harvard Univ. Press, 1981); according to Cavell, the comedies of remarriage evoke the "mystery of marriage. . . . [where] good dreams come true" (142). Note that important struggles, for example, struggles based on deep divisions of race or sexual orientation, are left out of Hollywood of the '30s and '40s, and may require a more radicalized notion of change than what I discuss here.

2. I use the term "rationalistic" in order to align Grant's character with a modernist, even Cartesian, formulation of a masculine reason. For an interpretation of Cartesian rationality in terms of a modernist conception of masculinity, see Susan Bordo's *The Flight to Objectivity: Essays on Cartesianism and Culture* (Albany: State Univ. of New York Press, 1987). Bordo concludes by endorsing the "contemporary feminist emphasis on the *insufficiency* of any ethics or rationality—'feminine' *or* 'masculine'—that operates solely in one mode without drawing on the resources and perspectives of the other" (114). I argue that among genres of comedy, only Hollywood screwball attempts to incorporate "feminine" and "masculine" perspectives in a dialectic.

3. I use the term "schizophrenic" to identify the orientation in postmodernism that celebrates freedom from the dominant, often phallogocentric codes. Gilles Deleuze and Felix Guattari romanticize a post-Oedipal schizophrenia in *Kafka: Toward a Minor Literature,* trans. Dana Polan (Minneapolis: Univ. of Minnesota Press, 1986).

4. I am agreeing with Drucilla Cornell and Adam Thurschwell, who argue: "There is an irony in an unbridled feminine negativity that Kristeva does not note explicitly. . . . The striving for absolute freedom in the form of abstract negation denies its relation to the Other." See "Feminism, Negativity, Intersubjectivity," *Feminism as Critique: Essays on the Politics of Gender in Late Capitalist Societies,* ed. Selya Benhabib and Drucilla Cornell (Minneapolis: Univ. of Minnesota Press, 1987), 153.

5. The mutual education that occurs in the dialectical comedies of Hollywood contrasts sharply with Bakhtin's more one-sided valorization of comedy. See M. M. Bakhtin, *The Dialogic Imagination: Four Essays* (Austin: Univ. of Texas Press, 1981), 23–24. Bakhtin argues that "in the comic world there is nothing for memory . . . to do. One ridicules in order to forget" (23). I argue that comic dialectic involves a two-sided transformation that supports not merely the lowering of the pretentious but also the elevating of the low. Screwball comedy supports not the low class, but the formation of an authentic and not yuppified middle class. The ethical education in Neo-Aristotelian comedy does not induce forgetfulness, but requires a crucial element of dialectic, namely, memory. This latter argument is developed in my earlier paper (see n.1 above).

6. Northrop Frye, *Anatomy of Criticism: Four Essays* (Princeton: Princeton Univ. Press, 1957), 169.

7. See also my "Hegel, Antigone, and the Possibility of Ecstatic Dialogue," *Philosophy and Literature* 14 (1990): 268–83.

8. Bill Martin, *Matrix and Line: Derrida and the Possibilities of Postmodern Social Theory* (Albany: State Univ. of New York Press, 1992), 27.

9. By "obscene," Jean Baudrillard signifies not pornography but the exposure of superfluous details, including arbitrary information without, for example, redeeming ethical or political value. See his "The Ecstasy of Communication," *The Anti-Aesthetic: Essays on Postmodern Culture,* ed. Hal Foster (Port Townsend, Wis.: Bay Press, 1983), 126–34.

10. For a Baudrillardian characterization of the aesthetic sensibility of the Soho of the mid- to late 1980s, see Arthur C. Danto's "The Hyper-Intellectual," *The New Republic,* 3.947 and 3.948 (September 10 & 17, 1990): 44–48.

11. Jane Gallop traces Baudrillard's own technique of ironic reversals in her "French Theory and the Seduction of Feminism," *Men in Feminism,* ed. Alice Jardine and Paul Smith (London: Methuen, 1987), 111–15. While it is clear that Baudrillard never allows reversals to be sublated, Gallop observes that he does forestall the complete reversal of at least one position—namely, his hostility to feminism.

12. See Francis Fukuyama's "The End of History?" in *The National Interest* 16 (1989): 3–35.

13. G. Reggio's 1983 film, *Koyaanisgatsi (Life Out of Balance),* illustrates how human beings disappear in the electronic networks of technological society.

14. Baudrillard, *Simulations,* trans. Paul Foss *et al.* (New York: Semiotext(e), 1983), 47. Abbreviated in the text as S.

15. Robert Frodeman suggests that the ready substitution of liposuction for "working out" by those who would redefine the contours of their body exemplifies the postmodern erasure of the value of labor.

16. Baudrillard, *For a Critique of the Political Economy of the Sign,* trans. Charles Levin (St. Louis: Telos Press, 1981), 169–70. Abbreviated in the text as CS. Douglas Kellner argues that passages like this one preclude what he considers to be a very real "possibility of 'responsible' or 'emancipatory' media communication" (*Jean Baudrillard: From Marxism to Postmodernism and Beyond* [Stanford: Stanford Univ. Press, 1989] 67). Kellner also points out that the failure of utopian theories in the 1960s persuaded leftists that "any reform whatsoever—economic, environmental, political and so on—strengthens the system of domination and should thus be denounced" (89). My argument—that classic Hollywood comedy provides a formula for social mediation and reform missing in postmodernism—supports Kellner's suggestion that media can be responsible.

17. Cf. Mark Poster: "What is at stake are new language formations that alter significantly the network of social relations, that restructure those relations and the subjects they constitute" ("Words without Things: The Mode of Information," *October* 53 [1990]: 68). A crucial moment of present history is what Poster labels "the electronic stage [in which] . . . the self is decentralized, dispersed and multiplied in continuous instability" (66). Poster argues against the possibility of an emancipatory meta/narrative, which could legitimate social action as well as the inevitable violence of change. This refusal to generate a narrative leaves Poster in the position of having to advocate change for the sake of change alone: "I choose discontinuity over continuity" (77).

18. For an analysis of the failure of the avant-garde effort towards political change see Peter Burger, *Theory of the Avant-Garde,* trans. Michael Shaw (Minneapolis: Univ. of Minnesota Press, 1984).

19. This is my paraphrase of remarks made in Karl Shapiro's introduction to Henry Miller's *Tropic of Cancer* (New York: Grove Press, 1961), v–xxx.

20. In the great "anti-epiphany" of the *Tropic of Cancer,* the narrator chants: "I made up my mind that I would hold on to nothing, that I would expect nothing, that henceforth I would live as animal, a beast of prey, a rover, a plunderer. . . . And if rape were the order of the day then rape I would, and

with a vengeance. . . . [For] at the extreme limits of his spiritual being man finds himself again naked as a savage. . . . Morally I am free" (98–99). And later: "I haven't any allegiance, any responsibilities" (153).

21. See Nancy Fraser's *Unruly Practices: Power, Discourse, and Gender in Contemporary Social Theory* (Minneapolis: Univ. of Minnesota Press, 1989) for an analysis of the claim that technological societies vanquish the political in favor of an " 'economic-socio-techno-cultural complex' " characterized by the "triumph of the *animal laborans*" and a common life "governed by considerations pertaining to subsistence" (84). She argues that postmodernism has failed to generate a narrative that could orient political change (11). Fraser does not contest Foucault's undialectical claim that "modern power is 'productive' rather than prohibitive" (18). Nor does she specify, at least in this book, a basis for formulating political goals that would exceed the clash of private interests. My reading of *After Hours* suggests that the resistance to dominant social practices can in part be legitimated by way of residual, relatively natural, desires of the social animal, desires that are not one-sidedly social products and that therefore might be repressed by social practices.

Agonal Politics in Space and Time: Arendt and Le Guin on World Creation

George A. Trey

In the beginning, God created the heavens and the earth. Or so the story goes. With a series of speech acts, primordial chaos was converted into nature. God, utilizing the linguistic tools that were at his disposal, transformed disorder into finely tuned systems that operated in perfect relational harmony. Nature was unilaterally spoken, not argued for. But, when language became the common bond of humanity, the art of agonistic speech came to be practiced. As such, culture was born. God, being jealous, recognized the threat that this posed to his reign over creation. When his human likenesses began to build the tower of Babel, he could see that things had gone too far.[1] God failed in his effort to stunt this activity. In fact his action merely intensified the problem. It was at this moment that the already naked truth became completely transparent: outside of discursive contexts, God could only use language to create nature; humans, on the other hand, can use language to create worlds.

In this chapter, I will discuss the respective ideas forwarded by Hannah Arendt and Ursula Le Guin on the way that "worlds" are created discursively in the agonal context of political debate. My use of the phrase "world creation" is influenced by the *Lebenswelt* tradition in German social thought. While problematic in a number of ways that cannot be addressed in this chapter,[2] I will largely be relying on Jürgen Habermas's version of lifeworld theory. It is his view that the lifeworld is essentially composed of intersecting speech acts that refer to the objective, subjective, and intersubjective elements of speech communities.[3] As Habermas has noted, his views complement Arendt's claim that "worlds" are always created, established, or constructed through human activity.[4] For her, this activity is paradigmatically modelled on the agonal context established by Athenian democracy. Le Guin, in her various novels, appears to share this view with several notable differences: (1) her models for world building are established on what I would call the logic of dispossession, which is predicated upon situational oppression and ultimately expulsion; (2) she advocates an egalitarian form of agonistics as opposed to the exclusive model advanced by Arendt; and (3) she attempts to deal with the difficulties of substantive democracy rather than resorting to an aristocratic conception of political debate. I will attempt to show in the course of this paper how these differences can be used to articulate critically the problems with Arendt's elitist conception of world creation.

Before proceeding, I would like to take note of the distinction between the genres that are utilized by Arendt and Le Guin. While I would be loath to make a sharp and misleading distinction between fictional and theoretical discourses, there are certain advantages and limitations that each affords. Insofar as the intent of this chapter is to be somewhat "utopian," it stands to reason that my own position is influenced more by the narrative structure of Le Guin's novels. I would, however, point out that there is a story-like character to much of Arendt's work as well. Further, there is clearly a normative, and even analytic, dimension to Le Guin's writings. In an attempt to lend integrity to my own text, I will highlight these "secondary" (the narrative in Arendt and the normative/analytic in Le Guin) elements in the works I discuss.

Hannah Arendt: The Rhetoric and Rationality of World Creation

In *The Human Condition,* Arendt presents a fascinating discussion of the agonal politics of Athenian democracy. Her analysis is rooted in the distinction between public and private life that she claims was fundamental to the vibrant political ethos of the city state. For her, the term "public" identifies two closely related phenomena. First, the public is accessible to anyone. It is the bright light of day, shielded by nothing. Second, and more importantly:

> [T]he term "public" signifies the world itself, in so far as it is common to all of us and distinguished from our privately owned place in it. The world, however, is not identical with the earth or with nature, as the limited space for the movement of men and the general condition of organic life. It is related, rather, to the human artifact, the fabrication of human hands, as well as to affairs which go on among those who inhabit the man-made world together.[5]

For her, the public space *par excellence* is the sphere of political discourse that played such an important role in the halcyon days of Athenian democracy. It is here that "men" presented themselves before their peers as they stated their political views. The manner in which they did so is particularly important in that the context was specifically agonal. This was not the realm of give and take; rather, the objective was to overcome opposition through superior self-presentation.

What intrigues Arendt about this scene pertains to the two levels on which political activity is creative. On the first level, the individual who presents him/herself develops her/his character in the process. By developing an ethos that is suitable for public display, the actor establishes an identity as she/he strives for excellence. Beyond this process of self-creation is the even more significant phenomenon of world building. This involves the aggregation of individual acts of excellence that form lasting political institutions. Arendt contrasts such activity with that conducted in the private realm. Here the aim is retreat, solace, and regeneration. Acts associated with the physical reproduction of the species are relegated to this domain. While the activities of the private sphere fade away into oblivion, public acts of excellence are immortalized in the life of the polis and the world that it represents. As Arendt puts it in *The Human Condition:* "It is the publicity of the public realm which can absorb and make shine through the centuries whatever men may want to save from the natural ruin of time. Through many ages before us—but now not any more—men entered the public realm because they wanted something of their own or something they had in common with others to be more permanent than their earthly lives" (55).

The world-building "action" that takes place in the public sphere is distinguished from work and labor. Labor is reproductive, work is productive, and action is creative. While all three are necessary for the task of world building, only action creates something out of nothing. Likewise, only action is unlimited by material constraints such as space and time. Hence, this is the activity of transcendence, through which mundane beings immortalize themselves: "By nature, men are like animals; they are transient members of a species, inhabiting an indifferent universe and possessing no more lasting significance than last summer's butterflies. Unlike butterflies, however, we can redeem our existence from futility precisely by means of the light of the public realm."[6]

Just as political debate in an agonal context fosters the development of the art of communication, so does a controllable form of power contribute to the creation of a world. Within the confines of the public sphere in the polis, it was unthinkable to attempt to advance one's interests by way of force. Power, as distinct from force, was channelled into the creation of the city state—a world where one could freely participate in the highest form of human activity. By advocating political action as more than a means to an end, Arendt emphasizes the qualitative distinction between participatory and non-participatory life. One must view political action to be a higher form of activity in order to sustain the type of commitment that is needed to construct a superior world.

Thus far I have isolated and highlighted those aspects of Arendt's conception of the public realm that have strong democratic resonances. As one commentator puts it: "Many of her insights are worth preserving and can become the basis of a democratic, participatory, and egalitarian conception of citizenship."[7] I want to consider how the creative interdependence of thought and action, deployed in the public sphere, indicates in an important manner the way in which worlds are created. This approach, however, requires that a number of the elitist, nostalgic tendencies of *The Human Condition* be ignored.

The interesting aspect of Arendt's interpretation of the agonal context in ancient Greece is her analysis of the way that conflictual political procedures result in the formation of a durable world. By focusing on the performative dimensions of political discourse, she shows how the public sphere functions creatively in the development of both an individual and a corporate character. This aside, she ignores both empirical and normative weaknesses of this model. Arendt advocates what I would call a politics of bravado. Such a politics is exclusive in a number of ways. On the empirical level, it is well known that the golden days of Athens were only rich for about ten percent of the population. This does not necessarily have normative implications; but in the case of Arendt's model, it clearly does. Her archetypical political actor is classically male, situated by class position, and culturally imbued with aristocratic tendencies that she accepts without question. Her defense of traditional dualisms such as public/private and political/social exacerbate this problem as they reproduce some of the most violently exclusive patterns of Western culture. Nonetheless, her insights into the quality of participatory life and the effect that this has on self-formation are invaluable. In order to develop and resituate this aspect of her analysis I will now turn to Ursula Le Guin. In doing so I will attempt to formulate a conception of an agonal politics that avoids these elitist tendencies.

Ursula Le Guin: Language and Life on Other Planets

A type of agonal tension does exist between Le Guin's and Arendt's notions of political discourse. One could say that this tension raises the issue about whether political discourse should be agonal at all. On the surface it would appear that Le Guin presents a view of discussion that eliminates "agony" from the agon. This strikes me as being a bit too simplistic and, in the discussion that follows, I will attempt to show that conflict, in the agonal sense, is an indispensable feature of Le Guin's model. The substantive differences between Arendt and Le Guin pertain to what it means to "win the contest" and the relationship between world creation and self-formation. My argument is that Arendt adheres rather rigidly to the notion of the "great man," whereas Le Guin is more interested in what it takes to form a great community.

The themes that I am going to extract from Le Guin's writings are central to most of her novels. In this chapter, I will focus on two—*The Dispossessed*[8] and *The Eye of the Heron.*[9] The unifying strands in her work that I will concentrate on are dispossession, discursive politics, and world creation.

The basic scenario for *The Dispossessed* and *The Eye of the Heron* is quite similar. In each case, communities of resistance are barred from their native world due to their disruptive political views. They are banished to other planets where it becomes necessary for them to create new worlds. The natural backdrop in either case is rather stark: the pilgrims have limited resources, harsh climates, and in the case of Victoria in *The Eye of the Heron,* domination by a community of co-inhabitants, to contend with. In order to face these conditions they rely on the one resource that bonded their communities prior to being dispossessed—political discourse. Le Guin provides this account of the procedure:

> On the porch, two groups formed: the explorers and other men and women, mostly young, around Vera, and a larger group around a fair, blue-eyed man named Elia. Down among the crowd this pattern was repeated, until it began to look like a ringtree forest: small circles, mostly young, argued passionately, yet without anger. (EH 12)

From this pattern—this feature of their past which sustained the resisters through their hardest times—their new world was created.

What takes shape in Le Guin's accounts of the development of new worlds out of no cultural artifacts other than language is a political ontology of dispossession. The constitutive ontological fabric of communities of outcasts is transformed into a new mode of being on an utterly different planet. A crucial component of this fabric is strife or struggle. Dispossessed communities are constituted in terms of the tension that exists between themselves and their oppressors. Often such a constitution has limitations that are quite obvious: once the oppression is overcome, the force that binds the community is annulled. In order to preserve the unity originally premised on violence, terror, and the instinct to survive, Le Guin's communities internalize conflict in the form of agonal discourse; Vera explains to Luz:

> We don't fight. Not with knives and guns. But when we've agreed that something ought to be done, or not done, we get very stubborn. And when that meets up with another stubbornness, it can make a kind of war, a struggle of ideas, the only kind of war anybody ever wins. (EH 44)

With a flair and passion that Heidegger only dreamed of, Le Guin shows that language is, in fact, the house of being. For her, however, language does not speak the world independent of the subjects that possess it and are under its possession. Out of an interchange of ideas that is framed by the language of discourse, the community emerges.

This model clearly overcomes some of the weaknesses that I identified with Arendt's. The paradigm for world creation is political opposition in the face of oppression. As such, the smug bravado that is characteristic of the ethos of Arendt's political actors is tempered by the high stakes of struggle not only as a way of life but also for a way of life, and often life itself. While Arendt would see this as a blurring of the all-important distinction between public and private activities, her attachment to this aspect of the Athenian model limits her ability to envision world creation as anything other than an exercise in self-presentation. For her, self-preservation is not a public activity and should be taken care of only in the hidden domain of the private sphere. For Le Guin, on the other hand, self-preservation and self-presentation are co-constitutive in that communal solidarity has to precede—both empirically and normatively—the assertion of self as a distinct character. This is clear in her depiction of a socialist society in *The Dispossessed*. The private activity of self-preservation is shared by the members of the community established on Anarres. Only under such conditions can personal excellence take shape in a way that is compatible with the political ethos being cultivated. An agon that encourages self-presentation at the expense of communal ties loses its practical orientation to the task of world creation and re-creation. It becomes a drama without purpose—art for art's sake. In contrast, Le Guin's conception of the agon transforms the contestatory dimensions of political debate into something more meaningful than immortality. Her concern is to show how conflict can be channelled into resistance movements that ultimately supersede the particularity of their own oppression. Hence, the world-creating force of Arendt's polis is kept intact without succumbing to the elitist, anti-egalitarian tendencies that permeate the Greek model.

Le Guin is astutely aware of the pitfalls of the model rendered by Arendt. In *The Eye of the Heron* she shows that political format is exclusive and self-destructive. The people of Victoria, a penal planet that restrains the "worst" criminals from earth, consist of two distinct communities—the city people and the residents of shanty. In the city, an elite group of male aristocrats runs the show. The aristocrats organize themselves hierarchically and their discussions concerning policy are characterized by the type of self-presentation described by Arendt—arrogant, verbose, and detached from the concerns of the community at large. The logic of this community is rooted in loci of power and tactics for preserving it as such. In contrast, the people of shanty conform to the egalitarian model that has as its basis the logic of dispossession. When compared like this, the normative weaknesses of the elitist model can be viewed in concrete terms:

> But Luz would not slow down for the poor squawking woman. She strode on, fighting tears that had come upon her unawares: tears of anger because she could never walk alone, never do anything by herself, never. *Because the men ran everything.* They had it all their way. And the older women were all on their side. So that a girl couldn't walk in the streets of the City alone, because some drunken working man might insult her, and what if he did get put in jail or get his ears cut off for it afterward? A lot of good that would do. The girl's reputation would be ruined. Because her reputation was what the men thought of her. The men thought everything, did everything, ran everything, made everything, made the laws, broke the laws, punished the lawbreakers; and there was no room left for the

> women, no City for the women. Nowhere, nowhere, but in their own rooms, alone. (EH 28–29; *my emphasis*)

In short, when world creation is limited to one sector of the world's population, only that sector will have a world. While shanty did not have the wealth or resources of the city, it was a richer world in that it was created by all, for all.

While it could be argued that the agonistic ethos is lost under egalitarian conditions—an argument, for instance, that someone like Nietzsche might make—this is not the case in Le Guin's characterization. The identity that characterizes her communities is rooted in a participatory struggle for a better world. As such, the creative vision is preserved, keeping intact utopian aspirations that translate into emancipatory action. In *The Eye of the Heron,* this leads to the establishment of a second community with the intent of strategically and geographically limiting the power of the city dwellers over the residents of shanty. Rather than succumb to either domination or to a mode of struggle—namely violence—that developed in the city community, a group of shanty dwellers sought to preserve the world that they had created by recreating it in another location. The mechanism by which the group did so remained constant; the tension that abounds in political debate was channelled into the creative ideas needed to meet the demands of a new set of conditions. But this is the only constant. In contrast to the quest for immortality—in other words, the desire to reify action—the egalitarian principles that undergird Le Guin's model of world creation embody the vibrancy needed to keep political life from stagnating or becoming conservative. Her communities are constantly operating within the framework of a progressive vision.

Creating Worlds with Words

Both Arendt and Le Guin offer interesting models of the way that worlds can be generated out of the agonal contexts of political debate. I have argued for the superiority of Le Guin's conception on the grounds that it is more egalitarian, has a practical orientation, and is substantiated by normative principles that mitigate against oppression and creatively envision emancipatory practices. In their own respective ways, both writers react negatively to modern notions of democracy. Arendt yearns nostalgically for a premodern agon that fails to benefit from the advantages of modernity. In contrast, Le Guin attempts to move beyond the limitations of modern democracy by shaping the most radical dimensions of modern thought into a utopian vision of what lies beyond the modern world. While her participatory aspirations are not burdened by the "realities" of the late-modern condition—which of course need to be reckoned with—it is refreshing to witness an alternative to what often amounts to sophisticated cynicism. Her radical egalitarianism is not tied to the logic of postmodernism; rather, it points to an alternative path. Perhaps her suggestion is that there awaits in the aftermath of modernity a way of being that celebrates human plurality. In the section that follows, I will discuss this possibility under the rubric of post-patriarchal socialism.

Post-Patriarchal Socialism

> There must be formed a sphere of society which claims no *traditional* status but only a human status, a sphere of society which is not opposed to particular consequences but is totally opposed to the assumptions of the German political system; a sphere, finally, which cannot emancipate itself without emancipating itself from all the other spheres of society, without, therefore, emancipating all these other spheres, which is, in short, a *total loss* of humanity and which can only redeem itself by a *total redemption of humanity*. This dissolution of society, as a particular class, is the *proletariat.*[10]

> "No," Atro went on, "you'll find the soul of the people true as steel, when the country's threatened. A few rabblerousers in Nio and the mill towns make a big noise between wars, but it's grand to see how the people close ranks when the flag's in danger. You're unwilling to believe that, I know. The trouble with Odonianism, you know, my dear fellow, *is that it's womanish.* It simply doesn't include the virile side of life. 'Blood and steel, battle's brightness,' as the old poet says. It doesn't understand courage—love of the flag." (D 230; *my emphasis*)

Up until this point, I have alluded to a patriarchal thread that runs through Arendt's conception of political discourse, and an alternative to that *imagined* by Le Guin. I want to emphasize the word "imagined" because that is precisely the mode of thought necessary for thinking the post-patriarchal socialist ideal that she develops in her brilliant novel *The Dispossessed.* Before turning to this work in an effort to thematize the philosophical outline that is contained in her narrative, I would like to comment briefly on the passages quoted above.

The first, from Marx's "Introduction to the Critique of Hegel's Philosophy of Right," situates the problem faced in imagining post-patriarchal socialism.[11] He begins with an unfathomably abstract question: where, within the distorted, maligned constructs that constitute human society, reside the kernels of human possibility that will enable us to sever ties with what we are, and become what we dream to be? This is not simply a naive, whimsical wish for some unattainable utopia; rather, it is an imperative to examine the possibilities buried beneath the debris of systemically dysfunctional modes of human interaction—an appeal to the hope that can be found in a simple moment of human solidarity. As Marx—and most other human beings—know, those moments are there. We experience them in the love between parent and child, between partners, friends, and within communities that situate our being in the world. Marx goes on to outline a procedure for opening up these possibilities by tearing away the veils with which they are occluded. In his particular context, it is the German political system that organizes these veils. In a more general sense, we might say that the various systems that govern our lives are the culprits—as well as the way in which they consolidate power, preserve economic injustices and, perhaps most importantly, destroy structures of meaning that provide our lives with a sense of integrity and mutual reliance.

Marx's claim seems to be that in order to get at these kernels of human possibility—which reside in the individual but only flourish within radically egalitarian contexts of intersubjectivity—it is necessary to break completely with the human condition as we know it and to recreate nothing less than humanity: this time in our own image. He seasons his remark with the religious theme of redemption—a retrieval of the irretrievable self through a miraculous act of grace on the part of the creator. In this case, the creator, as I have argued throughout, is not "God," as the religious traditions would have it, or "Man," as the humanist traditions have claimed, but rather humanity. It is intriguing to note the confluences that exist between Marx's notion of a totally redeemed humanity and Le Guin's scenarios. Her vision involves such a radical rupture with the human condition as we know it that a spatio-temporal difference is required. In both cases, it is the irredeemable present that contains the seeds of a redemption that is of an otherworldly nature. This is not to be confused with an anti-worldly, ontological difference such as we find in most religious notions of redemption. Rather, it is inspired by the recognition that the worlds we create are contingent, can be undone and reconceived in an image of ourselves that is closer to the "truth."

In the second passage, a remark by a character in *The Dispossessed*—who has been an interplanetary interlocutor of one of the main characters, Shevek the physicist, for many years—illuminates the aspect of this "total loss of humanity" which is passed over by most socialist thinkers. In this scene, which takes place on the planet Urras, the aging Atro explains to Shevek why the socialist-anarchist experiment that is in progress on the planet Anarres is untenable. For Atro, the final analysis of the problem rests in the gender of the body politic: " . . . it's womanish. It simply doesn't include the virile side of life." While the nation of Ioto is a staunchly patriarchal (hence politically legitimate) statist regime, and even the "socialist" nation of Thu is of the bureaucratic-patriarchal sort, Anarres is a political body not governed by a masculine organ. This of course means that it is disorganized, lacks a proper sense of structure, and ultimately is politically impotent. I will now argue that these patriarchal concerns are reflections of the notion of "the political" that Arendt affirms uncritically.

In *Acting and Thinking,* Leah Bradshaw situates Arendt's work in the following manner:

> Hannah Arendt . . . made the general claim that behind every theory there are incidents and stories that "contain in a nutshell the full meaning of whatever we have to say." In light of this

> remark one might say that the most important "incident" behind Arendt's theory is the twentieth-century experience of totalitarianism. She commented on more than one occasion that the experience of living in, and fleeing from, Nazi Germany was the formative experience of her life.[12]

While recognizing that this claim is a bit hyperbolic, it does offer an interesting and, to a certain extent, obvious perspective from which Arendt's views on public discussion, political action, and contemplative reflection can be approached. For Arendt, the locus of these activities is the public sphere: a domain within which discussions abound that depend upon thought and constitute action. Under conditions of "totalitarian" repression, such a sphere is impossible:[13] thinking takes place in one sphere; acting takes place in other spheres; intersubjective discussion does not take place at all. With this in mind, I will return briefly to *The Human Condition* in order to show how the egalitarian themes that are present in this text become overshadowed by the elitist, patriarchal tendencies as her later work unfolds.

Arendt's primary concern in *The Human Condition* is to consider what conditions must be met in order for political action to take place. As I noted earlier, in doing so she identifies three fundamental types of human activity: labor, which is reproductive; work, which is productive; and action, which is creative. Each of these activities, she accords, has an appropriate domain. In ancient Greek and Roman societies, the significance of maintaining a distinction between the two most important of these domains—the public and the private—was clearly understood: neither could operate effectively if the division became blurred. This distinction contributed to the maintenance of the public sphere as the proper domain for political action.

The fundamental question that Arendt deals with in her argument for distinct public and private spheres pertains to whether humans are fundamentally social or political animals. For the ancients, to engage in action is to act politically. This is distinguished from social activities intended for the efficient meeting of a particular group's needs. The necessities of life are more readily attained when laboring and working in unison with others. This requires, according to Arendt, a degree of cooperation but relatively little contemplation. We can see in the animal world numerous examples of social orders that function smoothly and effectively without ever raising questions about the purpose of their existence or the possibility of achieving a higher plateau. Animals are always satisfied as long as their basic needs are met. Humans are set apart from other animals in that they seek to use cooperation to get beyond the contingencies of any particular situation in order to establish a permanent, durable political body. For the ancients, this effort was undertaken through political dialogue. Using the capacity for speech as a mechanism for articulating ideas and thoughts, humans are able to advance their views rhetorically in the market place of ideas and develop political positions. This rational dimension of discourse, which emerges in the agonal context, provides the necessary checks and balances that render political actions legitimate.

The point that I want to emphasize here pertains to the aforementioned concern with Arendt's appropriation of traditional dualisms—particularly public/private and political/social. As numerous feminist theorists have pointed out, the construction and maintenance of these dualisms is patriarchal in foundation.[14] This specific group of dualisms has been particularly insidious in that it devalues the work and labor that most directly connect us to our material existence. Therefore, in spite of the egalitarian pretense of Arendt's conception of the public sphere, the only type of self-formation that could take place in this context is conventionally masculine, disembodied, and dependent upon an intricate network of oppressive practices. In the discussion that follows, I will show how this elitism becomes more pronounced in her later work as she attempts to preserve the spirit of the Greek agonal context in the domain of modern political life.

We should be reminded at this point that Arendt was no fan of modern society. She felt that the primacy of the social undermined the possibility for broad participatory democracy. The formal aura of democracy that exists in modern societies merely disguises the real lack of political engagement. As a result, political power becomes concentrated in the hands of an elite few. It seems that for Arendt, this is the logical consequence of the collapse of distinct public and private spheres into the social. The political ethos is pathologically dismantled and reformed into a set of technical skills for managing mass society. This collapse, which deeply disturbs Arendt, results in the virtual annihilation of the political character. As she writes in *On Revolution:* "For the qualities of the statesman or the political man, and the qualities of the manager or administrator are not only not the same, they very seldom are to be found in the same individual; the one is supposed to know how to deal with men in a field of human relations, whose principle is freedom, and the other must know how to manage things in a sphere of life whose principle is necessity."[15]

In response, Arendt suggests the need for a different type of political elite. This would involve establishing a ruling enclave that had no other concern than to practice statecraft. The closest thing that Arendt finds to this in history is the collective of political actors that framed the American Constitution. These men, at best, loved politics for the sake of politics. Arendt found this character best represented in Thomas Jefferson but saw its extension in the entire body of founding fathers. As Bradshaw explains: "The achievement of the Founding Fathers was that they sought revolution not for the sake of realizing any determinate end such as a just or equal society, but for the purpose of simply creating an open-ended public forum."[16] Arendt states that her ideal was that "[o]nly those who as voluntary members of an 'elementary republic' have demonstrated that they care for more than their private happiness and are concerned about the state of the world would have the right to be heard" (276). This ideal, however, was not realized, mainly because the new elite was unable to "spring" itself from the masses. What undermined the American experiment, she claims, was not the failure to affect substantive democracy but the inability to concede that democracy was neither possible nor desirable under modern conditions: "From the viewpoint of the revolution and the survival of the revolutionary spirit, the trouble does not lie in the factual rise of a new élite: it is not the revolutionary spirit but the democratic mentality of *an egalitarian society* that tends to deny *the obvious inability and conspicuous lack of interest* of large parts of the population in political matters as such" (281; *my emphasis*).

Arendt's shift from the pseudo-egalitarian polis to a political council model of the public sphere is caused by what she perceives to be a modern reality. If the modern condition is such that broad participation is no longer possible, then it is necessary to constitute spheres of political discourse independent of the public at large. The benefit of this from her perspective is that the distinction between public and private is in some odd sense preserved. In making this move, however, Arendt falls into the paradox of having a public sphere that, while accessible to the public in principle, effectively relegates the vast majority to a life of political privation. This discrepancy is exacerbated in her latest work, *The Life of the Mind,* resulting in the complete separation of political action from anything other than a patriarchal figurehead.[17]

Because Arendt's model of political participation does not absolve itself of patriarchal features, it evolves in an increasingly exclusive direction that leads to a distorted conception of the human being. Le Guin's model of political participation, on the other hand, is severely anti-patriarchal. The conditions under which this model takes shape include, as I noted above, situational oppression and ultimately dispossession. The logic of the effects of dispossession leads to a ferocious commitment to *communal* solidarity. I emphasize the word "communal" here because it breaks down Arendt's division between the social and the political, as well as the public and the private—consolidating them within a set of egalitarian practices. These practices, then, are correctly identified by Atro as being "womanish." This, in fact, seems to be the intent. The philosophical precepts that enable the development of the culture of Anarres were specifically configured to avoid the "virile side of life." In order to work in the direction of "a total redemption of humanity," it was necessary to experience "a total loss of humanity." This loss opened up the possibilities that I identify as post-patriarchal socialism.

Central to the development of post-patriarchal socialism are its constitutive elements. The most important of these is the dissolution of hierarchy. Contained in the term "hierarchy" is the notion of an overarching governing principle that is in all instances the final arbiter. In the case of a society dominated by men, the specific form this governing principle takes is patriarchy. Le Guin's solution to this problem is to imagine an "anarchic" form of socialism. This reflects an awareness that simply developing a socialist society does not necessarily do away with patriarchy. If there is hierarchy, and most existing models of hierarchy are at the very least tinged by patriarchy, then the only sure way to eliminate patriarchy is through the complete abolition of hierarchy. This imperative, of course, resonates with egalitarianism and communal solidarity—principles with which it is co-constitutive. With anarchy as its most basic principle—one managed through cooperation and mutual understanding—the tendency within communal movements for hierarchy-patriarchy to creep back in is at least in principle addressed.

The second constitutive feature of post-patriarchal socialism is flexibility in the division of labor. While citizens of Annares do become experts in their respective fields, everyone is likewise expected to take part in the maintenance of the community. This is a critical feature of the model insofar as much of the hierarchy in societies is the product of divisions of labor that distinguish between essential work and existential work. This dichotomy, too, is broken down by Le Guin's model in that existence itself becomes an essential concern of every member of the community. In addition to mitigating against hierarchy, it benefits the development of the person in a holistic manner, not only by valuing the mind and the body equally, but also by enabling self-formation through various types of activities and encounters with various types of people. The limited space in which Arendt conceives self-formation to take place leads to a limited conception of the self. It likewise leads to the degradation of existential activity. Le Guin clearly saw beyond this schema and attempted, through the development of a model of community (social-political), to frame the self in a broader context.

The third constitutive feature of post-patriarchal socialism is what I would call "social androgyny." Le Guin's interest in androgyny is first developed in her haunting novel *The Left Hand of Darkness*. Here, she imagines a type of being that is biologically androgynous. The only time that sexual difference is evident is when sexual and reproductive activity takes place. The following description by a student of this bizarre phenomenon is instructive in pointing out the way that this breaks down patriarchy:

> Our entire pattern of socio-sexual interaction is non-existent here. The Gethenians do not see one another as men or women. This is almost impossible for our imagination to accept. After all, what is the first question we ask about a newborn baby?
>
> Yet you cannot think of a Gethenian as "it." They are not neuters. They are potentials; during each sexual cycle they may develop in either direction for the duration of that cycle. No physiological habit is established, and the mother of several children may be the father of several more.
>
> There is no division of humanity into strong and weak halves, protected/protective. One is respected and judged only as a human being. You cannot cast a Genthenian in the role of Man or Woman, while adopting towards "him" a corresponding role dependent on your expectations of the interactions between persons of the same or opposite sex.[18]

The key feature of this description is found in the third paragraph. The androgyny here described—a biological feature of the species—has dramatic sociological repercussions. Insofar as gender and sexuality are fluid, there is no possibility for the establishment of a hierarchy based on gender or sexuality. As such, hierarchies generally based on gender—strong/weak, protected/protective—are nonexistent. This dismantling of hierarchy should likewise translate into the dismantling of hierarchies between public and private, as well as social and political.

There are problems with the model in *The Left Hand of Darkness* that Le Guin seems intent upon remedying in *The Dispossessed.* The first of these is that the form of government on Genthen is roughly that of a monarchy. This, of course, is a hierarchical form of government and its presence under these conditions demonstrates that gender roles are really rooted in social structures rather than biology. The second is that biological androgyny is somewhat implausible and not necessarily desirable. As Le Guin states in her introduction to the novel: "Yes, indeed the people in it are androgynous, but that doesn't mean that I'm predicting that in a millennium or so we will all be androgynous, or announcing that I think we damned well ought to be androgynous." In fact, to the extent that she takes up the theme of androgyny in *The Dispossessed,* the form that it assumes is "social androgyny." Social androgyny is much more complicated than biological androgyny in that it involves constantly addressing the questions, problems, and histories of sexual difference. In designing it in *The Dispossessed,* Le Guin does precisely this. We do not have a theory of social androgyny but rather the presentation of a set of scenarios that involve the dissolution and reappearance of defined gender roles. The condition that makes this possible is the radically egalitarian socialist system of Anarres. This is the necessary but not, as she shows, sufficient condition for a post-patriarchal form of socialism. In order for this final objective to be achieved, it is necessary to struggle with the development of social androgyny—a project that has to take shape within the contexts of critique and discourse that are the formative principles of this type of anarchism. While, as I have noted, redefining gender roles is not the only development that precedes the formation of an egalitarian social body, it is clear that for Le Guin that it is one of the most important. This speaks to the extent to which patriarchy limits participatory equality.

This also points to what I would refer to as the sustaining features of post-patriarchal socialism, which are, in fact, critique and discourse. Annares has an ideological framework—Odonianism—which is based on the work of Odo: a woman whose theories lead to the development of what I am calling the post-patriarchal world. What prevents this ideological framework from becoming *ideology* is its inherently critical-discursive character. Having discussed the form that this takes in earlier sections of the paper, I will simply refer now to what I take to be the fundamental insight concerning this character as exhibited in *The Dispossessed.* It has been noted by theorists from Plato to Dewey that the political culture of a society is going to be shaped by its educational culture. If principles of hierarchy and authority form the consciousnesses of children and young adults, principles of hierarchy and authority will likewise reveal themselves in political culture. Under such conditions, it is pointless to have a system of formal democracy insofar as there will be little understanding of, or basis for, democratic forms of life. Le Guin illustrates this through her descriptions of the interactive learning process that develops the sense of critical discourse that sustains Annares. This focus on the development of a world view, which is not based on hierarchical relations because it does not involve hierarchical relations, is what carries Anneres through its most difficult times. The implication is that the sustenance of a community defiantly opposed to any sort of *structure* involving hierarchy must be rooted in elemental *practices* that likewise defy authoritative hierarchies tainted with patriarchy.

Conclusion

My objective in this chapter has been to look at the creative possibilities that lie within agonal political discourse—how through processes of contention and response, we have the potential for shaping the worlds in which we live. I have further attempted to show that the form this assumes will be largely determined by the accessibility of the discursive forum. My argument against Arendt is that she has developed a model of political discourse that is unconcerned with participation—a problem I have organized around the theme of patriarchy. Le Guin, on the other hand, serves as an antidote to this problem. As such, it is possible to extract from several of her writings a basic notion of what a discursively created world that is not limited to hierarchical relationships would look like. My account, in some senses, is intended to be utopian. It is not, however, an account of some future *utopia.* Rather, the positions that I have developed here are intended to elucidate possibilities pertinent to the critical understanding of "what must be done" if the idea of a radically egalitarian community is ever to come to address the problems of social and political reality.

Notes

1. For an interesting discussion of the Tower of Babel and the linguistic turn in political philosophy, see Fred R. Dallmayr, *Language and Politics: Why does Language matter to Political Philosophy?* (Notre Dame: Univ. of Notre Dame Press, 1984), 1–28.

2. I discuss this at length in chapter 5 of my book, *Solidarity and Difference: The Politics of Enlightenment in the Aftermath of Modernity* (Albany: State Univ. of New York Press, 1996).

3. See Jürgen Habermas, *The Theory of Communicative Action*, vol. 2 (Boston: Beacon Press, 1987).

4. Habermas, "Hannah Arendt: On the Concept of Power," *Philosophical-Political Profiles*, trans. Frederick G. Lawrence (Cambridge: MIT Press, 1983).

5. Hannah Arendt, *The Human Condition* (Chicago: Univ. of Chicago Press, 1958), 52.

6. Margaret Canovan, "Politics and Culture: Hannah Arendt and the Public Realm," *History of Political Thought* 6.3 (1988): 681.

7. Maurisio Passerin d'Entreves, "Agency, Identity and Culture: Hannah Arendt's Conception of Citizenship," *Praxis International* 9.1–2 (1989): 2.

8. Ursula K. Le Guin, *The Dispossessed* (New York: Avon Books, 1974). Hereafter abbreviated as D.

9. Le Guin, *The Eye of the Heron* (New York: Harper Collins, 1978). Hereafter abbreviated as EH.

10. Karl Marx, *The Marx-Engels Reader*, 2nd ed., ed. Robert C. Tucker (New York: Norton, 1978), 64.

11. It might seem odd to invoke Marx in the context of a discussion of patriarchy. As feminist critics, too numerous to begin mentioning, have pointed out, there is a lack of concern with patriarchy in Marx's texts. There also seems to be an active disregard for the politics of identity, which has defined a good deal of feminism, throughout the history of Marxism. These are important criticisms and need to be taken into consideration. As is the case with any good criticism, however, it points us in the direction of reevaluating the objects of critique. The time seems to be ripe for a reevaluation of the Marxian corpus in terms of the light it might shed on the current world order. An important attempt to do so has been made by Jacques Derrida in his *Specters of Marx*, trans. Peggy Kamuf (New York: Routledge, 1994). In a more specifically feminist vein, see *Materialist Feminisms* by Donna Landry and Gerald Maclean (Cambridge: Blackwell, 1993).

12. Leah Bradshaw, *Acting and Thinking: The Political Thought of Hannah Arendt* (Toronto: Univ. of Toronto Press, 1989), 39.

13. Bradshaw makes this point as follows: " 'Terror,' Arendt wrote, 'is the very essence of (the totalitarian) form of government.' Terror *destroys the public space entirely* because it can literally prevent people from communicating with one another. Without the freedom to share their fears and concerns people are coerced by terror into the maddening isolation of their own thoughts or into the mute obedience of a mass" (41; *my emphasis*).

14. See, for example Charlene Haddock Seigfried, "Validating Women's Experiences Pragmatically," *Philosophy and the Reconstruction of Culture: Pragmatic Essays after Dewey*, ed. John J. Stuhr (Albany: State Univ. of New York Press, 1993), 111–29.

15. Arendt, *On Revolution* (New York: Viking Press, 1963), 278.

16. Bradshaw (54). Arendt's efforts to idealize the constitutional proceedings of the founding fathers is even more farfetched than her idealization of the polis. To say that they acted purely and simply for the sake of action, without any particular interests in mind, is debatable.

17. In the third volume of *The Life of the Mind,* which was published posthumously under the title *Lectures on Kant's Political Philosophy,* Arendt, I would argue, effectively separates thinking and acting in such a way that thinking is the territory of an intellectual elite and acting is the domain of their subordinates. Given the argument that I have presented relating hierarchy to patriarchy, the implications of this should be clear. Spelling this out in detail is beyond the scope of this chapter. I urge interested readers to pursue this issue and to delve into recent scholarship on Arendt's, as well as Kant's, political thought. For those interested in theorizing about the egalitarian possibilities in political life, I think that the direction this work (both Arendt's and those taking her cues) is taking will be disturbing.

18. Le Guin, *The Left Hand of Darkness* (New York: Ace Books, 1969), endpaper.

Notes on Contributors

MARCUS PAUL BULLOCK is Professor of German at the University of Wisconsin, Milwaukee. His interests focus particularly on the intersections between literature and philosophy. His books include *Romanticism and Marxism: The Philosophical Development of Literary Theory and Literary History in Walter Benjamin and Friedrich Schlegel* (1987), *The Violent Eye: Ernst Jünger's Visions and Revisions on the European Right* (1992), and the first section of the new Harvard edition of Walter Benjamin's work.

JORDAN DIETERICH works in administration at the University of Colorado at Boulder and is a freelance translator of German. He is a qualified US Army interpreter/translator and has taught for the Foreign Language Center, 101st Airborne. He has worked in Germany as a translator and interpreter.

LISABETH DURING teaches philosophy, gender studies and film theory at the University of New South Wales, Sydney. Among her recent publications are "The Failure of Love" (in *War, Violence, and the Structure of Modernity,* ed. Bernd Hüppauf) and "Clues and Intimations: Freud, Holmes, Foucault" *(Cultural Critique)*. She is completing a book called *Virtue and the Way of the World: Chastity, Marriage, and the Uses of Women.*

VOLNEY P. GAY is Professor of Religion, Anthropology, and Psychiatry at Vanderbilt University and Training and Supervising Analyst at the St. Louis Psychoanalytic Institute. His recent book, *Freud on Sublimation: Reconsiderations* (1992), won the 1993 Heinz Hartmann Award from the New York Psychoanalytic Institute. His current book in progress is on Freud, Lévi-Strauss, and narrative theory.

SANDER L. GILMAN is the Henry R. Luce Professor of the Liberal Arts in Human Biology at the University of Chicago. He is a cultural and literary historian and the author and editor of more than forty books, including *Smart Jews: The Construction of the Image of Jewish Superior Intelligence* (1996), *Picturing Health and Illness* (1995), *Jews in Today's Germany* (1995), and *Jewish Self-Hatred* (1986). He was the 1995 president of the Modern Language Association.

NANCY A. HARROWITZ is Assistant Professor of Italian at Boston University. She is the author of *Antisemitism, Misogyny and the Logic of Cultural Difference: Cesare Lombroso and Matilde Serao* (1994), the editor of *Tainted Greatness: Antisemitism and Cultural Heroes* (1994), and the co-editor of *Jews and Gender: Responses to Otto Weininger* (1995). She has written on Primo Levi and Margherita Sarfatti and is coediting a volume of essays on representing the Holocaust in art, literature, film, journalism, and video testimony.

JOHN HOBERMAN is Professor of Germanic Languages at the University of Texas at Austin. He is the author of *Sport and Political Ideology* (1984), *The Olympic Crisis: Sport, Politics and the Moral Order* (1986), and *Mortal Engines: The Science of Performance and the Dehumanization of Sport* (1992).

JANET LUNGSTRUM is Assistant Professor of German at the University of Colorado at Boulder and is currently writing a book entitled *Spectacular Surface: Urban Visual Culture in Weimar Germany.* She has published on Weimar film as well as on theories of creativity in Nietzsche and European modernity, architectural theory, and the philosophy of language. She is a member of the executive committee of the Kafka Society of America.

LORNA MARTENS, Associate Professor of German at the University of Virginia, is the author of *The Diary Novel* (1985) and of *Shadow Lines: Austrian Literature from Freud to Kafka* (1996). She has published articles on Butor, Freud, Schnitzler, Musil, Kafka, Zweig, Rilke, Hofmannsthal, and Valéry. Her research interests include narrative and narrative theory, lyric poetry, and literary theory.

CECILE MAZZUCCO-THAN is Assistant Professor of English at Assumption College. She has published articles on Cervantes, Angel

Ganivet, feminist theory, and Catharine Macaulay. She is at work on a book entitled *"A Form Foredoomed to Looseness": Henry James and the Anglo-American Preoccupation with the Gender of Fiction,* a study of gender antagonism as a self-reflexive theory of writing in the work of James.

JOHN A. MCCARTHY, Professor of German and Comparative Literature at Vanderbilt University, is writing a book on the nature of creativity in the physical and literary realms. He has authored numerous articles on eighteenth- and early nineteenth-century German and comparative literature and published several books on historical and theoretical topics; among them are *Crossing Boundaries: A Theory and History of Essay Writing in German 1680–1815* (1989), *Christoph Martin Wieland. Werk—Epoche—Wirkung* (with S. A. Jorgensen, H. Jauman, H. Thomé, 1994), and *Censorship and Culture from Weimar Classicism to Weimar Republic and Beyond* (coedited with Werner von der Ohe, 1995).

ARKADY PLOTNITSKY teaches English and Comparative Literature at the University of Pennsylvania and has published several books and numerous articles on British and European Romanticism, literary theory, continental philosophy, and philosophy of science, most recently *In the Shadow of Hegel, Complementarity: Anti-Epistemology After Bohr and Derrida,* and *Mathematics, Science, and Postclassical Theory,* which he co-edited with Barbara H. Smith. He is currently completing a study of Shelley, entitled *Physis, Noas, Eros: Shelley and Scientific Modernity.*

ELIZABETH SAUER, Associate Professor of English Literature at Brock University, Canada, is the author of *Barbarous Dissonance and Images of Voice in Milton's Epics* (1996) and the co-editor of *Milton and the Imperial Vision* with Balachandra Rajan (in progress). She is currently at work on a study of closeted performances and the politics of interpretation in writings by Milton and his contemporaries.

BENJAMIN C. SAX is currently an Associate Professor of History at the University of Kansas. He is the author of *Images of Identity: Goethe and the Problem of Self-Conception in the Nineteenth*

Century (1987) and as well as numerous articles on Hegel, Marx, Burckhardt, Nietzsche, and Foucault. A book entitled *The Radical Return: Postmodernity/Nietzsche/Modernity* is forthcoming.

ANDREW SCHMITZ is Assistant Professor of English at D'Youville College in Buffalo, New York. He has translated several interviews of Levinas to be included in a forthcoming volume by Stanford University Press. He is currently working on a translation of Paul Leppin.

GEORGE A. TREY, Assistant Professor of Philosophy at St. Mary's College of Notre Dame, is author of *Solidarity and Difference: The Politics of Enlightenment in the Aftermath of Modernity* (1996). He has published articles on critical social theory, Hegel, the Persian Gulf War, and Levinas. Currently he is working on a book entitled *Promised Lands: Critical Theory and the Religious Dimensions of Emancipation.*

CYNTHIA WILLETT is Assistant Professor of Philosophy at Emory University, where she teaches feminist, continental, and postcolonial philosophies. She has written articles on dialectic, deconstruction, tragedy and comedy, and a book, *Maternal Ethics and Other Slave Moralities* (1995).

Index